SCIENCE, THEOLOGY, AND ETHICS

Science challenges faith to seek fuller understanding, and faith challenges science to be socially and ethically responsible. This book begins with faith in God the Creator of the world, then expands our understanding of creation in light of Big Bang cosmology and new discoveries in physics. Examining the expanding frontier of genetic research, Ted Peters draws out implications for theological understandings of human nature and human freedom. Issues discussed include: methodology in science and theology; eschatology in cosmology and theology; freedom and responsibility in evolution and theology; and genetic determinism, genetic engineering, and cloning in relation to freedom, the comodification of human life, and equitable distribution of the fruits of genetic technology.

The dialogue model of relationship between science and religion, proposed in this book, provides a common ground for the disparate voices among theologians, scientists, and world religions. This common ground has the potential to breathe new life into current debates about the world in which we live, move, and have our being.

Ashgate Science and Religion Series

Series Editors:

Roger Trigg, *Department of Philosophy, University of Warwick, UK*
J. Wentzel van Huyssteen, *James I. McCord Professor of Theology and Science, Princeton Theological Seminary, USA*

Science and religion have often been thought to be at loggerheads but much contemporary work in this flourishing interdisciplinary field suggests this is far from the case. The *Ashgate Science and Religion Series* presents exciting new work to advance interdisciplinary study, research and debate across key themes in science and religion, exploring the philosophical relations between the physical and social sciences on the one hand and religious belief on the other. Contemporary issues in philosophy and theology are debated, as are prevailing cultural assumptions arising from the 'post-modernist' distaste for many forms of reasoning. The series enables leading international authors from a range of different disciplinary perspectives to apply the insights of the various sciences, theology and philosophy and look at the relations between the different disciplines and the rational connections that can be made between them. These accessible, stimulating new contributions to key topics across science and religion will appeal particularly to individual academics and researchers, graduates, postgraduates and upper-undergraduate students.

Other titles published in this series:

Scientism
Science, Ethics and Religion
Mikael Stenmark
0 7546 0445 4 (HBK)
0 7546 0446 2 (PBK)

Theology and Psychology
Fraser Watts
0 7546 1672 X (HBK)
0 7546 1673 8 (PBK)

Islam and Science
Muzaffar Iqbal
0 7546 0799 2 (HBK)
0 7546 0800 X (PBK)

Science, Theology, and Ethics

TED PETERS

ASHGATE

Published by
Ashgate Publishing Limited
Gower House
Croft Road
Aldershot
Hants GU11 3HR
England

Ashgate Publishing Company
Suite 420
101 Cherry Street
Burlington, VT 05401-4405 USA

Ashgate website: http://www.ashgate.com

British Library Cataloguing in Publication Data
Peters, Ted, 1941–
  Science, theology, and ethics. – (Ashgate science and
  religion series)
  1. Religion and science 2. Religion and ethics 3. Theology,
  Doctrinal 4. Science – Moral and ethical aspects
  I. Title
  261.5'5

Library of Congress Cataloging-in-Publication Data
Peters, Ted. 1941–
    Science, theology, and ethics / Ted Peters.
      p. cm. -- (Ashgate science and religion series)
    ISBN 0-7546-0824-7 -- ISBN 0-7546-0825-5 (pbk.)
      1. Religion and science. 2. Christian ethics. I. Title. II. Series.

  BL240.3 .P48 2002
  261.5'5 -- dc21

                                                              2002024889

ISBN 0 7546 0824 7 (HBK)
ISBN 0 7546 0825 5 (PBK)

Typeset by Tradespools, Frome, Somerset.
Printed by Antony Rowe Limited, Chippenham, Wiltshire.

I dedicate this book to my revered friends who have worked so closely with me during the four years of the 'Science and Religion Course Program' of the Center for Theology and the Natural Sciences at the Graduate Theological Union in Berkeley, California. United in a common mission with a vision nothing short of changing the world – of enriching the world of higher education through enhanced interdisciplinary teaching of the science–religion dialogue – we experienced together how shared dedication empowers our respective capacities for creativity. In our victories, we celebrated together. In our setbacks we got depressed together. Only posterity will be able to say retrodictively whether we made a difference.

In particular, I dedicate this book to our Principal Investigator, Robert John Russell, my teaching colleague, my close friend and my intellectual soul mate. Bob's vision for the field of science and theology, combined with his ingenious insights that issue from a profound inner faith in God has made it possible for me to enter this field and make a contribution.

I would also like to thank Whitney Bauman and Hiedi Hagg, who helped me to prepare and copyedit this manuscript; and Gaymon Bennett and Christin Quissell, who prepared the index.

Finally, I want to offer my thanks to Sir John Templeton and the John Templeton Foundation for the grant that funded this program. Our friends at the Foundation provided us with the academic freedom to think and plan for ourselves while providing support for a larger task that we share.

Contents

PART V   THE HUMAN BODY: A THEOLOGICAL PROGNOSIS

Previously Published Material

Chapter 1: 'Theology and Science: Where Are We?', *Dialog*, 34:4 (Fall 1995), 281–96.

Chapter 2: 'Scientific Research and the Christian Faith', *Thought*, 66:260 (March 1991), 75–94.

Chapter 3: 'The Terror of Time', *Dialog*, 39:1 (March 2000), 56–66.

Chapter 4: 'God as the Future of Cosmic Creativity', paper presented at the 'Accelerated Creativity' symposium sponsored by the John Templeton Foundation, Washington, DC (15 February 1999).

Chapter 5: 'David Bohm, Postmodernism and the Divine', *Zygon*, 20:2 (June 1985), 193–217.

Chapter 6: 'Exotheology: Speculations on Extraterrestrial Life', Chapter 8 in *The Gods Have Landed*, ed. by James R. Lewis (Albany: SUNY) 1995; and *CTNS Bulletin*, 14:3 (Summer 1994), 1–9.

Chapter 7: 'Genetics and Genethics: Are We Playing God with Our Genes?', published on the CTNS Web Site: *www.ctns.org* (1997).

Chapter 8: 'Cloning Shock: A Theological Reaction', *CTNS Bulletin*, 17:2 (Spring 1997), 1–9.

Chapter 9: 'The Stem Cell Debate: Ethical Questions', *CTNS Bulletin*, 19:2 (Spring 1999), 3–10.

Chapter 10: Excerpt from Chapter 4, 'Designer Genes and Selective Abortion', from *For the Love of Children*, Ted Peters (Louisville: Westminster John Knox, 1996)

Chapter 11: 'Multiple Choice in Baby Making', *Word and World*, XVI:1 (Winter 1996), 11–23.

Chapter 12: 'Playing God and Germline Intervention', *Journal of Medicine and Philosophy*, 20:4 (August 1995), 365–8; Swets & Zeitlinger Publishers ©, used with permission.

Chapter 13: 'Coevolution: Pain or Promise?', Nobel Conference XXXIV, Gustavus College (6–7 October 1998); and *CTNS Bulletin*, 18:3 (Summer 1998), 5–16.

Chapter 14: 'Whole and Part: the Tension between the Common Good and Individual Freedom', Paper presented at the 'New State Roles: Environment, Resources and the Economy' conference, HARC Woodlands, Houston, Texas (13–16 November 1988) (revised draft 30 November 1988).

Chapter 15: 'Not in My Backyard! The Crisis in Waste Siting', *The Christian Century*, 106:5 (15 February 1989), 175–7. Copyright 1989 Christian Century Foundation; reprinted by permission from the 15 February 1989 issue of *The Christian Century*.

Chapter 16: 'Wholeness in Salvation and Healing', paper presented at the 'Life and Wholeness in the Church' ELCS Sierra Pacific Synod Conference, Berkeley, California (14–17 June 1989) (paper draft 13 March 1989).

Chapter 17: 'The Physical Body of Immortality', *CTNS Bulletin*, 15:2 (Spring 1995), 1–20.

Introduction

It is exciting to live in revolutionary times. I had the privilege of finding myself on the firing line of one revolution, the dramatic renewal of the partnership between science and religion.

As a graduate student in the late 1960s at the University of Chicago, I treated natural science as a cultural phenomenon, as the driving force of the modern mind. Because the hermeneutical task involved contextualizing an ancient faith in the modern world, I found myself furthering the agendas of thinkers such as Paul Tillich, Langdon Gilkey, Wolfhart Pannenberg, Mircea Eliade and Paul Ricoeur. During the first decade of my university teaching, I gave special attention to the global ecological concerns of secular futurology in light of Christian concerns for eschatology and ethics, positing consonance and convergence regarding the exhortation to rescue the planet from human destruction.

The dominant view, articulated best by Langdon Gilkey, was the two-language view: science deals with natural facts, whereas religion deals with ultimate meanings. They belonged to two separate and non-overlapping domains.

After coming to the Graduate Theological Union in Berkeley and serving with Robert John Russell as midwife to the birth of the Center for Theology and the Natural Sciences (CTNS), my approach required modification. As what we affectionately call a hybrid, both a physicist and a theologian, Bob Russell demands that theologians engage scientists as laboratory researchers and as theoreticians who critically pursue truth about the natural realm. To treat science as a cultural phenomenon is derivative. What is primary is to treat scientists as they see themselves, as researchers producing new knowledge about physical reality. This knowledge about the physical world then becomes data for the theologian to assess, evaluate and incorporate into our understanding of God's creative and redeeming work.

The CTNS approach demands more than the two-language or separate domain model can bear. At CTNS, we press both science and theology into engagement, into mutual interaction and into pursuing creative development. That scientists and theologians around the world are ready for this mutual interaction constitutes the revolution we find ourselves in today.

A Revolution in the Relation of Science to Religion

We have become so accustomed to revolutions in science that we now expect them. At least, we expect progress, new developments. A revolution incorporates a turnaround, an unpredicted paradigm shift, a new lens through

1

which to view reality. Perhaps the conceptual revolution of Copernicus, wherein we shifted from geocentrism to heliocentrism, is the tacit model for subsequent revolutions. Einstein's relativity, Bohr's complementarity and Heisenberg's indeterminacy have fostered additional revolutions in the human mind.

Right now, we find ourselves in the midst of another revolution: the unpredicted shift in science's relationship to religion. It is a revolution in vision, the adoption of a new lens through which to view things. The new lens through which we have begun to peek is the lens of inquiry: many scientists among us want to inquire into religion's purchase on reality, while many theologians are inquiring what nature scientifically understood, means for their view of reality. If in the past we engaged in occasional warfare between science and religion, today's revolutionaries are pressing for peace. And they are pressing for more than merely peaceful coexistence wherein science and religion exist side by side in society without conflict. They wish to open science to questions of transcendence and open religion to a non-dogmatic appreciation of the natural world. And still more, some scholars are looking for consonance: shared domains of inquiry wherein the same subject matter is examined scientifically and theologically.

Our current revolutionary situation is complex, delightfully complex. I dub the situation complex because the global scope of communication includes a wide diversity of scientific disciplines, religious traditions, levels of sophistication and vested interests. I dub the situation delightful because of the pervasive positive spirit, the shared sense of excitement over the prospect that this diversity will lead us in a wholesome way toward a new level of shared unity.

The complexity requires us to pause on occasion to try to sort things out. I would like to identify four factors shaping what is becoming the science–religion dialogue: multireligious involvement, focus on a distinctively theological agenda, scientific challenges to theological thinking and implications for ethics and public policy. What I offer here will be both descriptive and prescriptive.

The Multireligious Factor

The first factor is multireligious involvement. Scientific research and its technological products are global, ubiquitous, present in every cultural setting. Every religious tradition with premodern ancestry confronts the challenge of modern materialist and reductionist ways of thinking that ride in on the scientific horse. In every clime, the current generation of educated intellectuals finds it must accommodate its thinking to the scientific worldview. The challenge is inescapable.

In some cases, the challenge is greeted less with fear and more with excitement. Cultural accommodation to technology comes relatively quickly and easily, accommodation to science much more slowly and with greater difficulty. Yet, for the intellectual prometheans in every tradition, the difficulty of the challenge makes science all the more enticing, inviting, thrilling.

The challenge requires a reassessment if not a *ressourcement* of the ancient traditions engaged in the dialogue: Hinduism, Buddhism, Islam, Chinese Confucianism–Taoism-Buddhism, Judaism, Christianity and others. Theologians or scholars of each discrete tradition have a responsibility to that tradition. In this sense, the dialogue with science is multireligious.

I employ the term *multireligious* to distinguish it from *interreligious*. This second term can be misleading if it directs our gaze toward what is *inter*, or standing between, the existing religious communions. An entire field has arisen over the last three decades that attends to interreligious dialogue and, more recently, interreligious cooperation on matters of ethics and social or ecological justice. Such interreligious enterprises are noble and high-minded. Yet, this is not where the science–religion dialogue should start. The science–religion dialogue, if it is to be authentic, must entice involvement first from the existing religious communities replete with their respective traditions of thought about reality. The science–religion dialogue should avoid asking a Muslim to be responsible initially for dialogue on behalf of any position other than his or her own Muslim tradition.

A second and related way in which the interreligious approach can be misleading is its covert and sometimes overt support for syncretism. New Age spirituality, for example, synthesizes the symbol systems of many of the world's religions into a single mystical vision. Looking much like perennial philosophy, what the New Age adopts includes Sri Ramakrishna's extended metaphor: the transcendent divine reality sits atop a mountain with the various religious traditions representing differing yet complementary pathways up the one mountain. A similar if not identical point of view is incorporated into the metaphysical commitments of many spokespersons for what is being called 'religious pluralism'. The various religions of the world are de-absolutized by religious pluralists: that is, each religion is ascribed a partial but distorted picture of a single ultimate reality that transcends its respective finite perspective, a reality that is also shared by other religions who hold quite different and perhaps contradictory perspectives. Such metaphysical commitments made by New Agers and by religious pluralists create an independent religious position. They create a *tertium quid*, a religious position that stands above the existing historical religions while claiming to include them in interreligious dialogue.

The pluralist and New Age motivations for the science–religion dialogue offer benefits and liabilities. The chief benefit is the respect given to diversity, the honoring of differing interpretations of reality. Because all truth claims are perspectival and relative, so the logic goes, we can respect one another even when views are incompatible. Yet, this benefit becomes the chief liability when religion engages science because science cannot afford to respect any claim to truth that does not pass the most ruthless empirical and rational testing. This is why the science–religion dialogue needs to be a science–theology dialogue: theology is that dimension within any religion where truth is rigorously and critically pursued.

A connected liability is that the pluralist and New Age approaches inadvertently dishonor the integrity of historic religious communities by substituting an inclusivist syncretism. Quite frequently, theologians in Islam or Christianity are pre-emptively written off as 'fundamentalist' and either excluded from the conversation or tacitly asked first to convert to some sort of liberal interreligious syncretism before they can be considered 'cleansed' enough to participate. Yet, it seems to me, dialogue should not require any prior liberal coversion or discriminatory selection that limits those admitted to participation. If the task of the science–religion dialogue is to address religious communities as they historically exist, then intellectuals from each respective religious community should enter such a dialogue presuming that others present will impute respect to the tradition they represent.

So, I recommend use of the term *multireligious* because it permits the various partners in the dialogue to retain the integrity of their respective traditional commitments. We expect dialogue to yield growth, to be sure; yet at the beginning we do not demand that those entering dialogue be anything other than what they are. Partners in the science–religion dialogue may maintain their initial allegiance to the particular theological tradition from which they have emerged and not convert prematurely to the contemporary ethos of a syncretistic metaphysical overlay.

Distinguishing Theology from Religion

This brings us to the second factor: the role of religion and the role of theology. The term *religion* is more encompassing, including a given tradition's symbols, rituals, spiritual practices, metaphysical beliefs, doctrines and political orientation. The term *theology* refers specifically to the rational reflection within a given religious tradition. The term literally means 'reasoning about God'. Theologians deal with conceptual issues, ask questions about ultimate reality, formulate doctrine and take up the intellectual challenges of each generation. Theologians raise the truth question, sometimes treating truth as a critical question. Even though some religious traditions such as Buddhism may not ascribe divinity to ultimate reality, I still tend to connect Buddhist philosophical speculation with theology because of the intellectual parallel.

Because natural science is rigorously rational and intellectual in character, it corresponds to the theological component within each religious tradition. Science is uncompromisingly dedicated to uncovering truth, even though this truth is restricted to the realm of nature. Both science and theology are dedicated to truth, even though the overlapping domains of truth may be distinguished as having separate centers. So, although many things could be discussed under the umbrella of science and religion, we have some reason to focus on the theological enterprise or its equivalent within each religious tradition.

Christian theologians, along with Muslim, Hindu and other theologians, have the right to engage science in the pursuit of expanded religious understanding. In fact, Christian theology may engage in two dialogues, or perhaps one large dialogue in two phases: the dialogue with natural science and the multireligious dialogue. Initially, these two might be approached separately. If the separate dialogue with science leads naturally toward a convergence, toward a second phase of multireligious dialogue, then this should be celebrated.

Among other things, this implies that Christian theologians can legitimately pursue the relation between natural science and Christian theology. Just as a Muslim theologian could pursue issues of science in relation to Islam without first sacrificing Islam on the altar of something *inter*religious, so also a Christian theologian could pursue distinctively Christian concerns prior to turning toward the interreligious phase of the dialogue.

The Challenge of Science to Theology

Turning to the third and fourth factors, theological and scientific domains, let me mention that my own field is Christian systematic theology. My work at CTNS includes opening up arenas for scholars in the various religions and the various sciences to converse with one another. In addition, I pursue scholarship as a Christian theologian and Christian ethicist.

Within Christianity, the systematic theologians over the millennia have provided us with a rich intellectual tradition for conceptualizing reality and raising critical questions regarding truth. In our own era, recent scientific discoveries and new theories press systematic theologians to rethink the grounds and implications of their inherited doctrinal commitments. I would like to identify some of the conceptual domains where science and theology seem increasingly to overlap and where theologians are challenged by science to engage in considerable rethinking of past modes of conceptualizing God's relation to the world. These challenges constitute the third and fourth factors that evoke theological and ethical responses, responses that should affect culture and public policy.

Methodology

Of the many developments in methodology, the single most prominent is the thrust to get beyond both the warfare model and the two-language model toward some form of consonance. Even though warfare between science and religion is the image preferred by the popular press, most intellectuals for the last two centuries have preferred the two-language view, according to which science and religion speak different and non-translatable languages. Sometimes called 'NOMA' for non-overlapping magisteria, this is a strategy of peaceful separation. Science is objective and religion subjective, according to this model. Science speaks of fact, whereas religion speaks of value. The recent acknowledgment that science is replete with values and that theology makes truth claims about reality, along with acknowledgment of trajectories within science that seem to press toward questions of transcendence, have compelled many to look for a better model.

The model I believe best describes this new era is *hypothetical consonance*, wherein we presume that both science and theology are concerned with truth about the one reality in which we live and that, at least hypothetically, we ought to be able to find a common domain of discourse about it. Hypothetical consonance does not claim at the outset that science and religion have already converged; but it provides sufficient warrant to set an agenda of inquiry.

Physics

Discoveries giving rise to relativity theory and especially quantum theory that severely challenged the mechanistic universe of Newtonian physics have similarly challenged theological assumptions about divine action in the natural world. The Newtonian view of a closed causal nexus governed deterministically and exhaustively by mathematizable laws became the Enlightenment's given to which descriptions of divine action had to accommodate. Might we think of God's action as miraculous, as an intervention that violates a law of nature? No, said the Enlightenment. After the Humean demolition of the concept of miracle and the reaffirmation of a mechanistic faith articulated by Alfred North Whitehead when he said that nature's laws never go on a holiday, theologians in the nineteenth century retreated to a second adaptive strategy.

This strategy became the Kantian and Schleiermachian retreat into subjectivity, into a religious consciousness that adds a subjective overlay of interpretation to the otherwise objective reality described by science. God's action in the world is discerned by looking at objective nature through the eyes of faith, from the perspective of religious consciousness. This leads to the two-language view, a peaceful coexistence between science and religion. Yet, the mechanistic assumption upon which the two-language détente was founded no longer holds at the micro and macro levels. With the mathematics of quantum theory permitting indeterminacy and contingency at the level of electron activity, a new openness in our physical substrate cracks the mechanistic picture of the universe upon which the two-language view was built. Is there room for divine action in the objective sense? Can we discern a non-interventionist yet objective form of divine action in the physical world?

Cosmology

Big Bang cosmology in its various forms has seemingly opened the window within science toward transcendent creation in the past while apparently closing the window to redemptive eschatology for the distant future. Openness toward divine creation in the past comes in two forms. First, when operating with the notion of an original singularity that exploded in the Big Bang some 15 billion years or so ago, this notion seems to put an edge to time, an edge beyond which we can peer into eternity. Science seems to have located a horizonal limit to nature, and this opens up questions regarding what might lie beyond.

Second, advocates of the Anthropic Principle provide stunning formulae to show how magnificently fine-tuned the initial conditions of the universe must have been to permit – even encourage – the long evolutionary development that has led to living creatures. Somehow, physicist Freeman Dyson remarks, the universe seemed to know that we would be coming. Such cosmological speculations rely on the perception of a *telos* or purpose within natural history; they point to a transcendent creator and designer. Here, we have theology arising from within science, independently of religion.

Looking toward the future, three scenarios have become the stock in trade of physical cosmologists. Each scenario depends upon a critical threshold regarding the density of all the matter in the universe, a threshold which is yet unknown. If, firstly, the density of matter exceeds this critical value, then we will have a closed universe wherein gravity is sufficient to cause a collapse, and this collapse may lead to a fiery implosion; perhaps, even precipitate a cycle of Big Bangs. If, secondly, the density of matter is less than the critical value, then the universe will be open and continue to expand virtually forever while cooling and disintegrating. If the density equals the critical value, thirdly, then we will have a flat universe, which will expand indefinitely but at a decreasing rate until it drifts into heatless equilibrium. According to the first model, the cosmos we know will end in a fiery apocalypse. According to the second two models, the law of entropy will see to it that the cosmos dissipates into a heat death. Whether fry or freeze, the only future of the universe is doom.

This evokes questions among theologians regarding the meaning of eschatological symbols such as 'new creation' and 'resurrection'. Symbols such as these are promises by God to make a 'new heaven and a new earth', a transformation that brings peace within nature and peace within human society. Little if not nothing in these projected scientific scenarios looks like transformation, like renewal of nature's life-giving power. Some physicists have speculated that human consciousness might in the far future escape our physical bodies and live on in a computer-like process of information processing. Yet, regardless of the scientific credibility of such speculations, this does not yet match what one would expect based upon divine promises for resurrection and harmonious fulfillment of body, soul and spirit.

This leads a number of theologians of the present era to admit that no obvious consonance between theological eschatology and cosmological eschatology seems to exist – only dissonance. Because what is at stake is a promised transformation of nature and perhaps the instantiation of new laws of nature, theologians simply cannot expect scientists to find in present principles what will take an independent act of God to bring about. This situation of dissonance is where the present discussion lies.

Big Bang-influenced theologies of creation tend to focus on the past, the point of origin, while ignoring the future. Christian theologians are quick to point out, however, that what constitutes the doctrine of creation is not limited to a single divine act at the beginning. God's creative activity is continuous. *Creatio ex nihilo* must be complemented by *creatio continua*. I predict that this commitment regarding continuing creation will soon be revived, stimulated once again by recent discoveries in physical cosmology, namely, vacuum energy. What is stimulating the scientific excitement is the observation that the expansion of the universe is speeding up. One would expect, if all cosmic matter and energy for the universe was already inherent in the Big Bang, that over time the speed of expansion would gradually slow down until it becomes inert. To the contrary, the universe seems to be increasing its rate of expansion, not slowing. Vacuum energy is the hypothesized explanation. From whence comes the energy to drive this acceleration?

Evolution

The Anthropic Principle notwithstanding, the dramatic challenge to theologians is the insistence on the part of evolutionary biologists on expunging the concepts of purpose and progress from their research. In contrast to the early Darwinians who established evolutionary theory within the wider cultural atmosphere of progress so that the human race could be seen as an advance, today's neo-Darwinian biologists attribute mechanisms such as genetic mutation and natural selection to brute contingency without any built-in *telos* or direction. Even self-organizing complexity proceeds without a prior design. Although theologians have no investment in the doctrine of progress, they certainly believe that the created world is the result of divine intention and divine purpose. What needs attention is the question: is the expunging of purpose within evolution a methodological commitment or an ontological state of affairs?

What the popular press believes to be the point of contact between science and religion is the fire lit by Scientific Creationists and inflamed by the Intelligent Design School. Although frequently depicted as a war that pits open-minded scientific appeals to empirical evidence against narrow-minded appeals to biblical authority, this depiction is misleading. A war is going on, to be sure; but, it is not a war over religious authority. It is rather a war over what constitutes good science. Both creationist and ID warriors claim that the evolutionary theory taught in universities and public schools is not strictly empirical, but rather ideological. Evolution is actually a materialist philosophy that repudiates belief in God and undermines charity in society by promulgating capitalist values such as the survival of the fittest.

This war is by no means boring. Fire and smoke light up the intellectual sky. This battle provides delight to postmodern voyeurs, because science and ideology are so mixed that no one can untangle them. Yet, the respective positions cannot be reduced to the social location of their advocates, because warriors in all armies share the same basic social location, namely, professors with doctorates in one or another natural science or related field.

In a subtler yet more profound manner, the challenge of evolutionary theory to theological anthropology comes from the sociobiologists, also known as evolutionary psychologists. Although claiming to base their view on empirical research into animal social behavior attributed to genetic determinants, sociobiology advances a philosophical ideology that attempts to describe and prescribe human behavior based upon certain genetic principles. The key principle is that of the 'selfish gene', according to which evolutionary development can be explained by the gene's desire to replicate itself. Evolution is now driven by the survival impulse of DNA. All that we know as human culture originates from this genetic determinism, according to this position.

Sociobiologists put back into evolution what the biologists had expunged – teleology, a primitive teleology focused on the selfish gene's agenda, which then gives birth to an increasingly complex teleology promulgated by human values.

The conundrums created by the assumptions of sociobiology combat boredom almost as effectively as the creationist controversy. A version of the naturalistic fallacy, which teaches that an 'ought' can be based upon what 'is', imbues sociobiology, so that the survival thrust of the gene becomes the ground of human valuing. The competition to survive through reproduction becomes the basis of culture, and the merit of a given religious tradition or ethical system becomes measured by its ability to enable its particular tribe to win in the competition. Yet, when a religious tradition teaches a value such as altruism or self-sacrificial love, then the sociobiologist is hard-pressed to find ad hoc auxiliary hypotheses to explain this contradiction. Finally, love risks being reduced to enlightened self-interest, a trick the selfish gene plays on the religious psyche. The result is scientized theology: that is, an evolutionary ideology claiming to be scientific that claims to explain religion better than theological representatives of religion can.

Genetics

This leads to what I call the *gene myth* in contemporary culture, the widespread belief that 'it's all in the genes'. By 'myth' here, I refer to a structure of interpretation, a socially constructed filter through which advances in molecular biology and related genetic sciences are interpreted. According to the myth of genetic determinism, three principles apply: first, puppet determinism, according to which the DNA, like a puppeteer, pulls strings and our phenotype, as well as personality traits, dance; second, promethean determinism, wherein we have confidence to ask our geneticists to enter our DNA with hammers and wrenches and redesign our evolutionary future; third, the myth admonishes us with a commandment – 'thou shalt not play God!' – which registers the Frankenstein or *Jurassic Park* fear that promethean manipulation will provoke nature to retaliate and become destructive to human well-being. This mythical belief structure is cultural and not theological in origin, even if the scientific community occasionally comforts itself by blaming conservative religion for cultural resistance.

The myth is not the science, of course. While the sociobiologists are pouring a steady stream of gasoline onto the cultural fire sparked by the specter of biological determinism, the genuinely interesting advances in genetic knowledge are taking place in the laboratories of the molecular biologists.

At this writing, Francis Collins and Craig Venter have announced the completion of the Human Genome Project. HGP has identified most of the nucleotides in the DNA sequence, while the final numbering of the genes and the determining of their function will take more time. Startling has been the new estimate for the number of genes in human DNA, only 30 000. Previous estimates were at 100 000, with the accompanying assumption that the number of genes determines the degree of an organism's complexity. Noting that a fruit fly has 13 000 genes and a grain of rice has 50 000 genes, the whole notion of genetic essentialism for human nature is being called into question. The statement, 'It's all in the genes', no longer looks confirmable. Perhaps we will see a diminishment of belief in genetic determinism in the near future.

Turning to ethics and public policy, the most dramatic advance in genetic research is the development of techniques for somatic cell nuclear transfer (cloning) and the establishment of immortal lines of stem cells. The potential for lengthening human life and increasing the level of human health while we live longer is enormous, with plans for genetic therapies to combat cancer, heart disease and brain disorders. Yet, a public outcry in North America and the United Kingdom is being raised up to veto cloning. This veto has two targets: outlawing reproductive cloning to make babies and outlawing the use of embryos in stem cell research.

Regarding the first issue, it is my own considered judgment that no theological principles forbid the bringing into the world of another human being through the use of nuclear transfer; yet, I support a moratorium against reproductive cloning on ethical grounds. The use of cloning and similar exotic reproductive technologies risks commodifying the child, rendering it a means to satisfy parental desires to replicate, rather than an end in itself, someone loved as an 'other' person. Regarding the second issue, it is my considered judgment that stem cell research should proceed even if it employs excess fertilized ova discarded from *in vitro* fertilization (IVF) procedures at reproductive clinics. The fertilized eggs in question have already been discarded and never would find their way into the womb of a mother. If not used in research, they would be poured down the drain. Due to circumstances, such fertilized ova could never become human beings, and their use in this research may indirectly lead to dramatic increases in human health and well-being.

Neuroscience

The new science on the block, which is about to enter the science–religion conversation, is brain research. Neuroscientific researchers to date have set rather specific agendas regarding the connection between neuron firing and mental function; they have not rendered their science accessible to philosophers dealing with the big questions about human nature. Nevertheless, the way resulting correlations are reported tantalize us with the thought that perhaps our brains make us who we are. Those who call themselves cognitive scientists are beginning to support a form of biological determinism parallel to the gene myth. For the near future, I predict that the specter of determinism in genetics and in the neurosciences will challenge culture and challenge theology in the same way.

Theological and Ethical Responses

With regard to theological anthropology, questions rightly arise regarding genetic determinism, with special focus on genes as determining brain function, and theologians are being called upon to retrieve and perhaps refurbish arguments of previous centuries defending human freedom and responsibility. With regard to ethics and public policy, questions arise about the ethical legitimacy of reproductive cloning, transferring genes from one species to another, the use of embryos in stem cell research, patenting raw genomic data and whether future distribution of genetic therapy will meet standards of economic justice. In my judgment, theologians should attend to both the hard science taking place in the laboratory and the gene myth operative in culture. Theologians should distinguish between the myth of determinism and what is actually being learned empirically about genes and their influence as they develop an anthropology. I further believe that in their role as ethicists, theologians must lift up the principle of beneficence: that is, rather than appeal to the naturalistic fallacy, theologians should direct our ethical gaze toward the contribution successful scientific research can make toward improving human health, well-being and flowering. Precautionary restrictions on research should be placed within the framework of a long-range commitment to beneficence.

Conclusion

We are living in a period of time when, despite the relativism and skepticism of deconstructionist postmodernism, our culture is seeking cooperation and integration in matters of knowledge. Our culture also holds in high regard cross-disciplinary and cross-cultural dialogue, working with the hidden assumption that finally truth is one and unity in truth provides strength for waging peace. Dialogue is something in which we implicitly place our trust.

Within this cultural context we press for the creative mutual interaction between natural science and critical theology. We begin with the assumption that dialogue is healthy and something worthy in its own right; yet, we press still further. We ask that this dialogue deepen the self-understanding of science and the self-understanding of theology, and we ask that both seek to deepen their respective purchase on the reality they study. In sum, our revolutionary vision sees the dialogue between science and theology as potentially a progressive research programme, as potentially yielding new knowledge about the world in which we live, move and have our being.

What is To Come

In what is to come, essays I have previously published and moderately edited for this volume will engage a number of subtopics within the larger dialogue between science and theology. The book will open with an overview of warfare and non-warfare models for describing the interaction, and this overview will be accompanied by a proposal for the pursuit of hypothetical consonance. Some level of consonance between the scientific apprehension of reality and the theological apprehension of reality is worth pursuing, because we might find that it was already presupposed. Regardless, the pursuit of consonance could possibly make both scientific research and theological reflection progressive – that is, fruitful with new insight and expanded understanding.

The essays dealing with physics, cosmology, and creation take up the complementary challenges to theology raised by Big Bang cosmology, especially the concomitant idea of an initial beginning to the cosmos and the idea that nature is undeniably historical. I say complementary because these two commitments have been resident in theology for a long time. With the ideas of a beginning to creation and historicity of nature, do we find ourselves in an orchard with the luscious fruit of consonance hanging on the intellectual tree just waiting to be picked?

The frontier of genetic research has been spreading across the scientific landscape like a field fire. At the Center for Theology and the Natural Sciences, I served as Principal Investigator on a grant from the US National Institutes of Health to study the 'Theological and Ethical Questions Raised by the Human Genome Initiative'. We put together a team of molecular biologists, behavioral geneticists, philosophers, theologians and ethicists to monitor the scientific research through the formative period of the 1990s. The first ethical issue demanding public policy response was genetic discrimination, formulated by many as the 'genetic privacy' issue. We, at CTNS, uncovered a whole nest of dragon's eggs about to hatch ethical monsters, and I enumerate them in these chapters. The final decade of the last century bequeathed to the present time the unresolved issues of human reproductive cloning and stem cell research. In this section, I try to describe the terrain and point out where the ethical dragons are hiding and ready to strike.

During the late 1970s and early 1980s, I worked on a contract with the US Department of Energy to provide an ethical framework for government policy regarding the siting of high level nuclear waste. This project fit well with my earlier work in what today we call 'ecology', but earlier was subsumed under 'futurology' – that is, a globe-wide concern for the health of the planet. Because the toxic radio activity of nuclear waste is so enduring, lasting perhaps a quarter million years, we desperately need a theology of nature, an ethical commitment and a public policy that will provide long-range vision and inspire long-range responsibility.

Finally, I note how contemporary theology has committed itself to a positive view of the human body, eschewing body–soul dualism and affirming the goodness of physical creation. Such a position leads to affirmation of holism, to an integrated view of the human person. It also raises difficulties for the Christian understanding of resurrection – or resurrection of the spiritual body – because what we learn from science regarding our present physical bodies makes it difficult to conceive of a future body that does not rely upon the killing of life to sustain its own biology, metabolic change over time, deterioration, and decay. What we may end up admitting here is dissonance; perhaps theological and scientific commitments may not find consonance as we project the divinely promised transformation of creation.

Whether consonance or dissonance, what fertilizes and nourishes the dialogue between science and theology is willingness to pursue truth wherever it might lead us.

I

FROM CONFLICT TO CONSONANCE

Chapter 1

Theology and Science: Where Are We?

Is the war being fought between evolution and creationism characteristic of the larger relationship between science and theology? Is warfare the best extended metaphor for understanding how scientific knowledge and Christian faith get along? The battle metaphor goes back to the late nineteenth century, most probably to the influence of the notorious book by A.D. White, *A History of the Warfare of Science with Theology*.[1] However, we will ask here: does the image of a declared state of war accurately describe the current interaction between theological thinking and natural science? No, not completely.

We could say that a revolution is underway, but this revolution is turning us toward greater peace, not toward new battles. It is a revolution that adds complexity and nuance so that it is no longer accurate to see science and theology merely as pitched enemies. The revolution is being led by an unpredicted and astounding intellectual trend, namely, the relocation of the God question within the orbit of scientific discussion about the natural world. The raising of theological questions within the scientific camp does not fit neatly into the warfare model.

The warfare model is not the only one. Some of us work with a model of separation. We assume that science and religion are separate, unable to conflict because they are soverign in different spheres. They allegedly speak different languages. So, we erect a high wall of separation between church and laboratory. Yet now, as the peaceful revolution is beginning to take hold, this separation is increasingly recognized as most unfortunate. It is unfortunate because we all are aware that there is but one reality. Sooner or later we will become dissatisfied with consigning our differences to separate ghettos of knowledge.

The pre-revolutionary separatists and the revolutionary scientists represent only part of the picture. There is another group of quiet revolutionaries who since the 1960s have been looking for parallels, points of contact, consonance, crossovers and conflations. Their emerging new discipline, as yet without a name, is studying developments in natural science – especially physics and the life sciences – and is engaging in serious reflection on various loci of Christian doctrine. Scientists and theologians are engaged in a common search for shared understanding. The search is not merely for a shared discipline. They are not looking merely for rapprochement between separate fields of inquiry. Rather, scientists and theologians are aiming for increased knowledge, for an actual advance in the human understanding of reality. Until a name comes along, we will refer to this new enterprise as *Theology and Natural Science*.

In this chapter, I will briefly outline eight different ways in which science and theology are currently thought to be related.[2] I will note that the dominant view in academic circles – the truce by separation view – is what I label the 'two-language theory', but I will go on to point out that the advancing frontier is taking us in the direction of hypothetical consonance. Then, I will turn to the central methodological issue, namely, the classic concern for the relation between faith and reason. I will conclude with my own observations regarding the merits of hypothetical consonance and the value of making a theological interpretation of nature so that we can see the natural cosmos as divine creation.

Who are the key partners in this emerging conversation between natural science and Christian theology? Rather than sharply contrasting what we can know by faith and what we can know by reason, Nancey Murphy and Wentzel van Huyssteen, along with others, are maximizing the overlap. Those looking for consonance in cosmology, evolutionary theory, genetics and other such subject areas include frontier thinkers such as Ian Barbour, Willem Drees, Philip Hefner, Wolfhart Pannenberg, Arthur Peacocke, John Polkinghorne, Robert John Russell and Thomas Torrance. In Australia, we must note that Paul Davies, Mark Worthing and Denis Edwards are emerging as world leaders in this growing field.

Eight Ways of Relating Science and Theology

Not everyone views the relation between science and religion the same. If we extend the metaphor of warfare, we can see that positions vary from pitched battle to an uneasy truce.

1   Scientism

Scientism, sometimes called 'naturalism', 'scientific materialism' or 'secular humanism', seeks war with total victory for one side. Scientism, like other '_isms', is an ideology. This one is built upon the assumption that science provides all the knowledge that we can know. There is only one reality, the natural, and science has a monopoly on the knowledge we have about nature.[3] Religion, which claims to purvey knowledge about things supernatural, provides only pseudo-knowledge – that is, false impressions about non-existent fictions.

Some decades ago, British philosopher and atheist Bertrand Russell told a BBC audience that 'what science cannot tell us, mankind cannot know'. At mid-century, astronomer Fred Hoyle argued that the Jewish and Christian religions have become outdated by modern science. He explained religious behavior as escapist, as pursued by people who seek illusory security from the mysteries of the universe.[4]

More recently, physicists Stephen Hawking and the late Carl Sagan have teamed up to assert that the cosmos is all there is or was or ever will be and to assert that there was no absolute beginning at the onset of the Big Bang. Why no beginning? Had there been an absolute beginning, then time would have an edge, and beyond this edge we could dimly glimpse a transcendent reality such as a creator God. But this is intolerable to scientism. So, by describing the cosmos as temporally self-contained, Sagan could write confidently in the introduction to Hawking's *A Brief History of Time* about 'the absence of God' on the grounds that there is 'nothing for a Creator to do'.[5] In the warfare between science and theology, scientism demands elimination of the enemy.

2   *Scientific Imperialism*

Scientific Imperialism is scientism in a slightly different form. Rather than eliminating the enemy, scientific imperialism seeks to conquer the territory formally possessed by theology and claim it as its own. Whereas scientism is atheistic, scientific imperialism affirms the existence of something divine but claims knowledge of the divine comes from scientific research rather than religious revelation. 'Science has actually advanced to the point where what were formerly religious questions can be seriously tackled [by] the new physics,' writes Adelaide physicist Paul Davies.[6] What Davies does is demonstrate how the field of physics transcends itself, opening us in the direction of the divine reality. 'I belong to a group of scientists,' he writes, 'who do not subscribe to a conventional religion but nevertheless deny that the universe is a purposeless accident.... There must, it seems to me, be a deeper level of explanation. Whether one wishes to call that deeper level "God" is a matter of taste and definition.'[7]

Physicist Frank Tipler takes imperialism to the academic extreme. Claiming that quantum theory combined with Big Bang and thermodynamics can provide a better explanation than Christianity for the future resurrection of the dead, Tipler declares that theology should become a branch of physics.[8]

3   *Ecclesiastical Authoritarianism*

Ecclesiastical Authoritarianism is the defensive tactic followed by some in the Roman Catholic tradition who perceive science and scientism as a threat. Presuming a two-step route to truth in which natural reason is followed by divine revelation, theological dogma is here granted authority over science on the grounds that science is founded on God's revelation. In 1864, Pope Pius IX promulgated *The Syllabus of Errors*, wherein item 57 stated it to be an error to think that science and philosophy could withdraw from ecclesiastical authority. A century later, the Second Vatican Council dropped the defenses by declaring the natural sciences to be free from ecclesiastical authority and called them 'autonomous' disciplines (*Gaudium et Spes*: 59). Pope John Paul II, who has a serious interest in fostering dialogue between theology and the natural sciences, is negotiating a new peace between faith and reason.[9]

4   *Scientific Creationism*

Scientific Creationism, sometimes called 'creation science', is not a Protestant version of church authoritarianism, even though it is frequently so mistaken. The grandparents of today's scientific creationists were fundamentalists, to be sure, and fundamentalism appealed to biblical authority in a fashion parallel to the Roman Catholic appeal to church authority. Yet, there is a marked difference between fundamentalist authoritarianism and contemporary creation science. Today's creation scientists are willing to argue their case in the arena of science, not biblical authority. They assume that biblical truth and scientific truth belong to the same domain. When there is a conflict between a scientific assertion and a religious assertion, we allegedly have a conflict in scientific theories. The creationists argue that the book of Genesis is itself a theory which tells us how the world was physically created: God fixed the distinct kinds (species) of organisms at the point of original creation. They did not evolve. Geological and biological facts attest to biblical truth, they argue.

With regard to theological commitments, scientific creationists typically affirm (1) the creation of the world out of nothing; (2) the insufficiency of mutation and natural selection to explain the process of evolution; (3) the stability of existing species and the impossibility of one species evolving out of another; (4) separate ancestry for apes and humans; (5) catastrophism to explain certain geological formations (for example, the flood explains why sea fossils appear on mountains); and (6) the relatively recent formation of the earth, about six to ten thousand years ago.[10]

Establishment scientists typically try to gain quick victory over creationists by dismissing them. Stephen Jay Gould, the colorful Harvard paleontologist, says the very term 'scientific creationism' is meaningless and self-contradictory.[11] Although the battle between scientific creationists and established scientists appears to be all-out war, this is not the case. The creationists, many of whom are themselves practicing scientists, see themselves as soldiers within the science army.[12]

5   The Two-language Theory

The two-language theory might appear to be the way to establish a truce with an enduring peace. This is because it respects the sovereign territory of both science and theology and because it is advocated by highly respected persons in both fields. Albert Einstein, remembered for his remark that 'science without religion is lame and religion without science is blind', distinguished between the language of fact and the language of value. 'Science can only ascertain what *is*, but not what *should be*,' he once told an audience at Princeton; 'religion, on the other hand, deals only with evaluations of human thought and action.' Note the use of 'only' here. Each language is *restricted* to its respective domain.

As of this writing, the current president of the American Association for the Advancement of Science, paleontologist Stephen Jay Gould, advocates the two-language view. Responding to Pope John Paul II's elocution on evolution, Gould argues that science and religion need not be in conflict because their teachings occupy different domains. Their respective *magisteria* (teaching authorities) are 'nonoverlapping'.[13]

Neo-orthodox theologian Langdon Gilkey argues for the two-language approach. Science, he says, deals only with objective or public knowing of *proximate* origins, whereas religion and its theological articulation deals with existential or personal knowing of *ultimate* origins. Science asks '*how?*' while religion asks '*why?*'[14] What Gilkey wants, of course, is for one person to be a citizen in two lands – that is, to be able to embrace both Christian faith and scientific method without conflict.[15] To speak both languages is to be bilingual, and bilingual intellectuals can work with one another in peace.

The modern two-language theory of the relation between science and theology ought not to be confused with the premodern concept of the two books. In medieval times, revelation regarding God could be read from two books, the *book of nature* and the *book of scripture*. Both science and theology could speak of things divine. Both natural revelation and special revelation pointed us in one direction: toward God.[16] The two-language theory, in contrast, points us in two different directions: either toward God or toward the world.

A problem I have with the two-language theory is that it gains peace through separation by establishing a demilitarized zone that prevents communication. In the event that a scientist might desire to speak about divine matters or that a theologian might desire to speak about the actual world created by God, the two would have to speak past one another on the assumption that shared understanding is impossible. Why begin with such an assumption? The method of hypothetical consonance makes just the opposite assumption, namely, there is but one reality and sooner or later scientists and theologians should be able to find some areas of shared understanding.

6   Hypothetical Consonance

Hypothetical consonance is the name I give to the frontier that seems to be emerging beyond the two-language policy. The term 'consonance', coming from the work of Ernan McMullin, indicates that we are looking for those areas where there is a correspondence between what can be said scientifically about the natural world and what the theologian understands to be God's creation.[17] 'Consonance' in the strong sense means accord, harmony. Accord or harmony might be a treasure we hope to find, but we have not found it yet. Now, we find ourselves working with consonance in a weak sense – that is, by identifying common domains of exploration. The advances in physics, especially thermodynamics and quantum theory in relation to Big Bang cosmology, have in their own way raised questions about transcendent reality. As Paul Davies has shown, the God question can be honestly asked from within scientific reasoning. Theologians and scientists may now be sharing a common subject matter, and the idea of hypothetical consonance encourages further cooperation.

Mark William Worthing at Luther Seminary in Adelaide challenges theologians to be theologically responsible by investigating what science is saying about the world, the world of which we believe God to be the creator and redeemer. 'Theology ... has the responsibility to demonstrate to what extent and in what ways Christian faith is compatible with cosmologies that may in fact prove to be an accurate description of the universe.'[18] Princeton theologian Wentzel van Huyssteen puts it this way: 'As Christians we should therefore take very seriously the theories of physics and cosmology; not to exploit or to try to change them, but to try to find interpretations that would suggest some form of complementary consonance with the Christian view-point.'[19]

Hypothetical consonance asks theologians to view their discipline somewhat differently. Rather than beginning from a rigid position of inviolable truth, the term 'hypothetical' asks theologians to subject their own assertions to further investigation and possible confirmation or disconfirmation. An openness to learning something new on the part of theologians and scientists alike is essential for hypothetical consonance to move us forward. Canberra systematic theologian Stephen Pickard 'suggests a more modest and humble theological task, willing to admit uncertainty and an appropriate provisionality in the results of theological enquiry, perhaps more so than has occurred in the past'.[20]

The new book by Flinders University/Adelaide School of Divinity theologian Denis Edwards, *The God of Evolution*, presumes hypothetical consonance when putting together evolutionary biology with Christian theology. As the 'of' in the book's title indicates, *The God of Evolution* does not hold that science and faith speak separate and untranslatable languages. Quite the contrary. The scientific theory of evolution provides actual knowledge about the way in which God works in nature to achieve divine purposes: 'There is every reason for a Christian of today to embrace *both* the theological teachings of Genesis *and* the theory of evolution. But holding together the Christian view of God and the insights of evolutionary science does demand a rethinking of our theology of the trinitarian God at work in creation.'[21]

It is my judgment that, at least for the near future, the model of hypothetical consonance should lead the conversation between natural science and Christian theology. Scientists are already recognizing the limits to reductionist methods and peering into the deeper questions about the nature of nature and the significance of all that is real. Theologians are mandated to speak responsibly about the natural world we claim to be the creation of a divine creator, and natural science has demonstrated its ability to increase our knowledge and understanding of this wondrous world. If God is the creator, we should expect growth in our understanding of God as we grow in understanding of the creation. Conversely, we should expect that, if the world is a creation, it cannot be fully understood without reference to its creator.

7 *Ethical Overlap*

Ethical overlap refers to the recognized need on the part of theologians to speak to the questions of human meaning created by our industrial and technological society and, even more urgently, to the ethical challenges posed by the environmental crisis and the need to plan for the long-range future of the planet. The ecological challenge arises from the crisis-crossing forces of population overgrowth, increased industrial and agricultural production that depletes non-renewable natural resources while polluting air and soil and water, the widening split between the haves and the have-nots around the world, and the loss of a sense of responsibility for the welfare of future generations. Modern technology is largely responsible for this ecological crisis, and theologians, along with secular moralists are struggling to gain ethical control over technological and economic forces that, if left to themselves, will drive us toward destruction.

An advocate of hypothetical consonance, I belong also to the ethical overlap camp. I believe that, at root, the ecological crisis poses a spiritual issue, namely, the crying need of world civilization for an ethical vision. An ethical vision – a vision of a just and sustainable society that lives in harmony with its environment and at peace with itself – is essential for future planning and motivating the peoples of the world to fruitful action. Ecological thinking is future thinking. Its logic takes the following form: *understanding–decision– control*. Prescinding from the scientific model, we implicitly assume that to solve the ecocrisis we need to understand the forces of destruction. Then, we need to make the decisions and take the actions that will put us in control of our future and establish a human economy that is in harmony with earth's natural ecology.

In order to bring theological resources to bear on the ecological challenge, most theologians have tried to mine the doctrine of creation for its wealth of ethical resources. It is my judgment that we need more than creation; we also need to appeal to eschatological redemption – that is, new creation. God's redeeming work is equally important when we begin with a creation that has somehow gone awry.

I believe the promise of eschatological renewal can provide a sense of direction, a vision of the coming just and sustainable society, and a motivating power that speaks relevantly to the understanding–decision–control formula. We need to combine creation with new creation. Theologians can make a genuine contribution to the public discussion if, on the basis of eschatological resources, we can project a vision of the coming new world order; that is, announce the promised kingdom of God and work from that vision backward to our present circumstance. This vision should picture our world as (a) a single, worldwide planetary society; (b) united in devotion to the will of God; (c) sustainable within the biological carrying capacity of the planet and harmonized with the principles of the ecosphere; (d) organized politically so as to preserve the just rights and voluntary contributions of all individuals; (e) organized economically so as to guarantee the basic survival needs of each person; (f) organized socially so that dignity and freedom are respected and protected in every quarter; and (g) dedicated to advancing the quality of life on behalf of future generations.[22]

8 New Age Spirituality

New Age spirituality is the last entry in our list of parties interested in the science–religion struggle. The key to New Age thinking is holism: the attempt to overcome modern dualisms such as the split between science and spirit, ideas and feelings, male and female, rich and poor, humanity and nature. New Age artillery is loaded with three explosive sets of ideas: (1) discoveries in twentieth-century physics, especially quantum theory; (2) acknowledgment of the important role played by imagination in human knowing; and (3) a recognition of the ethical exigency of preserving our planet from ecological destruction.

Fritjof Capra and David Bohm, who combine Hindu mysticism with physical theory, are among the favorite New Age physicists. Bohm, for example, argues that the explicate order of things that we accept as the natural world and that is studied in laboratories is not the fundamental reality; there is under and behind it an implicate order, a realm of undivided wholeness. This wholeness, like a hologram, is fully present in each of the explicate parts. Reality, according to Bohm, is ultimately 'undivided wholeness in flowing movement'.[23] When we focus on either objective knowing or subjective feeling, we temporarily forget the unity that binds them. New Age spirituality seeks to cultivate awareness of this underlying and continually changing unity.

A recent *Christian Century* article on science and religion promulgates such holism with a pantheistic overtone. 'When I am dreaming quantum dreams,' writes Barbara Brown Taylor, 'the picture I see is more like a web of relationships – an infinite web, flung across the vastness of space like a luminous net.... God is the web ... I want to proclaim that God is the unity – the very energy, the very intelligence, the very elegance and passion that make it all go.'[24]

By adding evolutionary theory to physics and especially to Big Bang cosmology, New Age theorists find themselves constructing a grand story – a myth – regarding the history and future of the cosmos of which we human beings are an integral and conscious part. On the basis of this grand myth, New Age ethics tries to proffer a vision of the future that will guide and motivate action appropriate to solving the ecological problem. Science here provides the background not only for ethical overlap, but also for a fundamental religious revelation. Brian Swimme and Thomas Berry put it this way: 'Our new sense of the universe is itself a type of revelatory experience. Presently we are moving beyond any religious expression so far known to the human into a meta-religious age, that seems to be a new comprehensive context for all religions.... The natural world itself is the primary economic reality, the primary educator, the primary governance, the primary technologist, the primary healer, the primary presence of the sacred, the primary moral value.'[25]

Now, I happen to find the ethical vision of the New Age inspiring. But I cannot in good conscience endorse its meta-religious naturalism. I find it contrived and uncompelling. Nearly the same ecological ethic with an even stronger emphasis on social justice can be derived from Christian eschatology.

Returning to the more theoretical tie between science and theology, I earlier recommended hypothetical consonance as the most viable option for the near future. Hypothetical consonance takes us beyond the limits of the two-language theory without initially violating the integrity of either natural science or Christian theology. Where the leading scholars find themselves, to my interpretation, is with one foot in the two-language theory and the other stretched for a stride to go beyond. That stride means we need to step back into an age-old theological concern, namely, the relation of faith to reason.

Faith and Reason in Science and Theology

The key development among those scholars who either strive for consonance or are at least in partial sympathy with consonance is the attempt to demonstrate overlap between scientific and theological reasoning. Two insights guide the discussion. First, scientific reasoning depends in part on a faith component, on foundational yet unprovable assumptions. Second, theological reasoning should be recast so as to take on a hypothetical character that is subject to testing. What is a matter of some dispute, however, is whether or not theological assertions refer – that is, is theology a form of realism? Do theological statements merely give expression to the faith of a religious community or do they refer to a reality beyond themselves such as God? Theologians are asking to what extent *critical realism* in the philosophy of science should be incorporated into theological methodology.

Langdon Gilkey has long argued that science, every bit as much as theology, rests upon faith. Science must appeal to some foundational assumptions regarding the nature of reality and our apprehension of it, assumptions which themselves cannot be proved within the scope of scientific reasoning. In its own disguised fashion, science is religious or mythical. 'The activity of knowing,' he writes, 'points beyond itself to a ground of ultimacy which its own forms of discourse cannot usefully thematize, and for which religious symbolization is alone adequate.'[26] Scientific reasoning depends upon the deeply held conviction – the passion of the scientist – that the world is rational and knowable and that truth is worth pursuing. 'This is not "faith" in the strictly religious and certainly not in the Christian sense,' he observes. 'But it is a *commitment* in the sense that it is a personal act of acceptance and affirmation of an ultimate in one's life.'[27]

On the scientific side, Paul Davies acknowledges the faith dimension to science in terms of assumptions regarding rationality. Presumed here is a gnostic-style connection between the rational structure of the universe and the corresponding spark of rationality in the human mind. That human reasoning is generally reliable constitutes his 'optimistic view'.[28] Yet he acknowledges that the pursuit of scientific knowledge will not eliminate all mystery, because every chain of reasoning will eventually hit its limit and force on us the meta-scientific question of transcendence. 'Sooner or later we all have to accept something as given,' he writes, 'whether it is God, or logic, or a set of laws, or some other foundation of existence. Thus "ultimate" questions will always lie beyond the scope of empirical science.'[29]

On the issue of faith at the level of assumption, theologians and scientists, at least philosophers of science, agree. This raises a second related issue: does theology, like science, seek to explain? If so, then theology cannot restrict itself to individual or even communal subjectivity or to authoritarian methods of justification that isolate it from common human reasoning. This is what Philip Clayton argues: 'theology cannot avoid an appeal to broader canons of rational argumentation and explanatory adequacy'.[30] Clayton proceeds to argue for intersubjective criticizability and to view theology as engaged in transcommunal explanation.

If theology seeks to explain, does it also refer? This is the question of critical realism to which we now turn.

Critical Realism and Theological Reference

Wentzel van Huysteen, professor in the first chair in the United States designated for Theology and Natural Science at Princeton, believes that theological statements about God refer to God. He advocates 'critical–theological realism' and a method for justifying theories in systematic theology that parallels what we find in natural science. Justification occurs through progressive illumination offered by a theological theory, not as traditionally done by appeal to ecclesiastical or some other undisputable authority. Van Huyssteen recognizes the relativistic, contextual and metaphorical dimensions of human speech that flood all discourse, theological and scientific alike. Progress toward truth requires constructive thought, the building up of metaphors and models so as to emit growing insight.[31] And, most significantly, theological assertions refer to God. They are realistic. 'Theology,' he writes, 'given both the ultimate religious commitment of the theologian and the metaphoric nature of our religious language, is scientifically committed to a realist point of view.... Our theological theories do indeed refer to a Reality beyond and greater than ours.'[32]

On the one hand, critical realism should be contrasted with non-literalist methods such as positivism and instrumentalism, because it recognizes that theories represent the real world. On the other hand, critical realism should be contrasted also with 'naïve realism', which invokes the correspondence theory of truth to presume a literal correspondence between one's mental picture and the object to which this picture refers. Critical realism, in contrast, is non-literal while still referential. The indirectness comes from the conscious use of metaphors, models and theories. Ian Barbour notes that 'Models and theories are abstract symbol systems, which inadequately and selectively represent particular aspects of the world for specific purposes. This view preserves the scientist's realistic intent while recognizing that models and theories are imaginative human constructs. Models, on this reading, are to be taken seriously but not literally.'[33] Urging the adoption of critical realism by theologians, Arthur Peacocke maintains that 'Critical realism in theology would maintain that theological concepts and models should be regarded as partial and inadequate, but necessary and, indeed, the only ways of referring to the reality that is named as "God" and to God's relation with humanity.'[34]

Not all theological voices chime in with harmony here. Nancey Murphy recommends that theologians avoid critical realism on the grounds that it remains modern just when we need to move toward postmodern reasoning. Critical realism remains caught in three restrictive elements of the modern mind: (1) epistemological foundationalism which attempts to provide an indubitable ground for believing; (2) representational thinking with its correspondence theory of truth; and (3) excessive individualism and inadequate attention to the community. The postmodern elements she lifts up for the theological agenda are (1) a non-foundationalist epistemological holism and (2) meaning as use in language philosophy.[35] What counts for Murphy is the progressive nature of a research program, and this is a sufficient criterion for evaluating theological research regardless of its referentiality.

Theological Assertions as Hypotheses: Wolfhart Pannenberg

Would the tasks of explanation and reference make theology itself scientific? Yes, answers Munich systematic theologian Wolfhart Pannenberg. Describing theology as the science of God, he contends that each theological assertion has the logical structure of a hypothesis.[36] This makes it subject to verification against the relevant state of affairs it seeks to explain. But how can we confirm or disconfirm an assertion about God? A theologian cannot follow a method of direct verification because the existence of its object, God, is itself in dispute and because God – defined by Pannenberg as the all-determining reality – is not a reproducible finite entity. An indirect method of verification is available, however. Building in part on Karl Popper's procedures for critical verification and falsification, Pannenberg submits that we can test assertions by their implications. Assertions about a divine life and divine actions can be tested by their implications for understanding the whole of finite reality, a wholeness which is implicitly anticipated in the ordinary experience of meaning.

Because of the temporal process in which the finite world is ever-changing, the whole, which is an essential framework for any item of experience to have a determinate meaning, does not exist yet as a totality. If there is a whole at all, then it must be future. So it can only be imagined, anticipated. As anticipation, the very positing of a temporal whole involves an element of hypothesis. Even the reality of God fits into this class. The reality of God is present to us now only in subjective anticipation of the totality of finite reality, in a conceptual model of the whole of meaning that we presuppose in all particular experience. Christians think of the whole temporally and eschatologically. The theological idea of the eschatological kingdom of God that arises from our historic religious tradition is subject to future confirmation or refutation by what happens. It is this openness to confirmation that makes theological assertions hypothetical and, hence, scientific.

The anticipation of wholeness of meaning within common human experience is the key that makes Pannenberg's method work. We anticipate a wholeness of meaning that is not yet fully present, a wholeness which we hypothesize will come in the future as the gift of an eschatological act of the one God. The *direct confirmation* of this hypothesis is dependent upon the actual coming of that eschatological wholeness. In the meantime, while we await the eschatological fulfillment, our faith in the future takes the form of a hypothesis that can gain *indirect confirmation* by the increased intelligibility it offers to our understanding of our experience of finite reality. If in fact God is the all-determining reality, then everything else we study, including the natural world, must eventually be shown to be determined by this reality. The very raising of the hypothesis of God as the all-determining one can be evaluated positively if it increases the intelligibility of the natural world we study through scientific disciplines.[37] It is this task of increasing the intelligibility of the natural world by considering it in relation to God that leads Pannenberg to engage in dialogue with scientists and to construct a theology of nature.

'Science and Religion' v. 'Science and Theology': Thomas F. Torrance

Pannenberg believes theology can be scientific if it makes hypotheses and seeks to confirm them. In complementary contrast, Thomas Torrance, who taught Christian Dogmatics at the University of Edinburgh from 1952 to 1979, argues that it is the objectivity of theology that makes it scientific.

The first and salient legacy of the Torrance approach is a key distinction: 'Science and Religion' versus 'Science and Theology'. These two labels are not the same. Religion has to do with human consciousness and human behavior. Theology has to do with God. 'Whenever religion is substituted in the place of God, the fact that in religion we are concerned with the behaviour of *religious people*, sooner or later means the substitution of humanity in the place of religion . . . '.[38] Torrance clearly prefers to take up the distinctively theological task, defining theology as a science. He describes theology (or a philosophy of theology) as a 'meta-science of our direct cognitive relation with God. Science and meta-science are required not because God is a problem but because *we* are . . . . It is because *our* relations with God have become problematic that we must have a scientific theology'.[39] One can see clearly here the influence of Karl Barth in getting beyond religious consciousness as the object of theology and allowing our consciousness to be shaped by the true object of theology, God. 'Scientific theology is active engagement in that cognitive relation to God in obedience to the demands of His reality and self-giving.'[40]

Torrance stresses that authentic inquiry, both scientific inquiry and theological inquiry, attend to what is, to what is actual, to what is real; this means that we should guard against superimposing upon reality an *a priori* or idealistic scheme. To this end, we allow our inquiry to be guided by its object, by the reality of the object under study. The transition from the Newtonian world-view to the Einstein revolution could take place only when science was authentic, only when it let nature tell us what nature is like.

In stressing this point, Torrance elegantly moves natural theology from its previous position of prolegomena into positive theology proper. This move parallels Einstein's treatment of geometry. The Euclidian geometry inherited with Newtonian physics provided a context for inquiry that presupposed absolute mathematical space and time with bodies in motion. For Einstein, this constituted an idealized presupposition detached from nature as he was studying it. Einstein's revolution in the theory of relativity consisted of placing geometry into the material content of physics. Rather than treating geometry as an idealized framework, Einstein brought it into the midst of physics where it became a natural science indissolubly united to physics.

Torrance wants to learn from Einstein's example. He puts natural theology where Einstein had put geometry. 'So it is with natural theology: brought within the embrace of positive theology and developed as a complex of rational structures arising in our actual knowledge of God it becomes "natural" in a new way, natural to its proper object, God in self-revealing interaction with us in space and time. Natural theology then constitutes the epistemological geometry, as it were, within the fabric of revealed theology.'[41] By making this post-Barthian move, Torrance denies natural theology any independent status while making it serve as an instrument for unfolding and expressing the knowledge content of Christian theology.

Authentic theology, then, attends to its object, God. It listens to what the Word of God tells us. This form of objectivity – listening to the object of inquiry – makes both science and theology scientific.

> Theology is the unique science devoted to knowledge of God, differing from other sciences by the uniqueness of its object [God] which can be apprehended only on its own terms and from within the actual situation it has created in our existence in making itself known.... Yet as a *science* theology is only a human endeavour in quest of the truth, in which we seek to apprehend God as far as we may, to understand what we apprehend, and to speak clearly and carefully about what we understand. It takes place only within the environment of the special sciences and only within the bounds of human learning and reasoning where critical judgment and rigorous testing are required, but where in faithfulness to its ultimate term of reference beyond itself to God it cannot attempt to justify itself on the grounds occupied by the other sciences or within their frames of interpretation.[42]

Torrance recognizes the finite and perspectival limits of human knowing as it operates in theology and the other sciences, and it is just this perspectival limit that mandates that authentic inquiry attend to its object and learn from its object.

Departing from Barth, for whom theology could be methodologically isolated from other disciplines, Torrance argues that theology should engage the natural sciences in conversation. Torrance affirms *creatio ex nihilo*, noting that the divine transcendence implied here renders the created world contingent. The contingency of the world requires that we study the world directly to unlock its secrets. No idealistic shortcuts or revelations about God can substitute for empirical research. This functions as a sort of theological blessing upon the scientific enterprise.

Torrance wants the theologian to broaden the scope of attention, to get beyond anthropology to include nature around and in us. Theology has been suffering from tunnel vision, he complains, wherein we have limited theology to the relationship between God and the human race. Theology cannot be restricted to the relationship of God to humanity. 'Theology has to do with the unlimited reality of God in his relations with the universe of all time and space.'[43] Hence the sciences broaden our knowledge of God's creation and provide an understanding of the arena within which incarnation and resurrection take place.

This enlargement of the scope of theology to include all space and time provides the framework for specifying just how God can be an object of inquiry and how knowledge of God can be objective. Torrance is a trinitarian theologian, and the finite objectivity of God incarnate grounds the objectivity of theology.[44]

> The framework of objective meaning which concerns the theologian here is bound up with the incarnation of the Son of God to be one with us in our physical human existence within the world of space and time in such a way that through his vicarious life and passion he might redeem human being and creatively reground it in the very life of God himself, and therefore it is also bound up with the resurrection of Jesus Christ in body, or the physical reality of his human existence among us, for it is in the resurrection that God's incarnate and redeeming purpose for us is brought to its triumphant fulfillment.[45]

One of the difficulties any Barthian theologian confronts when engaging in dialogue with the natural sciences is the apparent self-referentiality of the theological circle. The existence of the object of theological inquiry, God, is just what is in dispute in the modern world. To presuppose its truth and then contend that this produces knowledge seems to beg the question. Torrance is aware of the difficulty. He defends his method with a *tu quoque* argument, noting that all theories are circular and striving to establish themselves through coherence because they cannot be derived or justified on any grounds other than what they themselves constitute. In this regard, theology is no worse off than any other discipline.[46]

Science and Systematic Theology: Arthur Peacocke

For good or ill, it seems that within the subfields of theology one group, the systematic theologians, have taken the lead in developing a working relationship with the natural sciences. Biblical studies has long employed the investigative techniques of archaeology, to be sure, and Historical Theology and Ethics are coming to rely more and more on methods developed by the social sciences. But, it has been the systematic theologians who have carefully examined scientific methods, adopted some into theological methodology, and proceeded in certain cases to incorporate knowledge gained from natural science into the formulation of doctrinal beliefs.

Significant here is the creative work of Arthur Peacocke. A biochemist turned theologian, Peacocke is former Dean of Clare College at Cambridge, is retired from directing the Ian Ramsey Centre at Oxford, and is Warden Emeritus of the Society of Ordained Scientists. 'Theology needs to be consonant and coherent with, though far from being derived from, scientific perspectives on the world,' he asserts.[47] The task for theology is clear: to rethink religious conceptualizations in light of the perspective on the world afforded by the sciences.

This rethinking leads to questions about God. God is mysterious, affirms Peacocke. Natural theology paints a picture of an ineffable and transcendent God beyond human comprehension. The special revelation of God experienced in the person of Jesus Christ only enhances the mystery of the divine. Yet, mystery is by no means confined to theology. Twentieth-century science is characterized by a new appreciation of the mystery of existence. Such things as indeterminacy and vacuum fluctuations in quantum physics have increased our knowledge while at the same time they have humbled our previous *hubris* for assuming causal explanations would be right around the corner. The foundation of physical reality is more elusive than once thought. 'So the mystery-of-existence question becomes even more pressing in the light of the cosmic panorama disclosed by the natural sciences.'[48] Also mysterious is human personhood, arising as it does from the biological sphere to that of consciousness and then becoming itself a top-down cause. Peacocke believes that 'this recognition of an ultimate ineffability in the nature of the divine parallels that of our ultimate inability to say what even things and persons are in themselves'.[49]

Peacocke's rethinking of theological conceptions in light of natural science is leading him to assert certain things about God: beyond the eternity of the divine *being*, God is engaged in temporal *becoming*; beyond *creatio ex nihilo*, God is engaged in *creatio continua*; God creates and dynamically 'lets be'; God is the ultimate source and ground of both necessity and chance; God has a self-limited omnipotence and omniscience, thereby permitting necessity and chance in the history of nature; the divine act of self-limitation for the good of the creation warrants our saying that *God is love*. These reconceptualizations lead finally to a theopaschism: 'God suffers in, with and under the creative processes of the world.'[50]

Some interpreters of Peacocke assign the label 'temporal critical realism' to his work. Perhaps this is appropriate, for Peacocke writes, 'In giving being to entities, structures and processes *in* time, God cannot have a *static* relation to that time which is created with them. Hence we have to speak of a dynamic divine "becoming" as well as of the divine "being".'[51]

Bottoms-up Systematics: John Polkinghorne

Peacocke is a hybrid – that is, he is trained in both science and theology. Another hybrid is mathematician–physicist turned theologian John Polking-horne, now president of Queens' College, Cambridge. Polkinghorne pursues systematic theology with what he calls a 'bottom-up' method. The *bottoms* with which he begins are scientific data regarding the natural world, historical data regarding the biography of Jesus, the church's threefold encounter with the economic Trinity, and such. The *up* with which he concludes is a high degree of confidence regarding the fundamental commitments of the Christian faith, commitments that are completely compatible with the truths pursued in the field of science.[52]

Steadfast in affirming that epistemology models ontology, Polkinghorne begins methodologically with faith and reason. Faith is not merely a polite expression for unsubstantiated assertion or an excuse for believing in God as an irrational act. Rather, faith and reason belong together. Both reflect the quest for truth. Truth seeking is something shared by scientists and theologians alike. 'Although faith goes beyond what is logically demonstrable,' he writes, 'yet it is capable of rational motivation. Christians do not have to close their minds, nor are they faced with the dilemma of having to choose between ancient faith and modern knowledge. They can hold both together.'[53]

Polkinghorne is committed to *consonance*: theological reflection on creation must be consonant with what science says about Big Bang and evolution. This by no means requires that theological assertions be reducible to scientific assertions. The scientific world-view is itself subject to interrogation and expansion, and this is pursued through metaphysics.

None of us can do without metaphysics, he observes, and then admonishes us to do metaphysics deliberately. Rejecting Cartesian dualism in favor of what he calls 'dual-aspect monism', Polkinghorne opens biology to the existence of supraphysical consciousness or spirit; and he opens physics to a reality that transcends the world of the Big Bang and the evolution of conscious life.[54] At this point extrapolation and speculation from a scientific basis cease. Polkinghorne then turns to orthodox Christian commitments – such as a theistic understanding of God and *creatio ex nihilo* – and simply defends them against competing positions.

For example, he distinguishes his position from the deism opposed by Stephen Hawking and other physicists when discussing the onset of the Big Bang with its possible edge of time at the beginning, which implies that creation becomes limited to a single act at the beginning. From then on, God is presumed to let nature take its evolutionary course. But Polkinghorne is a theist who believes in an active God, so he combines *creatio ex nihilo* with *creatio continua* to emphasize God's continuing involvement in nature. Polkinghorne's active God is omnipotent, but is by no means a tyrant. God's power has been withheld to make room for freedom within nature. God still acts in nature without obviating this freedom. 'One is trying to steer a path between the unrelaxing grip of a Cosmic Tyrant and the impotence or indifference of a Deistic Spectator.'[55]

Then, looking in the other direction, Polkinghorne distinguishes his position from the panentheism of process theology, because the latter fails to provide sufficient grounds for hope. The God of Alfred North Whitehead, the leading process philosopher of the 20th century, can very well share our suffering, but there is no eschatological guarantee here that evil will be overcome. Being remembered by the consequent nature of God is unsatisfying to Polkinghorne. 'I do not want to be just a fly in the amber of divine remembrance,' he writes, 'I look forward to a destiny and a continuing life beyond death. To put it bluntly, the God of process theology does not seem to be the God who raised Jesus from the dead.'[56]

I wonder if this defense of theism, as clear and forceful as it is, actually needs the discussion of science. It seems to me that this classic debate between deists, theists and panentheists is only occasioned by issues rising out of Big Bang physics. The physics itself does not actually influence the direction let alone determine the destination of the debate as we find it in Polkinghorne.

Polkinghorne rightly defines his position sharply against panentheistic colleagues in the field such as Arthur Peacocke and Ian Barbour. The strength of Peacocke and Barbour is perhaps that they wrestle more thoroughly with the actual scientific ideas and seek a fuller integration with theological ideas. The strength of Polkinghorne is his confidence that the Christian faith, when subjected to the same rational scrutiny that science exacts upon its data and theories, exhibits an honest pursuit of truth accompanied by a confidence in its rational motivation.

Physical Cosmology and Divine Action: Robert John Russell

On the American side of the Atlantic, we find Robert John Russell, a hybrid physicist and systematic theologian, directing the program he founded in 1981: The Center for Theology and the Natural Sciences at the Graduate Theological Union in Berkeley.[57] Methodologically, Russell belongs to the consonance school, but in his own way he emphasizes a dialectic between consonance and dissonance. Science and theology can, at points, take different trajectories, and dissonance must be acknowledged. Like Polkinghorne, Russell is clear that scientific prognostications regarding the future of the cosmos do not square with Christian eschatology. A projected heat death due to entropy does not square with the promise of resurrection and new creation. Here is dissonance that needs to be acknowledged. Inspired by the work of his former student, Nancey Murphy, who employs the philosophy of Imre Lakatos for theological purposes, Russell seeks to embed the consonance–dissonance dialectic more tightly into a theological method that sees itself as a progressive research programme.[58]

In careful conversation with physical cosmologists and with theologians such as Ian Barbour and Willem Drees, Russell has pressed for consonance on understandings of the origin of the universe found in Big Bang cosmology and the Christian concept of creation.[59] The orienting question is this: is the Christian doctrine of *creatio ex nihilo* consonant with the Big Bang? Many answers have been given, all unsatisfying to Russell. The two-language answer is 'no', because this school believes in principle that no scientific picture of the universe's origin has any conceptual relevance for theology. It precludes looking for consonance at the outset. An alternative answer, a semi-literalist answer, would be: 'yes, they are consonant because the scientific discovery of a beginning to the universe corroborates the Christian view that the creation had a beginning boundary, before which there was nothing'. Two things make this unsatisfying as well. First, current conversations regarding quantum theory make it premature to say that the scientific consensus is that the universe – at least the original singularity – had an absolute beginning. Second, the force of the *creatio ex nihilo* idea is that the world is ontologically dependent upon God, and this could be the case even if there were no beginning boundary.

Russell feels the need to find his own answer. Following the Lakatos–Murphy distinction between the inner core commitment and the outer belt of auxiliary hypotheses in a research program, he posits the following as core:

creatio ex nihilo means ontological dependence. Then, he adumbrates three auxiliary hypotheses: (1) ontological dependence entails finitude; (2) finitude includes temporal finitude; and (3) temporal finitude entails past finitude – that is, going backwards in finite time must take us to a beginning, a $t = 0$ point. This fits with what we know from Big Bang cosmology in which the data of astrophysics, the theory of general relativity, and other factors point us to an initial singularity, $t = 0$. That this singularity may have a quantum life of its own does not stop Russell from tendering a modest conclusion: the empirical origination described by $t = 0$ in Big Bang cosmology tends to confirm what is entailed in this theory's core, namely, *creatio ex nihilo* means ontological dependence. This is not a proof, but it is a partial confirmation.[60]

Russell's contribution to the internal theological debate is the distinction he draws between finitude and boundedness. Traditionally, theologians have identified the two. But they are not identical. Ontological dependence upon God requires that the world be finite but not necessarily bounded. The initial singularity may have had a quantum life of its own and, hence, no temporal boundaries; yet, we can still say that the world has a beginning and that it is finite in time. Big Bang cosmology, even in its quantum form, becomes a character witness, even if not an eye witness, to the creation of the world.

The Created Co-creator: Philip Hefner

Like Russell, Philip Hefner picks up on the Lakatos–Murphy methodology with its core–auxiliary distinction. He puts God in the hard core, 'that to which all terrestrial and cosmic data are related'.[61] He adds seven auxiliary hypotheses, which I will not enumerate here. He believes that the test of theology is its explanatory adequacy, that it is subject to falsification by experience and that its relative success should be measured by its fruitfulness. 'What is at stake in the falsification of theological theories is not whether they can prove the existence of God,' he writes, 'but rather whether, with the help of auxiliary hypotheses, they lead to interpretations of the world and of our experience in the world that are empirically credible and fruitful – that is, productive of new insights and research.'[62]

Hefner is professor emeritus of systematic theology at the Lutheran School of Theology at Chicago, editor of the journal *Zygon* and director of the Chicago Center for Science and Religion. His career work in the field has been devoted less to physical cosmology and more to rapprochement between theology and the life sciences, especially evolutionary theory. He has sought to develop an anthropology and even a Christology in what he calls a biocultural evolutionary scheme. His is a grand vision, and at the focal center of this vision is the concept of the human being as the *created co-creator*. A basic element embedded within the core rather than located in an outer auxiliary hypothesis, the concept of the created co-creator is Hefner's central contribution to the Theology and Natural Science enterprise. He writes, 'Human beings are God's created co-creators whose purpose is to be the agency, acting in freedom, to birth the future that is most wholesome for the nature that has birthed us – the nature that is not only our own genetic heritage, but also the entire human community and the evolutionary and ecological reality in which and to which we belong. Exercising this agency is said to be God's will for humans.'[63]

Hefner has been criticized for advocating human hubris, for placing humanity on a level with the divine and overestimating the human potential for creativity. Such a criticism might apply to New Age thought, but not to Hefner. Hefner is clear that we human beings are creatures, brought here by God the creator even if God employed evolution to create us. This is what he means by *created* co-creator. Nevertheless, when explicating the biblical concept of the *imago dei*, Hefner wants to include creativity in the divine image and exhort us ethically to take responsibility for creating a future that is more human, more just and more loving.

Conclusion: Seeing Cosmos as Creation

We in the Christian tradition are used to speaking glibly of the natural world as God's creation. On what basis do we do this? It is not immediately obvious from observing the natural realm that it is the product of a divine hand or the object of divine care. Since the Enlightenment, we in the modern scientific world have been assuming that no footprints of the divine can be discerned in the sands of the natural world. Western science assumes that, if we study natural processes with the intention of learning the laws by which nature operates, what we will end up with is just a handful of natural laws. If we study natural processes with the intention of wondering about the magnificent mysteries that surround us, we will end up where we started, namely, with an imagination full of spectacular puzzles. If we study nature for her beauty, we will see beauty. If we study nature to see her violence, we will see her as did Tennyson, blood 'red in tooth and claw'. Nature, we have been assuming for a century or so now, does not seem to take the initiative to disclose her ultimate foundation or even her existential meaning. What natural revelation reveals is simply nature, not God. If we want to know more, we have to ask more questions. And we have to go beyond our natural relationship with nature to find the answers.

Christian theologians, seeing the limits to natural revelation in a modern world replete with naturalism, find they need to go to the historical events of the death and resurrection of Jesus Christ, the events that stand at the heart and center of God's special revelation. Good Friday and Easter do not reveal that God is the world's creator for the first time, of course. But these events do confirm what had already been suspected in ancient Israel, namely, that the creation of the world was the necessary first act in God's continuing drama of salvation. The world in which we live is not merely a conglomeration of natural laws or puzzles; it is not merely the realm of beauty or violence. The cosmos exists because it plays a part in the divine scenario of redemption. It is on the basis of what we know about the God who raised Jesus from the dead that St Paul can perceive how creation has been 'subjected to futility', that it 'has been groaning in travail' and that God has furthermore 'subjected it in hope' because it 'will be set free from its bondage to decay and obtain the glorious liberty of the children of God' (Rom.8:18–25).

Special experiences of God reveal special knowledge. We need to know, or at least need to hypothesize, that there is a God with divine intentions before we can see clearly that the world around and in us is in fact a creation. It is primarily on the strength of Israel's experience with the liberating God of the Exodus that the Old Testament writers could depict the world as God's creative handiwork. It is on the strength of our experience with the incarnate Lord that Christians in today's world can say that 'God so loved the world ...' (John 3:16). The New Testament promise of an eschatological new creation tells us something essential about the present creation. Theologically, it is God's promised kingdom that determines creation, and creation is the promise of the kingdom. Whether we interpret nature through the symbol of the Exodus, the incarnation, the kingdom or some other similar religious symbol, we find that we are dependent upon some form of revelation of God's purposes if we are to put nature into proper theological perspective – that is, if we are to think of nature as a creation.

So, curiously enough, we might consider the possibility of a reversal in natural theology. Traditionally, the aim of natural theology has been to ask what our study of nature can contribute to our knowledge of God. But might it work in reverse? Might we ask what our knowledge of God can contribute to our knowledge of nature? To know that God is the creator is to know that the world in which we live and move and have our being is *creation*.

We may not have to choose between the two methods, of course. We could begin with nature and then ask about God or we could begin with what we think we know about God and then ask how this influences what we think about nature. Or we could do both. Both should be on the agenda of those working in the field of Theology and Natural Science.

Notes

1   A.D. White, *A History of the Warfare of Science with Theology*, 2 volumes (New York: Dover, 1896; 1960).

2   The line-up of contending forces I offer here is revised from that sketched previously in the Preface to my *Cosmos as Creation* (Nashville: Abingdon Press, 1989), 13–17. It is also a more nuanced line-up compared to the one offered by Ian Barbour in his Gifford Lectures, *Religion in an Age of Science* (San Francisco: Harper, 1990), 3–30, wherein he identifies four ways: conflict, independence, dialogue and integration. My categories of scientism and church authoritarianism fit his conflict category, and the two-language theory is a model of independence in both schemes. Yet, Barbour's notions of dialogue and integration lack the nuance that I believe is operative under the notion of consonance. Consonance involves dialogue, to be sure, but it acknowledges that integration may be only a hope and not an achievement. Also, Barbour thinks of scientific creationism in terms of 'biblical literalism' and thereby places it in the conflict category, overlooking the fact that the creationists think of themselves as sharing a common domain with science; they see themselves in conflict with scientism but not with science itself.

John Haught offers up an aliterative four-unit typology – conflict, contrast, contact and confirmation – in his *Science and Religion* (New York: Paulist, 1995). Mark Richardson offers us a three-part typology: (1) integration, typified by the work of Lionel Thornton, William Temple, Austin Farrar, Arthur Peacocke and John Polkinghorne; (2) romantic, typified by poets Whitman or Wordsworth and by contemporary New Age figures such as Briane Swimme, Thomas Berry and Matthew Fox; and (3) scientific constraint, wherein one speaks univocally about the natural and transcendent worlds, typified by Paul Davies, Freman Dyson, Stephen Hawking and Frank Tipler. See Mark Richardson, 'Research Fellows Report', *CTNS Bulletin*, 14:3 (Summer 1994), 24–5. Philip Hefner cuts the pie six ways: (1) modern option of translating religious wisdom into scientific concepts; (2) postmodern/New Age option of constructing new science-based myths; (3) critical post-Enlightenment option of expressing truth at the obscure margin of science; (4) postmodern constructivist option of fashioning a new metaphysics for scientific knowledge; (5) constructivist traditional option of interpreting science in dynamic traditional concepts; and (6) Christian evangelical option of reaffirming the rationality of traditional belief. See Philip Hefner, 'Science and Religion and the Search for Meaning', *Zygon*, vol. 1 (1996), 307–21.

3   Langdon Gilkey, *Nature, Reality, and the Sacred: The Nexus of Science and Religion* (Minneapolis: Fortress, 1993), 14.

4   Fred Hoyle, *The Nature of the Universe* (New York: Mentor, 1950), 125.

5   Stephen Hawking, *A Brief History of Time* (New York: Bantam, 1988), 136; see Carl Sagan, *Cosmos* (New York: Random House, 1980). Co-discoverer of the double helix structure of DNA, Francis Crick reduces what religious people used to believe to be the disembodied soul to 'nothing but a pack of neurons'. All of our joys and sorrows, our memories and ambitions, our sense of personal identity and free will 'are in fact no more than the behavior of a vast assembly of nerve cells and their associated molecules' (*The Astonishing Hypothesis: The Scientific Search for the Soul*, New York: Charles Scribner's Sons, 1994, 3). For aggressive anti-religious secular humanism, see Paul Kurtz, *The Transcendental Temptation* (Buffalo: Prometheus, 1985) and the journal published by the Committee for the Scientific Investigation of Claims of the Paranormal, *The Skeptical Inquirer*.

6   Paul Davies, *God and the New Physics* (New York: Simon & Schuster, Touchstone, 1983), ix.

7   Paul Davies, *The Mind of God* (New York: Simon & Schuster, 1992), 16. In reviewing Davies' new book, *The Fifth Miracle: The Search for the Origin and Meaning of Life* (New York: Simon & Schuster, 1999), Philip Hefner alerts us to the manner in which Davies challenges science to go beyond its current limits: '*The Fifth Miracle* has an important subtext, which presses the claim: the current understanding of nature's laws is insufficient to understand the origin of life. Religious people have perennially perceived such insufficiencies as occasions to invoke the action of God' ('Mysterious Beginnings', *Christian Century*, 116:17, 522–623 (2–9 June 1999, 622). Davies does not invoke a religious God-of-the-gaps to fill the insufficiency, of course, but rather presses science to expand to fill this gap with a fuller understanding of nature.

8   Frank Tipler, *The Physics of Immortality* (New York: Doubleday, 1994), ix, 10, 17, 247. Tipler borrows some eschatological theology from Wolfhart Pannenberg and places it within the scientific eschatology of physicist Freeman Dyson, *Infinite in All Directions* (New York: Harper, 1988).

9   *John Paul II on Science and Religion: Reflections on the New View from Rome*, ed. by Robert John Russell, William R. Stoeger and George V. Coyne (Notre Dame:

University of Notre Dame Press, and Vatican City State: Vatican Observatory Publications, 1990). In October 1992, the pope completed a 13-year study of the Galileo affair, proclaiming that the church erred in condemning the atronomer for disobeying orders regarding the teaching of Copernicus' heliocentric theory of the universe. John Paul II described Galileo as 'a sincere believer' who was 'more perceptive [in the interpretation of Scripture] than the theologians who opposed him'. Because in the myths of scientism Galileo is touted as a martyr for truth over against the narrow-mindedness of theology, Owen Gingerich took the occasion to write to clear up the facts. One noteworthy fact is that Galileo was never condemned for heresy, only disobedience: 'How Galileo Changed the Rules of Science', *Sky and Telescope*, 85:3 (March 1993), 32–6.

10 See Duane T. Gish, *Evolution: The Fossils Say No!* (San Diego: Creation-Life Publishers, 1973) and Roger E. Timm, 'Scientific Creationism and Biblical Theology', in Peters, *Cosmos as Creation*, 247–64.

11 Stephen Jay Gould, *Hens Teeth and Horses' Toes: Reflections on Natural History* (New York: Norton, 1983), 254.

12 One could describe the war as a battle between atheistic science and theistic science. Langdon Gilkey suggests that scientism (what he calls 'scientific positivism') goes beyond the limits of science to propound an atheistic cosmology, and this initiates the reaction that results in scientific creationism. See Gilkey, *Nature, Reality, and the Sacred*, 55.

13 Stephen Jay Gould, 'Nonoverlapping Magisteria', *Natural History*, 106 (March 1997), 16–22.

14 Langdon Gilkey, *Creationism on Trial* (San Francisco: Harper, 1985), 49–52, 108–13.

15 In his more recent works, Gilkey has pressed for a closer relationship – a mutual dependence – between science and religion. Gilkey attacks scientism (what he calls 'naturalism' or 'scientific positivism') when it depicts nature as valueless, determined and void of the sacred, on the grounds that these are suprascientific or philosophical judgments that go beyond science itself. Science, therefore, must be supplemented by philosophy and religion if we are to understand reality fully (*Nature, Reality, and the Sacred*, 3, 11, 75, 111, 129).

16 The 'two books' approach is embraced today by the organization, Reasons to Believe, a publishing house that 'examines how the facts of nature and the truths of the Bible give each of us a reason to believe' (Reasons to Believe, P.O. Box 5978, Pasadena CA 91117, fax 818/852-0178).

17 Ernan McMullin, 'How Should Cosmology Relate to Theology?', in *The Sciences and Theology in the Twentieth Century*, ed. by Arthur Peacocke (Notre Dame: University of Notre Dame Press, 1981), 39. See Peters, *Cosmos as Creation*, 13–17.

18 Mark William Worthing, *God, Creation, and Contemporary Physics* (Minneapolis: Fortress Press, 1996), 193.

19 Wentzel van Huyssteen, *Duet or Duel? Theology and Science in a Postmodern World* (Harrisburg, Pennsylvania: Trinity Press International, 1998), 78.

20 Stephen Pickard, '"Unable to See the Wood for the Trees", John Locke and the Fate of Systematic Theology', in *The Task of Theology Today*, ed. by Victor Pfitzner and Hilary Regan (Adelaide: Open Book Publishers, 1998), 145.

21 Denis Edwards, *The God of Evolution* (New York: Paulist, 1999), 13.

22 See Ted Peters, *GOD – the World's Future: Systematic Theology for a Postmodern Era* (Minneapolis: Fortress, 1992), chapter 12; *Futures – Human and Divine* (Atlanta: John Knox Press, 1978).

23 David Bohm, *Wholeness and the Implicate Order* (London: Routledge and Kegan Paul, 1980), 11. See Fritjof Capra, *The Tao of Physics* (New York: Bantam, 1977);

Ted Peters, *The Cosmic Self: A Penetrating Look at Today's New Age Movements* (San Francisco: Harper, 1991), chapter four.

24 Barbara Brown Taylor, 'Physics and Faith: The Luminous Web', *Christian Century*, 116:17, 612–19 (2–9 June 1999), 619.

25 Brian Swimme and Thomas Berry, *The Universe Story* (San Francisco: Harper, 1992), 255. A variant would be the team work of physicist Joel R. Primack and musician Nancy Ellen Abrams, who are trying to construct a myth out of Big Bang inflationary cosmology and medieval Jewish Kabbalah, not because the myth would be true but because our culture needs a value-orienting cosmology ('In the Beginning...Quantum Cosmology and Kabbalah', *Tikkun*, 10:1 (January–February 1995), 66–73.

26 Langdon Gilkey, *Religion and the Scientific Future* (San Francisco: Harper, 1970), 41.

27 Ibid., 50.

28 Paul Davies, *The Mind of God* (New York: Simon & Schuster, 1992), 24; see also 232.

29 Ibid., 15. See Paul Davies, *Are We Alone?* (London and New York: Harper Collins, Basic Books, 1995).

30 Philip Clayton, *Explanation from Physics to Theology* (New Haven and London: Yale, 1989), 13; see Peters, *GOD – The World's Future*, 74–6.

31 The criterion for evaluating the progressive strength of a theory is fertility, and this constitutes the chief argument in behalf of critical realism for Ernan McMullin, 'A Case for Scientific Realism', in *Scientific Realism*, ed. by Jarret Leplin (Berkeley: University of California, 1984), 26. See Arthur Peacocke, *Intimations of Reality: Critical Realism in Science and Religion* (Notre Dame: University of Notre Dame, 1984).

32 Wentzel van Huyssteen, *Theology and the Justification of Faith* (Grand Rapids: Eerdmans, 1989), 162–3. 'I advocate a critical realism,' writes Ian Barbour, 'holding that both communities [scientific and religious communities] make cognitive claims about realities beyond the human world' (*Religion in an Age of Science*, 16).

33 Barbour, *Religion in an Age of Science*, 43; see Ian Barbour, *Myths, Models, and Paradigms* (San Francisco: Harper, 1974), 38; Sallie McFague, *Metaphorical Theology* (Minneapolis: Fortress, 1982), 133–4.

34 Arthur Peacocke, *Theology for a Scientific Age* (Oxford: Basil Blackwell, 1990, and Minneapolis: Fortress, enlarged edn, 1993), 14.

35 Nancey C. Murphy, 'Relating Theology and Science in a Postmodern Age', *CTNS Bulletin*, 7:4 (Autumn 1987), 1–10; see her Templeton Book Prize-winning work, *Theology in an Age of Scientific Reasoning* (Ithaca: Cornell, 1990).

36 Wolfhart Pannenberg, *Theology and the Philosophy of Science* (Louisville: Westminster/John Knox 1976); *Systematic Theology*, 3 volumes (Grand Rapids: Eerdmans, 1991–6).

37 See Wolfhart Pannenberg, *Toward a Theology of Nature*, ed. by Ted Peters (Louisville: Westminster/John Knox, 1993), chapter one. Similarly, John Haught expands on consonance with two nuanced categories, contact and confirmation. As a gesture of confirmation he contends that the theologian can contribute to the scientific apprehension of natural reality ('The theological notion that the world was created – and is therefore neither necessary nor eternal – gives a stature to empirical science that other ways of looking at the world do not', *Science and Religion*, 63).

38   Thomas F. Torrance, *Theological Science* (Oxford: Oxford University Press, 1969), iv–v.
39   Ibid., v.
40   Ibid., v.
41   Thomas F. Torrance, *Reality and Scientific Theology* (Edinburgh: Scottish Academic Press, 1985), 39. Karl Barth is reported to have granted full agreement to this new place for natural theology. See Thomas F. Torrance, *Space, Time and Resurrection* (Grand Rapids: Eerdmans, 1976), ix–xiii.
42   Torrance, *Theological Science*, 281–2.
43   Torrance, *Reality and Scientific Theology*, 67.
44   Thomas F. Torrance, *Space, Time and Incarnation* (Oxford: Oxford University Press, 1969).
45   Torrance, *Space, Time and Resurrection*, 13.
46   Ibid., 15. Wolfhart Pannenberg would fear that such a *tu quoque* ('you also,' says Brutus to Caesar) might become a rational excuse for an irrational commitment: *Theology and the Philosophy of Science*, 45.
47   Peacocke, *Theology for a Scientific Age*, x.
48   Ibid., 101.
49   Ibid., 102.
50   Ibid., 126.
51   Ibid., 184. Peacocke's early masterwork of 1979, *Creation and the World of Science* (Oxford: Clarendon, 1979), is organized somewhat like a systematic theology. Yet there the scientific agenda drove the project. More recently, in *Theology for a Scientific Age*, the theological agenda has taken the driver's seat. Distinctively theological commitments are being rethought in light of scientific apprehensions of nature.
52   John Polkinghorne, *The Faith of a Physicist* (Princeton: Princeton University Press, 1994), 193.
53   Ibid., 5.
54   Ibid., 21.
55   Ibid., 80.
56   Ibid., 68.
57   The Center for Theology and the Natural Sciences (CTNS) at 2400 Ridge Road, Berkeley CA 94709 is one of many active research and professional organizations pursuing science–theology dialogue. Philip Hefner directs the Chicago Center for Science and Religion at the Lutheran School of Technology at Chicago, 1100 E. 55th Street, Chicago, IL 60615. The annual Star Island conferences are sponsored by the Institute on Religion in an Age of Science (IRAS) headed by astronomer Ursula Goodenough of St. Louis. The American Scientific Affiliation (ASA) with Donald Munro as executive director is made up of scientists with evangelical Christian concerns and can be contacted at P.O. Box 668, Ipswich, MA 10938-0668. The Archbishop of York presides over the Science and Religion Forum, St Alban's Vicarage, Mercer Avenue, Coventry, CV2 4PQ, England. The European Society for the Study of Science and Theology (ESSSAT) is headed by Willem B. Drees, Högseröds Prästgard, S-240 33, Löberöd, Sweden, Fax +46-46-52975. Kevin Sharpe of the Institute on Religion in an Age of Science, 65 Hoit Road, Concord, NH 03301-1810 publishes an informative newsletter, *Science and Religion News*; and in Britain Peter E. Hodgson of Corpus Christi College at Oxford, OX1 4LF regularly publishes a book review service, *Science and Religion Forum*. The ELCA facilitates a working group on science and technology headed by Prof. Per Anderson, Concordia College, Moorhead, MN 56562.

58 See Imre Lakatos, *The Methodology of Scientific Research Programmes: Philosophical Papers*, vol. 1, ed. by John Warrall and Gregory Currie (Cambridge: Cambridge University Press, 1978).

59 See Barbour, *Religion in an Age of Science*; and Willem B. Drees, *Beyond the Big Bang: Quantum Cosmologies and God* (LaSalle, IL: Open Court, 1990).

60 See his work in Robert John Russell, William R. Stoeger and George V. Coyne (eds), *Physics, Philosophy and Theology* (Vatican City State: Vatican Observatory; and Notre Dame: University of Notre Dame, 1988) and Robert John Russell, Nancey C. Murphy and C.J. Isham (eds), *Quantum Cosmology and the Laws of Nature* (Vatican City State: Vatican Observatory; and Notre Dame: University of Notre Dame, 1993).

61 Philip Hefner, *The Human Factor* (Minneapolis: Fortress, 1993), 260. This book won the 1993 Templeton Book Prize in the field of theology and natural science.

62 Ibid., 261.

63 Ibid., 264; see also 32.

Chapter 2

Scientific Research and the Christian Faith

What is the relationship between scientific research and the Christian faith?[1] This is a multileveled question. At the theoretical level, where for so long we assumed science and theology were at war with one another, we are today discovering marvelous new areas of common concern. At the personal level, we are finding increased impetus for scientists to express their faith in ways that complement rather than conflict with their study of the natural world. At the church level, however, there seems to be some ambivalence, perhaps an unspoken hostility on the part of our church leaders aimed at scientific researchers. Then, finally, at the political level, we confront the moral issue of staggering importance, namely, the role of the scientist in the weapons industry.

Like creek water filled with silt after a spring rain, we cannot yet see through the flow of conversation to know what is at the bottom of it all. The general direction is toward increased communication and mutual respect, perhaps even common cause. At the same time, I fear that there may exist a subtle undercurrent, a hostility on the part of church leaders toward science and scientists. It is likely that most scientists are as yet blissfully unaware of their enemy lurking behind church doors. Our clergy and theologians may be unaware as well, having shielded themselves behind cloaks of prophetic self-righteousness. If it turns out that this is indeed what is happening, then I would recommend that church leaders re-examine their posture and ask openly whether we wish to greet the scientific community with open hands or closed fists.

All this and much more enters into the complex of issues which makes up the faith-and-science agenda in our time. In this chapter, we will look at the various levels of the science–faith relationship in turn. In doing so, we will observe that what is going on is anything but dull. Overall, this is an exciting epoch for pursuing partnership between scientific research and Christian faith.

New Horizons of Conversation between Science and Theology

Exciting things are happening, especially in physical cosmology. Twentieth-century scientific pictures of the cosmos are being drawn in such a way that it makes sense to ask: does God belong in the picture?

For too long in the modern world, we have assumed that natural science and religious faith are either antithetical or at least insulatable. Conservative and fundamentalist Christians have assumed that scientific method, as well as certain theories such as evolution, positively contradict the truth about the world witnessed to in Holy Scripture. In many cases, they have forced the human mind to choose: either science or faith, but not both. Neo-orthodox and liberal Christians have for the most part taken the two-language approach. They contend that science speaks about nature in empirical and rational language, whereas religion speaks about transcendent realities in poetic or symbolic language. Science speaks about fact, whereas religion speaks about value. People of faith, then, are simply bilingual. They speak both scientific and religious lingo.

Yet, neither of these approaches could anticipate what is happening now. New doors are being opened so that scientific and religious thinkers can talk with each other about common domains of knowledge. Let us note three examples.

First, the second law of thermodynamics has drawn attention from Christian theologians because it seems to make nature historical. The principle of entropy entailed in the second law seems to indicate that there is an arrow to time. Time runs in only one direction. Events are single and unrepeatable. And nature is composed of events, not just universal principles endlessly repeating themselves. The work of Ilya Prigogine and others on the thermodynamics of non-equilibrium systems has shown quite convincingly that, on the macro scale, time moves from a finite past toward a finite future. Time is irreversible.[2] We may now think in terms of a history of nature.

This could be significant because theologians in this century have been thinking of God's relation to the world in terms of historical acts. God acts in history. The Exodus is a historical act. So is the incarnation, death and resurrection of Jesus Christ. So will be the consummation. Temporal history may become a common category wherein both scientists and theologians will pursue their research.[3]

Second, Big Bang cosmology has raised again the reasonableness of talking about the Christian doctrine of creation out of nothing, of *creatio ex nihilo*.[4] The red shift, noted when observing distant galaxies moving away from us and from each other, has led us to conceive of the universe as expanding. As we speculate backwards in time, we envision a point – perhaps 20 billion years ago – at which everything belonged together. The second law of thermodynamics leads us to pursue the logic of finite time. The bang began hot, exploded, and is now cooling off as it expands. There must have been a very hot beginning, a point at which it all began. There must have been a point at which time began, when $t=0$.

Where did this beginning come from? If there was nothing before $t=0$, can we talk again about an origin of all things out of nothing? Can we talk about *creatio ex nihilo* or about God lighting the fuse on the Big Bang? Regardless of how one answers such questions, we must recognize that the discipline of physical cosmology itself has pushed us to the edge of thinking about the world. It has pushed us to the brink of finite reality and is inviting us to look for the infinite. Physicist Stephen Hawking says that 'the odds against a universe like ours emerging out of something like the Big Bang are enormous. I think there are clearly religious implications'.[5]

Third, scientific discussions of the Anthropic Principle are raising again the prospect of a design argument for the existence of God. Two centuries ago, when the universe was thought of mechanistically and likened to the precision workings of a watch, natural theologians argued that this necessitated someone to design the world machine: it necessitated a divine watchmaker. Something similar may be happening today. As we shift from the mechanical model to the historical model of the universe, the question arises as to whether or not the history of nature is subject to divine guidance. What is significant to note here is that the question of a divine designer is being raised by scientists, not theologians.

The argument begins by noting how the facts of astronomy seem to involve an incredible combination of numerical accidents which readies the universe for the evolutionary appearance of life. Only the slightest change in the physical constants would have resulted in an uninhabitable universe. Take, for example, the expansion rate. If the early rate of the expansion following the initial bang had been slower by even one part in a thousand billion, the universe would have collapsed again before temperatures had fallen below 10 000 degrees. On the other hand, if the rate had been faster by one part in a million, the universe would have expanded too rapidly for stars and planets to form. Given all the factors determining the expansion rate – such as the total mass of the universe, the initial explosive energy, the strength of gravitational forces, and so on – it appears that everything was finely tuned just to make coalescing planets hospitable for living creatures.

Similarly, the minuscule asymmetry in the ratio of particles to anti-particles is another amazing feature. For every 1 000 000 000 anti-protons in the early universe, there were 1 000 000 001 protons. The billion pairs annihilated each other, producing radiation. Only one remained. Yet these one in a billion particles made the material world possible.

In addition, we note that the weak interaction force keeps the sun burning at a slow and steady rate. A slight change in strength either way would destroy the delicate relationship between sun and earth. And, further, if the strong nuclear force were slightly weaker than it is, we would have only hydrogen in the universe. If it were slightly stronger, all the hydrogen would turn to helium. In either case, stable stars and compounds such as water could not have formed. Without water, no life ... at least life as we know it.

This remarkable collection of unexplained coincidences leads physicist Freeman Dyson to remark, 'the more I examine the universe and study the details of its architecture, the more evidence I find that the universe in some sense must have known that we were coming'.[6] If the cosmos is so finely tuned to life, does this mean there is a divine tuner? Regardless of how one answers it, the question is alive again.

What all this is pointing to is the revival of conversation about theological matters within the domain of scientific inquiry. There certainly remains considerable rivalry between scientists and theologians, of course. Paul Davies brags that 'science offers a surer path to God than religion'. Nevertheless, what is significant is that 'what were formerly religious questions can be seriously tackled' by the new physics.[7]

Astronomer and agnostic Robert Jastrow created quite a stir some time ago
by arguing that 'the astronomical evidence leads to a biblical view of the origin
of the world'. Probably intending to goad the likes of Paul Davies, cited above,
Jastrow wrote the now oft-quoted lines:

> at this moment it seems as though science will never be able to raise the curtain on
> the mystery of creation. For the scientist who has lived by his faith in the power of
> reason, the story ends like a bad dream. He has scaled the mountains of ignorance;
> he is about to conquer the highest peak; as he pulls himself over the final rock, he is
> greeted by a band of theologians who have been sitting there for centuries.[8]

Some of our church leaders are rising to the occasion. In September 1987,
Pope John Paul II convened a study commission to commemorate the 300th
anniversary of the publication of Isaac Newton's *Principia*. He told the
physicists and theologians gathered at the Vatican that 'reality is one and the
truth is one; and we claim that there is an intrinsic call for unity of knowledge
whether it comes from experimental science or from theology'. Then in a
preface he wrote for the commission report, the Holy Father called upon both
the church and the scientific community to 'intensify their constructive
relations of interchange through unity'.[9]

The Roman Catholic Church is not the only Christian group interested.
Protestant and ecumenical Christians are ready as well. Institutes for the
purpose of bringing scientists into conversation with theologians are being
established in the United States and elsewhere. Princeton University has a
center. The Lutheran School of Theology at Chicago has now set up the
Chicago Center for Religion and Science. At the Graduate Theological Union
in Berkeley, California, the Center for Theology and the Natural Sciences
pursues research regarding the potential integration of the disciplines. The
Presbyterians have a task force to deal with it. The former Lutheran Church in
America and the Lutheran World Federation sponsored a major international
conference on 'The New Scientific–Technological World: What Difference
Does it Make for the Churches?' at Cypress in November 1987.[10] Credentialed
scientists in evangelical churches have formed a society, the American Scientific
Affiliation.

In sum, we find ourselves today in an exciting time, a time when natural
scientists and Christian theologians are finding that they have a number of
important things to talk about.

The Personal Faith of the Scientist

There is a widespread myth afoot in modern culture that a full-scale war is
going on between science and religion. Both disciplines are allegedly competing
for the allegiance of the human mind. Sometimes, the scientist is pictured as the
defender of rational truth leading the forward advance of our civilization,
whereas the religionist is pictured as one steeped in outdated superstition while
fighting for narrow-mindedness and intolerance. At other times, the scientist is

pictured as the godless naturalist who is threatening to undermine religion's claim to transcendental knowledge, whereas the person of faith is pictured as devoutly defending the truths and values which make life wholesome and meaningful. Although the reality of the situation hardly even approximates the myth of warfare, there is just enough truth to the pictures to make people think they must choose sides.

Usually during the years of higher education, the student begins to sense that he or she is coming to a fork in the road where the choice is one or the other, but not both. For some, of course, the fork is identified as a mirage and the student proceeds to embrace both the principles of scientific research and religious faith. The split is by no means inevitable; yet, many of us operate with the assumption that scientists are non-religious, if not downright anti-religious.

A psychometric study was performed by Bernice Eiduson on the generation of experimental physicists who broke open the twentieth-century mind with such discoveries as relativity and quantum mechanics, the same generation which pooled its mental resources to produce the atomic bomb. They had a surprising number of characteristics in common, such as that almost all were first-born sons of professional fathers.[11] The IQs of experimental physicists clustered around 150, whereas the theoretical physicists clustered at 170. Numerous factors were taken into account. Relevant to our discussion here is a section of the composite portrait of the male scientist at the prime of his career:

> He works hard and devotedly in his laboratory, often seven days a week. He says his work is his life, and he has few recreations.... The movies bore him. He avoids social affairs and political activity, and religion plays no part in his life or thinking. Better than any other interest or activity, scientific research seems to meet the inner need of his nature.[12]

Note: 'religion plays no part in his life or thinking'. It appears that scientific research is thought to replace religious devotion because it better meets the needs of our inner nature. In particular, science allegedly meets more adequately than religion our need for truth. Perhaps Albert Einstein represents the composite best. As a student in a German Gymnasium reading the works of Kant and Darwin, he reported, 'I soon reached the conviction that much of the stories in the Bible could not be true.'[13] With this as the operative stereotype, it is understandable that people today entering research may assume that they must choose between science and faith.

In one of his early movies, *Heavens Above*, famed comedian Peter Sellers played the role of a village vicar who diligently but somewhat naively was calling the people in his parish back to a personal trust in God. Among other things, he asked the rich to share their wealth with the poor. This got him into trouble with the business community and a forced transfer away from his vicarage. His new post was that of chaplain to Britain's space program. In one scene near the end of the movie, a number of scientists and technicians are sitting at their stations to monitor a rocket launch. One reports that the chaplain – Peter Sellers – has refused to make the official Church of England blessing of the rocket ship. 'Why won't he do it?' they ask. Because, the chaplain was reported as saying, he wants to bless people, not machines. Furthermore, he is concerned about their relationship with God. 'What,' one scientist exclaims, saying in effect, 'doesn't he know that we don't believe any more?'

Some scientists, of course, do believe. They embrace both a personal faith in God and a commitment to a life of research. A sterling example is Vincent Titanji, Senior Lecturer of Biochemistry and Molecular Biology at the University of Yaoundé in Cameroon. A man of firm Christian faith, Dr Titanji believes he has been called by God to pursue biochemical research into the causes of river blindness. This disease affects 40 per cent of the population of Cameroon, causing some to die and many to live their senior years without benefit of sight. The discovery of a cure could revolutionize health in his homeland. He works year in and year out, both on site as well as in laboratories in Sweden, to find the answer. This is his life's vocation.[14]

But, understanding such research as a divine call was not easy to maintain. As with so many young Africans who show promise in missionary boarding schools, there was no money for him to advance his education in North America or Europe. So, he accepted a full scholarship to the University of Moscow where he eventually earned his doctorate. During every year of his seven-year stint in Moscow, he was obliged to hear weekly lectures on atheism and dialectical materialism. The anti-religious propaganda was strong and incessant. This puzzled him. Even after a half-century of communist rule, the Soviet Union still perceived religion to be such a threat that there was no letting up on the pressure. Why such a reaction? he quizzed himself. Later, through contacts set up by the Lutheran World Federation, he met some biologists in Sweden who have continued to support him in his work in central Africa. They also support him in his self-understanding as a scientist who is working in the service of God.

Dr Titanji is a scientist who is a faithful Christian layman. There are many like him. The American Scientific Affiliation is an organization of evangelical (not fundamentalist) Christians who are trained scientists. In addition to lay people, at the present time they are seeing a growing number of science–theology hybrids, that is, individuals who are taking the matter so seriously that they are combining scientific credentials with theological training and in some cases even ordination. William Stoeger, SJ, is a priest and physical cosmologist doing research at the Vatican Observatory. Stanley Jaki at the Princeton Center for Theological Inquiry is a physicist and a Benedictine monk.[15] Lindon Eaves, genetics researcher at the University of Virginia, is also an Anglican priest. Robert Russell, who directs the Center for Theology and the Natural Sciences in Berkeley, holds a doctorate in physics and is an ordained minister in the United Church of Christ. Oxford scholar Arthur Peacocke is a biochemist as well as a theologian and heads a recently founded order for hybrids called the Society of Ordained Scientists.

Just how the individual integrates the two disciplines into a single life is a continuing agenda. It was said a century ago of physicist Michael Farraday, who was a strong Christian believer, that when he went into his laboratory he forgot his religion and when he came out again he forgot his science. 'I hope that is not true,' pines John Polkinghorne, Cambridge professor of theoretical physics and Anglican priest. He says, 'despite the obvious differences of subject matter, the two disciplines have in common the fact that they both involve corrigible attempts to understand experience. They are both concerned with exploring, and submitting to, the way things are'.[16]

What all this means, I think, is that we are entering a period where the mirage of the conflict between science and faith is being penetrated. If we allow ourselves the time and effort to get beyond the stereotype of the non-believing scientist, the opportunities for an integration of research and faith may appear.

The Scientist and the Church

Although the scientist may have achieved a harmonious integration between work and personal faith, his or her relationship to the church may be ambiguous. It is the case, of course, that professional scientists in our congregations are lay people and as such have much in common with all other lay people. Yet, there may be some characteristics of the scientist as scientist which affects his or her relationship to the church. On occasion, that relationship may lead to frustration. Let us explore just how and why.[17]

In 1982, I heard a Lutheran research geneticist from Boston describe his laboratory work as the 'passion' of his life, as the place where he puts his heart, mind, body and soul. He has invested years in postgraduate education and in grant applications, and he drives himself to stay at the frontier of new developments. 'But when I go to church,' he pines, 'the pastor asks me to pass out bulletins. No one in my congregation has the slightest idea what I do. My passion is not expressed or even acknowledged there.'

'Why is it this way?' I queried.

'Well, it's not that my pastor doesn't care. I think he's intimidated by science. So, he doesn't risk talking on my turf. I guess asking me to hand out bulletins is all he dare do.'

This is a mild, but significant criticism of pastor and congregation. We might call the problem here a failure in pastoral care. Whenever the deepest passions of a Christian individual's life are ignored by the Christian community, there is something wrong. Of course, practically speaking, we must recognize that it would be difficult to integrate such a highly specialized discipline as genetics research into the common life of a parish. Nevertheless, the sense of alienation expressed by this lay person needs to be heard.

Yet, there is more to it than just this. There may exist a subtle hostility on the part of church leaders aimed at scientists. I find it significant that when the geneticist is in church he is asked to pass out bulletins. Regardless of his personal background, he like everyone else in the congregation is asked to express his stewardship according to the list of activities we identify as church activities. When in church, do as the church people do. He is operating on the pastor's turf so he conforms to the pastor's routine understanding of what church is all about. This way the scientist as scientist cannot influence congregational life.

Is this enough evidence of hostility against scientists? No, not in itself. But if we combine this observation with what we know about the training of our clergy over the last few decades, perhaps a pattern of antipathy may become visible. Let me offer a couple of observations.

First, the senior generation of today's clergy and theologians went through seminary when neo-orthodoxy was dominant. We learned about the power of The Word, about preaching the kerygma, and about the centrality of faith. We learned to pit faith against knowledge of things in this world. We agreed with the modern atheists that scientific knowledge should be secular, neutral, objective and divorced from any taint of a faith perspective. The neo-orthodox theologians showed a healthy respect for the natural sciences, but they put up a high wall of separation between lab stool and pew. Many of us pastors have simply grown accustomed to this separation.

We take it for granted that Søren Kierkegaard is the grandparent to neo-orthodox and existentialist theology. We inherit from this great Dane more than a mild antipathy toward science. 'It is no good trying to cope with natural science,' he wrote; 'one finds oneself standing there defenceless and in no position to control. The researcher immediately begins to dissect with his details ... now it is time to use the telescope now the microscope; who the hell can stand that!' What Kierkegaard feared was the steady advance of the scientific mind which would eventually reduce matters of spirit to matters of matter. 'Physiology will eventually be so comprehensive that it swallows up ethics as well,' he pined. It is a combination of respect, but also fear of science which led neo-orthodox theology to distance itself from the modern enemy.

Second, the most recent generation of today's clergy has been more influenced by liberation theology than by neo-orthodoxy. This group may be overtly negative toward scientists. Whereas the neo-orthodox had respect for science, the liberation theologians do not. There are two reasons. The first reason is that liberation theology is anti-theoretical. The emphasis on praxis, on changing the world instead of understanding it, leaves the scientific researcher – whose primary task is to understand the world – out in the cold. The second reason is that those first-world theologians who try to tie the ecology movement with third-world liberation end up making the scientists their enemy. They conflate technology with science – in some cases deliberately refusing to distinguish the two – and then condemn technology for destroying the environment and becoming a weapon whereby the first world exploits the third world. So, the scientists become identified as the enemies of oppressed humanity as well as of mother earth.

We might call this liberation-based antipathy a 'moral' or 'prophetic' argument against science. This moral argument is not limited to clergy, however. It is broader. This brings us to the third cause of anti-scientism. There is widespread in Western culture a growing disenchantment with research science. After all, science produced the bomb! Whereas a century ago we believed that science, along with industry, would soon create Utopia on earth, we now worry that nuclear war may leave us with an earth which is uninhabitable. And even if we never get to nuclear annihilation, we know that many scientists earn their living by working on government contracts;

government contracts mean weapons research; weapons research means not only war, but also the unnecessary diversion of funds which could go to aid the poor. In effect, research scientists are integral to the structures of social evil.[18]

We clergy, of course, always want to stand up for what is moral. We want to oppose war and economic injustice. This is proper, I suppose. Yet, I wish to pause and ask: is it possible that we have created an atmosphere of moral self-righteousness such that, whenever we engage scientists on scientific matters, we carry the air of moral condemnation? Do we tacitly blame the individual scientists we know for the so-called 'structures of evil' in such a way that an intangible tension creates a separation, a separation which makes pastoral ministry impossible? Does it appear that we have reserved our ministry to the rightous among us and that scientists do not fit that category?

I am reminded here of Kurt Vonnegut's *Cat's Cradle*. The narrator is a journalist interviewing the director of a nuclear research laboratory. He writes,

> every question I asked implied that the creators of the atomic bomb had been criminal accessories to murder most foul.
>
> [The director] Dr Breed was astonished, and then he got very sore. He drew back and grumbled, 'I gather you don't like scientists very much.'[19]

No clergyperson is likely to say publicly that she or he does not like scientists. It may not even be admittable to the pastor herself or himself. Yet, the message comes through to the scientist. To be liked by the pastor, the scientist needs to pass out bulletins; the scientist needs to play the game on the pastor's turf.

What can we do to remedy the situation? One suggestion comes to mind: use the church as a forum for discussing the implications of the scientific research in which our people are engaged. Whether in an individual congregation, in consortia of congregations or at special conferences designated for this purpose, we ought not continue leaving things unsaid. We need to open doors, so to speak, so that the scientists among us can express their concerns and perhaps guide the church into new realms of responsibility. Such open discussion may meet some of the personal needs of the scientists, as well as serve the mission of the church as a whole.

I have spoken with Tom Gilbert. Formerly a research chemist with Argonne National Laboratories, Gilbert, along with Philip Hefner, now directs the Center for Religion and Science at the Lutheran School of Theology at Chicago. He said he once was a Methodist. He would sit in worship Sunday after Sunday listening to inanities from the pulpit that seemed to be forcing him into a *sacrificium intellectus*. So he quit. He dropped out of church activities altogether, thinking of himself as an atheist (although he wants to give a very specific meaning to his kind of atheism). He knew religious questions were very important, but he was not sure how to bring them to articulation. Sometime later, a few of his friends who were engineers and research scientists invited him to a Presbyterian church to talk about these matters. A discussion group formed, and this made the difference. Gilbert became a Presbyterian.

Gilbert is now a Lutheran and carrying on what he consideres to be important conversations regarding the relationship between God and the world. I find his biography significant, because he tells us one thing which the church can do; namely, provide a place where these matters can be explored in an intelligent fashion.

I asked Lindon Eaves, an aforementioned researcher in human genetics at the Medical College of Virginia and an Anglican clergyman, what he wants out of his church. 'First,' he says, 'I want good liturgy. Second, good preaching. Now, the preacher need not be sophisticated in science, but he or she should not say things which are palpably false.' He went on to add that, when matters of science and faith are discussed within church circles, we should address issues which are already on the minds of the scientists. 'Thank God,' he exclaims, 'we don't have to talk about evolution versus creationism any more!'

Science and the State

Scientists are citizens. Their incumbent moral imperatives are for the most part shared with every other citizen. There may be certain notable exceptions, however. These exceptions center upon weapons research. One issue is this: should scientists in the pursuit of truth sell their skills to national governments for the purpose of developing new weapons for destruction? A closely related but distinguishable issue is this: should scientists, whose morality of knowledge requires the open sharing of information on behalf of the pursuit of truth, engage in secrecy?

Many scientists, just like philosophers and theologians, are idealists for whom world peace is the primary goal of statesmenship. The vision of world peace is a universal vision, of course. Yet, the universality of that vision is challenged if not compromised when the scientist's daily employment is aimed at providing a military advantage of one nation over all the others.

Perhaps the most horrible chapter in the story of World War I was the development of poison gas. The German army introduced chemical warfare against Canadian and French African troops on 22 April 1915. It was chlorine gas, caustic and asphyxiating. Soldiers clawed at their throats, stuffed shirt-tails and scarves into their mouths, and buried their faces in the dirt. Writhing in agony, 5000 died and another 10 000 were damaged for life. A similar attack was launched against the Russians in June, a complete success.

Soon the allies appeared in the field wearing gas masks. Then things began to escalate. The French, who had already used tear gas, retaliated with phosgene artillery shells. These were ten times more toxic than chlorine. The Germans accelerated the development of ever more lethal gases, using chlorpicrin (Klop in German) against the Russians. Then, during an artillery bombardment against the British on the night of 17 July 1917 they introduced dichlorethyl sulfide. It had a horseradish- or mustard-like smell and so became known as 'mustard gas'. It penetrated the gas masks. The victims began vomiting. Then their skin reddened and blistered. Finally their eyelids inflamed and swelled shut. Blinded, they were no longer able to fight.

The director of chemical warfare research for the German military command was Fritz Haber. Haber justified his work, saying that 'it was a way of saving countless lives, if it meant that the war could be brought to an end sooner'. As the casualties began to mount and the atrocities became so horrendous, Haber's wife Clara Immerwahr, also a chemist, became melancholy. She complained to her husband that the production of poison gas was a perversion of science as well as a sign of barbarism. She demanded that her husband abandon his work. He refused, saying that a scientist belongs to the world in times of peace, but to his country in times of war. Then he went to the Eastern front to supervise a gas attack. Dr Clara Immerwahr Haber committed suicide that night.[20]

I find the Haber philosophy haunting: a scientist belongs to the world in times of peace, but to his or her country in times of war. This seems to have been the fate of the researchers who laid the groundwork for the Manhatten Project and the raising of the curtain on the dramas of the nuclear age. Hungarian expatriot Leo Szilard believed the liberation of atomic energy could actually save humankind. It would save us from confinement on earth and open up space travel.[21] It was he, along with Edward Teller and Eugene Wigner, who spearheaded the move to persuade Albert Einstein to write the famous letter to then President Franklin Roosevelt. This letter began the government-subsidized work on the atomic bomb. These scientists realized full well that, should atomic weapons be developed, no two nations would be able to live in peace with each other unless military forces were controlled by a common higher authority. And, further, if such an international control could abolish atomic warfare, it would be effective enough to abolish all other forms of warfare as well. In short, they hoped that the production of weaponry made from uranium would in itself hasten the advent of world peace.[22]

Szilard, along with Teller, helped the prestigious Einstein to compose the letter on 2 August 1939. They gave it to Alexander Sachs, a confidant of the president, for delivery. Sachs was not received by the president until 11 October. Sachs opened with a story about a young American inventor, Robert Fulton by name, who wrote a letter to Napoleon. The inventor proposed to build the emperor a fleet of ships that carried no sail but could attack England in any weather. With such engine-driven ships, Napoleon's armies could travel to and from England without fear of wind or storm. Napoleon scoffed: ships without sails? 'Bah! Away with your visionists!'

Roosevelt laughed.

Then Sachs cautioned the president to listen carefully as he presented the Einstein letter requesting the United States government to support research into energy drawn from uranium. Sachs handed over the letter wrapped around a bottle of Napoleon brandy. After two glasses of brandy were poured, the president began to pay concentrated attention.

'Alex,' said Roosevelt finally, 'what you are after is to see that the Nazis don't blow us up.'

'Precisely,' Sachs said.[23]

Eventually, Roosevelt became convinced and supported the research. He then needed to enlist the scientific community in the war effort. In a conversation with Edward Teller, the president said: 'If the scientists in the free countries will not make weapons to defend the freedom of their countries, then freedom will be lost.'[24] He was offering absolution in advance to those researchers whose consciences might be challenged by making weapons of death.[25] How does this compare with the position of Fritz Haber: the scientist belongs to the world in times of peace but to his or her country in time of war?

In addition to the humanitarian isssue whether scientists should invent machines of death, there is a closely allied issue regarding secrecy, of doing research behind 'closed doors'. In principle, scientific research, if it is to be true to its very nature, should be open and public. Knowledge advances more rapidly when discoveries are shared among the community of scholars. Each builds upon the other.

This certainly was the case among physicists around the world up to 1939. Communication was maximized. Whether a successful experiment was executed in Germany by Lise Meitner and Otto Hahn, in England by Ernest Rutherford, in Denmark by Niels Bohr, in Italy by Enrico Fermi, in the Soviet Union by Georg Flerov, or in America by Albert Einstein or Ernest Lawrence, it was written up and published in an international journal such as *Physical Review*. Conferences gathered these scientists together annually, usually in Copenhagen at Niels Bohr's invitation. When, in 1940, Igor Kurchatov, a nuclear physicist in the USSR, noted how the names of prominent physicists, chemists, metallurgists and mathematicians had disappeared from international journals, he deduced that bomb research was well underway. Secrecy itself gave secrecy away. This, in turn, accelerated the Russian research on nuclear explosives which had begun in 1939.

The achievement of secrecy in the United States was not easy to accomplish. The idea of secrecy arose once the idea became implanted that German research on nuclear weaponry was proceeding toward strengthening the Nazi war machine. People such as Enrico Fermi and Edward Teller advocated secrecy, meaning that fission research results would no longer be published, in an attempt to isolate German physics. People such as Leo Szilard and Niels Bohr insisted that secrecy must never be introduced into the discipline of physics. Bohr argued on behalf of complete openness as an operational necessity. Openness, fragile as it might be, is as essential to scientific progress as freedom of speech is to democracy. The scientist should publish all his or her results, favorable and unfavorable, where all could read them, making possible continuous correction of error. The advent of secrecy would not only retard the growth of science; it would subordinate science to someone's political system.

Once the war had arrived on America's doorstep, so did secrecy. At first, it took the form of an informal code. Plutonium became known as copper. U235 was called magnesium, and uranium generically was dubbed 'tube alloy'. The attempt at Columbia University to create a chain-reacting pile was known as 'the egg-boiling experiment'. Eventually, secrecy became official policy, and some scientists suspected of espionage were followed by undercover agents.

The issue of who enforces secrecy – whether it is enforced by the scientists themselves or by the military – only extends the concern. When Robert

Oppenheimer was traveling the country recruiting scientists to join in the research at Los Alamos in 1942 and 1943, a potential conflict arose. General Leslie Groves wanted the scientists commissioned into the military. This would help to insure security. Very few of the scientists were attracted to the notion of joining the Army. Some revolted. Science should remain autonomous, they argued. The execution of secrecy and security could be left to the military, they said, but decisions as to what should be applied in the laboratory must remain strictly in the hands of the laboratory. Oppenheimer feared a rebellion would delay the work and so convinced Groves to compromise. The Army would administer the facility and surround it with a fence. But freedom of speech was retained within the laboratory itself.[26]

Much has changed over the past half-century. Much has also stayed the same. It appears that nuclear weapons have not brought us world peace. They certainly have not eliminated non-nuclear war, and we believe we are threatened daily by nuclear holocaust. What has not happened is the rising of a common higher authority to insure protection from such weapons. In its place we have substituted the policy of deterrence, the policy of control through fear.

Church Statements on the Ethics of Nuclear War

Fear abounded in the decade between Ronald Reagan's first presidential campaign in the late 1970s – when he stated that the United States could win a limited nuclear war – and the dramatic Soviet shift toward rapprochement in 1989. The whole world asked: if our political leaders think we can survive a limited nuclear war, might they try it? Anxiety was high. Self-appointed prophets flailed about looking for someone to blame.

Church leaders came out squarely in opposition to nuclear war.[27] In 1984, the Twelfth Biennial Convention of the Lutheran Church in America (LCA), a predecessor body to the Evangelical Lutheran Church in America, approved a statement on peace which said: 'we declare without equivocation that nuclear war, with its catastrophic devastation of the earth, is contrary to the good and gracious will of God for the creation'.[28] Given this global repudiation of nuclear war, we need to ask what this means for research scientists employed by the government-sponsored weapons industry.

When we take a look at what our church leaders have been saying specifically about deterrence and its relationship to the threat of nuclear war, certain implications for scientists working in the weapons industry can be dimly discerned. These implications are not always drawn out. But the logic, I think, is identifiable. It goes like this:

What is said:
On the basis of both the pacifist and just war traditions, it would be immoral to engage in strategic nuclear war under any conditions, even in self-defense.

If we on our side should declare never to use a nuclear weapon under any condition, then we would no longer pose a nuclear threat to our enemy.

If we are no longer a nuclear threat to our enemy, then we must give up (or at best, give only conditional approval of) the policy of deterrence.

What is not usually said yet seemingly implied:
If we commit ourselves never to employ a strategic nuclear weapon and thereby abandon the policy of deterrence, then we would no longer need scientific researchers who are trying to improve on these weapons.

Or, as a corollary, engaging in such scientific research would itself be immoral.

The logic hinges on the acceptability or unacceptability of the policy of deterrence. Let me cite a couple of examples. On 3 May 1983, the National Conference of Catholic Bishops (NCCB) issued its controversial Pastoral Letter on War and Peace. This letter, it condemns totally any strategic use of nuclear weapons against population centers because such use would kill millions of innocent people: 'Under no circumstances may nuclear weapons or other instruments of mass slaughter be used for the purpose of destroying population centers or other predominantly civilian targets.'[29]

What the bishops oppose here is 'total war'. More specifically, it is opposition to nuclear weapons for strategic warfare on the grounds of the just war theory regarding proportionality, according to which the damage to be inflicted must be proportionate to the good expected by taking up arms. Because of the massive destructiveness of today's weapons, no proportional good could possibly emerge from their use. The opposition is based in addition on the principle of discrimination, according to which we should discriminate between combatants and non-combatants. Thus the bishops may be silently approving of the tactical use of nuclear weapons directed solely at combatants, but the strategic use is clearly condemned.

> Response to aggression must not exceed the nature of the aggression. To destroy civilization as we know it by waging a 'total war' as today it could be waged would be a monstrously disproportionate response to aggression on the part of any nation.... To wage truly 'total' war is by definition to take huge numbers of innocent lives. Just response to aggression must be discriminate; it must be directed against unjust aggressors, not against innocent people caught up in a war not of their own making.[30]

What this leads to is 'a strictly conditional moral acceptance of nuclear deterrence'.[31] Insofar as deterrence actually functions to prevent the outbreak of war, the bishops can accept it. But insofar as it functions to encourage the arms race with its ever-increasing refinement and stockpiling of weapons of destruction, they reject it. Or, more precisely, they view deterrence as an interim strategy for peace in a time when there exists no international authority strong enough to defuse international hostilities.

> The moral duty today is to prevent nuclear war from ever occurring and to protect and preserve those key values of justice, freedom, and independence which are

necessary for personal dignity and national integrity. In reference to these issues, Pope John Paul II judges that deterrence may still be judged morally acceptable, 'certainly not as an end in itself but as a step on the way toward a progressive disarmament'.[32]

Now, in light of this wholesale rejection of strategic nuclear warfare and partial rejection of deterrence as national policy, what do the bishops say about scientists and others working in the defense industries? Not much. They leave professional, financial and moral choices up to the individual. They 'recognize the possibility of diverse concrete judgments being made in this complex area'.[33] To the scientists specifically, the bishops write:

> We appreciate the efforts of scientists... Modern history is not lacking scientists who have looked back with deep remorse on the development of weapons to which they contributed, sometimes with the highest motivation, even believing that they were creating weapons that would render all other weapons obsolete and convince the world of the unthinkableness of war. Such efforts have ever proved illusory. Surely, equivalent dedication of scientific minds to reverse current trends and to pursue concepts as bold and adventuresome in favor of peace as those which in the past have magnified the risks of war could result in dramatic benefits for all of humanity.[34]

One might have expected more from the bishops. Given the premises of the argument, it would seem to follow that it would be morally unacceptable for scientists to continue to refine nuclear weapons if such refinement has potential for going beyond the temporary need for deterrence. But the bishops stop short of rendering such a judgment, turning moral responsibility over to the scientists themselves.

In 1986, the United Methodist Council of Bishops followed, with a similar statement with similar arguments. But, rather than embrace conditional acceptance of deterrence, they totally repudiate it. The logic seems to be that, if we commit ourselves to avoid using nuclear weapons, we have no ground for threatening their use through a policy of deterrence. In addition, the Methodist bishops accuse the American establishment of idolatry on the grounds that we place our trust in weapons instead of in God. Deterrence equals idolatry.

> Deterrence has too long been reverenced as the unquestioned idol of national security. It has become an ideology of conformity too frequently invoked to disparage dissent and to dismiss any alternative foreign policy proposals... Our vulnerability is mutual. Our security must be mutual.... Deterrence must no longer receive the churches' blessing, even as a temporary warrant for the maintenance of nuclear weapons.[35]

With regard to specific implications for scientists who engage in weapons research and manufacturing, the advice of the Methodists parallels that of the Roman Catholics: 'We know that scientists, engineers, and other workers in defense industries face difficult questions of conscience. We want our churches to help such persons confront these questions ethically; we urge the churches to provide a supporting fellowship for such persons in whatever vocational choices they make.'[36]

Now, after the Methodist bishops condemned the whole of society for a national idolatry, one might have expected something more specific to be said regarding the contribution of scientists to deterrence. Yet, both groups of bishops appeal finally to the individual conscience of the scientist in question rather than to the same broad principles appealed to earlier.

Having discussed these church pronouncements with chemists, physicists and engineers working in the weapons industry, I offer some preliminary and as yet informal observations. I note three reactions among scientists who are committed members of Christian congregations. Some scientists are simply willing to ignore what church spokespersons say about such matters. Another group is willing to reject what church leaders say on the grounds that, in the words of one woman chemist, 'they just don't know what they're talking about. They are such asses they don't deserve the waste of our energy'. A third group pines pathetically that they have been betrayed. In the words of a plasma physicist: 'it hurts to think that our own church leaders consider us as contributors to national idolatry'.

What is needed here, I think, is a couple of things. First, church leaders need to investigate the situation to find out just what our scientists are thinking and feeling. Second, we need to examine our pastoral responsibility toward the scientists among us. I wonder if the strength of our prophetic pronouncements regarding God's will for world peace may have so focused our vision that the pastoral needs of this important group of people have escaped our purview.

Conclusion

The coming decade could be an exciting one. If we remain on the present trajectory, we will find more and more conversations taking place between natural scientists and Christian theologians. The mood will be one of genuine openness, characterized by the free play of imaginations that wish to explore new frontiers. Creative opportunities abound. Unless this movement is cut short by a sudden return to rigidity by church theologians or a similar return to rejection of religion by the scientific milieu, we may soon wake up to some new and exciting convergences of thought.

On another front – the relationship between the prophetic and pastoral responsibilities of the church – I believe we need to examine a bit more closely the nature of the present situation. Perhaps the dismantling of the Soviet empire and the declaration by Mikhail Gorbachev that the cold war is over will permit us a brief interlude in which to make some reassessments. The nuclear crisis is by no means over. It remains the single most potent threat to human and natural existence on the planet. Yet, the factors that define the crisis may be undergoing a shift. During this period of shifting, we will have to readjust our prophetic posture. This may give us as well an opportunity to readjust our pastoral posture and add the church's relationship to the scientists within and without to this agenda.

Notes

1   This chapter was first delivered as the Graduate Theological Union Distinguished Faculty Lecture, Berkeley, California, 28 November 1990.

2   Ilya Prigogine and Isabelle Stengers, *Order Out of Chaos* (New York: Bantam, 1984).

3   See Wolfhart Pannenberg, *Basic Questions in Theology*, 2 volumes (Philadelphia: Fortress Press, 1970–71), I, 15. 'History is the most comprehensive horizon of Christian theology,' writes Pannenberg in his programmatic essay, 'Redemptive Event and History'. Pannenberg is inspired in part by the respected German physicist, C.F. von Weizsäcker, who wrote *The History of Nature* (Chicago: University of Chicago Press, 1959).

4   For much of the twentieth century, theologians tended to give up on the doctrine of *creatio ex nihilo*, presumably because it lacks scientific intelligibility. The idea of continuing creation has taken its place. Now, however, physical cosmologists are exploring the idea of creation out of nothing in a number of areas, including the notion of a sudden beginning to all things. The relationship between *creatio ex nihilo* and *creatio continua* is one of the themes uniting the essays in *Cosmos as Creation: Theology and Science in Consonance*, ed. by Ted Peters (Nashville: Abingdon, 1989).

5   Cited by John Boslough in *Stephen Hawking's Universe* (New York: Quill/William Morrow,1985), 121. Hawking recognizes the religious implications, then he moves to try to reconceive of $t=0$ so as to eliminate the need for God. Carl Sagan, a religious skeptic, tries to draw out the implications of the Hawking cosmology when introducing a Hawking book: 'This is also a book about God ... or perhaps the absence of God,' in Steven Hawking's *A Brief History of Time From the Big Bang to Black Holes* (New York: Bantum, 1988), x. What is important is that the question of God is unavoidable in the scientific discussion.

6   Freeman Dyson, *Disturbing the Universe* (New York: Harper & Rowe, 1979), 250. Cf. John Barrow and Frank Tipler, *The Anthropic Cosmological Principle* (New York: Oxford, 1986); Ted Peters, (ed.), *Cosmos as Creation: Theology and Science in Consonance* (Nashville: Abingdon, 1989), 129–31.

7   Paul Davies, *God and the New Physics* (New York: Simon & Schuster, 1983), ix.

8   Robert Jastrow, *God and the Astronomers* (New York: W.W. Norton, 1978), 116.

9   Robert Russell, William R. Stoeger, SJ and George V. Coyne, SJ (eds), *Physics, Philosophy and Theology: A Common Quest for Understanding* (Notre Dame: University of Notre Dame, 1988).

10   John M. Magnum, *The New Faith–Science Debate* (Geneva: WCC; Philadelphia: Fortress, 1989).

11   Some of the major contributors to the scientific advance have been women, of course, such as Marie Curie, Irene Joliot-Curie and Lise Meitner. The particular study noted here finds that generally American male physicists came from Protestant or Jewish background, not Roman Catholic, and were sickly in their youth. It also found that scientists think about problems in much the same way artists do.

12   Richard Rhodes, *The Making of the Atomic Bomb* (New York: Simon & Schuster, 1988), 142.

13   Ronald W. Clark, *Einstein* (New York: Avon, 1971), 36.

14   Magnum, *The New Faith–Science Debate*, 85–9.

15   Stanley L. Jaki argues that what science and Christian faith have in common is the demand for intellectual honesty. 'In fact,' he writes, 'science is as closely related to

religion, and especially to Christian religion, as a child is to the womb out of which it came forth and with full vitality.' Stanley L. Jaki, 'Science: From the Womb of Religion', *The Christian Century*, 104:28 (7 October), 851.

16 John Polkinghorne, *One World: The Interaction of Science and Theology* (Princeton: Princeton University Press, 1986), 97.

17 Ted Peters, 'The Scientist Among Us', in *Lutheran Partners*, IV:5 (September–October 1988), 18–22.

18 We will see below in the section 'Church Statements on the Ethics of Nuclear War' that official statements by church leaders do not overtly blame scientists for the evils of the bomb. The logic of ecclesiastical condemnations of the bomb, however, cannot but help implicate the scientists. What we are exploring here is the possibility that such condemnation is an undercurrent in church life.

19 Kurt Vonnegut, *Cat's Cradle* (New York: Dell, 1963).

20 Rhodes, *The Making of the Atomic Bomb*, 90–95.

21 Ibid., 14, 25, 107, 442.

22 Ibid., 308. When in March 1944 Robert Oppenheimer was deciding on the use of the code word 'Trinity' to name the test site for the first nuclear explosion, he had in mind a poem of John Donne, 'Hymne to God My God, in My Sicknesse'. It was a poem about death and resurrection held in paradox. Death is the path to resurrection. Oppenheimer, along with Niels Bohr, was trying to affirm the paradox that the invention of a weapon of massive death might actually win the war and redeem the human race for world peace (571f).

23 Ibid., 314.

24 Ibid., 336.

25 Absolving scientists of their possible guilt seems to be the accepted norm in public discussion even today. See Johnathan Shell, *The Fate of the Earth* (New York: Alfred A. Knopf, 1982). In his bestselling bombshell denouncing the nuclear threat, Jonathan Shell writes: 'although it is unquestionably the scientists who have led us to the edge of the nuclear abyss, we would be mistaken if we either held them chiefly responsible for our plight or looked to them, particularly, for a solution' (103). Well, if we cannot blame the scientists, then whom do we blame? Shell faults the applied scientists who make technological application of what the pure scientists discover, plus the political decision makers. He says that 'the scientists in the Manhattan Project could not decide to make the first atomic bomb; only President Roosevelt, elected to office by the American people, could do that' (105). And finally he says, 'all of mankind threatens all of mankind' (107).

26 Rhodes, *The Making of the Atomic Bomb*, 454. Oppenheimer, along with Szilard and Bohr, in their own respective ways defended the sharing of scientific knowledge even amidst the pressures of making war decisions. They believed that the USA could not maintain a monopoly on nuclear knowledge and that other nations, especially the USSR, would soon catch up. They could foresee an arms race. So they argued for a pre-emptive sharing of knowledge with the USSR to help reduce suspicion and competition (529–38, 620, 644).

27 Along with church leaders, many scientists have engaged in public protests against flirting with the nuclear threat. The March 4th Movement, begun on that date in 1969 at the Massachusetts Institute of Technology, initially focused on the Vietnam war, but then expanded to express concern toward general abuses of science and technology. This led to the formation of two groups dedicated to confronting the responsibilities of scientists in the weapons industry, the Union of Concerned Scients and Science for the People. The task here, says Robert Jay Lifton, is 'to separate science from scientism and technology from technocism' and to break the

collusion between the scientists 'with the nuclear deity – so that they can reconstitute themselves into an open brotherhood and sisterhood committed to the survival and growth of human beings'. Robert J. Lifton, *The Future of Immortality and Other Essays for a Nuclear Age* (New York: Basic Books, 1987) 169.

28 LCA, 'Peace and Politics' (Division for Mission in North America: Lutheran Church in America, 1984), 5. Although the LCA social statement covers many aspects of the nuclear threat, it does not directly speak to the role played by scientists engaged in weapons research, nor does a corresponding statement in 1982 by the Eleventh General Convention of The American Lutheran Church, 'Mandate for Peacemaking'. The closest is to say that 'the ALC encourage exploration of economic conversion in regions dependent on defense-related industries'. See the ALC 'Mandate for Peacemaking' (The American Lutheran Church, 1982).

29 NCCB, 'The Challenge of Peace: A Pastoral Letter by the National Conference of Catholic Bishops' (Washington, DC: US Catholic Conference, 1983), vi.

30 Ibid., 79. The problem with an outright endorsement of tactical use of nuclear weapons is that innocent civilians in the vicinity would get caught up in the conflagration. The USA has named 60 military targets within the city limits of Moscow alone. Thus, 'even with attacks limited to "military" targets, the number of deaths in a substantial exchange would be almost indistinguishable from what might occur if civilian centers had been deliberately and directly struck' (78).

31 Ibid., p. 79. 'Deterrence' is defined as 'dissuasion of a potential adversary from initiating an attack or conflict, often by the threat of unacceptable retaliatory damage' (ibid., 69). The Lutherans add a risk calculus and a principle of reciprocity to the concept of deterrence, saying: 'it is of vital importance for the near future that nuclear deterrence be stabilized at the lowest possible level of risk. Such stabilization requires the political recognition by both parties of the reciprocity of the deterrence situation. Reciprocity means that what is to be deterred is not only the other's capacity for aggression, but also one's own. Each side must restrain its own capacity for aggression to the satisfaction of the other' (LCA, 'Peace and Politics', 7).

32 NCCB, 'The Challenge of Peace', 74f.

33 Ibid., 129.

34 Ibid., 130.

35 UMCB (United Methodist Council of Bishops), *In Defense of Creation: The Nuclear Crisis and a Just Peace* (Nashville: Graded Press, 1986), 46, 48.

36 Ibid., 87.

II

PHYSICS, COSMOLOGY, AND CREATION

Chapter 3

The Terror of Time

Time terrifies us. It terrifies us because there is not enough of it. We want more time. The time we have seems too little for what we want to fill it with. We want to put a gallon of living into a quart of time.

Worse. Time terrifies us because it signals change. Specifically, time signals deterioration, dissolution and death. St Augustine asks rhetorically, 'Does it not follow that we can truly say that it is time, only because it tends towards non-being?'[1]

Can we find security in the present moment, in the now? Perhaps it seems that way. We can remember our past and imagine our future. It is by looking through the lens of the present that the past is past and the future is future. The present is concrete, while past and future are abstract. The present is solid and stable and here now. Therefore, what is present – what is in the now – must be reality. It is in the present that we find being, the solid ground on which we stand. We can find security in the face of time's terror by fixating ourselves in the present moment, by eternalizing the present moment. Right? Does this seem right?

The problem, of course, is that the present does not stand still. It is constantly moving. What a moment ago was future is now present, and what was present is now past. There is no stopping this movement. Time is a brutal, invincible reality that renders every present moment ephemeral. No amount of whining or flailing or cursing can alter time's incorrigibility.

If there is to be salvation, it will have to be found, not in the non-being of the now past past, nor or in the ephemerality of the passing present. If there is to be salvation, it will have to come to us from the future. If there is to be salvation, we will have to be greeted by a future of wholeness rather than deterioration, of fulfillment rather than dissolution, of life rather than death.

It seems to me that the Christian promise of salvation comes in this form. Rather than shoring up the present by eternalizing it and thus protecting it from past and future non-being, the Christian promise is that the power of being comes to us from the future, from God's future. It is the transformatory power of God's eschatological future that overcomes the terror of time, because it makes the ephemerality of the present moment temporary rather than final. Deterioration, dissolution and death are temporary. What is final is God's promised new creation and our resurrection into it.

As we draw out implications from God's eschatological promise, we see that we can look at time without terror. We can distinguish between passage and deterioration. Finite passage or the one-after-the-otherness of events does not need to be abrogated to enjoy the fruits of God's redeeming accomplishments. Eternity need not be conceived as an eternal present moment, as timelessness.

Eternity, if it is to incorporate the reality of the redeemed creation, cannot be simply timeless. Would it be better, I wonder, to avoid speaking of a timeless eternity and to speak rather of the everlastingness of God's promised new creation?

The Temptation to Timelessness

In an essay in *Dialog*, Jürgen Moltmann says that eternity has nothing to do with timelessness; rather, eternity is fulfilled life. Moltmann also places this fulfillment in the momentary experience.[2] Yet I wonder: if we collapse eternity into the momentary experience, are we not inadvertently appealing to timelessness?

In the face of time's terror, the temptation is to rid ourselves of time. We can see the temptation at work in Martin Luther's speculation that our future life in God's heaven will be without time. Luther writes:

> We recall early childhood to some extent; but we do not remember nursing at our mother's breasts, although we did have life at that time. The reason is that we lacked the ability to count. This is also why beasts have no knowledge of time, just as infants have no knowledge of it either.... We see Augustine gladly extolling this endowment of our nature and proving the immortality of our souls from it... Here some raise a question concerning the future life: Will this service of the heavenly bodies come to an end? However, that future life will be without time; for the godly will have an eternal day; the wicked will have everlasting night and darkness.[3]

Such an assumption that we need to disconnect eternity from time recalls Augustine. In his honest wrestling with the impenetrable conundrums surrounding the concepts of time and eternity, Augustine at one point contrasts them. 'No times are coeternal with you,' he says to God.[4] Might this imply that God's eternity is divorced from the world's temporality, and from our personal temporality? If so, then no salvation could lodge here in God's eternity. Yet, elsewhere, Augustine emphasizes that the problem is not with time per se, but with passage into non-being so that, if God could keep what is past present, then eternity would be redemptive. 'In the eternal nothing can pass away, but the whole is present.'[5] If the whole of which the Hippo bishop speaks is the whole of creation's history, then God's eternity is redemptive of all that is.

I applaud Augustine's inclusion of the whole of time in his understanding of history. What needs to be added is acknowledgment that the whole of history is not at the present moment done; it is not over. No whole of creation's history – nor even of your and my individual history – exists yet. Our time is yet open. If God's eternal present is coterminus with our present, then it could not be redemptive. Somehow, any definition of eternity with which we work must include our future, a future that is yet to be determined. This seems to be just what St Paul is saying in the Corinthian correspondence.[6] So, would it be too crude conceptually to say that eternity cannot begin until the whole of time is complete? Would it be too crude conceptually to say that eternity depends upon a prior eschatological consummation?

We may add another somewhat speculative argument for incorporating temporality into an eternity that God will share with us and with the whole of creation. As Christians, we tacitly affirm that the personal interaction between God and ourselves is fundamental and real. This implies that God is personal. It implies further at least some form of temporal passage, because interpersonal interactions have a built-in sense of continuity, sometimes even growth and development. If we were to conceive of heaven without interpersonal interaction, could it look fulfilling? If we were to conceive of heaven as futureless, would it then look more like eternal death than eternal life?

John D. Zizioulas recognizes the personal in the eternal: 'The life of God is eternal because it is personal, that is to say, it is realized as an expression of free communion, as love.'[7] If love between God and God's creatures as well as love among us creatures will imbue heaven for eternity, then might some sort of open future be included within eternity? Right now, on this side of the promised eschatological reality, we are oriented toward the future. 'It is God's promises which may be considered as ultimate truth, and these promises coincide with the goal or fulfillment of history. It is in short an eschatological truth which orients the human spirit toward the future.'[8] Might interpersonal loving characteristic of life in eternity itself also require some sort of temporal, even future, dimension?

What is to Come?

These questions regarding the internal nature of eternal reality are beyond my ability to answer. Tendering cautious speculations is the best I can offer. Yet, speculating on the nature of eternity or everlastingness has the value of turning our attention once more to what lies closer to hand, namely, the nature of time. Like Augustine, we assume we know what time is. We live with time every day, all day long. Yet, when we try to explain it, we find it quite difficult to articulate. Despite the difficulty, exerting some effort to articulate it could yield some worthwhile insight.

In what is to come in this chapter, I would like to look briefly at the intermixing of certain understandings of time pertinent to theological thinking: linear or historical time, mythical or cyclical time, and calendar time. In so doing, I would like to ask how such understandings of time illuminate the notion of an eschatological future. I will argue that the notion of linear time frequently ascribed to the Bible needs augmentation to account for two things: an openness to future newness that avoids predestination, plus a conceptual ordering that sees actual events as ontologically prior to the time by which we conceptually organize them. I will note that we can find significant continuity and consonance between the biblical notion of time and what modern natural scientists think. Then, I would like to turn to an example of theological reflection which, to my reading, prematurely and unnecessarily collapses the eschatological future into an eternal present, a sacramental present. John

Mbiti, a theologian from the East African Akamba people, will be my example here. In all of this I plan to argue for an eschatological ontology that invites us to trust the reality of the present to its dynamic dependence upon God's power to establish a redemptive future.

Is Linear Time Really Linear?

Paul Sponheim asserts that faith has an essential connection to irreversible time. Time has to do with freedom, 'for we give our deeds to the future irreversibly.... If the spacetime is truly in us, surely we cannot simply be saved "out of" it, "departing" at some point, as it were'.[9] This leads to the question of linear time.

It has become customary recently to contrast the linear conception of time presumed in the Bible with the cyclical conception of time of the Greek myths and of archaic mythological thinking generally. With this contrast we are given to understand that linear time is open to newness in the future, whereas mythological time always seeks return to an eternal point of origin and is thereby closed.[10] This conceptual contrast is helpful, to be sure, but it may be insufficient. The notion of linear time may be insufficient on two counts: it may need to add openness toward newness in the future and it may need to assess just which comes first, events or the time within which events take place.

First, we consider linearity and openness. Linearity all by itself does not guarantee openness to the future. Reality could be fated or even predetermined by parameters and principles fixed at the beginning. We find a closed future theologically in the doctrine of predestination, and we find it scientifically in reductionistic naturalism. Here, linear time may be reduced to a sequence of past causes and present effects that is closed to genuine newness; it may incorporate growth while being closed to an eschatological renewal. In sum, the concept of linear time may include either an open and contingent future or it may include a predetermined, fated one.

Now, the concept of time presupposed by the ancient Hebrew consciousness is linear, right? Well, sort of. I would describe it as punctiliniar or stochastic and epochal; that is to say, time moves in a monolinear direction, but it is punctuated by significant events. We might say further that in the ancient world, significant events probably had a greater impact on temporal consciousness than did time's monolinear direction.

The Hebrews were always living amidst or between significant events. They lived between the Exodus of yesterday and the promised land of tomorrow; they lived between promise and fulfillment. Time was conceived as a series of moments or seasons or epochs, each of which was initiated by an act of God. There can be no time without an event and no event without time.[11] The Israelites used festivals and Scripture to remember the saving activity of God on their behalf and in this way began to think historically. Religious ceremonies commemorated past events such as the Exodus, while the prophets looked forward to a new Exodus. Time for the Hebrews runs in one direction:

from past events toward future ones. More importantly, time is open for the God of promise to bring about new events.

We moderns share the ancient Hebrew understanding of time as monolinear, running in one direction from past, through the present, toward the future, with each event on the line being unique and unrepeatable. This concept of time may be more than just the cultural preference of the modern mind. It may be the way the physical world itself works. Physical scientists who stand on the frontier of modern science and who are looking at possible postmodern reconceptualization seem to agree: the course of natural events is irreversible and time runs in one direction from the past toward the future. Space physicist C.F. von Weizsacker has argued for nearly four decades that we should think of nature in terms of history.[12] Cambridge astronomer Arthur Eddington gave us the concept of time's arrow more than a half century ago, and today Nobel Prize winner Ilya Prigogine continues the argument that the second law of thermodynamics requires that we think of time within natural processes as stochastic, future oriented and irreversible.[13] Ian Barbour sums it up: 'Astrophysics adds its testimony to that of evolutionary biology and other fields of science. Time is irreversible and genuine novelty appears in cosmic history. It is a dynamic world with a long story of change and development.'[14]

Thus, there seems to be a convergence between our modern concept of historical time and our understanding of the natural world – especially through physical cosmology and evolutionary biology – and monodirectional time marks the point of convergence. On this point the ancient Hebrew world-view is not simply outdated and ought not be consigned to the irrelevant past.

Which Comes First: Time or Events?

Second, we consider time and events. Which comes first? For the ancient Hebrews, events come first. Whatever concept of time they worked with was derivative from their experience with events. The events are ontologically prior. Interestingly, this too seems to have a counterpart in modern physics through Albert Einstein's theories of relativity. According to the Newtonian world-view that preceded Einstein, the natural world exists within a container of time and space, so to speak. In the Newtonian world we can start with calendar and map and then locate material objects within an otherwise empty container of time and space.

With Einstein, we begin not with empty time or empty space, but rather with physical actualities. In Einstein's theory of general relativity, time is tied to gravity. In his theory of special relativity, time is tied to each inertial frame of reference, and these inertial frames of reference can be multiple. The old Newtonian picture of 'a fixed transcendent spacetime which is ontologically prior to the material contents of the universe', notes theoretical physicist Christopher Isham, is confronted with the subtlety of understanding causality as effective only within its respective reference frame.[15] What this implies scientifically is that natural events have an ontological priority, that time is event-dependent. Theologically, events arising from divine action come ontologically prior to the time in which they take place. Robert John Russell first notes temporal openness to creative newness in the natural world: 'The future is ontologically open, influenced, of course, but *under*determined by the factors of nature acting in the present.'[16] He follows this up: 'The basic argument is that God acts together with nature to bring about a quantum event. Nature provides the necessary causes, but God's action together with nature constitutes the sufficient cause of the occurrence of the event. In short, and metaphorically, what one could say is that what we normally take as "nature" is in reality the activity of God + nature.'[17] Whether the events are natural or historical, whether divine or human, it is the actuality of the events that elicits time.

Apocalyptic Fatalism

As I pointed out earlier, theological literature over the last half-century has indulged in the frequent contrast between the Hebrew notion of linear time and the cyclical or repetitive notion of time indicative of myth-oriented cultures, especially as espoused in Greek thought. There is some truth to this contrast, of course, but it is not subtle enough. The contrast is not so much between linear and cyclical models as it is between freedom and determinism, between open history and fate.

The cyclical notion of time expressed in the myth of the eternal return presupposes a fixed reality, an eternal design established once and for all by the gods *in illo tempore*, in the eternal time before there was any time. According to the mythical world-view, we may of course wander away from the divine source of being while in profane time, but sooner or later we must return to what has been originally established or else we risk dropping off into non-being. Nothing really new happens in the story of being. Ultimate reality has already been determined, and the cycles simply bring us back to the source of this determination.

But such deterministic thinking is not limited to the myth-oriented mind. Determinism in the form of fate can also imbue a linear notion of time. This is what happens in the apocalyptic. In apocalyptic literature, the history of the world is conceived as a single whole, running from an absolute beginning to an absolute end. God is pictured as having a single design for the whole, so that the individual events within the course of history are not of real consequence. The one-after-the-otherness of the series of happenings which we experience is simply the execution of an already established divine plan. Time's arrow flies in only one direction and it will not stop until it hits God's target. And the original aim is sure. Nothing we do can alter its course, and God has no plan to change its direction while it is in flight. It is all predetermined.

The Old Testament prophets, in contrast, look to a future in which God will do something new. They remember the past when God stepped into the course of history to change its direction. They then ponder the direction things are following at the present moment, noting especially when this direction goes against the divine will. What they report is God's promise to act again in the future, to re-establish his will and to change the direction of current trends and trajectories. On this count I here favor the prophetic over the apocalyptic mode of thinking about time.

Futurum v. Adventus

But, apocalypticism does make a contribution too. The concept of the two eons is indispensable to apprehending the significance of Jesus. The apocalypticists have divided the history of the world into two ages: the present evil age with its sorrows, and the future age of God's reign with its accompanying joy. Just prior to the coming of Jesus the two eons were thought to be opposites, separated by an invincible wall of time. What happens with the incarnation, however, is that the wall is penetrated. The New Testament draws us a picture in which the age to come has intercepted the present age. The future enters the present and becomes interwoven with it. The present reveals the future, whereas the future unlocks and opens up the present.

Our ontological question is this: from where comes the power of being, from the past or the future? The different answers can be distinguished by two Latin words for the future, *futurum* and *adventus*. The idea of *futurum* entails the assumption that the future will be the result of causative forces coming from the past. Here the future actualizes a potential that is already present, just as a cherry tree actualizes the potential already in the stone we plant in the ground. With the term *adventus*, in contrast, we think of the appearance of something radically new. The new here is not merely the effect of past causes or the actualization of existing potential. The kingdom of God which cleanses our world of its original sin, for example, cannot be simply the product of present causes, because all such present causes are corrupted and unable to shed their corruption. The kingdom of God must then come as an advent, as an act of divine grace whereby the creation undergoes genuine renewal. The future renewal of all things, which the advent of the divine kingdom will bring, has already appeared ahead of time in the person of Jesus from Nazareth, the proleptic advent of the ultimate rule of God.

Easter as Prolepsis

In this way, time itself becomes Christologized and eschatologized. This interweaving of future and present in the Christ event cannot be explicated fully within the strictures of the notion of linear time if this notion assumes that the future is the product of the past. The Easter resurrection did occur at one point on the line, to be sure, but it also transcended the circumscription of its own historical period. Something genuinely new happened on the first Easter. Somehow the eschatological future was collapsed and compressed and appeared in seed form within the soil of that temporal moment. Therefore celebrating Easter in Sunday worship is not simply a matter of remembering it. It is rather a matter of participating in an as yet outstanding universal reality, of anticipating the eternal and everlasting kingdom which has taken on the limits of temporality and ephemerality. Just as in Christ himself, so also in our Eucharist, the future arrives ahead of time but is not exhausted upon its arrival. It is the proleptic presence under humble conditions of the yet to be consummated fulfillment of all things in their ultimate glory. As in the first Easter so also in our Eucharist, the future is present in the flesh.

It is important to stress here that, although the future is present in the now, it is not exhausted by the now. Something remains outstanding, waiting to be realized. In the Pauline literature the point at which the present eon must make room for the future eon is the cross and resurrection of Jesus Christ. With him the new creation has arrived (Gal. 1:4; 6:15; II Cor. 5:17; Eph. 6:12). But, this is not realized eschatology if by that we mean nothing remains outstanding. Christ will come again, not to deal with the sin he has already forgiven, but to grant fulfillment to those who wait for him (Heb. 9:28). We live between Easter and the Parousia. The new eon will come in its fullness in the future. Hence, we now live between the times, on the margin of overlap between the future eon and the present. What that future time will bring, and its impact on us while we anticipate it, is the subject matter of eschatology.

Calendar Time as Empty Time

I find it fascinating that we can identify so much continuity of conceptuality between us today and the Hebrews of yesterday regarding time's directionality and the priority of events. However, at the level of culture it seems that the Newtonian notion of time as an empty container dominates our modern consciousness. Modern consciousness has objectivized and mathematized time so that the relation between event and epoch has been reversed, making calendar time a sort of receptacle into which we place and order significant events.

The use of calendars and the writing of history books along with the projections of futurists all seem to give primary ontological status to the relentless sequence of days, months, years and centuries. We scribble appointments on our calendars to organize our thoughts about the near future. We make time-lines to conceptualize the past and generate scenarios for what is to come. These provide the categories into which we drop our knowledge of events like filling containers on the assembly line at a canning factory. Calendar time in itself cannot distinguish between significant and trivial events. In our modern consciousness the abstract has taken priority over the concrete, the method of measure over what is measured. In the biblical period, in contrast, people oriented themselves temporally in relation to significant past and future acts of God.

Because calendar time for us today is linear in character, we seem pleased to think that it was linear for the ancient Hebrews as well. And time is certainly linear, according to the Old Testament, in the sense that there is a continuity of reality, a one-after-the-other series of covenantal epochs. In the present the past is remembered and the future anticipated. But, linear continuity in the

Bible surrenders priority to the events themselves. Each time God acts decisively he virtually creates reality anew. He establishes what will be. He acts out of his freedom and his power, evidently unconstrained by what has gone on before. His interventions into history demonstrate the same newness as that demonstrated in the creation of the world at the beginning, *creatio ex nihilo*.

Akamba Eschatology

I find fascinating and relevant the understanding of time within Akamba culture at the point where the traditional Akamba world-view incorporated Christian belief. Many among the Akamba of Eastern Kenya converted to Christianity shortly after the turn of the twentieth century. Now Christian and non-Christian Akamba live together in a single society.

In his very telling study of the concept of temporality among the Akamba people, John Mbiti, himself an Akamba, observes that time as the succession of events moves not forward, but backwards. History here does not move forward towards any goal still to come in the future. Rather, it points backwards to the origins and roots of present existence in the departed spirits called *Aimu* who are dead, but still with us. There is no concept of the end of the world. There is no abstract or mathematized concept of a time line or calendar, nor is there a *telos* or purpose built into history as a whole that is taking us toward the future. The verb structure of their language, Kikamba, is such that they cannot think abstractly of projected events more than two years into the future. And even this is considered a stretching of the present. Akamba do not learn about the future unless they study foreign languages such as English. Mbiti is convinced that our three-dimensional notion of linear time, with its past, present and future, is incomprehensible to these people who have only a past and a present.

Mbiti wants Christian eschatology to be meaningful to the Akamba. He wants to adapt it, but by no means is he suggesting an unauthentic accommodation or compromise. He begins by observing that, when the Akamba are confronted with Christian teaching in general, what interests them first and foremost is the complex of eschatological concepts – especially parousia, resurrection of the dead, heaven, hell and so on, – and these are quickly transmuted into Akamba conceptuality. What these doctrines lose in the transmutation, of course, is their tie to the Western notion of linear or calendar time. What the Akamba gain is a strong feeling of imminence, an intense expectation of the parousia. Their present is stretched by the Christian eschatological symbols so that a tension is felt between what is and what is now just about to happen.

Mbiti's thesis is that the eschatology of the New Testament is not dependent upon linear time and that it is possible to explicate the gospel symbols adequately without an exclusively 'futurist' conceptuality. Nevertheless, Mbiti is convinced that inherent in New Testament eschatology is a metaphysical commitment, which precludes demythicizing.[18] He must take a stand with regard to the nature of reality as a whole. So, what he intends to do is 'horizontalize' the Christian symbols through a sacramental understanding, and this will permit us to recognize the continued 'nearness of the spirit world' in a much more intensified present.[19]

Mbiti fixes on the phrase 'in Christ' with which he identifies the sum total of salvation. This is reminiscent of some neo-orthodox approaches to eschatology, which in a non-mystical way emphasize that the event of faith within time is the eschatological event, and that the fullness of being 'in Christ' means there is no as yet outstanding future. The future is collapsed into a very pregnant present, a present which never really gives birth to anything further. Karl Barth's approach, for example, did not use the term 'to horizontalize' but 'to eternalize' time, so that 'this event is that of a present without a future'.[20]

Mbiti's subtle but extremely important objective here is not actually to arrive at the correct understanding of time. It is rather to facilitate fellowship with God. The Akamba know what it is to have fellowship with the web of kinship which includes the living-dead, but such kinship has never been extended to the creator, to their high god Mulungu. The presence of Christ in the physical elements of the sacraments and the unity with God this signifies have 'stupendous implications' which are potentially within the grasp of Akamba thinking.[21] The sacraments form the connective nexus between the physical and the spiritual worlds. Through the concrete and material elements of the sacraments eschatological realities become evident and available in the temporal and physical realm.[22] It is this which Mbiti, motivated as much by pastoral as by theological concerns, wishes to develop further in the Akamba context.

The Challenges of John Mbiti's Eschatology

There is an immense hermeneutical problem, however, which confronts the Mbiti proposal. Namely, the Akamba have no traditional sacramental concepts or practices on which to build. Mbiti complains that they are too literalistic and materialistic, unable to perceive the transcendent spiritual realities associated with the sacramental elements. Further, the Akamba proclivity to magic makes it difficult for them to discriminate between magical manipulation and divine grace. Hence, it appears that the teaching task regarding the sacraments is just as formidable as that regarding the nature of the future.

This reveals something important about Mbiti. He is not a nativist or chauvinist arguing for isolating traditional tribal thinking from external encroachment. He does not intend to leave the traditional Akamba world-view intact. He is willing to alter the Akamba conception of reality – and his own conception of reality because he himself is an Akamba – if the alteration consists in a necessary explication of the gospel. His criterion, then, is the gospel, and he believes the gospel is better explicated in terms of being 'in Christ' through the sacraments than through a linear conception of time with its outstanding future.

Despite the care and clarity with which Mbiti examines the issues in his otherwise very fine study of eschatology, I for one cannot share his conclusion. This is the case for a number of reasons. First, the rejection of a still outstanding future on the grounds that living 'in Christ' is the more accurate eschatological concept I believe is fallacious. It involves the fallacy which blurs clarity through the unwarranted substitution of a more comprehensive but more abstract category. Of course we assert with Mbiti that being 'in Christ' constitutes salvation. But a significant question is: what does this mean? Does it mean 'in Christ now'? Or 'in the Christ of Calvary in the past'? Or 'in the Christ of the future kingdom'? Or all of these? Raking through the New Testament shows that there are both present and future dimensions to living in Christ, and the fullness of our union with him awaits the transformation. Sacramental presence is proleptic presence, in my judgment, not consummate presence. The Mbiti proposal would lose this complementary distinction between present and future maintained in the concept of prolepsis.

Second, if eschatological reality can be reduced to sacramental presence, we face another problem: we end up teaching the salvation of individual souls apart from the renewal of the cosmos. While Mbiti's Christians are eating the bread and drinking the wine at Eucharist, the pain of disease and hunger along with the threats of marching armies and nuclear destruction still plague the rest of our planet. Over these things the gospel promises complete victory, a victory which we still await. Even if one extends this sacramental theology beyond the individualism of faith to the communion of saints, we are still speaking about only a part of the creation rather than the whole. It seems clear that the Christian understanding of salvation still awaits a further and more comprehensive act on the part of God. Thus, sacramental indulgence by the Christian community ought not to be an end in itself.

Third, if Mbiti is willing to try to change the Akamba perception with regard to sacramental understanding, why is he unwilling to do so with regard to time? The Akamba world-view just might be one of those cases where evangelical explication implies a change or expansion in world-view. We need not embrace nativism wherein worldviews are considered sacrosanct and immune from alteration by the gospel. Mbiti himself agrees. He is willing to use methods of teaching to alter the Akamba perception of reality so that they will better understand God's grace working through the sacraments. So we must ask: if he is willing to do this with regard to the sacraments, why is he unwilling to teach the Akamba about the existence of the future? Is Mbiti consistent?

Mbiti believes it to be unnecessary and inappropriate to force the Akamba to believe in the Western linear concept of calendar time in order to present the gospel effectively. But could there be a straw-person fallacy here? Do we all agree that the gospel requires that we embrace calendar time? No, not necessarily. As we have seen, the biblical – and traditional Akamba – conception of time is not identical with abstract calendar time which cannot distinguish between important and trivial events. Christian faith has no stake in simply keeping date books or calendars. But, it does have a stake in the beforeness and afterness of events. We have to be able to think of ourselves as living between the times, between incarnation and consummation, between cross and kingdom, between promise and fulfillment, between the old and the new. These things cannot be collapsed without remainder into the present moment, even a sacramental moment.

The eschatological position I suggest we develop here does not have as its purpose the imposition of the modern Newtonian assumptions regarding a container of time on other cultures. But there are some things at stake in defending the one-after-the-otherness quality of events. For one, unless there is a past past, we cannot speak of genuine freedom on the part of God to create *ex nihilo* or, for that matter, to redeem what already exists. And the loss of divine freedom usually ends up with the loss of human freedom to change and create things as well.

In addition, the loss of a future pulls the rug out from under an ethics of planning, of any long-range vision of stewardship. If we are to think globally and holistically, what we need in our generation is a proleptic ethic, an ethic of long-range planning. This ethic begins with a vision of the positive future and then seeks to actualize that future ahead of time.

This leads to practical considerations which are associated with ethics and politics. There may be some practical value for the Akamba to learn how to think in terms of calendar time and how to master the challenges it poses. Whether the Kikamba language allows for it or not, the reality is that scientific futurists can and do make forecasts regarding the depletion of non-renewable natural resources and population growth, and such factoring just may spell life or death for the whole Akamba people over the next few decades. Advancing desertification and the loss of food-bearing land is on the way, and along with it is likely to come more and more starvation. Plans need to be made to insure the well-being if not the very existence of such peoples in proximity to the African Sahara. The relevant factors can and must be analyzed in time periods much longer than two years. On ethical grounds alone it just may be advisable to teach the Akamba some degree of future consciousness as a means to their very survival. But we must acknowledge that with such teaching comes the terror of time. Only an eschatological promise can meet such terror with comfort.

The Whole of Time

What we need to construct is a concept of eternity that does more than merely escape the terrors of a present that passes into the non-being of the past. We need an understanding of eternity that incorporates the temporality of creation without losing it to the dead past. To which theologians might we turn?

Could Paul Tillich help? Tillich may appear at first to try to escape from the terror of time by hiding in the *eternal now*. The eternal now, says Tillich, is found 'above' time or in the 'depth' of time. Eternity may be above or below time, but certainly not subject to a future that would turn the present into the past. 'The eternal is not a future state of things. It is always present.'[23] Yet, on the other hand, Tillich cannot divorce eternity completely from time. 'What happens in time and space, in the smallest particle of matter as well as in the greatest personality, is significant for eternal life. And since eternal life is participation in the divine life, finite happening is significant for God.'[24] So, just what is Tillich's commitment: a time-less eternity of a time-filled eternity? Tillich seems to advocate a futureless eternal present that takes finite events seriously. Yet, I ask, can eternity take finite events seriously without a future of its own?

More helpful here is the contribution of Wolfhart Pannenberg. Pannenberg's alternative to eternity residing above time or in the depth of time is to conceive of eternity as the whole of time. This is because the essence of anything, especially the essence of our personhood, is contextual. Who we are is determined by the whole context of which we are a part, and the meaning of the present moment is determined by the whole context of our personal history. The meaning of our individual personal history is determined by the whole context of cosmic history.

> The end of worldly history will bring fully to light all of its events and the life of each individual human being. But the end of history is not nothingness. The end of time ... is eternity. It is from the standpoint of this end that the essence of each individual thing, the manner in which it has anticipated eternity, will be decided.[25]

This means that eternity as the whole of time is dependent upon the consummation of time, both existential time and cosmic time. This is what resurrection and new creation beyond the end make possible, for Pannenberg.

> In life in the present the past is no more and the future has not yet come. This separateness means that the totality of our life constantly evades us. Hence time is no more a theologically neutral thing than death.... The finitude of the perfected, when this corruptible will have put on incorruption (1 Cor. 15:53), will no longer have the form of a sequence of separated moments of time but will represent the *totality* of our earthly existence.[26]

In short, our future end is not the cessation of being but rather the fullness of being. God's eschatological future is the ground of the being of all that is.[27]

Conclusion

In sum, I argue that we think of the future as the gravity of being which is drawing us toward God's eschatological consummation. Although this Christian understanding of time shares with the modern mind – with both the Newtonian and post-Einstein modern minds – the concept of linearity, the views are not in every respect identical. Whereas the biblically based view orients us between significant events, the modern Newtonian view of calendar time is abstract and unable to distinguish the significant from the trivial. Therefore, when it comes to contextualization in the third world, Christians are not theologically obligated to force premodern peoples to adopt the calendar view of time. Nevertheless, just any old framework for temporal thinking will not do. The communication of the gospel requires at least a minimum of temporal consciousness so that we can see ourselves as living between the Easter of yesterday and the consummation of tomorrow. And, once the eschatological tomorrow comes, the eternal life we will share with God will transcend not temporal passage but rather deterioration, dissolution and death. Confidence in this divine promise offers confidence in the face of time's terror.

To be is to have a future. We sense this existentially. To lose our future is to die. The threat of losing our future elicits anxiety. Without a future we feel depressed, lonely and angry. Hope for the future elicits joy, confidence and energy. The dialectic between future and present is the dialectic between being and non-being. We may try to escape this anxiety through flight into mythology or sacramentology. Mythologies that carry us back to our origin or sacramental theologies that export the terrifying present into an eternal present risk conceptual denial, denial of the reality of temporal passage with tomorrow's decay and death. To seek the ground of being in the past or in the present fails to come to grips with the terror of the future and the grace of the future.

A theological ontology based upon the Easter eschatological promise implies, I believe, that the power of being comes from the future, God's future. We and all that exists in the cosmos experience the power of being as a draw toward the future. This is the way God, the ground of being, cedes being to the world: God grants the world a future. When we think of *creatio ex nihilo* – creation at day one in the book of Genesis or lighting the fuse on the Big Bang – I believe we could say this: the first thing God did for the universe was to give it a future. God bestows future by opening up the possibility of becoming something it had never been before and by supplying the power to change. The power of God is experienced in the creation as the power to become something new. Until it has become something new, it has not become what it essentially is. Creation and redemption have this in common: both receive a future from God.

In the present moment we experience the power of being as a draw toward future reality. The present never stands still. It is constantly moving. What we call the 'now' is really an abstraction, a mentally conceived discrete moment. The underlying actuality from which we abstract it is an ever-moving frontier of time. As the frontier moves, what we think of as the present is dropping off into the past, dropping into the non-being of the past. The power of being is constantly drawing us from the present moment toward the next, while allowing all other reality to drop into the non-being of the past. To fail to be drawn forward is to allow the past to overtake us, to cease to be.

What I am describing here is the pre-eschatological relation of time to being as experienced by the created cosmos. The eschatological dimension, as Christian theology conceives it, anticipates a fulfillment of time and being. The eschatological end – both *telos* and *finis* – will constitute the fulfillment of time. Rather than a cessation of time wherein everything drops into the non-being of the past, the eschatological end will constitute the consummation of time, the gathering up of all that has been the history of reality into eternal life. What has been fragmentary and partial will, according to Christian soteriology, become healed and whole.

Notes

1 Augustine, *Confessions*, XI, 14.
2 Jürgen Moltmann, 'What is Time? And How Do We Experience It?', *Dialog*, 39:1 (March 2000), 27–34.
3 Martin Luther, *Luther's Works: American Edition* (vols 1–30: St. Louis: Concordia, 1955–67; Vols 31–55: Minneapolis: Fortress, 1955–86), I, 44.
4 Augustine, *Confessions*, XI, 14.
5 Augustine, *Confessions*, XI, 11. Boethius provides the West with the classic definition of eternity as 'the simultaneous and complete possession of infinite life' (*The Consolation of Philosophy*, V, 6).
6 For further discussion on this point, see David Fredrickson, 'Paul Playfully on Time and Eternity', *Dialog*, 39:1 (March 2000), 21–6.
7 John D. Zizioulas, *Being as Communion* (Crestwood, NY: St. Vladimir's Seminary Press, 1993), 49.
8 Ibid., 68.
9 Paul Sponheim, *Faith and the Other* (Minneapolis: Fortress, 1993), 28.
10 Mircea Eliade describes the structure of mythological time with its security in the eternal return. He then describes the *terror of time* at the appearance of historical consciousness in biblical religion: 'Definitely desacralized, time presents itself as a precarious and evanesent duration, leading irremdiably to death.' *The Sacred and the Profane* (New York: Harcout, Brace & World, 1959), 113.
11 See Gerhard von Rad, *Old Testament Theology*, 2 volumes (Edinburgh: Oliver & Boyd; New York: Harper & Row, 1962–5).
12 Carl Friedrich von Weizsacker, *The History of Nature*, tr. by Fred D. Wieck (Chicago: University of Chicago Press, 1949).
13 See Ilya Prigogine and Isabelle Stengers, *Order Out of Chaos* (New York: Bantam, 1984). The startling 1998 discovery in physical cosmology that the expansion of the universe is accelerating only re-enforces the concept of the arrow of time. The distant galaxies are not slowing down because of gravity, as earlier Big Bang theories predicted; rather, they are accelerating in speed, indicating a possible vacuum energy operative. Some scientists are identifying this vacuum energy with Albert Einstein's notion of the cosmological constant, lambda. Initial data suggest that 70 per cent of the universe's energy is in the form of lambda and only 30 per cent in matter. See James Glanz, 'Cosmic Motion Revealed', *Science*, 282:5397 (18 December 1998), 2156–7; Martin A. Bucher and David N. Spergel, 'Inflation in a Low-Density Universe', *Scientific American*, 280:1 (January 1999), 63–9.
14 Ian G. Barbour, 'Creation and Cosmology', in *Cosmos as Creation*, ed. by Ted Peters (Nashville: Abingdon Press, 1989), 143. See 'The Ever-Presence of Eternity' by J.T. Fraser where temporal consciousness is tied to evolutionary biology, *Dialog* 39:1 (Sping 2000), 40–5.
15 C.J. Isham, 'Creation of the Universe as a Quantum Process', in *Physics, Philosophy, and Theology*, eds Robert John Russell, William R. Stoeger and George V. Coyne (Vatican City State: Vatican Observatory; Notre Dame: University of Notre Dame Press, 1988), 388. Shifting from relativity theory to quantum physics and thermodynamics, Robert John Russell shows how new understandings of

nature are openings to seeing God's continuing creative activity. 'Rather than saying that God creates order in place of chaos, from a quantum perspective we could say that God creates order by displaying the properties of chaos. In addition we can now think of God the Creator as immanent in the world such that events which are physically separate are somehow co-present or coherent to God' ('Quantum Physics in Philosophical and Theological Perspective', ibid., 367).

16   Robert John Russell, 'Does the God Who Acts Really Act in Nature?', in *Science and Theology: The New Consonance*, ed. by Ted Peters (Boulder: Westview Press, 1998), 85.

17   Ibid., 89.

18   John Mbiti, *New Testament Eschatology in an African Background!* (Oxford: Oxford University Press, 1971), 57.

19   Ibid., 61, 156.

20   Ibid., 99, 108, 153; Karl Barth, *Church Dogmatics*, 4 volumes (Edinburgh: T.&T. Clark, 1936–62), III: 2, 624.

21   Mbiti, *New Testament Eschatology*, 123.

22   Ibid., 125.

23   Paul Tillich, *Systematic Theology*, 3 volumes (Chicago: University of Chicago Press, 1951–63), III, 400.

24   Tillich, *Systematic Theology*, III, 398. Raymond F. Bulman presses Tillich's notion of *kairos* or fullness of time in the direction of prolepsis: 'A *kairos* is always a fragmentary breakthrough of the divine power into history: it may last only for a moment in time. At any point in history, we can only hope for a partial victory, but all such victories are real anticipations of the coming reign of God at the end of history and bear important witness to its ethical demand.' *The Lure of the Millennium* (Maryknoll, NY: Orbis, 1999), 199.

25   Wolfhart Pannenberg, *Metaphysics and the Idea of God* (Grand Rapids: Eerdmans, 1990), 109.

26   Wolfhart Pannenberg, *Systematic Theology*, 3 volumes (Grand Rapids: Wm. B. Eerdmans, 1991–8), III, 561 (original emphasis).

27   Pannenberg makes eternity inclusive of time as infinity is inclusive of finitude: 'The thought of eternity that is not simply opposed to time but positively related to it, embracing it in its totality, offers a paradigmatic illustration and actualization of the structure of the true Infinite which is not just opposed to the finite but also embraces the antithesis' (ibid., I, 408).

Chapter 4

God as the Future of Cosmic Creativity

The question of creativity, especially advancing or accelerating creativity, can be posed cosmologically or anthropologically. Did the cosmos already exhibit creativity prior to the appearance and evolutionary development of *homo sapiens*? Or is creativity something introduced for the first time by human imagination and invention? Is human creativity itself an emergent phenomenon, or does it depend on a prior creative advance that makes it possible? To these questions we might want to add a theological one: is human creativity tied in any essential way to divine creativity?

My answer to the final question is yes; human imagination and invention issue from an inner sense of being drawn toward a new and better future, a sense evoked within the human soul by our interaction with a creative God. God does new things and we, made in God's image, are capable of transforming the old into the new. God creates *de novo* and *ex nihilo*: God creates brand new things out of nothing. We, God's creatures, cannot by any means mimic God in creating out of nothing, to be sure; yet, God's power to renew and redeem can work around us and through us to bring about a future that goes beyond the potentials of the past.

My interest in this subject has an autobiographical component. My father was an automotive engineer in the Detroit area. Every day he would awaken, shave, catch breakfast and go the General Motors Tech Center. There he would try to invent something that hitherto had never existed in the history of the world. He and 40 000 other engineers nonchalantly went about their business day after day creating technologies that, in each instance, brought something brand new into the reality that is our world. When he retired, 22 patents had my father's name on them. Though proud of his patents, he thought of his work as routine. It may look routine to the engineer at work, but philosophically, much is at stake here.

What is present in our culture that stimulates such systematic creativity and yet assumes it to be routine? My father, like myself, is heir to three plus millennia of Western culture that inherits the rational mind of the Greeks and the promising God of the Hebrews. The God of ancient Israel would make promises. Then God would fulfill them. This God did not settle for things the way they were. This God did not restrict divine activity to a one-time act at the beginning, nor did this God ask us to return to realities of the past. This God promised the people of Israel a new land, a new covenant, a new life and a new creation. Once we today put such promises of newness together with the human capacity to reason, we get invention. We can imagine a new world different from the present one, and we can begin to take steps to transform present reality. If we begin with tacit faith in the God of new things – if we tacitly assume that newness is normal, so to speak – then human imagination and ingenuity are set free to be creative.

Was it the experience of a promising God that let loose human creativity for the first time? Probably not. We might surmise that something was already present within the human soul that rose up to greet the divine promise positively. A quiet voice within us says 'yes' to the image of a future better than the present. Perhaps God placed the sense of draw toward the new within the nascent human psyche early in the evolutionary process.

Getting Ready: Consonance and Dissonance between Science and Theology

My plan here is to set forth a number of theses regarding God's relation to the world understood primarily in terms of future orientation and continuing creativity. These will be primarily theological theses; yet, they will be cognizant of correlate concepts based upon the natural sciences. I will look for consonance and dissonance between science and theology.[1] In some cases what we say theologically will fit consonantly with current scientific thinking, while in other cases we may find little if any correspondence or perhaps even incompatible perspectives.

What we are after is not merely the melding of disciplines. Rather, we are after an understanding of reality, the reality of nature that the scientist studies. Physicist Charles Townes speaks eloquently:

> Although science and religion are frequently separated and contrasted, I believe they can provide overlapping ways in which we apprehend the one universe of which we are a part. Nature gives voice to beauty, and beauty to meaning and purpose. The language of science may appear lifeless or deadening to some poets; but the scientist himself or herself is often sensitive to the beauty of nature, immensity of space, and the complexity of the material world.[2]

The truth of nature transcends what can be learned through science, and the aesthetic sensibilities of the scientist makes him or her aware of it.

This suggests that we should be cautious about overestimating the contribution of science to our understanding of God. If science stops a bit short of fully understanding nature, the theologian cannot expect science all by itself to discover and describe God. Certainly, the scientific study of nature cannot match what is revealed in a symbol or event, such as the cross or Easter. Yet, science can point beyond itself, beyond the natural world. At this point, the theologian offers distinctive resources to the discussion. Theologian Mark Worthing acknowledges that 'science can legitimately address questions related, at least indirectly, to the existence and role of God in the world'.[3] Although science may examine the physical and suggest things metaphysical, we must eventually appeal to extra-scientific knowledge. Philip Clayton points out that 'physics (and biology and neurophysiology) *underdetermines* its metaphysics; multiple metaphysical perspectives can interpret the results'.[4] So, when science poses questions that go beyond itself, then we need to employ distinctively theological resources to speak to those questions.

Be that as it may, we theologians find that we cannot pursue our craft honestly without giving serious consideration to the world as natural science perceives it. What science and theology have in common is commitment to truth, to following whatever path truth leads us down. There is but one world, one reality. We theologians believe that this one reality is God's creation, so any truth about the world should in principle complement what is true in our beliefs about God. Even if now we only see through a clouded window, we have confidence that the pursuit of good theology and the pursuit of good science will gradually dispel the cloudiness.[5]

This confidence requires that the theologian seek out the best of science. 'The dialogue partner of theology should primarily be the most established scientific theories representing the best available truth-candidates,' says Niels Gregersen.[6] Pastor–physicist George Murphy puts it this way: 'It is important for the mission of the church that it support good science and oppose bad science, pseudo-science and the opponents of science. Why? In the first place, the Christian doctrine of creation implies that the world makes sense .... [Second] the church itself will be discredited among scientifically literate people if it is identified with scientific ignorance and incompetence.'[7]

Five Theses about God as the Source of Cosmic Creativity

I put forth the following theses as hypothetical propositions for discussion. In some instances, they begin with the faith commitments of the theologian and expand by looking for consonance and dissonance. In other instances they begin with scientific observations about nature and then draw implications for theological conceptualizing.

1 The Concept of 'Integrative Wholeness' will be Fruitful for Theology

Epistemological and even ontological holism have much to offer theological reflection. Building upon genuine scientific knowledge about the natural world, yet avoiding the pitfalls of reductionism, holistic thinking allows us to recognize emergence within nature and spurs us to consider the value of projected future evolutionary and cosmological transformations.

The cardinal principle of holistic thinking is this: *the whole is greater than the sum of the parts.* Nancey Murphy, in her relentless rebuttals of reductionism, recommends a new 'thinking strategy' that begins by 'recognizing *a complex mutual conditioning between part and whole*'.[8] With this in mind, research might find fruitful a guided examination of phenomena, looking for the whole–part interaction and expect, on occasion, to find it.

An important corollary to the cardinal principle is this: *everything is related to everything else.* This is the principle of connectedness, of relationality. It prescinds from an intuitive metaphysical insight regarding the necessity for all things to be united. The logic goes like this: if there is one God, then there must be one world, one creation standing over against, but in relation to the one God. In addition, any images we work with regarding eschatological redemption will include the qualities of peace and harmony, and these qualities require integration, wholeness.[9]

Of course, it is one thing to look for integrative wholeness; it is quite another to find it in the physical world.[10] Recent discoveries and speculations in cosmology draw our attention in this direction. Is the cosmological constant making a comeback? In 1917, Albert Einstein had modified his gravitational equations in general relativity theory to include a 'cosmological term' representing a force of repulsion at great distances. This anti-gravitational force would allegedly hold the universe in a constant shape, avoiding collapse due to gravity. When it was proved that the universe is expanding, Einstein gave it up. If there is no quasi-static world, he said, then away with the cosmological term. Without this cosmological constant, Big Bang theory could describe a universe spreading out and out and never regaining what once might have been its state of singularity.

With new discoveries of distant supernovae accelerating, however, perhaps we will see a version of the cosmological constant invited back into the equations. Although one would expect on the basis of the standard Big Bang model that distant stellar clusters would slow down over time, new evidence suggests that the expansion is actually accelerating with time. A universe made up only of normal matter/energy could not grow in this fashion, because gravity is always attractive. Expansion could speed up only if some form of exotic energy fills the apparently empty space everywhere. What physicists are now referring to as 'vacuum energy' looks curiously akin to Einstein's discarded cosmological constant. Vacuum energy is roughly calculated at 120 orders of magnitude larger than the energy contained in all the known matter of the universe. Unlike ordinary forms of mass and energy, vacuum energy adds gravity that is repulsive and can drive objects within the universe apart at increasing velocities.[11]

Physical connectedness, if it exists, would be found not in the stellar objects separating from one another as a result of accelerating expansion; rather, it would be found in the ubiquitous exotic energy. One ought not to jump to metaphysical conclusions here; yet, we can project significant metaphysical implications if the new cosmology gains empirical confirmation.

This is philosophically reminiscent of, but not identical to, the revisionist physics of David Bohm. Like Einstein, Bohm's proclivity is to see cosmological unity in hidden variables. But, more relevant to our discussion here is the connection Bohm draws between cosmological unity, holism and healing. Bohm notes that 'health' in English is based on the Anglo-Saxon word 'hale' meaning 'whole'. Therefore, he argues, healthy thinking will be holistic thinking. The entire Bohm project of reconstructive physics is based on the thesis that the explicate order of things, the order at which we can discriminate one thing from another, is not the fundamental reality. There is under and behind it an implicate order, a realm of undivided wholeness – he calls it the 'multidimensional ground' – which is present in each of the explicate parts.[12] In short, Bohm believes holistic thinking is redemptive because it reflects what is really real, namely, a holistic reality which encompasses and includes the thinker. Our certainty as to whether the physical world is or is not actually as Bohm describes it awaits further scientific confirmation. While waiting, we might want to push on to describe speculatively this multidimensional whole which, it is hoped, can heal our brokenness. Hence there is a soteriology implicit in holism; namely, if we think holistically we will not only reflect reality better but we will also heal the lack of wholeness.

Note the path I have trod. I began with the intuitive sense that the holistic principle should guide our observations about the physical cosmos. Empirical research and cosmological theory in the field of physics may (or may not) corroborate the postulate that all things are connected. The field of evolutionary biology, to which we turn now, gives rise to holistic reflection because of the emergence of living organisms that transcend their chemical make-up.[13] We will note that emergence incorporates temporality and, hence, creativity – that is, integrative wholes developing over time.

2 Holism, Combined with Temporality, Implies the Emergence of Something New

The whole of which holistic thinking speaks is not static; it is dynamic. It implies movement, change, transformation. It implies the emergence of something whole out of what was previously fragmented or merely aggregated. Living organisms, for example, develop capabilities and functions at levels of complexity beyond what can be accounted for by the aggregate of their chemical components.[14] Nothing physical is *added*; yet the organism emerges as an integrated whole with a dynamic life over time.

Although emergence can be recognized in many domains of reality, the idea arises most vividly in evolutionary biology.[15] The basic principles of holism in its current twentieth-century form were developed by South African philosopher, Jan Smuts. Smuts sought to conceive philosophically of the whole of things based upon the model of biological evolution. He observed that things move through time. They change and develop. What makes temporal movement significant, according to Smuts, is that it is accompanied by genuine creativity, by what we call 'epigenesis'. The result is a holism that is creative.

As I see it, there are two basic and perhaps incompatible ways of conceiving creative activity within the cosmos. They are the *unfolding view* and the *epigenetic view*. According to the first view, everything is in one way or another given at the beginning. The universe consists in an unfolding or realization of potentialities already present at the starting point. This view assumes the created order was in principle complete and final at the point of origin. This would mean that all subsequent events and changes consist only in rearrangements and reshufflings of the original material and forms. Present and future events have been predetermined or at least delimited by the past. All fresh initiative, novelty or creativeness are effectively banned from such a universe. I refer to this unfolding view as the *archonic view*, using the Greek root *arché*, which means both 'beginning' and 'rule'. Archonic thinking tacitly presumes that the past rules the present, and religions based upon it seek to find the real or the sacred by returning to the moment of origin.

In contrast, Smuts proffers an epigenetic view of reality. Evolutionary theory emerging from the nineteenth century rejects the notion of a completed beginning in the past. Instead we have 'a real progressive creation still going forward in the universe' so that 'the sum of reality' is not constant but is 'progressively increasing in the course of evolution.... Evolution is not merely a process of change, of regrouping of the old into new forms; it is creative, its new forms are not merely fashioned out of the old materials; it creates both new materials and new forms from the synthesis of the new with the old materials'.[16] This gives rise to the view that evolutionary development is an epigenesis rather than an unfolding of a previously fixed genetic reality. Epigenetic movement is understood as creative of the new, as displaying novelty and initiative, as opening up new paths and rendering possible new choices, as creating freedom for the future and in a very real sense breaking the bondage of the past and its fixed predeterminations.[17]

Significant here is how epigenesis and *emergent* holism presuppose temporality. We are not talking about a realm of eternity where everything is fixed. Nor are we thinking in terms of cyclical time where we occasionally return to the nascent beginning of things, to the *illud tempus*. Physicist Ilya Prigogine, researcher on the thermodynamics of non-equilibrium systems, contends that on the macro scale time is monodirectional and irreversible. This makes the universe finite in time. It had a beginning, and it will have an end. The idea that time moves from the past through the present and toward the future is not just a product of human subjectivity. Nature herself reveals this fact. '*Science is rediscovering time*,' he writes.[18] Hence, if we want to know what the real world looks like to scientific and theological eyes, we must think in terms of a temporal and creative holism.

When combining essential temporality with this emergent creativity, we find ourselves moving rapidly away from the holism characteristic of classical ontology. The metaphysics of the ancient Greeks was certainly holistic, but it was an archonic holism. The monistic question was constantly raised: how are all things finally related to one another? Simplicity was the answer. Plato argued that oneness was prior to plurality. Plurality was a fall from a prior simplicity. Anything that is a composite of two or more elements is subordinate, because it is dependent upon each of those elements for its reality. Therefore, what is simple, indivisible and indestructible is ultimate.

Today's discussion centers upon a concept of emergent holism, wherein composite actualities produce new wholes which are not simple, but which represent higher levels of complex and integrated being. Whereas for classical ontology the move from the simple to the composite is almost a degeneration, for epigenetic holism ever new composites – if they become genuine wholes and not mere aggregates – constitute an achievement. The ancient metaphysic left virtually no room for change or development. It consisted in a form of the unfolding view of creation. The evolutionary and epigenetic metaphysic, however, incorporates temporal movement and foresees new and equally ultimate realities appearing in the future. 'The pull of the future' is as essential to the life of an organism as 'the push of the past', and the new wholes which arise are the center and creative source of reality.[19] The position I develop here does not depend upon a principle of progress built into the natural processes. Sufficient here for my argument is the principle of epigenesis, of newness in nature. The question of purpose requires the introduction of notions such as divine providence.

3   God Creates from the Future, not the Past

Building upon the first two theses, perhaps we could transmute classical commitments regarding God as creator. What all this implies, it seems to me, is that serious consideration should be given to what we might call a *retroactive ontology* – that is, an ontology that begins with the future and works backward to interpret the past and present. Hence the thesis: *God creates from the future, not the past.*[20]

The notion that God's creative work consists of the impact of the future on us now in the present may seem counterintuitive, at least to begin with. It may seem to contradict the commonly accepted Christian view – as well as our commonsense view – of temporal causality. Our commonly accepted idea of temporality is that time consists of a linear one-way passage from the past, through the present, toward the future. And, when it comes to causality, we are archonic. We assume that the power of being comes from the past. We assume that everything that exists is due to a past cause and a present effect. The power of being, it is commonly assumed, comes in the form of a push from the past.

This push from the past is an idea held in common by both Western theology and Big Bang cosmology. Whether the *creatio ex nihilo* (creation out of nothing) of the patristic theologians or the Big Bang of the astrophysicists, creation is assumed to be a single event which happened once upon a time – at the beginning of time – long ago. God, say our forerunners, created all things once and for all at the onset of time. What is widely believed is that out of abject nothingness God built a lovely machine complete with parts and principles of operation, wound it up, and has let it run ever since. In short, our commonsense view is at best deistic and most assuredly archonic.

So, to reverse this and speak of the power of being coming from the future would upset this scheme. Yet, the idea of a retroactive ontology may be well worth considering. Let us ask: does this image that locates the power of being in the ancient past adequately describe how we actually experience time and creativity? I suggest not. Yes of course we experience some current effects due to past causes. Yet, we also recognize a certain priority given to those things which have the power of creativity for the future. Without a future, present realities drop into non-existence. Without a future, the present moment becomes a death trap.

We can add this: because we accept as axiomatic that all things are always in the process of changing, the future which sustains existence must be thought of as a creative future. I believe we sense this implicitly. We preconsciously understand the power of being as that which can comfort us in our anxiety by assuring the future, especially a future which is not stuck by the precedents of the past or subject to death. To be is to have a future. To lose one's future and to have only a past is to die. Deep down we know this. The dynamic perdurance of the present moment is contingent upon the power of the future to draw us into it.

When we think of God's initial activity as described in the book of Genesis or when associated with the singularity at the moment of the Big Bang, I would like to consider the following thesis: the first thing God did for the world was give it a future. Without a future it would be nothing. When referring theologically to the absolute beginning with the phrase *creatio ex nihilo*, then, we are referring to God's first gracious gift of futurity. When referring scientifically about the unfathomably dense ball of proto-hydrogen at the onset of the Big Bang, we could think of God's first cosmogonic act as bestowing on the universe an open future. God bestows the future by opening up the possibility of its becoming something it never had been before and by supplying it with the power to change.

What we find in Big Bang cosmogony and in biological evolution is that everything we know in nature is contingent and finite, having come into existence at a particular point in time and without any previous precedence.[21] Not only does God release the exploding energy which drives the universe, but God also opens up the future so that new things can occur. This ontological gift of the future is the very condition for the coming into existence and the sustaining of any present reality. From our perspective today, of course, we have the sense that we are looking back upon this first divine act. It seems now to be a part of the dead past. But, we need to be careful, because God is continuing to bestow upon us a future, even at this very moment. It is the continuing divine work of future giving which is the source of all life and being.

To think in terms of God as the power of the future has existential value. When in the present moment we feel overwhelmed by trends set in motion by past causes, we feel cramped, contained and constrained. To look at a future we believe to be archonically predetermined is to feel that life has been lost. It could be good news to hear that God's power comes to us not as a brute determination from the past, but as that which counters such determinations. Each moment God exerts divine power to relieve us from past constraints so as to open up a field for free action, for responsible living, for new creation.

4   *God Creates by Integrating into Wholeness*

Against an archonic view of being as a push from the past, I am suggesting here that we think of God's creative activity as a pull from the future. This brings us to the next principle: *God's creative activity within nature and history derives from the redemptive work of drawing contingent and free beings into a harmonious whole.* Recall that the cardinal tenet of holism is that the whole is greater than the sum of the parts. It is this 'greater than' which distinguishes a whole from a simple totality or aggregate of otherwise individual things. Corollary to this is the idea that the parts are defined by their relationship to one another and by the whole which frames that relationship. We may borrow these insights to help illumine the divine destiny which determines God's past and present activity.

This is an anti-reductionistic approach. We are combating two forms of reductionism here. We seek to avoid first the fallacy of reduction to origin, the archonic fallacy, wherein all of reality is thought to be determined by what happened at the point of origin in the past. The archonic view is problematic because it precludes the coming into being of anything fundamentally new: most importantly, the new creation. When imported into Christian theology the archonic view risks deism, that is, belief in a quiescent God. The archonic view does not lead us toward theism, that is, belief in an active God.

The holism component of our retroactive ontology also helps us avoid a second fallacy, namely, atomic reductionism. This fallacy assumes that the macrocosm is simply a composite of much more fundamental building blocks – atoms – at the microcosmic level. The problem with this assumption is that it fails to recognize as ontologically significant the patterns and interactions which exist only at more complex and comprehensive levels of reality. Adherents to the concept of integrative holism posit that emergent wholes are just as real as the reducible atomic units that make them up. 'One cannot say that ... atoms and molecules are *more* real than cells, living organisms, or ecosystems,' writes Arthur Peacocke.[22]

The concept of integrative holism united with retroactive ontology might help us to untie the knotty problem of the relationship between freedom and natural causation. The mechanistic model of Enlightenment physics could not account for human freedom, or even randomness in nature for that matter. Archonic thinking finds it difficult to explain exhaustively free human acts on the basis of their antecedent efficient causes. Where holism helps is that, by avoiding atomic reduction, it affirms equal reality to complex forms of interrelationship. Freedom is exercised at these more complex levels. Integrative holism provides an explanation that does not deny efficient causation at relatively more simple levels.

A common everyday example may be illustrative. Suppose I am confronted with the option of going either to the refrigerator to eat some leftover apple pie or to the athletic field for jogging. If I devour the apple pie, my body will start processing its sugars and I will begin to feel sleepy. My breathing rate and skin reaction to the environment within the house will remain the same, but my metabolism will shoot up and my heart will beat faster for a brief period. Then, everything will slow down and I'll feel like taking a nap. Eventually, this will result in my loosening my belt to one notch larger. On the other hand, if I decide to jog around the athletic field, my breathing will become very rapid and my skin will react to the cold outside air. My heart rate and metabolism will increase as they process the fats already present in my body. This activity will be sustained for a long period of time, and I will feel energetic and ready for hard work. Eventually, I may be able to tighten my belt one notch.

The point is that freedom – consisting of deliberation, decision and responsible action – operates at a high level of complex integration, at the level of the human self as a whole. The decision I make as a whole human self becomes an ordering factor in the causal nexus constituting my bodily activity. Even though my body operates according to established natural principles governing breathing cycles, skin reaction, heart and metabolism rate and such, my decision introduces an independent but inclusive or top-down factor which reorders the actual pattern of causal interaction. A decision of the whole has reordered the interrelationship of the parts. But, we need not say the causal chain has been broken. We need only say that the lower-level causal nexus is less than completely determined and that human freedom is not reducible to the level of biophysical causes.

How might this look from the point of view of the part rather than the whole? How might this look from the point of view of the heart within the body? I suspect it would be impossible for the heart to comprehend the whole person of which it is a vital part. The heart is an organ – it is not a machine even though the machine model helps us to understand the heart – which responds to stimuli by serving the various needs of the body as a whole. It will respond somewhat differently if stimulated by the digestion of apple pie than it would if stimulated by jogging. The heart by itself cannot comprehend the deliberative processes of the person whose decision will determine which stimulus will come its way. The heart does not know if I am making a decision on behalf of good health or on behalf of culinary pleasure. Certainly, there is reciprocity between the life-giving work of the heart and the health decisions made by the person, but the whole–part dialectic gives a certain prerogative to the whole personality which the heart cannot govern or understand.

Having described the determining power and influence of more comprehensive wholes on their respective parts, holism can approach an account for human freedom that does not break the nexus of finite relations at the physiological, biochemical or physical levels. Having observed this, we may now pose the theological question: can we by analogy see ourselves as part of a still larger whole, the whole of reality? Can we, like the heart, accept the fact that there is a more comprehensive freedom and governing power than we can understand? Can we affirm that through the macro whole God acts to alter the course of historical events but does not break what to our observation is the causal nexus?[23]

Our method now appeals to the principle of analogy, because we cannot experience what we are talking about directly. If the whole person is someone who is more than the sum of his or her constitutive parts, heart included, then we can understand how the larger whole of which we are a part is not reducible to the human level of reality. As human beings we retain our integrity and a degree of freedom, to be sure. But, as part of a larger whole, which in itself is greater than the sum of its parts and enjoys still greater freedom, we must realize that there is a level of reality which simply remains beyond our grasp. It follows that we cannot fully comprehend that whole itself. It must remain mysterious. Our knowledge of its existence is a formal construction of the human imagination, and its material content must remain partially known yet elusive in its fullness. Nevertheless, it is quite understandable how this whole can be determinative of who and what we are.

This line of thinking finds resonance with the concept of the 'master act' in the theology of Gordon Kaufman.[24] God's primary creative action, according to Kaufman, is his master act. This is the single act by which God creates and consummates the whole cosmos. En route to the completion of this work, God engages in many subacts, of course. A carpenter, for example, may build a house. The house is his or her master act. But, in the process of completing it the carpenter must perform certain subacts, such as examining the blueprints, delivering materials to the site, measuring, sawing, hammering and cleaning up. There is one master act, but it incorporates numerous subacts all of which can be identified by their contribution to the purpose of bringing a brand new house into existence.

We cannot say we have a house – a whole – until the creative work is completed. So also, God's act consists in a purposive event of creation which will not become an event of its own until its completion, until the eschatological consummation. There is no whole of all things as we look strictly from our present perspective. The uniting and determining whole is yet to come. Here a curious paradox presents itself: our knowledge of God's subacts depends upon our prior knowledge of God's master act, but the master act is not yet complete. For us to be able to discern an event to be a subact within the divine master act would require that we have the eschatological completion in sight.

Is it possible to have the end revealed ahead of time? Yes, the creator of the world has revealed to us creatures that God has a purpose which is being brought toward fulfillment. This purpose can be discerned in the ministry, death and resurrection of Jesus Christ. In Jesus Christ, we see proleptically God's intention for the whole, God's single purpose which runs from alpha to omega, from beginning to end. 'For in him all things were created, in heaven and on earth, visible and invisible .... He is before all things, and in him all things hold together' (Col. 1:16–17). Wolfhart Pannenberg applies the notion of anticipation or prolepsis to spell this out in temporal and eschatological terms.

> The future of God is not merely disclosed in advance with the coming of Jesus; it is already an event, although without ceasing to be future. The future of God has already dawned. In its own way the Christian Easter message corresponds to this structure of the proclamation of Jesus, for it declares that the saving future of the resurrection life of Jesus has come already, and that in him it has broken in for us.[25]

As a consequence of all this, perhaps we could think of the whole of cosmic history as a single divine act of creation, a whole of which our own personal histories are minute but indispensable parts. Just as the operations of the human heart are drawn up into the decisions and purposes of the human personality as a whole, our personal lives will be drawn up into and find their proper definition through their relationship to the whole of God's creative work. Yet, because God's creative history has not yet come to its completion, it is not yet whole. The future is for us still open. Reality is on the way to being determined and defined in mutual reciprocity between the actual course of

finite events and the overall divine design. What permits us to think holistically
is the promise of the future completion of God's master act. In the meantime,
we find ourselves within the creative work of God, a work yet to be completed,
and hence appropriately called from our point of view *creatio continua*
(continuing creation).

Is such a vision of eschatological wholeness consonant with projections in
physical cosmology?[26] Physicist–priest John Polkinghorne, though a strong
advocate of consonance between science and faith, sees dissonance when it
comes to eschatology. Polkinghorne embraces a vision that looks forward to a
new creation. The present natural world 'must be delivered from the frustration
of its impending mortality, just as Jesus was delivered from the bonds of death
by his resurrection'.[27] Yet, cosmological or evolutionary optimism provides
insufficient strength for embracing such a vision. He depicts the battle between
open and closed cosmologies, between freeze and fry scenarios, as evidence that
science falls short of providing what we need theologically.

> Cosmologists do not only peer into the past. They can attempt to discern the future.
> On a cosmic scale, the history of the universe is a gigantic tug-of-war between the
> expansive force of the big bang, driving the galaxies apart, and the contractive force
> of gravity, pulling them together. These two effects are so evenly balanced we cannot
> tell which will win .... Nevertheless, one way or the other, the universe is condemned
> to ultimate futility, and humanity will prove to have been a transient episode in its
> history.
>   It may seem a melancholy prospect, a clear denial of those religious assertions of a
> purpose at work within cosmic history.[28]

Finding little or no consonance in scientific projections, Polkinghorne turns to
the resources of faith. Our ultimate hope can rest only on what we believe
about ultimate reality, he says. We will have to put our faith in the eternal God
and not in the temporal creation.

Another physicist–pastor, George Murphy, still holds out hope for
consonance, pressing for the possibility that a retroactive ontology could
make scientific sense. Although disavowing connection with physicist Frank
Tipler's views, Murphy speculates on prolepsis in terms of an intracosmic
retrieval of the past on behalf of future redemption. 'Modern physics must
consider the possibility of signals which travel backward in time, such as the
advanced potentials of electromagnetic theory .... we may imagine that God
could use the advanced technologies of the future to bring about a general
resurrection, *and that this resurrection state could be retrojected into the first
century*. The raising of Jesus from the dead would be a very real foretaste of the
general resurrection.'[29]

5   *God's Faithfulness is Expressed through Law*

On the basis of what we have said, it is clear that creation is not something that
is over and done; it is still going on. We need to affirm *creatio continua* right
along with *creatio ex nihilo*. *Creatio continua* is necessary if we are to recognize

that God's creative work still awaits completion and that, from the point of view of the present time, genuinely new things can still happen. Yet, the stream of cosmic history is not made of only new things. There is continuity too. If there were no continuity of events, we could not even recognize that such a thing as a single history of creation exists. If there were only creativity, there would be nothing to connect past events with future events. If everything has the quality of newness, the old would cease to exist. There would be no such thing as constancy, normativity or order. Creativity without continuity would make temporality and history vacuous. This raises the question: is God responsible for the continuity of creation as well as its newness? Our answer will be affirmative, and we will say that the means by which God maintains the continuity of creation is law.

Would it make sense to say this: *God's faithfulness to creation is expressed through the impartation of law?*[30] Traditional dogmatics took up this concern under doctrinal *loci* such as preservation or governance, *conservatio* or *gubernatio*, and providence.[31] Faith affirms that the regularities and causal connectedness between otherwise contingent events are gifts from God's continued work of preserving what is, while in the midst of creating what is yet to be. Although we find ourselves amidst a stream of events through time, each event is unique. This stream of events, moreover, seems to have a structure. The task of the scientist is to discover the laws that apparently govern this structure. Such laws are formulated inductively after observing a single pattern frequently repeated.

Arthur Peacocke argues that creativity within cosmic evolution is the result of the interplay between law and chance. One without the other would not produce any emerging newness. Looking back upon the immense journey of nature from origin to present, it has been the creative interaction of law and randomness which has made possible the emergence of life forms where previously there had been none.[32] Peacocke goes on to argue that the impartation of randomness and chance in the developmental process is the act of God whereby creation continues. Peacocke has a valuable insight, I believe. Yet, I would suggest that the presence of law, not just randomness, is also the work of God.

Are the laws of nature eternal or temporal? Not eternal. The laws of nature or the laws of God are not necessarily eternal or everlasting. It is a frequent mistake to think so. Although laws cover the scope of our reflection on any natural (or moral) topic, it does not follow that they must have always existed in the past or that they must continue to exist into the indefinite future. They are contingent. The universe could have been otherwise. Things have not always been the way they are now. The validity of natural laws is time-dependent. What we know as the regularities of nature are here for a season, but then they too are subject to subsumption into future contingent and perhaps more comprehensive events.

The thesis here is that these principles of regularity by which we recognize the continuity of otherwise contingent events are the result of God's faithfulness to God's world. God, of course, is *a se*. God is not bound to the cosmic order. God is free to relate *to* the created order as a whole, whereas we experience freedom only *within* the order and not *over against* the order. We are subject to the regularities of law. What we experience as governing principles within nature are ordinances freely imparted by God to keep the world in being, to keep it organized as a single cosmos, for a given duration. Because we always look at such law from the side of the governed, it is difficult if not impossible for us to imagine what things were like before there was the particular natural order within which we live. Because we always look at things from within the cosmos, we can barely imagine how things could operate lawfully in any other cosmos not subject to the form of governance by the natural laws we have come to know. Much less can we comprehend the freedom of the governor, the God who is beyond.

Freedom is a category of mystery here. Theologically, we affirm that God acts out of a higher freedom. The ancient Hebrews understood the continuity of the world's existence to be a fruit of God's freely expressed faithfulness. The Hebrew mind did not see nature as ordered by eternal or immutable laws; rather, the future could be trusted because God could be trusted. We learn that someone is faithful only after an experience over time with his or her loyalty. Although ancient Israel's Near Eastern neighbors conceived of nature as governed by eternal archetypes fixed by the gods *in illo tempore*, Israel was given promises that new things would happen. These promises were fulfilled. Israel experienced this curious combination of divine newness and faithfulness, both freedom and law. Our understanding of continuous creation is an extrapolation based upon this experience of Israel with God.

Today we find ourselves between promise and fulfillment, a period of tension that is calling us to relate to God's faithfulness through faith. Faith is understood as trust in the God of the future. The final evidence of God's trustworthiness will be available only at the end of cosmic history.[33] In the meantime, this can be made intelligible by noting the temporality, if not ephemerality, of natural law, the constant contingency of the cosmos as we know it. Hence, the call to faith is a call to place our trust not in the ordered cosmos, but rather in the faithfulness of the transcendent God who has committed the divine self to determine a future that is redemptive. In short, trust God, not nature!

Conclusion

We began with the suggestion that human creativity – that is, human imagination and invention – issues from a sense of being drawn toward a new and better future. We asked whether this human experience of creativity is grounded in something *extra nos*, grounded in God's relation to the world as creator to creature. We then lifted up for consideration five theses that develop a retroactive ontology, according to which God's creative work regarding the world draws all of finite reality toward newness, toward the new creation. This newness is holistic and integrative and, thereby, redemptive. Although we can find some scientific theorizings that provide tantalizing areas of possible consonance with these theological hopes, finally our theology of a transformed eschatological future will have to be rooted and grounded in the resources of faith. This faith includes within it the hope that consonance with science could grow.

We explored for theology the implications of the overarching concept of wholeness which is qualified and developed in terms of temporality and continuing creativity. We saw how the realm of nature can be understood epigenetically rather than archonically. We then explored the possibility that this configuration of ideas might help us to explicate the Christian doctrine of creation, especially if we take as our point of departure the symbol of new creation. Where we end up is with a proposed vision of continuing creation tending toward a consummate whole of wholes, the final fulfillment of all things at the completion of God's one comprehensive act of creation. Where we find ourselves now is somewhere along the way, anticipating the fullness and the wholeness yet to come.

Notes

1   Wentzel van Huyssteen argues similarly for consonance: 'As Christians we should therefore take very seriously the theories of physics and cosmology: not to exploit or to try to change them, but to try to find interpretations that would suggest some form of complementary consonance with the Christian viewpoint, *Duet or Duel: Theology and Science in a Postmodern World*, (Harrisburg PA: Trinity Press International, 1998), 78.

2   Charles Townes, 'Logic and Understandings in Science and Religion', in *Science and Theology: The New Consonance*, ed. by Ted Peters (Boulder CO: Westview Press, 1998), 45.

3   Mark William Worthing, *God, Creation, and Contemporary Physics* (Minneapolis: Fortress Press, 1996), 4.

4   Philip Clayton, *God and Contemporary Science* (Grand Rapids: Eerdmans, 1997), 238, Clayton's italics.

5   The seeking of truth requires humility on the part of the seeker when confronted by growth in knowledge and understanding. 'The models we derive in science, or the doctrines we distill out of our collective religious insights, are only partial because both science and religion depend on continuing revelation,' writes Pauline M. Rudd ('The Science and Spirit Quest', *Science and Spirit*, 9:5 (December 1998), 2). Short of attaining truth, some debate exists whether science still has an indefinite future for pursuing truth – that is, pursuing new knowledge about the natural world. 'Could scientists, in effect, learn everything there is to know? Could they banish mystery from the universe?' asks John Horgan, suggesting that pure science might be over. (*The End of Science*, (Reading MA: Addison-Wesley, Helix Books, 1996), 3. Robert M. Hazen and Maxin Singer disagree, pointing out that we confront things we know, things we know we do not know, and as yet things we do not know we do not know. Science is not at an end, because the questions are endless. See *Why Aren't Black Holes Black?* (New York: Doubleday, Anchor, 1997), xvi–xvii.

6   Neils Henrik Gregersen, 'A Contextual Coherence Theory for the Science–Theology Dialogue', in *Rethinking Theology and Science*, ed. by Niels Henrik Gregersen and J. Wentzel van Huyssteen (Grand Rapids: Eerdmans, 1998), 226.

7   George Murphy, 'Fake Science, Anti-Science, and the Church', *Works: The Newsletter of the Evangelical Lutheran Church in America Work Group on Science and Technology*, 5:4 (January–February 1997), 6–8.

8   Nancey Murphy, *Anglo-American Postmodernity* (Boulder CO: Westview Press, 1997), 34; Murphy's italics.

9   'Whoever uses the word "God", writes Wolfhart Pannenberg, 'particularly as a singular, makes a claim at the same time about the totality of what exists finitely' (*Metaphysics and the Idea of God*, tr. by Philip Clayton, Grand Rapids: Eerdmans, 1990, 142). See Ted Peters, 'Clarity of the Part versus Meaning of the Whole', in *Beginning with the End: God, Science, and Wolfhart Pannenberg*, ed. by Carol Rausch Albright and Joel Haugen (LaSalle IL: Open Court, 1997), 289–301.

10 Robert M. Hazen raises the as yet unanswered preliminary question, namely, is there homogeneity in the universe? He answers: we must assume it. 'Observational data cannot prove homogeneity . . . . It requires a leap of faith to assume that every place is the same . . . Nevertheless, that assumption of homogeneity is central to all current cosmological models,' *Why Aren't Black Holes Black?* (New York: Doubleday, Anchor 1997), 32.

11 Craig J. Hogan, Robert P. Kirshner and Nicholas B. Suntzeff, 'Surveying Space-time with Supernovae', *Scientific American*, 280:1 (January 1999), 46–51; Lawrence M. Krauss, 'Cosmological Antigravity', ibid., 53–9.

12 David Bohm, *Wholeness and the Implicate Order* (London and Boston: Routledge & Kegan Paul, 1980). Theologian Wolfhart Pannenberg eschatologizes the healing dimension of wholeness: 'In German the word "Heil" carries the sense of wholeness or integrity of life, even in the sense of achieving wholeness in the course of our history. Similarly *soteria* has the wholeness or integrity of life in view (cf. simply Mark 8:35). It refers not merely to the process of saving but also to the result, to the saved and newly regained life. In the latter respect it is close to the comprehensive sense that the word for peace (*shalom*) bears in the OT. The wholeness of life that a word like "Heil" denotes cannot be achieved, however, in the process of time. It may even be felt to be absent, or at least to be threatened, in the march of history, with no final security. Hence the salvation of human life depends on the future' (*Systematic Theology*, tr. by Geoffrey Bromiley, 3 volumes (Grand Rapids: Eerdmans, 1991–8), II, 399).

13 The inner drive for a unity of truth is reflected in sociobiologist (or evolutionary psychologist) Edward O. Wilson's concept of consilience. More than mere coherence, by *consilience* Wilson means a 'jumping together of knowledge by the linking of facts and fact-based theory across disciplines to create a common groundwork of explanation' (*Consilience: The Unity of Knowledge* (New York: Alfred A. Knopf, 1998), 8). Even if scholars disagree as to just what the unity of truth entails, they can agree that pursuing such unity of truth is worthwhile.

14 Arthur Peacocke defines 'emergence' as 'the entirely *neutral* name for that general feature of natural processes wherein complex structures, especially in living organisms, develop distinctively new capabilities and function at levels of greater complexity. Such emergence is an undoubted, observed feature of the evolutionary process . . . ['emergence' is being used] *not* in the sense that some actual entity has been *added* to the more complex system' ('A Map of Scientific Knowledge: Genetics, Evolution, and Theology', *Science and Theology*, 191), Peacocke's italics. Mathematician Ian Stewart says, 'emergence is not the absence of causality; rather, it is a web of causality so intricate that the human mind cannot grasp it' (*Life's Other Secret* (New York: John Wiley & Sons, 1998), 7). Stewart believes that DNA constitutes only one of life's secrets, mathematics the other one. Mathematical rules

in nature make the evolution of emergent life forms possible; then the creativity of evolution takes over on its own. When referring to brain development, he writes, 'so, universal mathematical features of neural nets provided the bag of computational devices for evolution to build on. And once evolution gains a toehold, it soon takes over completely; it's getting started that counts' (ibid., 164).

15   'Are we still evolving?' asks evolutionary biologist Christopher Wills. 'It is very lucky for us that we are' (*Children of Prometheus: The Accelerating Pace of Human Evolution* (Reading MA: Perseus Books, Helix Books, 1998), 271).

16   J.C. Smuts, *Holism and Evolution* (New York: Macmillan, 1926; and Capetown, South Africa: N.&S. Press, 1987), 89. Edward O. Wilson's use of the term *epigenesis* focuses specifically on gene–culture coevolution. Though human culture is genetically determined, he can add a 'parallel track of cultural evolution'. He writes, 'Culture is created by the communal mind, and each mind in turn is the product of the genetically structured human brain. Genes and culture are therefore inseverably linked. But the linkage is flexible, to a degree still mostly unmeasured. The linkage is also tortuous: Genes prescribe epigenetic rules, which are the neural pathways and regularities in cognitive development by which the individual mind assembles itself. The mind grows from birth to death by absorbing parts of the existing culture available to it, with selections guided through epigenetic rules inherited by the individual brain' (*Consilience*, 127). The appeal to epigenetic rules shifts Wilson's discipline from 'human sociobiology to gene–culture coevolution. In this new phase of research, the definition of epigenetic rules is the best means to make important advances in the understanding of human nature' (ibid., 150). My own use of the term *epigenesis* follows that of Smuts in order to emphasize openness to creative advance; I am not inclined to follow the reductionism inherent in Wilson's genetically determined rules for culture.

17   Central to evolutionary biology is the principle of natural selection. How is this creative? Francisco Ayala says, 'Natural selection is thus creative in a way. It does not create the entities upon which it operates, but it produces adaptive genetic combinations that would not have existed otherwise, owing to the enormous improbability of their coming about by chance. Natural selection generates novelty in the form of accumulated hereditary information that is expressed in organisms and their functional attributes' ('Chance and Necessity: Adaptation and Novelty in Evolution', *An Evolving Dialogue*, ed. by James B. Miller (Washington, DC: AAAS, 1998), 234).

18   Ilya Prigogine and Isabelle Stengers, *Order Out of Chaos* (New York: Bantam, 1984, xxviii), Prigogine's italics.

19   Smuts, *Holism and Evolution*, pp.115f; cf. 102. Emergent holism draws our attention to the evolutionary advance toward complexity in individual organisms. What remains in dispute is whether one can discern purpose operative within the whole scope of evolutionary history so that some sort of progress can be measured. Stephen Jay Gould rejects the application of the doctrine of progress to evolution, seeing it as a superimposition of value based on excessive human pride. Gould argues that we should 'abandon progress or complexification as a central principle and come to entertain the strong possibility that *H. sapiens* is but a tiny, late-arising tail on life's enormously arborescent bush – a small bud that would almost surely not appear a second time if we could replant the bush from a seed and let it grow again' ('The Evolution of Life on Earth', in *An Evolving Dialogue: Scientific, Historical, and Theological Perspecitves on Evolution* (Washington, DC: AAAS, 1998), 167).

20   My discussion here expands on principles enunciated in earlier works such as chapter 4 of *GOD – The World's Future: Systematic Theology for a Postmodern Era*

(Minneapolis: Fortress 1992) and 'The Real World is the Yet-To-Be Whole World', *Dialog*, 26:3 (Summer 1987), 167–4.

21 Robert John Russell proposes 'that the concept of contingency is central to the doctrine of creation, both as *creatio ex nihilo* and *creatio continua*, and to contemporary scientific cosmology.... These results are aimed at consonance between theology and science in which the empirical test of science will strengthen and trim the theological meaning of contingency' ('Cosmology, Creation, and Contingency', in *Cosmos as Creation*, ed. by Ted Peters (Nashville: Abingdon Press, 1989), 205).

22 Peacocke, 'Genesis, Evolution, and Theology', *Science and Theology*, 194; Peacocke's italics.

23 The relations between the whole or finite reality and the whole of reality inclusive of God need to be sorted out with care. Although it is important to see the natural world as an integrated whole, as creation, in itself it is distinguishable from God, the creator. 'God is not the whole of what exists finitely, and the concept of the whole does not include God within it as one of its parts,' says Pannenberg. *Metaphysics and the Idea of God*, 142.

24 Gordon Kaufman, *God the Problem* (Cambridge: Harvard University Press, 1972), 137. For a similar position, see Wolfhart Pannenberg, *Toward a Theology of Nature: Essays on Science and Faith*, ed. by Ted Peters (Louisville: Westminster/ John Knox Press, 1993), chapter 3.

25 Pannenberg, *Systematic Theology*, III, 247.

26 Robert Hazen, recognizing that the planet earth will have been burned up by the sun long before entropy determines the ultimate fate of the universe, poses the existential question: 'That we should ask with something more than idle curiosity about this unimaginably distant fate of the universe – that we should care about an end that in all probability no member of our species will witness – says much about ourselves and our aspirations. Something deep inside each of us yearns to know. Science can hypothesize about reality's future demise, but equations do little to help us deal with the implications of that seemingly inevitable total obliteration of everything that is human. *Why Aren't Black Holes Black?*, 47.

27 John Polkinghorne, *The Faith of a Physicist* (Princeton, NJ: Princeton University Press, 1994), 169.

28 Ibid., 162.

29 George Murphy, 'What Can Physics Contribute to Eschatology?', *Dialog*, 38:1 (Winter 1999), 35–39: 39, Murphy's italics.

30 See Wolfhart Pannenberg, 'On the Theology of Law', in *Ethics* (Philadelphia: Westminster, 1981).

31 'If creation stresses that God is the cause of the existence of all that is, providence stresses that God is the cause of the meaning and purpose of all that is. God not only creates but guides and directs the universe towards the fulfilling of God's purposes.' Robert John Russell, 'Does the "God Who Acts" Really Act in Nature?' in *Science and Theology*, 81.

32 A.R. Peacocke, *Creation and the World of Science* (Oxford: Clarendon Press, 1979), 103.

33 The truth that undergirds our trust in God remains dependent upon the very existence of a God who makes promises and fulfills them, a truth that in principle could be disconfirmed. 'The future that will reveal the truth about the present remains open and ahead of us,' writes Pannenberg. 'The truth of this anticipation hinges on the still-absent future.' *Metaphysics and the Idea of God*, 96.

Chapter 5

David Bohm, Postmodernism and the Divine

The cosmological speculations of physicist David Bohm represent among other things a probe into what might become the postmodern world of tomorrow. The world of modernity, which Alvin Toffler dubs 'the second wave', has dominated Western consciousness since the Enlightenment. That wave is receding now and leaving on the beach the debris of abstract thinking, compartmentalized knowledge, warring specialisms, fragmented facts and a general sense of alienation between human consciousness and wider reality. A new, third wave is about to break upon us, and we are thirsting for it. What we desire is synthetic thinking, a putting back together what we have rent apart.[1] In short, the thirst for postmodernity is the thirst for a renewed sense of the whole.

Bohm thirsts for wholeness, and the reason is that we in the world of Isaac Newton and René Descartes are plagued by a drought because there is fragmentation strewn across the landscape, unnourished by the rains of holistic thinking. He believes fragmentation is a confusion of the mind which creates an endless series of problems and interferes with our clarity of perception so as to prevent us from solving them. We divide subjects and objects and cannot put them back together again. We divide mind and matter, the human and the natural, and we end up with separation and alienation. This way of life has brought about pollution, destruction of the balance of nature, overpopulation and the threat of worldwide economic and political disorder.

The fundamental cause of this fragmentation is the modern Western habit of divisive thinking or, more precisely, we assume that the fragmentary nature of our thinking corresponds with an actual fragmentariness indicative of reality itself. 'Since our thought is pervaded with differences and distinctions, it follows that such a habit leads us to look on these as real divisions, so that the world is then seen and experienced as actually broken up into fragments.'[2] Hence the cure for the ills of modernity must begin with healthier thinking. And, noting that *health* in English is based on the Anglo-Saxon word *hale*, meaning whole, healthy thinking will be (w)holistic thinking. This sets the agenda for the Bohm project, namely, to understand the nature of reality in general and conscious thought in particular as a coherent whole.[3] It is Bohm's thesis that the explicate order of things which we accept as part of our everyday world and which is studied by modern scientists is itself not the fundamental reality. There is under and behind it an implicate order, a realm of undivided wholeness which is present in each of the explicate parts.

Our task in this chapter will be to examine the Bohm cosmology in light of the transition from modernity to postmodernity. We will thank him for trying to put the broken Humpty Dumpty of modernity back together again. In doing so we will amplify his cosmology a little by drawing some comparisons with a theorist who holds similar views, Arthur Koestler. We will then analyze his concept of the 'immense multidimensional ground' in light of theological concerns regarding monotheism and the unity of the whole of reality. We will conclude by thanking Bohm for refraining from labeling his key concept, the holomovement, 'God'.

Beyond Newton and Descartes

From the point of view of the revisionist or postmodern physicist, the now effete modern mind of the last three centuries is characterized by atomism, mechanism and objectivism. The problem is not, of course, that the mind thinks objectively about atoms and mechanics; the problem is that it mistakenly assumes that reality itself is so constituted. The result is fragmentation in the sense that reality is assumed to be composed of separate atomic objects functioning according to mechanical laws, externally related to one another as are subjects and objects. The theories of relativity and quantum mechanics upset this world-view a half century ago, because they suggest that 'the world can not be analyzed into separate and independently existing parts'.[4] This insight is the heart of the new vision, which Bohm wishes to explore.

The world-view which constitutes the framework of Newtonian physics is based upon the three-dimensional space of Euclidean geometry and the notion of the mathematically calculable and constantly reliable flow of time from past to future. In this receptacle of absolute space and time there move material elements or particles, the small, solid and ultimately indestructible objects out of which all matter is made. These material atomic units can be located in space and time. Their velocity and size can be measured. They are basically passive, their relationships to one another being determined by external forces of nature such as gravity. These forces or laws of motion presume a closed causal nexus or mechanistic structure. Any definite cause gives rise to a definite effect, and the future of any part of the world system could be, in principle, predicted with certainty should one know the details of the causes. This leads to the image of the world as a machine, to an implicit and rigorous mechanical determinism.

Descartes, usually considered the father of modern philosophy, paved the way for our understanding of the world machine by distinguishing sharply between the world of extended objects out there and the world of subjectivity in here, in our own mind. Despite the thoughts and feelings endemic to human consciousness, we may observe the mechanistic workings of objects in the external world without influencing them as long as we think objectively, as long as we do not personally participate in those workings, as long as we simply conceive accurately in our mind how objects relate to one another. The net effect of Cartesianism over the last three centuries has been for us to separate human consciousness from the world process and, in addition, by concentrating on the plurality of objects to miss seeing the world process as a single process at all.

Big changes came during the first quarter of the twentieth century. Albert Einstein's special theory of relativity dispossessed the framework of absolute space-time, at least when dealing with very high velocity movements that approach the speed of light. Quantum theory similarly disrupted the Newtonian view, perhaps even more so. There are three reasons. The first is that atomic particles such as electrons are not things which can be described by concepts such as location, velocity or size. Thought of as particles, they travel from one location to another without traversing the distance in between. They move discontinuously. They do not appear to function at all like the material objects we understand at the commonsense level. Thus understanding them as particles of matter can be misleading. It is helpful, say the new breed of physicists, to understand them also as waves or wavicles.

Second, there is no apparent structure of efficient causation belonging to individual subatomic events. We must study them in groups. Individual subatomic events are not predictable and do not even seem to be individually causally determined. What we can do is predict what will happen on the basis of a statistical analysis of a given quantum of atomic activity. In the case of radioactive decay, for example, the point in time in which a particular radioactive atom will suddenly disintegrate is totally unpredictable, but the overall half-life or rate of decay of radioactive substances is knowable. Bohm uses the actuarial predictions of insurance companies as an analogy. Statistical laws predict with a high degree of approximation the mean number of people in a given class of age, height, weight, and so on, that will die of a certain disease in a specified period of time. Even though no one can predict the precise time of death of an individual policyholder, the statistical laws are counted as knowledge.

Third, there are subatomic experiments that demonstrate non-local relationships between electrons. Einstein, B. Podolsky and N. Rosen have shown that, when two electrons from a single atom have interacted and then flown off in opposite directions, interference with one will instantly affect the other, regardless of the distance between them. This seems to indicate a sort of telepathy between the particles, an intimate interconnection between particles that are not in spatial contact: a non-causal non-material, yet influential relationship.[5]

In short, quantum theory takes us away from a material notion of matter and from a closed nexus of efficient causation, away from a strictly mechanistic picture of the world, away from the world of Descartes and Newton. University of California physicist and popular author Fritjof Capra describes the significance of these new perspectives: 'The first three decades of our century changed the situation in physics radically. Two separate developments – that of relativity theory and atomic physics – shattered all the principal concepts of the Newtonian worldview: the notion of absolute space and time, the elementary solid particles, the strictly causal nature of physical phenomena, and the ideal of an objective description of nature.'[6] Arthur Koestler sums it up similarly: 'the strictly deterministic, mechanistic worldview can no longer be upheld; it has become a Victorian anachronism. The nineteenth-century model of the universe as a mechanical clockwork is a shambles and since the concept of matter itself has been dematerialized, materialism can no longer claim to be a scientific philosophy'.[7] And Buckminster Fuller says it, in 'Intuition':

> In short, physics has discovered
> That there are no solids,
> No continuous surfaces,
> No straight lines.
> Only waves,
> No things,
> Only energy event complexes,
> Only behaviors,
> Only verbs,
> Only relationships ...

The new physics has brought us to the brink of a new postmaterialist and relationalist era. Where do we go from here? Koestler wants to take these insights in the direction of a holism that establishes the credibility of parapsychology. Capra is trying to lead the new physics in the direction of Asian mysticism.

Bohm's agenda is not as specific as that of Koestler or Capra; nevertheless, he does have an agenda. Although not wishing to return to a cause–effect determinism, he wants to take us beyond the present state of quantum theory with his own notion of 'hidden variables'. The problem is that at present there is no consistent notion at all of what the reality might be that underlies the universal constitution and structure of matter. Quantum physicists tend to avoid the issue by concentrating on mathematical equations that permit us to predict and control the behavior of large statistical aggregates of particles, while adopting an attitude that any overall view of the nature of reality is of little or no importance. On this count, the practicing quantum physicists are still positivistic and hence still modern, still just calculating the position and momentum of fragments even though the fragments are of a different scale.[8]

By focusing on the quantum as an indivisible unit amidst a plurality of such quanta and assuming only indeterminacy within the unit itself, we may miss other hidden factors that might open us to seeing the fundamental unity behind all things. Bohm wants to open us up to those hidden factors by contending that the electron has more properties than can be described in terms of the so-called observables characteristic of quantum theory. There are hidden variables which influence the directly observable behavior of the quantum unit or system. His thesis is that, 'in a deeper sub-quantum level, there are further variables which determine in more detail the fluctuations of the results of individual quantum-mechanical measurements'.[9] What are these variables? The answer partially proposed by Bohm is to be found as much in philosophy as in physics. While accepting quantum theory as satisfactory for its domain, the search for hidden variables must be pursued in a different domain. They are to be found in reconceiving our world-view, in speculating about the underlying unity of the whole of reality. It is to Bohm's specific cosmological speculations that we now turn.

Flow, Flux and Holomovement

Heraclitus wins! Reality, according to Bohm, is fundamentally '*Undivided Wholeness in Flowing Movement*'.[10] This harkens back to the ancient Greek philosophers and their debate as to which is prior, being or becoming. For Parmenides of Elea there is one fundamental reality, being, that is through and through one in kind, homogeneous with itself, uncreated, complete and unchangeable. Heraclitus, in contrast, gives priority to becoming. All flows. The universe as a whole and everything in it is engaged in perpetual motion, ceaseless process. You cannot step into the same stream twice, he is quoted by Plato to have said (Cratylus 402A). Bohm has taken sides with Heraclitus in this classic debate.

And in doing so, Bohm has sided with one aspect of the modern mind as well. Interpreters of Western culture attest to the triumph of Heraclitus in the age of science. Yale historian of ideas Franklin L Baumer says the 'sense of becoming is at the heart of what we mean by modernity, or "the modern mind"'.[11] University of Chicago theologian Langdon Gilkey says that, 'for moderns, time is the most fundamental structure of all experienced being.... Almost every significant aspect of the modern spirit – its sense of contingency, of relativity, of temporality, and of transience – moves in exactly the opposite direction from the concept of a necessary, self-sufficient, changeless, unrelated, and eternal being'.[12] Although, in saying this, we should also note that, within the modern period, the triumph of time consciousness occurs in the later phase, more in the nineteenth century, and does not in quite the same way dominate the mindset of Descartes and Newton in the formative period of the seventeenth and eighteenth centuries. Nevertheless, the notion of flowing movement belongs to the modern era and in itself does not represent something peculiarly postmodern.

What does Bohm mean by it? Flow means that everything is changing. But, it is not a single homogeneous or undifferentiated flow, which would be undiscernible from static being. It is rather a flux, a movement of forms and shapes and units. Despite the undivided wholeness in the overall flowing movement, we can with the tools of thought abstract from it patterns, objects, entities, conditions, structures and so on, and these will have a certain autonomy and stability. What Bohm wants to stress here is that the flow as an unknown and undefinable totality is prior, whereas the flux of describable events and objects are considered abstractions. This means that our knowledge of the laws of physics deals with abstractions; it deals with events and objects having only relative independence and existence from their ultimate ground in the unknown totality of the universal movement.

It follows that human knowing is both an abstraction from, yet a participant in, the total flux. It is an abstraction because, when we focus on either subjective knowing or objective knowledge, we temporarily forget the wider unit that binds them. We mentally extricate them from the single flow of which they are a part. Although the distinction between mind and matter is described by Bohm as an abstraction from a prior unity in the universal flux, such things as mind and matter do exist. But, they do not exist by themselves, independently, in isolation; they are each modes of the one common underlying reality. This is not the bifurcated world of Descartes in which thought in the mind views the reality of objects out there, as if thinking consisted in viewing reality as an audience views a drama. Here thought is part of the reality that is the continuing flow. Because reality is inclusive of thought, reality itself must be thoughtful. It thinks through us. It has consciousness. It belongs to us and we to it. The flow consists in a single holomovement.

Holomovement and the Implicate Order

There is more than just flow, flux and consciousness in the holomovement. There is also a microcosm–macrocosm correlation, a sort of presence of the whole within and implied by the part. Bohm's notion of cosmic order as flow is not to be understood solely in terms of a regular arrangement of objects (for example, in rows) or as a regular arrangement of events (for example, in a series). Rather, the total order of the holomovement is contained in some implicit sense in each region of space and time. He refers to this as the 'implicate order'.

Bohm observes that the verb *to implicate* means to fold inward or to enfold, as the term 'multiplication' means to fold many times. The implicate ordering of the cosmos means that the total structure is enfolded within each region of space and time. So, whatever part, element or aspect we may abstract in thought, this still enfolds the whole and is therefore intrinsically related to the totality from which it has been abstracted. 'In terms of the implicate order one may say that everything is enfolded into everything. This contrasts with the *explicate order* now dominant in physics in which things are *unfolded* in the sense that each thing lies only in its own particular region of space (and time) and outside the regions belonging to other things.'[13]

Another term for these regions is *subtotalities*. The relationship between subtotalities and the whole is governed by holonomy, that is, the law of the whole. The law of the whole has a looseness about it, permitting a certain autonomy on the part of regions within it. The exact nature of the law of the whole is not known and may even be unknowable, but what we do know is that it includes an overall sense of necessity while avoiding any mechanicalism. 'In the holomovement, there is still an overall necessity ... but its laws are no longer mechanical. Rather ... its laws will be in a first approximation those of the quantum theory, while more accurately they will go beyond even these, in ways that are at present only vaguely discernible.'[14] The net effect of holonomy is to establish the implicate order, to foster subtotalities which provide access to the whole.

Manifestation and the Explicate Order

Although the non-manifest implicate order is primary, the explicate order of manifestations perceptible through the human senses is authentic for Bohm. What is manifest is literally what can be held with the hand – something solid, tangible and visibly stable. The manifest world consists in the external unfolding or explication of the implicate order. The holomovement emits 'verration', that is, the act of perceiving truth as well as attending to what truth means.[15] In other words, the forms of flux themselves do not leave us abandoned in a world of illusion. Illusion occurs only when we mistake the forms of flux for the fundamental reality, that is, when we assume that what is explicate is all that there is.

> '*What is* is the holomovement and ... everything is to be explained in terms of forms derived from this holomovement. Though the full set of laws governing its totality is unknown (and, indeed, probably unknowable) nevertheless these laws are assumed to be such that from them may be abstracted relatively autonomous or independent subtotalities of movement (e.g., field, particles, etc.) having a certain recurrence and stability of their basic patterns of order and measure.'[16]

Bohm believes that the notion of an implicate order becoming explicate gives a more coherent account of the quantum properties of matter than does the traditional mechanistic order. For example, it solves the problem of discontinuities in the track of an electron particle. Where the electron seems to pass from one state to another without traversing the states between, Bohm can say this is possible because the electron itself is only an abstraction from a much greater totality of structure. If we assume that the electron as a particle is the primary reality, then it appears to drop out of existence and then come back into existence. But, this is something impossible. However, if we assume a hidden implicate order to be the primary reality, and that this implicate order provides the continuity, we can accept that what is manifest to our senses (or to laboratory instruments) does not itself have continuous movement or continuous existence. The disappearance and reappearance of the particle represent multiple projections of a single higher-dimensional movement, the unfolding and enfolding of the single more comprehensive holomovement.

Scientists may very well study the manifest explicate order of electron particles and even employ mechanistic concepts as far as they are helpful, according to Bohm. But, they should avoid the mistake of assuming that the explicate order is the fundamental reality. Science here, understood as the human process of pursuing knowledge, ought not to begin from an examination of the parts and then attempt to derive all wholes through abstraction, explaining wholes as simply the results of interactions of the parts.

> On the contrary, when one works in terms of the implicate order, one begins with the undivided wholeness of the universe, and the task of science is to derive the parts through abstraction from the whole, explaining them as approximately separable,

stable, and recurrent, but externally related elements making up relatively autonomous sub-totalities, which are to be described in terms of an explicate order.[17]

We have a move here from one point of departure to another that parallels the move from nominalism to realism, from beginning with the part to beginning with the whole. Some might say that it represents a move from physics to philosophy. It may also represent a move from the modern to the postmodern.

Part, Whole and Holarchy

A question we might pose at this point is: what is the relationship between the parts and the whole? In one sense Bohm resists any sort of hierarchy of relationships; there is no great chain of being from lower to higher. Animate matter is not a higher form of being than is inanimate matter for him. To say that inanimate matter is dead or that it exhibits no intelligence is not to place it lower on the ladder of being. It is rather to think abstractly.[18] Bohm begins with the whole of matter, and he holds that this whole unfolds itself – becomes explicate – in a variety of media, some intelligent and some not, some conscious and some not. To focus our attention on either the animate or the inanimate is to abstract, to divide and separate by means of thought. Yet, in saying this Bohm does not want to say that abstract thought is simply illusion. There really is an implicate order making itself explicate. He is not a simple monist believing that the parts are swallowed up in a mystical blur. It is really the case that the whole is immanent in the parts.

Consequently, we might press the question of the relation of whole and parts in the explicate order. Will a strictly inanimate part contain the whole which has animate qualities? Bohm seems to answer this indirectly with his notion of region or subtotality. It should follow from the above that a subtotality would necessarily contain both animate and inanimate dimensions if it is authentically to re-present the whole. However, Bohm describes inanimate matter as a relatively autonomous subtotality in which life is not manifest. This raises questions. If life is characteristic of the whole but not the inanimate subtotality, then how can the whole be wholly present in the subtotality? Is life left out? Or is it just not manifest? Does he mean to say that life is present implicately even when only inanimate matter is explicate? If so, then how do we know? By faith? That is, do we believe in the non-manifest whole even when it is not manifest? In addition, we wish to ask about the relationship between various subtotalities. Do they relate directly and solely to the whole, or is there an intermediate relation which they share with one another that qualifies their relation to the whole?

We might refer briefly here to the work of Koestler, whose cosmology at this point seems to run somewhat parallel to Bohm's. What Bohm refers to as a subtotality corresponds roughly to Koestler's notion of the 'holon'. Like Bohm, Koestler is seeking a holistic worldview. He defines *holism* as the belief that the whole is more than the sum of the parts, and in modern physics it consists in the insight that the whole is as necessary for understanding the parts as the parts are necessary for understanding the whole.[19] A whole is considered something complete in itself which needs no further explanation. The whole – part relationship, contrary to widely held thought, is not just that. There are no completely distinguishable parts and wholes in any absolute sense; they mutually define and depend on one another. Furthermore, all things are held together by an intermediate reality, the subwhole or 'holon'. The holon is a stable, integrated structure, equipped with self-regulatory devices and enjoying a considerable degree of autonomy, of self-government.

Holons are part of an inclusive hierarchy. Koestler offers the example of cells of tissue and the heart. Each cell is capable of functioning in vitro as a quasi-independent whole. The heart is made up of such cells, but it too is a quasi-independent whole, functioning according to its own somewhat autonomous principles. Each of these are subwholes which function as subordinated parts of a yet more inclusive whole, namely, the human organism. 'The term "holon" may be applied to any stable sub-whole in an organismic, cognitive, or social hierarchy which displays rule-governed behavior and/or structural Gestalt constancy.'[20] Koestler's concept of the holon serves to supply the missing link between atomism or fundamental pluralism, on the one hand, and a holism which swallows everything individual up into mystical absorption, on the other.

Koestler's holons recall the mythical god Janus. That is, holons face in two directions within the holarchy, internal and downward as well as external and upward. Internally, the holon integrates its parts into itself as a whole. Externally, it is self-assertive, preserving its individual identity, while it itself becomes integrated into a more inclusive hierarchy. Holons 'are Janus-faced. The face turned upward, toward higher levels, is that of a dependent part; the face turned downward, towards its own constituents, is that of a whole of remarkable self-sufficiency'.[21]

It seems that Bohm would probably follow the Koestler development, agreeing that the concept of subtotalities denies that the whole of reality is simply an aggregation of elementary parts. The whole determines the parts as much as the parts determine the whole, perhaps even more so for Bohm. And at times Bohm will speak of an infinite regress of implicate orders, wherein a given order will be implicate to the explicate order dependent on it, and at the same time it itself will be explicate to a higher order which is its implicate. This parallels roughly Koestler's holarchy.

But, there are some contrasts. Bohm does not apparently develop the notion of holarchy with reference to the explicate world, which appears to be what Koestler does. Koestler proffers a broader application of the notion by stating that holarchy applies not just to the realm of subatomic physics but also to biological and social organisms. In addition, Bohm may be asking more from his subtotalities than Koestler does. To get from the part to the whole in Koestler's holarchy one must climb the ladder one holon at a time until reaching the comprehensive top, whereas for Bohm, in contrast, one goes directly from part to whole and back again. Bohm holds that access to one subtotality or integrated region provides us with a material door that opens directly out onto the whole, that the very nature or character of the largest whole can be revealed in the smallest holon.

The Immense Multidimensional Ground

Now we ask of Bohm: what is the nature of the whole itself? For starters, it is not limited to the four dimensions of space-time common to our everyday experience. Electromagnetic fields which obey the laws of quantum theory have already provided us with one example of reality that transcends the four-dimensional frame of reference. And, Bohm argues, quantum theory in turn is limited to a certain domain so that hidden variables must be sought elsewhere, providing us with a second example. In short, 'the implicate order has to be extended into a multidimensional reality. In principle, this reality is one unbroken whole, including the entire universe with all its fields and particles. Thus, we have to say that the holomovement enfolds and unfolds in a multidimensional order, the dimensionality of which is effectively infinite'.[22]

Occasionally, Bohm refers to this as a background reality of 'higher dimensional' space. What does he mean here? Could it be a form of space that transcends, yet is inclusive of our three-dimensional space? What are the alternatives? One alternative is to conceive of the inclusive background reality as an empty receptacle, as a void. There are premodern precedents for this conception, which became dominant during the modern period. Leucippus and Democrates divide material being into a plurality of imperceptibly small atoms (*atomoi*), each one eternal and indivisible. These atoms can be separated from one another and relate to one another because they are set within a wider background of empty space, the unlimited (*apeiron*). Because true being is associated with the atoms and not with the empty receptacle, the spatial background itself cannot function as a cause or influence in the material world; it is only present owing to its absence.

The other alternative is to fill the background with being. For this alternative we can thank both Parmenides and Heraclitus. Bohm, curiously enough, identifies himself with the school of Parmenides in holding that space is a filled plenum.[23] Space is a filled plenum for Parmenides because outside it there can be only nothing. 'What is, is,' he writes, which implies that there is no such thing as empty space either within or outside the being of the world. All things are finally reduced to one thing, and that great One is described as never having come into being from a previous state of non-being. It is eternal, imperishable, unitary and complete. Parmenides goes on to argue that, if there is a single substance behind all things, then the concept of change is logically absurd and the phenomenon of change is an illusion. To get beyond opinion to truth is to get beyond illusory change to eternal and unchangeable being.

One would think Bohm would be more interested in Heraclitus than in Parmenides on this score. With Heraclitus, Bohm could have both fundamental unity plus change. According to Heraclitus, there is only one basic reality in the world, which is the source for all things, and the process by which this reality becomes a plurality of things is the process of change. The never-ending flux consists in differing forms of a continuing single reality variously described as fire, *logos* or God. Materially conceived, all things are a different form of the ever-living fire. Rationally conceived, all things are expressions of the divine. Because God is reason (*logos*) and since God is the One which permeates all things, pantheist Heraclitus holds that all things move and change in accordance with the *logos* as the universal law immanent in the process. What we perceive to be disorder and strife between opposites will ultimately find a higher harmony in the continuing life of the divine unity.[24] In addition to comprehensive unity and flux, Heraclitus should also have appeal for Bohm because his unifying reality, God, has the ability to influence individual events.

How does Bohm describe his own notion of the filled plenum? He describes it as a sea of energy. The forms of the flux appear as ripples or wave patterns on the surface of this sea.

> What is implied by this proposal is that what we call empty space contains an immense background of energy, and that matter as we know it is a small quantized wavelike excitation on top of this background, rather like a tiny ripple on a vast sea ... this vast sea of energy may play a key part in the understanding of the cosmos as a whole. ... what we perceive through the senses as empty space is actually the plenum; which is the ground for the existence of everything, including ourselves.[25]

The sea of energy is immense, so immense that when Bohm discusses the Big Bang theory of cosmogenesis, he says, 'this big bang is to be regarded as actually just a little ripple'.[26] The whole 20 billion year history of the multigalactic cosmos is just a little ripple! When Bohm says his sea of energy is immense, he means it.

Bohm's plenum is not to be conceived as a material medium such as Heraclitus' fire or the 19th-century concept of a pervasive ether, both of which were regarded as moving only in three-dimensional space. Bohm wants more. This energy sea is to be understood in terms of a multidimensional implicate order, while the universe of matter manifested to our sense experience is to be treated as a comparatively small pattern of excitation. This excitation pattern is relatively autonomous and gives rise to our experience of subtotalities and the notions of three-dimensional and quantum space.

From this point on, Bohm's multidimensional sea of energy begins to pick up character and personality. As we mentioned before, because this grand reality is inclusive of human consciousness – which Bohm takes to include thought, feeling, desire, will and so on – in itself it cannot be less than conscious. The holomovement must be the source of life and itself be living. Furthermore, the absence of life is dubbed by Bohm as an abstraction: 'In its totality the holomovement includes the principle of life as well. Inanimate matter is then to be regarded as a relatively autonomous sub-totality in which, at least as far as we now know, life does not significantly manifest. That is to say, inanimate matter is a secondary, derivative, and particular abstraction from the holomovement.'[27]

Bohm, like other postmodernists, strives to get beyond the dualism bequeathed us by Descartes, for whom consciousness or 'thinking substance' is sharply distinguished from matter or 'extended substance'. The problem this dualism creates is that we need a basis for relationship between matter and consciousness. Descartes clearly understands this difficulty and proposes its solution with his doctrine of God. God, being transcendent to both matter and consciousness, is able to provide clear and distinct ideas to consciousness that correspond to extended objects. During the intervening centuries since Descartes, the notion of God has dropped out of modern cosmology, leaving the now divorced mind and matter to go their separate ways. Bohm wants to reunite them with a common higher-dimensional ground, so, his notion of holomovement performs the job done by God in Descartes' system.[28]

In uniting mind and matter the holomovement is not simply passive, waiting for conscious thought to manipulate it. Bohm says it projects. It presses itself into human consciousness through memory, wherein a single moment consists in the co-presence of a series of interpenetrating and intermingling elements in different degrees of enfoldment. Bohm is making the startling claim that human memory is not the projection of subjectivity out toward the world but rather the projection of the world itself into our subjectivity. The holomovement actively prompts human consciousness.

Thus, each moment of consciousness has an explicit content, which is a foreground, along with an implicit content, which is a corresponding background. But, the holomovement here is not restricted to the implicit background; it also manifests itself in the explicit foreground. It projects its own implicate order in the process of becoming the explicate manifestation.

> The more comprehensive, deeper, and more inward actuality is neither mind nor body but rather a yet higher-dimensional actuality, which is their common ground and which is of a nature beyond both. ... In this higher-dimensional ground the implicate order prevails. Thus, within this ground, *what is* is movement which is represented in thought as the co-presence of many phases of the implicate order. ... So we do not say that mind and body causally affect each other, but rather that the movements of both are the outcome of related projections of a common higher-dimensional ground.[29]

And Bohm goes even further in his concept of projection. He says the inclusive ground is creative.

> Such a projection can be described as creative, rather than mechanical, for by creativity one means just the inception of new content, which unfolds into a sequence of moments that is not completely derivable from what came earlier in this sequence or set of such sequences. What we are saying is, then, that movement is basically such a creative inception of new content as projected from the multidimensional ground. ... This we may call the ground of all that is.[30]

In sum, the all-inclusive holomovement can be understood as the sea of energy or the multidimensional ground from which all things derive. It is living.

It actively projects its own implicate order in and through human consciousness, thereby becoming manifest and explicit. In doing so it is creative, because what it unfolds in a sequence of moments is not simply derivable from what came earlier.

Holomovement and Holes in the Argument?

One might ask at this point if Bohm has fallen into the fallacy of composition when one reasons without warrant from the properties of the parts to the properties of the whole. The whole, if understood as more than simply the sum of its constituent parts, will have a character or integrity of its own that is not simply the transfer of the character of the parts; it will be a composition and not merely an aggregate. A particularly flagrant example of the fallacy, which appears in logic textbooks, is the argument that, if every part of a certain machine is light in weight, then the machine as a whole is light in weight. The error is that the machine may contain a very large number of parts and may as a whole be quite heavy. In the case of Bohm's holomovement, he argues that, because individual human beings are conscious, the universe as a whole is conscious. Does it follow necessarily that if the individual parts are conscious – which implies intelligence, self-awareness, identity over against other identities, and so on – that the whole *qua* whole has a parallel consciousness? It is in principle possible that the whole is as Leucippis and Democrates thought it is, namely, an empty receptacle containing individual atomic units. Instead of a whole the cosmos might be simply an aggregate, a large collection of individual entities, some of which are conscious.

Bohm, of course, means what he says. He understands the holomovement on the model of the hologram. The term *hologram* is derived from the Greek *holo*, meaning whole, and *gram* meaning to write. Holography is the construction of a kind of three-dimensional picture produced by lensless photography. By letting light fall on a photographic plate from two sources (from the object itself and from a reference beam, which is light deflected by a mirror from the object onto the plate) a three-dimensional likeness can be reconstructed. What is important for the present argument is that every part of the resultant hologram contains the entire image. If the hologram is broken, any piece of it will reconstruct the whole. This is the model for the universe employed by Bohm in his notion of the holomovement.[31] The whole is fully present in the part.

But we might ask whether or not there might be some fallacious reasoning involved. In this case it would be the reverse of the composition fallacy, namely, the fallacy of division when the properties of the whole are attributed without warrant to the parts. An example would be to argue that, because a million dollars has a lot of buying power, so also does each of the million dollars. According to the holographic model the qualities of the whole seem to be present without remainder in each of the parts. Yet, holistic thinking ordinarily requires as one of its premises that the whole is greater than the sum of the parts – or, to phrase it more accurately, that the whole has an integrity (integrating power) of its own. This is something which the parts on their own do not possess. This premise would permit the influence of the whole to be present in each of the parts, but the whole itself would not be exhausted in each of the parts. The problem of the parts for Bohm is just that they are parts; they are perceived and thought of as separate and distinct from one another. What Bohm wants to affirm is unity, wholeness. Whatever unity or wholeness there is, then, is a quality that by definition belongs not to the parts but to the whole. The parts even just formally cannot contain all the qualities of the whole. It seems that the holographic model might be leading Bohm away from his target, because this model implies that all of the qualities of the whole are exhaustively present in the part.

Is the Holomovement Divine?

Could we consider the holomovement divine? Bohm refers to it as the 'higher-dimensional ground' of all things, the implicate order underlying the explicate order, or even the non-manifest which moves what is manifest. Corresponding notions in the philosophies of Descartes and Spinoza are labeled 'God'. What functions as God and the divine subjective aim in Alfred North Whitehead's system has an ordering responsibility akin to Bohm's implicate ordering. John B. Cobb, Jr. refers to Whitehead's God as an 'energy-event' which gives rise to both matter and human consciousness.[32] Hence, should Bohm wish to attribute divine qualities to the holomovement, there would be some precedent.

But Bohm hesitates to follow this precedent. He is willing to speculate on the nature of the implicate order, but then he adds a caution: 'we have to be careful not to linger on that too long'.[33] He wishes to keep theological speculation to a minimum.

Bohm is willing to describe the implicate order as holy but is less willing to describe it as sacred. The term *sacred* has an etymological history going back to ancient religious sacrifice. This makes Bohm nervous because it is too closely associated with organized religion. The term *holy*, in contrast, comes from the same root as *whole*; therefore, he is quite happy thinking of the whole as holy.[34]

We are a long way from formulating what looks like a doctrine of God. The implicate order for Bohm is matter, not spirit. The term *spirit* in languages such as Hebrew and Greek means breath or wind. It became associated with the divine because, though in itself it was not manifest, it appeared to move what is manifest when blowing things around. Modern science upset the phenomenological basis for such a theology, however, by discovering that breath and wind are themselves matter. All this brings Bohm to the frontier of theology without crossing over. 'All we can say is that this view is consistent with the notion that there's a truth, an actuality, a being beyond what can be grasped in thought, and that is intelligence, the sacred, the holy.'[35]

In thinking this way, Bohm follows other philosophers who have similarly hesitated at this point. Parmenides, whom Bohm mentions, refrained from referring to the plenum as divine and may even have refrained from referring to it as being. Parmenides' phrase *estin a ouk estin* is grammatically ambiguous, so that it can be translated as either 'it is or it is not' or 'what is, is'. The rendering 'it is' makes one ask what *it* is referred to here. Some translators answer: being. The term for being, *eon*, appears in other Parmenidean texts, but not here. Why? And why does he avoid the term *god*, which was so commonly used by other presocratic thinkers? Eric Voegelin speculates that it is because of a mystical tendency in Parmenides, and the term *god* is typically used to refer to an object of thought.

> We suspect that there was a good reason for the hesitation to use the subjection and that in this hesitation the true philosophical genius of Parmenides reveals itself. ... To name the subject 'God', as is done in Christian theology, is a convenience, but quite unsatisfactory in critical philosophy. With great circumspection Parmenides has resisted the temptation of calling his Being God. ... The progress on the way toward the light culminates in an experience of a supreme reality that can only be expressed in the exclamatory 'Is!'[36]

Although it is worthy of note that Parmenides did not dub his unifying reality divine, it may have been for reasons that do not apply to Bohm. If Voegelin is correct that Parmenides was a mystic and that mystic reality transcends divinity, we should note that Bohm does not seem to develop his notion of the multidimensional ground in a traditionally mystical direction. There is a hint of mysticism, although he restricts himself to scientific and speculative procedures and avoids any appeal to direct mystical experience or to mystical philosophy. Bohm's theory of the implicate order is a theory about matter, not spirit. Should there be a realm of supramatter beyond the holomovement – which the Bohm theory does not forbid – then the discussion would be open for religious speculation. In the meantime, there is no mixture of physics and theology in Bohm's work.[37]

Another reason that might be given for avoiding the attribution of divinity to the holomovement is that in doing so we might fall into the god-of-the-gaps trap. Koestler, whose position is quite similar to the one under discussion, is cautious here while being critical of Bohm's hidden variables theory.

> Einstein, de Broglie, Schrödinger, Vigier, and David Bohm, who were unwilling to accept the indeterminacy and acausality of sub-atomic events ... were inclined to believe in the existence of a sub-stratum below the sub-atomic level, which ruled and determined those seemingly indeterminate processes. This was called the theory of 'hidden variables' – which, however, has been abandoned even by its staunchest supporters because it seemed to lead simply nowhere.
>
> But although unacceptable to the physicists, the hidden variables provided a fertile field for metaphysical and parapsychological theorizings. Theologians proposed that Divine Providence might work from within the fuzzy gaps in the matrix of physical causality ('the god of the gaps').[38]

Although Bohm does not advocate a god-of-the-gaps position, he does advocate something parallel: a ground-of-the-gaps or holomovement-of-the-gaps position. The Newtonian physics of the modern era and the quantum physics of the approaching postmodern era have left gaps that Bohm wants to fill. The fragmentation of modern thinking and its corresponding breakdown of social and natural relationships has sent Bohm on a search for a holistic actuality which can unite the fragments. He has not sought out divine revelation or even mystical experience, but has sought rather to observe what is manifest in the explicate order, to observe the spatial gaps between what is explicate, and then to render a synthetic judgment positing an all-inclusive and implicate order belonging to the whole of reality.

Whether or not Bohm himself engages in theological inquiry, we must recognize that talk about the whole suggests talk about God. To raise the question of the whole of reality is to ask about the divine. In Jewish and Christian tradition, all that is real is the product of God's creative work. The cosmological speculations of theorists such as Bohm raise the kind of issues that prompt questions about monotheism.

Monotheism is the belief in one God as the ultimate reality that normally includes a distinction between God and the created order which is not sufficient unto itself. Even if we conceive of it as a whole, as the totality of finite reality, we must recognize that we can then conceive of something outside or beyond it. In fact, wholes which we have experienced (Bohm's subtotalities) are constituted as specific wholes by being separated from something else, by drawing the line between what is integrated and what is left outside, by distinguishing one totality from another. Unless the cosmos be an exception to the rule, a transcendent God is required for it to attain its own wholeness.

Christians have historically made certain commitments regarding such a doctrine of God that usually puts them in the camp of monotheism. The primary religious sentiment is to affirm that God is the ultimate reality. Regardless of how it is rationally depicted, this affirmation of God's intimacy is expressed by Paul for whom God is all in all (I Cor. 15:28), by Augustine's doctrine of *creatio ex nihilo*, and by Anselm's notion of God as 'that than which nothing greater can be conceived'. Note, for example, how H. Richard Niebuhr communicates this sense of divine ultimacy when depicting 'radical monotheism'.

> For radical monotheism the value-center is neither closed society nor the principle of such a society but the principle of being itself; its reference is to no one reality among the many but to One beyond all the many, whence all the many derive their being, and by participation in which they exist. As faith, it is reliance on the source of all being for the significance of the self and of all that exists. It is the assurance that because I am, I am valued, and because you are, you are beloved, and because whatever is has being, therefore it is worthy of love. It is the confidence that whatever is, is good, because it exists as one thing among the many which all have their origin and their being, in the One – the principle of being which is also the principle of value.[39]

For Niebuhr, radical monotheism has to do with the ultimate being and value of all things. It is also more: that 'One beyond all the many' Christians call God.

It is in principle possible to solve the problem of the relationship between the one and the many without recourse to the Christian God. A monism would do. Monism is the view that the plurality of things in the phenomenal world are ultimately part of a single reality. Parmenides and Heraclitus provide us with examples. In more recent times, monism has become attractive as a tool for overcoming the dualism of mind and body, because one can posit a more primary reality of which both mind and body are modes. This seems to be what attracts Bohm.

The problem with monism in all its forms is that it denies the Christian belief in a radical distinction between God and the creation. This distinction functions to affirm divine ultimacy. God transcends the world. This means among other things that the creature can never become totally divine. Although God as immanent can and does participate in the creation, that which has been created will remain the created.

The distinction between God and the creation has two corollaries in Christian monotheism. First, God is not thought of as simply a craftsperson who molds, shapes and directs an already existent world stuff. Rather, God creates *ex nihilo*, out of nothing. He summons the universe into existence and should he not so summon it, then there would be only God.

Second, the created realm is entirely dependent upon God as the source and power of its continued existence. We have a part in the universe not by some natural right, but only by the grace of God. Life is a gift. The proper creaturely response is to be thankful.[40] The purpose of Bohm's *Wholeness and the Implicate Order* is not to render thanksgiving for the cosmos, of course. But perhaps the theological reader can be thankful that Bohm successfully avoids a clash with Christian theology that would result from dubbing the holomovement divine.

History and the Whole

There is another related issue: can Bohm's holographic microcosm–macrocosm correlation be made compatible with the Christian emphasis on historical reality? The idea that reality is history and that such things as creativity and irrevocable change occur within history is an idea that modernity shares with ancient Israel and the New Testament. Because of the movement in holomovement, it would seem that Bohm is accepting of the modern understanding of reality as processive, temporal and historical. But just how far is he in fact willing to go with this? Speculations on the microcosm–macrocosm correlation have a tendency to deny genuine historicity to events, to dissolve everything into a timeless unity. When he speaks directly to the issue, he speaks of time in the holomovement in terms of 'recurrence' on the analogy of the changing seasons.[41]

Bohm's notion of implicate causation carries his theory in the direction of an achronic or suprahistorical whole that minimizes the importance of the course of individual events. In the explicate order, current events do not cause or influence future events directly; each event is enfolded into the implicate order, into the whole. The next or subsequent event emerges from the implicate order and is not the direct product of its predecessor. All of history is analogous to a film. Each frame is a still picture, but owing to its speed through the camera we perceive the movie as continuous. So also in history each event is a unit unto itself produced by the implicate order becoming explicate. It only appears to be a sequence of causally related events. To exaggerate a little: in order to kick the dog, one must first kick the implicate order, then the implicate order kicks the dog and in a subsequent event, it prompts the dog to yelp. Kicking, feeling the kick and yelping all belong to the immense multidimensional whole and simply become explicate at arbitrary times. It just appears to us that they are causally related.

The advantage in such a theory is that we are no longer the victims of a strict nexus of efficient causation. Individual events are related to the whole. Should one want to describe divine activity in the ordinary course of events, the concept of the implicate order might be a vehicle for doing so. However, there may be a disadvantage as well. By eliminating entirely the direct continuity between the sequence of events, temporality and historicity risk being swallowed up in the achronic abyss of the implicate order.

There are grounds for taking history seriously in both natural science and theology. It has been traditionally assumed that history belongs peculiarly to the human condition and that nature functions in some achronic realm, subject to unchanging laws. What is beginning to dawn on modern consciousness is the comprehensiveness of the category history. Nature, too, is historical. It is not timeless. Astrophysicist C.F. von Weizsacker argues the point forcefully. 'Man is indeed a historic being, but this is possible because man comes out of nature and because nature is historic herself. ... History in the broadest sense is the essence of what happens in time. In this sense, nature undoubtedly has a history since nature herself is in time. History of nature, then, would be the totality of what happens in nature.'[42] If von Weizsacker is correct, that the natural realm is historical and hence subject to newness and to irrevocable changes, then the whole of nature is neither directly accessible through mental holography or micro-cosm–macrocosm correlation, nor is temporal passage a totally discontinuous product of a supratemporal whole.

If one were to take history seriously, so that what is engaged in temporal passage is understood as what is real, and if one were similarly open to the future and to the possibility of a genuinely new reality resulting from the processes, one would have to deny that the whole of reality currently exists anywhere. Even if the whole of space were present, certainly the whole of time would not be. In any given moment in which one focuses on one of the parts, the whole could not become present in any complete sense. It could not do so because it is not yet the whole which it someday will be. There cannot be a microcosm which fully represents the macrocosm, because the macrocosm is itself still in process, still becoming, still incomplete. To assert that the whole is fully present holographically implies a denial of temporality; it implies that reality as a whole is achronic and unchanging. The only authentic way in which the whole can become present in the part is for the final future to become present in the moment.

Bohm believes he handles this problem by distinguishing between flowing 'wholeness' and static 'totality'. Totality includes the notion of completeness. What is whole, in contrast, is incomplete.[43] By the whole, he refers to what is at the present moment in its incompleteness and without regard to its future. But, we might ask, what kind of a whole is it that is an incomplete whole? Can the whole understood this way be equated with what is real? Is not the future of the holomovement constitutive of its reality? Is not Bohm himself doing what he has warned us against, namely, abstracting and isolating the present whole from the more inclusive reality?

The concept of totality is not necessarily static as Bohm believes. If it includes the aspect of temporal passage, then totality is located in the future and stands over against the present in creative tension. It constantly draws the present beyond itself towards ever new reality, towards fulfillment. Without the notion of future totality, the notion of wholeness is abstracted from time and becomes vacuous.

At the present moment the totality of reality does not exist anywhere in its completeness. We can only anticipate it. In fact, that is what we do. In isolated moments of meaningfulness, we implicitly anticipate the completed whole, the total reality which will finally put all things into their respective place. To see meaning in the present moment is an act of unconscious faith. It is an act of trust that the future will confirm and extend the meaning we currently perceive and experience.

There may be deep mystical experiences which give an individual a sense of cosmic unity. There also may be theories such as Bohm's which posit at the level of metaphysical discourse belief in cosmic unity. They are not holograms in the sense that they reveal a currently existing wholeness to all things. Rather, such experiences and theories are proleptic, that is, they anticipate future wholeness. Ordinary events – as well as mystical experiences and metaphysical theories – are both causative and yet open to the future, making them reciprocally related to the future whole. Present events, or parts and subtotalities, gain their own present identity from the final future of all things, and the final future will be determined in part by present events. Meaningful events may be revelatory, that is, they may manifest wholeness, but they do so not because they are microcosms of the whole. They do so, rather, because by faith we recognize their dependence upon the whole to make them what they are. They point to the whole while not in themselves embodying all that the whole will ultimately include. Instead of holograms we should speak of proleptograms.

Theologian Wolfhart Pannenberg contends that the essence of all things is yet to be determined. It will not be determined until the eschatological future. The meaning we find in the present moment is dependent upon an implicit faith that includes a fore-conception of what is to come.

Only from such a fore-conception of a final future, and thus of the still unfinished wholeness of reality, is it possible to assign to an individual event or being – be it present or past – its definitive meaning by saying what it is. Thus, when someone names a thing and says, 'this is a rose,' or 'this is a dog,' he always does so from the standpoint of an implicit fore-conception of the final future, and of the totality of reality that will first be constituted by the final future. For every individual has its definitive meaning only within this whole.[44]

It is at the point of this defining whole in the final future that we will find God. All events are moving ahead to meet a common future, a common future that is the reality of God. There is no whole at present. There really do exist separate subjects and separate objects and the consequent uncertainty in human knowing. We must live in part by faith and in part by reason until the process is complete, until the advent of God's consummate future, at which time faith and reason will themselves be united.

Conclusion

In conclusion, theologians should give ear to what Bohm says because he raises a scientific voice on behalf of the widespread yearnings for wholeness that characterize the emerging postmodern consciousness. Postmodernity has yet to make it on the agenda of present-day theologians. So preoccupied have the church's twentieth-century intellectuals been with making the gospel relevant to the modern mind that they have scarcely noticed that the modern mind itself is now breaking down and giving way to something new. When postmodernity finally does begin to draw the belated attention of the church, we can expect that one of the first things systematic theologians will do is search for a philosophical system that is both authentically postmodern and potentially compatible with the Christian faith. At that time Bohm's scientific theory will quite likely be considered as an aid to theology in a manner parallel to the roles previously played by the systems of Aristotle and Whitehead.

It is with this possibility in mind that we have raised a few theological questions and suggested some cautions. Although Bohm's cosmology might very well become allied to Christian theology in the mind of some theorists, it is fortunate at this point that Bohm has refrained from simply labeling his holomovement 'God'. Whether by accident or design he shows wisdom in following Parmenides in this regard. To call it God would be to produce another god of the philosophers, a divine principle posited to save the other principles of the system from collapse. It would be a god-of-the-gaps philosophy. Now there is nothing in principle wrong with a god-of-the-gaps philosophy, especially if it is done with coherence and elegance. The problem from the Christian point of view is that, once one is secure in a sound system with a built-in divinity, one's ears are less likely to be open to the revelatory word coming from the transcendent God, the word that takes us beyond every system into the as yet open future.

Notes

1 Toffler writes, 'Today I believe we stand on the edge of a new age of synthesis. In all intellectual fields, from the hard sciences to sociology, psychology, and economics – especially economics – we are likely to see a return to large-scale thinking, to generating theory, to the putting of the pieces back together again', in Alvin Toffler, *The Third Wave* (New York: William Morrow, 1980), 146. Bohm's work represents one of the attempts at large synthetic thinking.
2 David Bohm, *Wholeness and the Implicate Order* (London and Boston: Routledge and Kegan, 1980), 3; cf. xi, 206–7. Cf. also Renee Weber, 'The Enfolding–Unfolding Universe: A Conversation with David Bohm', in *The Holographic Paradigm and Other* Paradoxes, ed. by Ken Wilber (Boulder: Shambala, 1982), 44–104. Bohm's position here regarding the self-deception created when we mistakenly assume conceptual distinctions are fundamental to reality itself seems to be at minimum an attempt to avoid Whitehead's fallacy of misplaced concreteness and at maximum a flirting with Asian mysticism wherein the phenomenal world of multiplicity and distinction is illusory.
3 Bohm, *Wholeness and the Implicate Order*, ix, 172.
4 Renee Weber, 'The Physicist and the Mystic – Is Dialogue Between Them Possible? A Conversation with David Bohm', in *The Holographic Paradigm and Other Paradoxes*, 190.
5 Bohm, *Wholeness and the Implicate Order*, 71–6, 175.
6 Fritjof Capra, *The Tao of Physics* (New York: Bantam, 1977), 50. Cf. Fritjof Capra, *The Turning Point* (New York: Bantam, 1982), 74–8.
7 Arthur Koestler, *Janus* (New York: Random House, 1978), 249–50.
8 Bohm, *Wholeness and the Implicate Order*, xii, 75, 175–6.
9 Ibid., 85.
10 Ibid., 11.
11 Franklin L. Baumer, *Modern European Thought: Continuity and Change in Ideas 1600–1950* (New York: Macmillan, 1977), 21.
12 Langdon Gilkey, *Naming the Whirlwind* (Indianapolis: Bobbs-Merrill, 1969), 54.
13 Bohm, *Wholeness and the Implicate Order*, 177 (emphasis original); cf. 149, 185.
14 Ibid., 181; cf. 156.
15 Ibid., 42.
16 Bohm, *Wholeness and the Implicate Order*, 178. Cf. Weber, 'The Physicist and the Mystic', 204. The degree of reality attributed to concrete experience with distinction and multiplicity is not clear here. The option taken by Asian philosophy – an option at times resisted by Bohm – is to treat the explicate order as illusion. New Age commentator Marilyn Ferguson employs the work of Bohm along with that of Karl Pribram of Stanford University in speculating on a microcosm–macrocosm correlation following the holographic model. 'If the nature of reality is itself holographic, and if the brain operates holographically,' she writes, 'then the world is indeed, as the Eastern religions have said, maya: a magic show. Its concreteness is an illusion,' quoted in Bohm, *Wholeness and the Implicate Order*, 180.
17 Bohm, *Wholeness and the Implicate Order*, 179.
18 Weber, 'The Physicist and the Mystic', 191.
19 Koestler, *Janus*, 26, 256.
20 Ibid., 293; cf. 26–7, 37, 304.
21 Ibid., 27; cf. 301.
22 Bohm, *Wholeness and the Implicate Order*, 189.
23 Ibid., 191.

24 Heraclitus writes, 'Things taken together are whole and not whole, something which is being brought together and brought apart, which is in tune and out of tune: out of all things there comes a unity, and out of a unity all things,' in G.S. Kirk and J.E. Raven, *The Presocratic Philosophers* (Cambridge: University Press, 1960), 191.

25 Bohm, *Wholeness and the Implicate Order*, 191–2.

26 Ibid., 192.

27 Ibid., 195.

28 Ibid., 196–7.

29 Ibid., 209.

30 Ibid., 212.

31 Ibid., 145, 177.

32 John B. Cobb, Jr., *God and the World* (Philadelphia: Westminster, 1969), 71.

33 Weber, 'The Enfolding–Unfolding Universe', 71, 83.

34 Weber, 'The Enfolding–Unfolding Universe', 69–70; 'The Physicist and the Mystic', 194.

35 Weber, 'The Enfolding–Unfolding Universe', 70. On one occasion, Bohm describes the holomovement as an interpenetration of matter and spirit, but on no occasion does he give ontological priority to spirit. See Weber, 'The Physicist and the Mystic', 206–7.

36 Eric Voegelin, *The World of the Polis* (Baton Rouge: Louisiana State University, 1957), 210–11.

37 Ken Wilber, 'Physics, Mysticism, and the New Holographic Paradigm: A Critical Appraisal', in *The Holographic Paradigm and Other Paradoxes*, 168–9. On at least one occasion Bohm tiptoed so close to the edge of theology that he could not prevent himself from falling in. The reason he gave the people assembled at Saint James's Church in London for declining to apply the term *God* to the multidimensional ground has a mystical tone to it. He said that the voice which spoke to Moses in the burning bush referred to itself simply as 'I am'. Bohm believes the 'I am' without predicates places it beyond all limits of time, space and condition. It would be wrong to add predicates to the 'I am' as Christians and other religious people do, he says, because this would lead to religious belief and then to theology and then to interreligious fighting over competing theologies. Religious people who fight with one another contribute to the fragmentation which postmodernity seeks to supersede. Therefore, Bohm himself wishes to avoid any predication by identifying Moses' 'I am' with 'a universal energy pervaded with intelligence and love, which is the ground of everything' (Bohm, 'Fragmentation and Wholeness in Religion and in Science', in *Zygon: Journal of Religion and Science*, 20 (June 1985), 125–33); cf. David Bohm, 'Hidden Variables and the Implicate Order', in *Zygon: Journal of Religion and Science*, 20 (June 1985), 111–24. But, one must ask immediately, what are 'universal energy', 'intelligence', 'love' and 'ground', if not predicates? Just how is Bohm's approach non-theological? In effect, Bohm has a god here, whether he admits it or not. This may mark somewhat of a departure from his position on non-theology. See Bohm, 'Fragmentation and Wholeness', 125–33.

38 Koestler, *Janus*, 250–51.

39 H. Richard Niebuhr, *Radical Monotheism and Western Culture* (New York: Harper, 1943), 32.

40 John Hick, *Philosophy of Religion* (Englewood Cliffs, NJ: Prentice-Hall, 1973), 8.

41 Weber, 'The Enfolding–Unfolding Universe', 89–90.

42   C.F. von Weizsacker, *The History of Nature* (Chicago: University of Chicago Press, 1966), 7.
43   Weber, 'The Physicist and the Mystic', 203.
44   Wolfhart Pannenberg, *Basic Questions in Theology*, 2 vols (Philadelphia: Fortress, 1970–71), 2, 62; cf. 1, 156–7, 229–30.

Chapter 6

Exotheology: Speculations on Extraterrestrial Life

Astronomer and exobiologist Carl Sagan wrote: 'Space exploration leads directly to religious and philosophical questions.'[1] Just what are these questions? Unfortunately, some of the first questions typically asked are very misleading. At the top of the list is a question posed all too frequently by skeptical scientists and tabloid journalists. The question goes like this: 'If we discover living beings in outer space as intelligent or more intelligent than we, will the Christian religion collapse?' Physicist and popular science author Paul Davies provides an example. In his *God and the New Physics*, he lays down the gauntlet:

> The existence of extra-terrestrial intelligences would have a profound impact on religion, shattering completely the traditional perspective on God's relationship with man. The difficulties are particularly acute for Christianity, which postulates that Jesus Christ was God incarnate whose mission was to provide salvation for man on Earth. The prospect of a host of 'alien Christs' systematically visiting every inhabited planet in the physical form of the local creatures has a rather absurd aspect. Yet how otherwise are the aliens to be saved?[2]

What is misleading here is the assumption that the Christian religion is fragile, that it is so fixed upon its orientation to human beings centered on earth that an experience with extraterrestrial beings would shatter it. An alleged earth centrism renders Christianity vulnerable. Yet, I find little or no credible evidence that such a threat exists. To the contrary, I find that when the issue of beings on other worlds has been raised it has been greeted positively. Nevertheless, it is important to observe that the issue has only seldom been raised; so, to Davies' credit, it is not crystal clear how theologians would react should extraterrestrial intelligence (ETI) suddenly become part of our everyday world. I believe the theological community should view the Davies challenge as an opportunity to think more deeply about the matter. I advocate *exotheology* – that is, speculation on the theological significance of extraterrestrial life.

In what follows, it is my task to show that theologians following philosophers in the ancient and medieval periods consciously confronted the prospect of life on other worlds and on more than one occasion actually integrated such thinking into their theological understanding. Then, I will survey examples of modern religious and theological spokespersons who represent Roman Catholic, evangelical Protestant, liberal Protestant and

Jewish theological perspectives. Here, we will find that the topic of extraterrestrial intelligence is seldom raised; but, when it comes up, it seems to present no significant difficulty. Nevertheless, such a study would not be complete without examining the fundamentalist literature of the 1970s that may have contributed to the misunderstanding alluded to above. This literature sought to demonize the UFO phenomenon – presuming that UFOs are associated with extraterrestrial intelligence – and this literature might have given the impression that the Christian faith is more fragile than it in fact is. To this agenda we now turn.

Historical Theology: Might God Create Many Worlds?

The question of the existence of extraterrestrial intelligent life as we pose it today was, in the ancient world, subsumed under a slightly broader question: are there many worlds or only one? The story begins prior to the Christian era. It begins during the rise of philosophy in Greece in the fourth century before Christ.

Yes, there are many worlds, said the atomistic philosophers Democritus (460–370 BC) and Epicurus (341–270 BC). The basic assumption of atomism is that the things we know in the world are the result of chance. They are formed by the chance coalescence of atoms moving about within the void, within empty space. Atoms are in constant motion, colliding, sticking together and forming things. This is how our world came into existence. Because the number of atoms is infinite, it follows that there is an infinite number of other worlds (*aperoi kosmoi*) resulting from the same cause-and-effect chance formations. A Roman disciple of these earlier Greeks, Lucretius (98–54 BC), wrote in his famous *On the Nature of Things*: 'since there is illimitable space in every direction, and since seeds innumerable in number and unfathomable in sum are flying about in many ways driven in everlasting movement', the existence of other worlds must be admitted, 'especially since this world was made by nature'.[3] Just as there are many kinds of fish, there are many earths. Just as there are many kinds of life on earth, there are many kinds of worlds.

What about life in those other worlds? Epicurus and Lucretius positively asserted the existence of plants and living creatures on other worlds. Speculation on this question sometimes focused on the moon. One late Greek source known as pseudo-Plutarch says that 'the moon is terraneous, is inhabited as our earth is, and contains animals of a larger size and plants of a rarer beauty than our globe affords'.[4] Note the assumption that we live on a global, not a flat, earth. Note also the hint of utopianism: the 'rarer beauty than our globe affords'.

No, answered the towering giant of ancient philosophy, Aristotle (384–322 BC); there is only one world and not many. He rejected the arguments of the atomists, especially the idea of chance formation. Aristotle's primary argument was based on his belief that all things naturally seek their proper place. The motions of the four simple elements which make up reality – earth, air, fire and water – were governed by two principles. They would move toward their natural place by nature, or they would move away from their natural place by violence. The natural place for the earth is the center of the world, and the other elements are oriented accordingly. Fire seeks its natural place by ascending to the heavens, while water and air seek their places in between. What results is a cosmological vision of a single reality with the earth at its center. Extending out from the center we find concentric spheres until we reach the one and only heaven. The heart of the argument is what we might call a 'natural centrism' toward which all of nature tends. And, of course, there can exist but one center. Therefore, there can exist one and only one world.[5]

It is well known that Aristotle's philosophy made a significant impact on Christian theology. It dominated the medieval tradition of scholasticism. Perhaps this accounts for the assumption made by Paul Davies and others that Christian theology thinks of the earth or humanity as the center of the universe. Although Aristotle's influence was doubtless formidable, nevertheless, it would be simplistic to say that Christians say it just because Aristotle said it. There was a good deal more flexibility and even controversy than we might assume.

St Thomas Aquinas (1224–74) of the University of Paris is the best known and most influential of the scholastic theologians; he was dedicated to reconciling the Christian faith with Aristotelian philosophy. The particular question he confronted which leads into our topic here was this: is God's omnipotence compromised if God creates only one world? The counter-assumption seems to be that an omnipotent God could, if God so desired, create an infinite number of worlds. Thomas' position is that 'it is necessary that all things should belong to one world'.[6] The key premise is that perfection is found in unity. One world which is constituted of everything that exists would be perfect, a definition which, by the way, derives from Plato. In sum, it would be more in accord to say that God has created a single perfect world than a great number of necessarily imperfect worlds. Hence, divine omnipotence and the existence of only one world are compatible.

Note what is missing here. Thomas does not argue according to some principle of earth chauvinism that the earth must be the center because it is the best. He does not argue that the human race is the be-all and end-all. Rather, he explores where the logic of certain premises might take him. He agrees with Aristotle that our world is ordered, not by chance as Democritus and the atomists said, but by the principle of unity tending toward perfection. Be that as it may, the Thomistic view is definitely in favor of one world, not many.

But Thomas was not the only one to consider this issue. Others did, with other opinions. John Buridan (1295–1358), also at the University of Paris, said, 'we hold from faith that just as God made this world, so he could make another or several worlds'.[7] Note that Buridan's position is based upon faith, not philosophy. Yet, Buridan did not want to fly in the face of Aristotle's arguments. So, he added a premise. Different elements which operate according to different laws could be produced in other worlds. Other worlds, then, would not have to obey what we earlier identified as Aristotle's law of natural centrism. This would permit God to create another world, and God could order the things in it to that world and not to the center of ours. Thus, Buridan could meet the demands of both faith and philosophy.

Nicole Oresme (1320–82), Bishop of Lisieux, extended Buridan's thinking in his treatise, *De coelo de mundo*. But, rather than make peace between faith and Aristotle, Oresme simply repudiated Aristotle. To do so he reformulated the definitions of 'up' and 'down', the directional indicators for the movement of light and heavy things. Heavy things go down, toward the center of the earth. According to Oresme's reformulation, however, no longer do 'up' and 'down' refer only to the center and circumference of our world alone. Another world with another center could have its own version of up and down. All things do not have to orient themselves to our world's center. There could exist a plurality of centers. This denies the position of both Aristotle and Thomas that all things in the same universe must have a relation to one another. Two worlds sufficiently removed need not have a relation to one another, but only relations between their own respective parts. In the 14th century it was easier to disagree with Aristotle than it would be later, when Aristotle's metaphysics became almost a criterion of Christian orthodoxy.

So, Steven Dick unraveled a litany of medieval theologians prior to the Copernican revolution who could accept the many worlds idea, including Albertus Magnus, John Major, Leonardo da Vinci and Spanish Jewish scholar Hasdai Crescas. With some theologians, such as Nicholas of Cusa (1401–64), we get not only a plurality of worlds but also extraterrestrial life.

> Life, as it exists here on earth in the form of men, animals and plants, is to be found, let us suppose, in a higher form in the solar and stellar regions. Rather than think that so many stars and parts of the heavens are uninhabited and that this earth of ours alone is peopled – and that with beings perhaps of an inferior type – we will suppose that in every region there are inhabitants, differing in nature by rank and all owing their origin to God, who is the center and circumference of all stellar regions.[8]

This is what we find in the medieval period. What happened at the dawn of the modern period? What happened to religious thinking about life on other worlds in the wake of the Copernican revolution and the heliocentric theory of the universe where each planet, including earth, has its own center of gravity?

This heliocentric view, of course, met with resistance from some church leaders. Not all church theologians objected, of course, only those who had committed themselves to Aristotelian metaphysics. We recall here that heliocentrism was condemned in 1616. Yet, it is important to note that this condemnation was not based directly on the issue of many worlds. In his defense of Galileo, Tommaso Campanella in effect gave support to the many worlds point of view. He made it clear that the idea of multiple worlds violated no decrees of the Roman Catholic Church and certainly was not contrary to Scripture. It was contrary only to the opinion of Aristotle. Then, lifting the argument to a higher level, he pointed out that Galileo's heliocentric view does not actually posit a plurality of worlds; rather, it discloses one world, the universe, with many subsystems within it.

Theological accommodation to the new science and the vast view of the universe opened up by astronomy moved sufficiently rapidly for Arthur Lovejoy to be able to write, 'by the first or second decade of the eighteenth century not only the Copernican theory of the solar system but also belief in other inhabited planets and in the plurality of worlds seems to have been commonly accepted even in highly orthodox circles'.[9]

In his important study on the history of Protestant thought and natural science, John Dillenberger reports how the debate over many worlds continued in the Reformation churches. 'The debate hung on the assumption that human life existed on other planets,' writes Dillenberger. A second and more troubling assumption was that Scripture nowhere mentions extraterrestrial life. In the event that life on other planets is discovered through science, this significant truth about our universe would be revealed apart from Scripture. The recognition of this possibility could mean a shift in the focus of Christian theology toward creation; creation would be thought to be more extensive than redemption. In the tradition of the Two Books – Scripture and Nature – nature seemed to be revealing more about creation than Scripture about redemption. 'Now creation, interpreted as the wisdom of God in His works, was more significant than redemption. ... there was an entire realm where science was valid and where the Biblical tradition had nothing to say.'[10] The significance of this historical observation for our study here is that, although a theological debate took place, the theologians did not deem it important to reject the notion of other worlds with living creatures.

So, Steven Dick listed numerous natural theologians of the 17th and 18th centuries, following the Copernican revolution, who could affirm many worlds – Richard Bentley, John Ray, William Derham, Immanuel Kant and others. Similar to Nicholas of Cusa, Richard Bentley, a theologian and contemporary colleague of Isaac Newton, posited the existence of ETI. As he did so, he anticipated contemporary ethical concerns regarding the centrality or non-centrality of the human race on our planet. He prepared to combat what we might today call 'earth chauvinism'.

> we need not nor do not confine and determine the purposes of God in creating all mundane bodies, merely to human ends and uses ... all bodies were formed for the sake of intelligent minds: and as the Earth was principally designed for the being and service and contemplation of men; why may not all other planets be created for the like uses, each for their own inhabitants which have life and understanding?[11]

In sum, during the formidable period of medieval scholasticism, despite the forceful impact of Aristotelian philosophy, Christian theology was by no means wedded to the idea that God created only one world. An honest debate raged that carried on well past the Copernican revolution into the modern era. More than one position was put forth. Not only did some of our best minds affirm the idea of multiple worlds, some even spoke positively regarding the existence of extraterrestrial life.

Contemporary Theology: What about ETI?

The period of history following World War II is the space age in many respects. We have put satellites in orbit and astronauts on the moon, and we have sent probes to Venus, Mars and beyond. We have searched for extraterrestrial life with radio telescopes.[12] Budgetary arguments regarding space exploration rage annually in the US Congress. Our theaters have shown sci-fi films depicting interplanetary space travel and even wars between extraterrestrial civilizations. Nine per cent of the US population claims to have seen what they believe to be a UFO, and half the people who think of UFOs as a reality believe they come from outer space.[13] Our culture is shot through and through with space consciousness.

One would expect, therefore, that theological leaders would want to respond to the rise in space consciousness by providing some intellectual guidance. Yet, surprisingly, relatively little is being done. The subject is too widely ignored, in my judgment.[14]

Be that as it may, in those instances during the post-World War II period when the subject has been seriously taken up, the possibility of the existence of ETI is positively affirmed. Beginning with the Roman Catholics, a theologian of the manualist tradition which extends scholasticism down to the present day, George van Noort, has held that it is not in the least incompatible with faith to admit that rational beings exist on other heavenly bodies.[15] Fr. Theodore Hesburgh, past president of the University of Notre Dame, served on a NASA commission and argued that he could legitimately accept the possibility of life on other planets. His argument was that, because God is infinite in intelligence, freedom and power, we cannot take it upon ourselves to limit what God might have done.[16] Notorious German theologian Hans Küng, while making an argument to decenter the place of humanity on planet earth, says, 'we must allow for living beings, intelligent – although quite different – living beings, also on other stars of the immense universe'.[17] And Karl Rahner, whom many see as the theological giant of Catholicism in the 20th century, refers to 'the many histories of freedom which do not only take place on our earth'.[18] Francis J. Connell, C.S.S.R., dean of the School of Sacred Theology at the Catholic University of America during the 1940s and 1950s, sums the matter up: 'it is good for Catholics to know that the principles of their faith are entirely compatible with the most startling possibilities concerning life on other planets'.[19]

Turning to the conservative wing of Protestantism, evangelical preacher Billy Graham welcomes the prospect of both ETI and UFOs. 'I firmly believe there are intelligent beings like us far away in space who worship God,' he told an interviewer. 'But we would have nothing to fear from these people. Like us, they are God's creation.'[20] In his book on angels, Graham writes,

> Some ... have speculated that UFOs could very well be part of God's angelic host who preside over the physical affairs of universal creation. While we cannot assert such a view with certainty ... nothing can hide the fact that these unexplained events

are occurring with greater frequency around the entire world.... UFOs are astonishingly angel-like in some of their reported appearances.[21]

Moving a little more to the center of mainline Protestant theology, we find New Testament scholar Krister Stendahl, former Bishop of Stockholm and former dean of Harvard Divinity School. At a NASA-sponsored symposium in 1972, Stendahl was asked about communication with ETI. 'That's great,' he said. 'It seems always great to me, when God's world gets a little bigger and I get a somewhat more true view of my place and my smallness in that universe.'[22]

A. Durwood Foster poses the very question central to this chapter. Given the prospects of contact with extraterrestrial intelligent beings, 'is faith in any way threatened by the possibilities here in view? Why should it be?' He answers that a faith already steeped in God's mystery should be prepared for the unexpected and even affirmatively open to it. He goes on to cite the New Testament recognition that there are other sheep of which we know not (John 10:16). Then he concludes, 'The love of God manifest in Jesus Christ has surely not remained unknown wherever there is spiritual receptivity.'[23]

Paul Tillich would agree. Tillich, the renowned systematic theologian with one foot in neo-orthodoxy and the other in liberal Protestantism, takes the question of ETI quite seriously. The prospects of extraterrestrial life raise important issues for the doctrines of creation, anthropology and Christology.

> A question arises which has been carefully avoided by many traditional theologians, even though it is consciously or unconsciously alive for most contemporary people. It is the problem of how to understand the meaning of the symbol 'Christ' in the light of the immensity of the universe, the heliocentric system of planets, the infinitely small part of the universe which man and his history constitute, and the possibility of other worlds in which divine self-manifestations may appear and be received.
>
> ... our basic answer leaves the universe open for possible divine manifestations in other areas or periods of being. Such possibilities cannot be denied. But they cannot be proved or disproved. Incarnation is unique for the special group in which it happens, but it is not unique in the sense that other singular incarnations for other unique worlds are excluded ... Man cannot claim to occupy the only possible place for incarnation.[24]

The issue Tillich debates here is the one cynically referred to as 'absurd' by Paul Davies. The issue is this: does the existence of multiple worlds of intelligent life require multiple divine incarnations and multiple acts of redemption? Tillich seems to be answering in the affirmative.[25] Tillich so conflates the doctrines of creation and redemption that he believes God's saving power would already be at work regardless of the situation in which ETI find themselves. One implication of this position is that we earthlings would not necessarily need to send missionaries to initiate aliens into God's plan of salvation.

Returning to the Roman Catholics for a moment, two contemporary scholars have tackled this issue and, at some variance with Tillich's position, argued for the universal efficacy of the Christ event on earth. In an interview, Jesuit journalist L.C. McHugh was asked: what would be the relation of intelligent beings inhabiting a far corner of the cosmos to Jesus Christ? McHugh responded by saying that such people 'would fall under the universal dominion of Christ the King, just as we and even the angels do'.[26] Similarly, J. Edgar Bruns, a New Testament scholar and president of Notre Dame Seminary in New Orleans, writes that 'the significance of Jesus Christ extends beyond our global limits. He is the foundation stone and apex of the universe and not merely the Savior of Adam's progeny'.[27] This position would probably imply that, should ETI be discovered, missionaries would be called for, much as they were when Europe discovered the Western hemisphere.

This is not the case for Roman Catholic Karl Rahner, who seems to side more with Tillich. Rahner, as mentioned earlier, argues that the possibility of extraterrestrial intelligent life 'can today no longer be excluded'. Then he raises the question of 'Christ as head of all creation'. He speculates: 'In view of the immutability of God in himself and the identity of the Logos with God, it cannot be proved that a multiple incarnation in different histories of salvation is absolutely unthinkable.' He concludes that theologians on earth will 'not be able to say anything further on this question', because they are limited by revelation. The purpose of Christian revelation is limited to 'the salvation of humankind, not to provide an answer to questions which really have no important bearing on the realization of this salvation in freedom'.[28]

In this debate over the need for multiple incarnations, we need to keep one item in mind. Even though there are slight differences of opinion regarding the relationship between ETI and the historical event of redemption here on earth, what is important is the common assumption that possible ETI belong within the realm of God's creation and are well worth serious theological consideration.

Back to the Protestants. Moving a step in the liberal direction on the spectrum, German theologian Wolfhart Pannenberg affirms at least the vague possibility of intelligent life living in other solar systems in our own or in remote galaxies. With regard to redemption, however, he differs from Tillich. Pannenberg understands Jesus Christ to be the incarnation of the eternal *logos*, and the eternal *logos* is the medium through which the whole of creation has come into being. The significance of Jesus Christ extends to the farthest reaches of the universe, because through Christ God has promised to draw the whole of time and space into a consummate unity.[29]

The issue of the universality of earth's Christ event is taken up as well by Lewis Ford, a spokesperson for the school of process theology. Disciples of the philosophy of Alfred North Whitehead, process theologians usually find themselves on the liberal end of the Protestant spectrum. Ford begins by stating that 'salvation is not just limited to men but applies to all intelligent beings wherever they may dwell'.[30] Ford embraces the concept of evolution, applies it to every location in the universe, and then asserts that God is always and everywhere drawing the evolutionary process toward greater complexity and higher value.

> we may define God as that dynamic source of values which lures the evolutionary
> process to an ever-richer complexity productive of increasing freedom and intensity

of experience. As such, God is necessarily operative in the development of every life and in every culture, whether terrestrial or extraterrestrial.[31]

The Ford position is close to Tillich's. It virtually collapses salvation into creation. As with Tillich, Ford affirms multiple manifestations of the divine, each one appropriate to the species for which redemption is aimed. Jesus Christ constitutes the incarnation aimed at the human race on earth. Other parallel incarnations are then possible for other intelligent races. In every instance, however, operative is the same creative and redeeming work of the same God.

Although I wish more theologians would take the matter of other worlds and ETI seriously, I still find the spectrum of theological considerations of ETI and even UFOs impressive.[32] Yet, the above-mentioned theologians are all Christians. When researching this topic, I began to wonder what a Jewish theologian might say. So, I telephoned my friend and colleague, Rabbi Hayim Perelmuter. Dr Perelmuter is former president of the Chicago Board of Rabbis and a professor at the Catholic Theological Union in Chicago. He is one of those renaissance people who covers the waterfront: he is an author, a scripture scholar, knowledgeable about the history of intellectual thought, experienced in Jewish–Christian dialogue, up to date on the politics of Israel, and most apt to know the broad sweep of current Jewish thinking. I described the issue on which I was working. His response was forthright and clear. Contemporary Jewish theology would have no difficulty whatsoever in accepting new knowledge regarding the existence of extraterrestrial life. In fact, it would simply broaden the scope of our understanding of God's creation. Then he added a note of tragic humor: 'We Jews have had to adjust to all kinds of things in history, including Nazi Germany and the difficulties with Israel. I am sure we could adjust to space beings emerging from flying saucers as well.'[33]

Fundamentalist Literature: UFOs as Chariots of Satan

During the decade of the 1970s numerous magazine articles and books appeared that dramatically challenged the alleged existence of UFOs and depicted the entire phenomenon as a Satanic plot. This literature sought to frighten Christian readers into disbelief in ETI, and in doing so to capitalize on the fascination that usually accompanies fright. The literature influenced many conservative and evangelical clergy and eventually found its way into sermons and Christian education programs. This approach was most likely stimulated by the wide publicity given to the Pascagoula, Mississippi abduction of Charles Hickson and Calvin Parker on 11 October 1973 as well as the extremely large sales of books such as *Chariots of the Gods?* by Erich von Däniken. A brief upsurge in fright publications followed the release of Spielberg's movie, *Close Encounters of the Third Kind* in December 1977, but then it died down. In the 1980s and 1990s, anti-New Age and then anti-Satanism literature seems to have rushed in to fill the gap in Christian terror literature.[34]

Puzzled at such extremism at a time when Billy Graham had spoken so favorably about ETI, I engaged these proponents in conversation. As best I can reconstruct it, their theological argument follows three steps that lead us to the question of biblical authority. First, there can be no life on other planets because the Bible has not revealed this to be the case. Because the Bible does not anywhere mention life on other worlds, belief in ETI is anti-biblical.

> If there were intelligent beings with origins in outer space, we would expect the Bible to support the fact. However, the Bible takes no such position ... the Bible doesn't even mention the existence of other planets. ... the person of Jesus Christ and His redemptive work underscore the uniqueness of life to the planet earth. He came to die for man's sins, exclusively.[35]

Note how blatantly this argument commits the fallacy of *argumentum ex ignorantia*, the argument from ignorance: because the Bible ignores UFOs and ETI, therefore, UFOs and ETI do not exist. This is fallacious because no one has ever claimed that the Bible constitutes the exhaustive supply of all knowledge that can be known. It is logically possible for things to exist that are not mentioned in the Bible. Toyotas, Swiss watches and Big Mac hamburgers exist indisputably, but they are not mentioned in the Bible.

Note also the earth-centrist assumption here. Perhaps this shows that Paul Davies has some grounds for predicting a radical challenge to Christian belief – at least this brand of Christian belief – should the existence of ETI be empirically confirmed.

The second step in the fundamentalist fright argument is to acknowledge that belief in ETI seems to presuppose the theory of evolution. This observation is correct. The UFO phenomenon and the concept of evolution converge in our culture to form a kind of mythical view of reality.[36] Since the 1950s and perhaps even before, a myth has been under construction in our society that pictures Ufonauts as coming from a civilization in outer space that is further advanced than ours – further advanced in science, technology and morality. This means they have evolved further than we on earth. According to this emerging myth, the Ufonauts are traveling to earth to teach us how to evolve faster, to save ourselves from disaster as we cross the nuclear threshold. The space beings constitute our own future coming back in time as well as space to rescue us, to save us.[37] What the fundamentalist interpreters believe they see in this emerging UFO myth is the human imagination gone wild. By presuming validity to the theory of evolution, earthling imagination has projected evolutionary advance to the point of developmental salvation onto imaginary civilizations in outer space. What we find here, complain the fundamentalists, is a subversive plot to convince our people to believe in evolution and, of course, then to deny the authority of the biblical account of creation in the book of Genesis.

The third step in the argument is to declare all this demonic. Scientists who propound the theory of evolution have with some frequency in the past been denounced by fundamentalists as enemies of the Bible. Indirectly, this denouncing is repeating itself between the lines of anti-UFO literature. Further and more decisively, the UFO phenomenon with its accompanying evolutionary myth provides a temptation for earthlings to look for salvation in someone other than the biblical Jesus Christ. Responding specifically to the movie, *Close Encounters of the Third Kind*, as well as to the generic cultural UFO myth, Frank Allnutt considers the implications of believing in a race of ETI who are 'smart enough to have outlawed crime and war'. He goes on, 'That line of reasoning sees the possibility that these extraterrestrials have become masters over those things which cause death and that they hold the key to the mysteries of immortality. And, maybe, they intend to teach us the secret way to obtain eternal life.'[38] Allnutt can only conclude, then, that 'the UFO phenomenon is being caused by Satan and his demons. Their purpose is to confuse people about the true source of salvation, the Lord Jesus Christ'.[39]

It seems to me that the fundamentalist interpreters perceive with accuracy the salvific structure inherent to the developing UFO myth in our society and, further, that this myth stands at some variance with what Christians want to teach. For this the appropriate response is Christian apologetic theology, to be sure. Yet, the apologetic argument as actually raised here is unnecessarily confused with fallacious appeals to the exclusive authority of the Bible.[40]

Conclusion

In sum, although there are partial grounds for thinking the Christian faith is so earth centrist that it could be severely upset by confirmation of the existence of ETI, an assessment of the overall historical and modern strength of Christian theology indicates no insurmountable weakness. The Aristotelian metaphysical tradition within medieval theology and recent fulminations by fundamentalists have admittedly propounded versions of earth centrism that might give one pause in this regard. Despite St Thomas' use of Aristotelian arguments against many worlds, however, Christian theologians have routinely found ways to address the issue of Jesus Christ as God incarnate and to conceive of God's creative and saving power exerted in other worlds. This applies, of course, to historic Christianity in its present-day Roman Catholic, evangelical Protestant and liberal Protestant forms. Although Paul Davies' challenge does apply to some expressions of fundamentalism, we must note that, in the giant story book that constitutes the 2000 year history of the Christian religion, fundamentalism makes up at best one tiny subchapter. It would be a mistake to take the fundamentalist fright as representative of Christianity as a whole.

At this point in time we can only speculate. The UFO mystery remains unsolved. The question of the actual existence or non-existence of ETI remains open. Should contact between terrestrials and extraterrestrials occur, we cannot predict with certainty how hitherto earthbound society will react. Some scenarios present themselves as likely. In the event that the ETIs appear rich, friendly and benevolent, we will at first greet them with open arms. In the event that the ETIs appear to be warlike conquerors or disease-ridden contaminators or in some other way a threat, we may see the diverse peoples of earth uniting in a common defense. In the event that the ETIs appear to be much like us, we can expect both of the above reactions initially, and then we will eventually see the development of alliances and counter-alliances between segments of both earth and ETI populations. In all three cases, alert Christian theologians will attempt to extrapolate on the basis of existing knowledge of earthling behavior and try to guide us all toward a peaceful and fraternal bond of friendship. Such theologians would affirm with St Thomas that 'all things should belong to one world', and this one world would include both earthlings and extraterrestrials. In the meantime, while we wait for contact, I recommend that some scholars take up Paul Davies' challenge and engage in a preliminary form of exotheology.

Notes

1   Carl Sagan, *The Cosmic Connection* (New York: Dell, 1973), 63.
2   Paul Davies, *God and the New Physics* (New York: Simon & Schuster, Touchstone, 1983), 71.
3   Lucretius, *On the Nature of Things*, Book II, lines 1052–66. See the overall account of the development of the idea of many worlds by Steven J. Dick, *Plurality of Worlds: The Origins of the Extraterrestrial Life Debate from Democritus to Kant* (Cambridge: Cambridge University Press, 1982); hereinafter abbreviated, *PW*. For his citing of Lucretius, see p.11. After the rediscovery of Lucretius' book in medieval Europe in 1417, there was considerable Christian opposition raised against atomism. The heart of the opposition did not stem from the many worlds theory per se, but rather from Lucretius' overt atheism.
4   Cited by Dick, *PW*, 19.
5   Aristotle, *On the Heavens*, books 8 and 9. Dick argues that in only one place does Aristotle commit himself to one world only (*PW*, 193, n.18). But the texts he gives as evidence of variation (*Physics*, II, 196a, 25–30; III, 203b, 20–30; IV, 218b, 4–10; VIII, 250b, 20–23) do not, in my judgment, support Dick's claim. In fact, what Aristotle says in *Metaphysics*, XII, 1073a, 33–40 reiterates what he said in book 9 of *On the Heavens*.
6   Thomas Aquinas, *Summa Theologica*, First Part, Question 47, Article 3. Shortly before his death, Thomas wrote a commentary on Aristotle's *On the Heavens*, *Aristotelis libros de caelo et mundo, generatione et corruptione, meteorologicorum expositio* (Rome, 1952).
7   John Buridan, *Quaestiones super libris quattuor de caelo et mundo*, cited by Dick, *PW*, 29.
8   Nicholas of Cusa, *On Learned Ignorance*, trans. Fr. Germain Heron (New Haven: Yale, 1954), 114f, cited by Dick, *PW*, 41. It was Nicholas, in discussing the boundlessness of God's universe, who gave us the line which Carl Jung likes so well, its 'center is everywhere and its circumference is nowhere'.
9   Arthur O. Lovejoy, *The Great Chain of Being* (New York: Harper and Row, 1936), 130.
10 John Dillenberger, *Protestant Thought and Natural Science* (New York: Doubleday, 1960), 136.
11 Richard Bentley, *A Confutation of Atheism from the Origin and Frame of the World* (London, 1693), reprinted in *Isaac Newton's Papers and Letters on Natural Philosophy*, ed. by I.B. Cohen (Cambridge, MA: Harvard University Press, 1958), 356–8.
12 The US NASA project known as SETI (Search for Extra-Terrestrial Intelligence) under the leadership of Frank Drake at the University of California at Santa Cruz

began using radio telescopes in 1960 to listen for signals coming from various locations in our galaxy. So far no contact. On 12 October 1992, NASA added new channels and upgraded its technical listening capabilities by a factor of 10 000. SETI has also been renamed the High-Resolution Microwave Survey. See 'SETI Faces Uncertainty on Earth and in the Stars', *Science*, 258:5079 (2 October 1992), 27.

13   In his fascinating study of the UFO phenomenon in terms of the classical mythical structure of human experience, Keith Thompson recognizes the already widespread public acceptance of the idea of extraterrestrial intelligence: 'The main significance of UFOs for society may well rest not so much in their extraterrestrial origins, or lack thereof, as in the fact that a sizable segment of society believes and behaves as if they are real, regardless of the available evidence. Public opinion surveys show an increasing willingness of Americans to believe we are not alone in the universe', *Angels and Aliens: UFOs and the Mythic Imagination* (Reading, MA: Addison-Wesley, 1991), 244–5.

14   There are some exceptions, of course. Jack Finegan and, later, A. Durwood Foster, both theological professors at the Pacific School of Religion in Berkeley, California, tried to provide such guidance in their respective books, *Space, Atoms, and God* (St. Louis: Bethany Press, 1959) and *The God Who Loves* (New York: Colliere-Macmillan, Bruce, 1971), esp. 118–26. Jack A. Jennings, a Presbyterian campus minister, contends that both UFOs and ETI should become items of theological debate; but, unfortunately, the debate is not being carried on in the learnèd journals. Because the church ignores the topic, we find it being considered in the marketplace. Jennings recommends that the main bodies of orthodox Christian believers begin getting ready: 'UFOs: The Next Theological Challenge?', *Christian Century* (22 Feb. 1978), 184–9.

15   The fifth edition of Msgr. Van Noort's *Tractatus de Vera Religione* comes in nine volumes. In the English rendering, he points out that we can expect progress in Christian theological thinking if we grant one fundamental principle: 'dogmatic progress, i.e., progress in faith, can go in only one direction: a deeper, fuller explanation of one and the same revealed truth, without any change in the essential meaning of a dogma', *Dogmatic Theology*, Volume III (Westminster, MD: Newman Press, 1961), 394. Applied to the question of ETI, we may expect progress insofar as it is a deepening of our essential apprehension of the fullness of God's creation.

16   Reported by Alan Lightman, 'In His Image: Reflections on Other Worlds', *Books and Religion*, 13:6 (September 1985), 1.

17   Hans Küng, *Eternal Life?* (New York: Doubleday, 1984), 224.

18   Karl Rahner, *Foundations of Christian Faith* (New York: Crossroad, 1978), 446. See Denis Edwards, *Jesus and the Cosmos* (New York: Paulist Press, 1991), 89.

19   Francis J. Connell, C.S.S.R., 'Flying Saucers and Theology', in *The Truth About Flying Saucers*, ed. by Aime Michel (New York: Pyramid Books, 1967), 258.

20   *National Enquirer* (November 30, 1976).

21   Billy Graham, *Angels: God's Secret Agents* (Garden City, NY: Doubleday, 1975), 9–14, *passim*. In a fine article on the social implications of UFOs and ETI, James M. McCampbell comments skeptically on the Graham book. If the primary duty of both angels and UFOs is to protect the faithful, he says, then they are not doing a very good job. 'Unfortunately, they seem to be off playing golf during wars, earthquakes, famines, epidemics, tidal waves, tornadoes, hurricanes, volcanoes, murder, and airplane accidents. Perhaps somebody should fire about 200,000,000

c134   *Science, Theology, and Ethics*

dangels and hire some reliable replacements,' 'Significance for Society if UFOs are Extraterrestrial', unpublished paper, (1988), 12.

22 *Life Beyond Earth and the Mind of Man*, ed. by Richard Berendzen (Washington: NASA Scientific and Technical Information Office, 1973), 29. Even God-is-dead theologian William Hamilton agrees that there may be ETI. But Hamilton says so minus the 'that's great!' enthusiasm of Stendahl. He writes, 'I see no objection to saying that God may have created other worlds than this one. I see no objection to saying that a savior may have visited other places in other times. I see no objection, but neither do I see a point,' William Hamilton, 'The Discovery of Extraterrestrial Intelligence: A Religious Response', in *Extra-Terrestrial Intelligence: The First Encounter*, ed. by James L. Christian (Buffalo: Prometheus Books, 1976), 108.

23 Foster, *The God Who Loves*, 125. A century earlier, Albrecht Ritschl approached the matter similarly. Ritschl announced his acceptance of the Copernican revolution and the decentering of planet earth and then speculated about 'the development of a spiritually-endowed race of organisms' living on other worlds. 'Thus it is possible that the earth is not the only scene of the history of created spirits,' *The Christian Doctrine of Justification and Reconciliation*, volume III of *The Positive Development of the Doctrine*, tr. by H.R. Mackintosh and A.B. Macaulay, (Clifton, NJ: Reference Book, 1874, 1966), 614–15. The continuity here is the notion that there could exist on multiple planets spiritual beings who are receptive to divine grace.

24 Paul Tillich, *Systematic Theology*, 3 Volumes (Chicago: University of Chicago Press, 1951–63), II, 95f.

25 Positions taken on this issue vary. William of Vorilong, a contemporary of Nicholas of Cusa, could affirm many worlds but only one Christ event. The death and resurrection of Jesus Christ on earth is sufficiently efficacious for the redemption of extraterrestrial civilizations. Jesus would not have to die again, *Sentences*, book I. Philip Melanchthon, sixteenth century Reformer and compatriot of Martin Luther, would deny the existence of many worlds on the ground that there could be only one redemptive event: 'Therefore it must not be imagined that there are many worlds, because it must not be imagined that Christ died and was resurrected more often, nor must it be thought that in any other world without the knowledge of the Son of God, that men would be restored to eternal life,' *Initia doctrinae physicae* (Wittenberg, 1550), fol. 43. See Dick, *PW*, 42f, 87f.

26 'Life in Outer Space? An Interview with Rev. L.C. McHugh, S.J.', *Sign*, 41:5 (December 1961), 29. In this interview Rev. McHugh uses the term 'exotheology' for what is to my knowledge the first time it has appeared in print. A similar term, 'exochristology', appears in an article by Andrew J. Burgess, 'Earth Chauvinism', *Christian Century* (8 December 1976), 1098–1102.

27 J. Edgar Bruns, 'Cosmolatry', *The Catholic World*, 191:1 (August 1960), 286.

28 Karl Rahner, 'Natural Science and Reasonable Faith', in *Theological Investigations*, 22 volumes (New York: Crossroad, 1961–88), XXI, 51–2.

29 Wolfhart Pannenberg, *Systematische Theologie*, 3 volumes (Göttingen: Vandenhoeck und Ruprecht, 1988–91), II.

30 Lewis S. Ford, 'Theological Reflections on Extra-Terrestrial Life', *Raymond Review*, 3:1 (Fall 1968), 2.

31 Lewis S. Ford, *The Lure of God* (Philadelphia: Fortress Press, 1978), 63; cf. 54ff. John Hick, a liberal Protestant, though not of the process school, believes similarly that 'God could become incarnate more than once – and indeed, in principle, an indefinite number of times – for the sake of separate groups of people … on other planets of other stars', 'A Response to Hebblethwaite', in *Incarnation and Myth:*

The Debate Continues, ed. by Michael Goulder (Grand Rapids, MI: Eerdmans, 1979), 192.

32 Some theology is more serious than others. A book widely ignored in theological circles yet fascinating to a large number of readers in other circles is Barry Downing's *The Bible and Flying Saucers* (New York: Avon, 1968 and Berkeley, 1989), wherein Downing acknowledges the hermeneutics of existentialist and death-of-God theology and then proceeds to interpret the Bible in such a way as to discern repeated ETI visits in UFOs. Less serious is the spate of literature that tried to superimpose a scientific naturalism upon the scriptural witness, turning God into a technologically advanced Ufonaut. See R.L. Dione, *God Drives a Flying Saucer* (New York: Bantam, 1969) and *Is God Supernatural? The 4,000 Year Misunderstanding* (New York: Bantam, 1976). See also the notorious Erich von Däniken, *Chariots of the Gods?* (New York: Bantam, 1970), *Gold of the Gods* (New York: Bantam, 1974) and *Gods from Outer Space* (New York: Bantam, 1970).

33 This theme of creative survival under the worst imaginable conditions unites the various chapters of Jewish history for Perelmuter, whether this be the rise of Rabbinic Judaism in the ancient world or survival under the Nazi assault in the twentieth century. See his epilogue to *This Immortal People: A Short History of the Jewish People*, by Emil Bernhard Cohn, revised and expanded by Hayim Goren Perelmuter (New York: Paulist Press, 1985) and the book he authored, *Siblings: Rabbinic Judaism and Early Christianity at Their Beginnings* (New York: Paulist Press, 1989).

34 A relevant example is William M. Alnor, *UFOs in the New Age: Extraterrestrial Messages and the Truth of Scripture* (Grand Rapids: Baker, 1992), 133, see 15. Alnor cannot make up his mind as to whether or not ETI exist. He is waiting for more facts. Yet, he is confident that a combined UFO–New Age conspiracy seeks to entice us away from orthodox Christian beliefs into a vague mystical and universalistic religion: 'Their foremost concern seems to be to change the way we think about God. They are almost equally interested in changing God's Word, the Bible, and inserting in its place a type of universalism that says it really doesn't matter what one believes in matters of religious faith as long as one is sincere. Truth is irrelevant.

35 Frank Allnutt, *Infinite Encounters: The Real Force Behind the UFO Phenomenon* (Old Tappan, NJ: Fleming H. Revell, 1978), 80. In the same genre, see John Weldon with Zola Levitt, *Encounters with UFO's* (Irvine, CA: Harvest House, 1975), reprinted as *UFOs: What On Earth is Happening?* (New York: Bantam, 1975); Clifford Wilson and John Weldon, *Close Encounters: A Better Explanation* (San Diego, CA: Master Books, 1978).

36 I outline this emerging myth in Ted Peters, *UFOs – God's Chariots: Flying Saucers in Politics, Science, and Religion* (Louisville: Westminster/John Knox Press, 1977). The thesis I develop in this book follows the trail blazed by Carl Jung in *Flying Saucers: A Modern Myth of Things Seen in the Sky* (Princeton: Princeton University Press, 1973) and expanded by incorporating the methods of Mircea Eliade, Paul Tillich and Langdon Gilkey so as to uncover the covert religious dimensions of an otherwise apparently secular phenomenon. The previously mentioned work by Keith Thompson, *Angels and Aliens: UFOs and the Mythic Imagination*, follows a different path. Thompson's fascinating thesis is that the very unsolvability of the split between surface appearance and mysterious underlying reality of UFOs provides the driving energy that keeps the UFO myth alive and generates its continuing symbolic power.

37 New Age spirituality is also cultivating evolution in mythological ways. In modern literature we find an interesting synthesis of UFOs and evolutionary spirituality in the work of psychologist Kenneth Ring. Ring compares and contrasts UFO experiences with Near Death experiences and suggests that both are precipitated by what philosopher Michael Grosso calls the 'Mind at Large'. UFO aliens enter our imagination through the Mind at Large, and our imagination becomes an 'objectively self-existent' reality with a purpose, namely, to transform human consciousness. To what end? To persuade the human race to take responsibility for the ecological health of the planet. This leap in human consciousness constitutes a psychospiritual evolutionary advance, says Ring. 'We are in the midst of an evolutionary spurt toward greater spiritual awareness and higher consciousness – and the occurrence of UFOEs and NDEs is an integral part of that progression' (*The Omega Project: Near-Death Experiences, UFO Encounters, and Mind at Large*, New York: William Morrow, 1992, 186). In contrast to the contactees of the 1950s for whom UFOs would save us from nuclear destruction, Ring says the UFOs will save us from ecological destruction (p.180). And, because Ring incorporates an eschatological vision of a new heaven and a new earth (pp.235f), I believe he represents a nuanced example of the celestial savior model of UFO interpretation I outline in *UFOs–God's Chariots?*, chapter 7.

38 Allnutt, *Infinite Encounters*, 72.

39 Ibid., p.122.

40 I am not challenging the authority of the Bible here. I am challenging the fallacious form of arguing for application of biblical authority to UFO–ETI claims.

III

GENETICS, ETHICS, AND OUR EVOLUTIONARY FUTURE

Chapter 7

Genetics and Genethics:
Are We Playing God with Our Genes?

New knowledge gained from genetics research is raising a host of challenging ethical questions, and these ethical questions are prompting theological reflection. The dramatic scale of the biomedical challenges throws us back upon first principles, back to questions about the nature of human nature, about our relationship to ourselves and to our divine source, God. In the popular press the issue is formulated this way: are we playing God? We formulate it this way: how might theological reflection on the frontier of genetic research guide and direct ethical deliberation?[1]

The ethical questions emerging from the field of genetics create a sense of urgency due to the enormous scale of research associated with the Human Genome Project (HGP), sometimes referred to as the Human Genome Initiative (HGI). Begun in 1987 and virtually completed in 2001, HGP was a 'big science' project, international in scope, involving numerous laboratories and associations of scientists strewn across the landscape. The HGP had a 15-year time line and a $3 billion total price tag.[2] The scientific goal was to map and sequence the human DNA. Mapping will tell us the position and spacing of the predicted 100 000 genes – which actually turns out to be about 30 000 genes in each of our body's cells; and sequencing will determine the order of the four base pairs (the A,T,G and C nucleotides) that compose the DNA molecule. The primary motive is that which drives all basic science, namely, the need to know.[3] The secondary motive is perhaps even more important, namely, to identify the 4000 or so genes that are suspected to be responsible for inherited diseases and prepare the way for treatment through genetic therapy. This will be the social benefit, the connection between laboratory and society. The new knowledge will require new thinking about the ethical, legal and social dimensions of life for the human beings whose cells contain the DNA being studied.

It is significant to note that in the case of the HGP, the scientists involved were already aware that their research would impact surrounding society and were willing to share responsibility for it. When James Watson counseled the US Department of Health and Human Services to appropriate the funds for what would become the HGP, he recommended that three per cent of the budget be allotted to study the ethical, legal and social implications of genome research. 'We must work to ensure that society learns to use the information only in beneficial ways,' says Watson, 'and, if necessary, pass laws at both the federal and state levels to prevent invasions of privacy ... to prevent discrimination on genetic grounds.'[4] Watson, who along with Francis Crick is famed for his discovery of the double helix structure of DNA, was the first to head the Office of Human Genome Research at the National Institute of Health (NIH). He recently resigned amidst a dispute with former NIH director Bernadine Healey over the morality of patenting DNA sequences. Moral controversy has already broken out on this and numerous other issues. Hence, we can expect *genetics* and *ethics* to court one another for the next few years, leading perhaps to a marriage, to *genethics*.[5]

My task here will be to identify and formulate eight of the major ethical questions which are already appearing on the genetic horizon and to help bring them into focus by drawing out their theological implications.[6] In doing so, I will cast an eye in the direction of religious communities in North America on whom an awareness has dawned that something significant is happening here. The controversy that broke out over recombinant DNA in the late 1970s and early 1980s precipitated an initial awareness on the part of theologians and other church leaders that research in genetics might require ethical monitoring. Since then a handful of theologians and ethicists have begun a serious dialogue with research scientists to sort through the issues.

Genetic Discrimination

One ethical issue on the genetic horizon has already begun to take focus, namely, genetic discrimination.[7] A possible scenario runs like this. In the next few years researchers will identify and locate most if not all genes in the human genome that either condition or in some cases cause disease. Already, we know that the gene for cystic fibrosis is found on chromosome seven and Huntington's chorea on chromosome four. Alzheimer's disease is probably due to a defective gene on chromosome 21 and colon cancer to a gene on chromosome two. Disposition to muscular dystrophy, sickle-cell anemia, Tay Sachs disease, certain cancers and numerous other diseases have locatable genetic origins. More knowledge is yet to come, which may be accompanied by an inexpensive method for testing the genome of each individual to see if he or she has any genes for any diseases. Screening for all genetic diseases may become routine for newborns just as testing for phenylketonuria (PKU) has been since the 1960s. A person's individual genome would become part of a data bank to which each of us as well as our health care providers would have future access. The advantage is clear: alert medical care from birth to grave could be carefully planned to delay onset, treat appropriately and perhaps even cure genetically based diseases.

This is an unlikely scenario, however. As good as it may sound, the specter of genetic discrimination may slow it down if not retard it completely. Any grand plan to employ new genetic knowledge for preventive health care is likely to be impeded if not blocked entirely for Americans by the US system of financing medical care through commercial insurance. The problem begins with insurability and may end up with a form of discrimination that for genetic reasons prevents certain individuals from obtaining employment and, hence, obtaining medical services. Even with a government-regulated program of access to basic health services, the need to purchase supplemental insurance to cover serious diseases makes many of us with certain genetic configurations vulnerable to discrimination.

Insurance works by sharing risk. When risk is uncertain to all, then all can be asked to contribute equally to the insurance pool. Premiums can be equalized. Once the genetic disorders of individuals become known, however, this could justify higher premiums for those demonstrating greater risk. The greater the risk, the higher the premium. Insurance may even be denied those whose genes predict extended or expensive medical treatment.[8]

For three-fourths of Americans, medical insurance is tied to employment. Among *Fortune*'s 500 top companies, 12 already report using genetic screening for employment purposes. Although screening in the past was justified initially for public health purposes, increasingly employers may be motivated to use screening to cut premium costs for the medical insurance they pay on behalf of employees. Underwriters already deny or limit coverage to some gene-related conditions such as sickle-cell anemia, atherosclerosis, Huntington's chorea, Down's syndrome and muscular dystrophy.[9] This list could increase. Individuals with genetic dispositions to expensive diseases may become unemployable, uninsured and finally become unable to acquire medical care. Between 30 and 40 million persons in the United States currently live with insufficient or no medical coverage, and, despite its promises for a better life, the HGP could inadvertently create a whole new class of poor people.

Many pieces of proposed legislation in the US Congress plus many state initiatives include provisions aimed at protecting us from genetic discrimination. Prompted by ethicists operating out of rights theory, these proposals invoke the principles of confidentiality and privacy. They argue that genetic testing should be voluntary and that the information contained in one's genome be controlled by the patient. This 'privacy defense' argument presumes that, if information can be controlled, then the rights of the individual for employment, insurance and medical care can be protected. There are some grounds for thinking this approach will succeed. Title VII of the 1964 Civil Rights Act restricts pre-employment questioning to work-related health conditions, and its paragraph 102.b.4 potentially protects coverage for the employee's spouse and children. Current legislative proposals seem to favor privacy.[10]

Nevertheless, I believe the privacy defense can at best be a mere stopgap effort. In the long run, it will fail. Insurance carriers will press for legislation more fair to them, and eventually protection of privacy may slip. In addition, the existing state of computer linkage makes it difficult to prevent the movement of data from hospital to insurance carrier and to anyone else bent on finding out. In addition, in my judgment, the most important factor is the principle that genome information should finally not be restricted. The more we know and the more who know, the better the health care planning can be. In the long run, what we want is *information without discrimination*. The only way to obtain this is to restructure the employment–insurance–health care relationship. The current structure seems to make it profitable for employers and insurance carriers to discriminate against individuals with certain genetic configurations: that is, it is in their best financial interest to limit or even deny health care. A restructuring seems called for so that it becomes profitable to deliver, not withhold, health care. To accomplish this the whole nation will have to become more egalitarian – that is, to think of the nation itself as a single community willing to care for its own constituents.[11]

Where is the nation's church leadership now that this debate is beginning to heat up? It is clear that religious ethicists oppose genetic discrimination. In 1989, the Church and Society commission of the World Council of Churches released a study document, 'Biotechnology: Its Challenges to the Churches and the World', which draws attention to 'unfair discrimination ... in work, health care, insurance and education'.[12] Similarly, in the proposal approved by its 1992 General Conference, the United Methodist Church Genetic Task Force listed prominently among possible HGP repercussions 'discrimination: the suffering and/or hardship that may result for persons with late-onset disease like Huntington's or Alzheimer's disease, or with a genetic predisposition to diseases like high cholesterol levels or arteriosclerosis'.[13] And in 1989, the Seventeenth General Synod of the United Church of Christ meeting in Fort Worth, Texas, approved a Pronouncement which included a rejection of 'screening as a basis for determining civil, economic, or reproductive rights'.[14] A resolution passed at the 70th General Convention of the Episcopal Church in July of 1991 states forcefully: 'the use of results of genetic screening of adults, newborns and the unborn for the purpose of discrimination in employment and insurance is unacceptable'. This clear stand against genetic discrimination provides a solid foundation from which to build an ethical proposal, but it stops here. There are hints that church ethicists will side with those who advocate privacy; and there are hints that they favor some sort of national program guaranteeing health care to everyone. What we do not see as yet among religious leaders is any overall vision regarding the potential value (or nonvalue) of widespread use of genome information for health care delivery.

The Abortion Controversy Intensifies

Perhaps the most divisive moral issue in America is the practice of abortion on demand. The advance of genetic knowledge and the development of more sophisticated reproductive technologies will only add nuance and subtlety to an already complicated debate. Techniques have been developed to examine in vitro fertilized (IVF) eggs as early as the fourth cell division in order to identify so-called 'defective' genes such as the chromosomal structure of Down's syndrome. Prospective parents may soon be able to fertilize a dozen or so eggs in the laboratory, screen for the preferred genetic make-up, implant the desired zygote(s) and discard the rest. What will be the status of the discarded pre-embryos? Might they be considered abortions? By what criteria do we define 'defective' when considering the future of a human being? Should prospective parents limit themselves to eliminating defective children, or should they go on to screen for positive genetic traits such as blue eyes or higher intelligence? If so, might this lead to a new form of eugenics, to selective breeding based upon personal preference and prevailing social values? What will become of human dignity in all this?[15]

The ethical question we face here (by what criterion do we deem a genetically defective or undesirable fetus abortable?) was not addressed by *Roe* v. *Wade* in 1973. The present practice of abortion by choice prior to the third trimester locates the choice in the pregnant woman (actually her doctor); but it does not provide distinctively ethical criteria for distinguishing better from worse choices.

The Roman Catholic tradition has set strong precedents regarding the practice of abortion. The precedent against aborting the unborn is clear from the Second Vatican Council: 'from the moment of its conception life must be guarded with the greatest care, while abortion and infanticide are unspeakable crimes'.[16] The challenge to ethicists in the Roman Catholic tradition in the near future will be to examine what transpires at the pre-implantation stage of the embryo (or pre-embryo) to determine if the word 'abortion' applies. If it does, this may lead to recommending that genetic screening be pushed back one step further, to the gamete stage prior to fertilization. The genetic make-up of sperm and ovum separately could be screened, using acceptable gametes and discarding the unacceptable. The Catholic Health Association of the United States pushes back a step still further by recommending the development of techniques of gonadal cell therapy to make genetic corrections in the reproductive tissues of prospective parents long before conception takes place – that is, gametocyte therapy.[17] Other issues such as the criteria for genetic acceptability remain, to be sure, but the problem of post-conception abortion may be solved in this way.

Patenting God's Creation

One might think that the controversy over whether we should patent knowledge of DNA sequences would be limited to an argument among scientists, biotechnology companies and the government. Yet, religious voices have been raised. The louder religious voices have shouted 'No!' to patenting intellectual property regarding genes on the grounds that DNA belongs to God's creation. Where are we on this? Let me try to explain briefly this third issue.

The 1990s chapter in the larger story of the controversy over patenting life forms began with the initial filing in June 1991 for patent property rights on 337 gene fragments and a second filing in February 1992 on 2375 more partial gene sequences by J. Craig Venter. Venter, at that time, was pursuing research at the NIH's National Institute of Neurological Disorders and Strokes. His aim was to locate and sequence the 30 000 or so complementary DNAs, or cDNAs, from the human brain.

Venter's method, based on a deceptively simple insight, was key. The task of the Human Genome Project was to sequence the entire three billion nucleotides in the DNA and to locate where on the DNA the genes are sited. Relatively speaking, only a small portion of the DNA functions as genes, about three per cent. The non-genetic material has been affectionately labeled 'junk DNA'. If one wants to find only the genes, thought Venter, then why bother with plodding through all the junk DNA? Noting that only the genes, not the junk DNA, code for proteins by creating messenger RNA (mRNA), Venter set his focus on mRNA. He began making sturdier clone copies of the otherwise fragile mRNA, and he called these stronger and analyzable copies cDNAs. By sequencing only the cDNAs, he could be assured that he was gaining knowledge of actual genes. By focusing the research this way he brought the price of sequencing down dramatically.

These clones made from messenger RNAs represent a part of the coding region of genes on the DNA chain. By sequencing a short stretch of cDNA clones – about 300 to 500 bases and not necessarily the entire gene – Venter created what he called an 'expressed sequence tag', or EST. Venter had begun using automatic sequencing machines to the limit of their capacity and was churning out 50 to 150 such tags per day.

In the fall of 1992, the US Patent and Trademark Office made a preliminary ruling that denied the applications on the grounds that gene fragments could not be patented without knowing the function of the gene. NIH director at that time, Bernadine Healy, pressed for an appeal. When Harold Varmus took over the helm from Healy he withdrew the applications, saying that patents on partial gene sequences are 'not in the best interests of the public or science'.[18] This threw the ball into the court of the private sector where similar patent applications have been filed. Some have been filed by Venter and his colleagues since he left the NIH, after having garnered $70 million in venture capital to start a private biotech company, The Institute for Genomic Research (TIGR).[19] The result has been controversy with numerous hotly debated questions.

Two of the many hotly debated questions are the following. Should patents be granted for knowledge of gene sequences at all? And, if so, should they be granted to a government-funded agency such as NIH or only to the private sector? We will not take up the question as to whether the government or the private sector should own the patents, because the owner of the patent is irrelevant to what has become the religious issue.

The first question is this: should knowledge of DNA sequences in the original or natural human genome be patentable? In order to qualify for a patent, an invention must meet three criteria: it must be novel, non-obvious and useful. At this writing, in 1997, the US Patent and Trademark Office has issued more than 1200 patents of the type mentioned above, assuming that these patents meet the three criteria. Do they?

Relevant here is a philosophical question: should intellectual knowledge regarding natural processes in principle be patentable? Does witnessing an existing natural phenomenon in itself warrant patent protection for the witness? Should an astronomer be able to patent every new galaxy he or she discovers? No, would be the answer someone like Justice Douglas would give. Writing for the majority in the 1948 US Supreme Court case of *Funk Brothers Seed Co.* v. *Kalo Inoculant Co.*, he wrote: 'patents cannot issue for the discovery of the phenomena of nature. ... [Such] are manifestations of laws of nature, free to all men and reserved exclusively to none'.[20]

Are cDNAs a natural phenomenon or a human invention? The cDNA is not a gene per se. Rather, it is a copy version of a gene with the introns edited out. It does not occur naturally. It is coded into messenger RNA by the process that reads the raw cellular DNA. This fact leads to an interesting double-mindedness on the part of Daniel Kevles and Leroy Hood. On the one hand, they argue: 'since it can be physically realized by a devising of human beings, using the enzyme reverse transcriptase, it is patentable'. On the other hand, Kevles and Hood are troubled. 'If anything is literally a common birthright of human beings, it is the human genome. It would thus seem that if anything should be avoided in the genomic political economy, it is a war of patents and commerce over the operational elements of that birthright.'[21]

In 1995, the Human Genome Organization (HUGO) issued a statement opposing the patenting of cDNAs because it would impede the free flow of scientific information.

> HUGO is worried that the patenting of partial and uncharacterized cDNA sequences will reward those who make routine discoveries but penalize those who determine biological function or application. Such an outcome would impede the development of diagnostics and therapeutics, which is clearly not in the public interest. HUGO is also dedicated to the early release of genome information, thus accelerating widespread investigation of functional aspects of genes.[22]

In sum, cDNAs may prove patentable on the grounds that they are the product of a humanly devised process of gaining intellectual knowledge. But, at the present moment this appears inappropriate, because the only value of cDNAs is that they tell us what is in the original DNA. As long as the Douglas principle holds, that processes already occurring in nature are exempt, the human genome itself will not become patentable.

This became a religious issue on 18 May 1995 at a Washington Press Conference where it was announced that religious leaders representing more than 80 different groups had signed a statement opposing patenting. Numerous Roman Catholic bishops, along with Jewish, Protestant, Islamic, Hindu and Buddhist leaders, signed the following statement:

> We, the undersigned religious leaders, oppose the patenting of human and animal life forms. We are disturbed by the U.S. Patent Office's recent decision to patent human body parts and several genetically engineered animals. We believe that humans and animals are creations of God, not humans, and as such should not be patented as human inventions.[23]

The press conference, called the 'Joint Appeal Against Human and Animal Patenting', included Rabbi David Saperstein, Director of the Religious Action Center of Reform Judaism; Abdurahman Alamoudi, Executive Director of the American Muslim Council; Wesley Granberg-Michaelson, Secretary General of the Reformed Church in America; Richard Land, Executive Director of the

Christian Life Commission of the Southern Baptist Convention; and Kenneth Carder and Jaydee Hanson of the United Methodist Church. 'By turning life into patented inventions,' said Jeremy Rifkin, whose Foundation on Economic Trends orchestrated the event, 'the government drains life of its intrinsic nature and sacred value.'

'Marketing human life is a form of genetic slavery,' Richard Land was quoted as saying, in papers across the country. 'Instead of whole persons being marched in shackles to the market block, human cell lines and gene sequences are labeled, patented and sold to the highest bidders.' Land added a prophet-like judgment against playing God in the laboratory: 'We see altering life forms, creating new life forms, as a revolt against the sovereignty of God and an attempt to be God.'[24]

This event marks a point of public meeting between the religious and scientific communities, a meeting that quite unfortunately has the appearance of a battle. That the religious community would enter into a battle over patenting is most unfortunate, in my judgment. The main problem with the statement is that it is vague and inflammatory. The statement fails to make clear what the Patent and Trademark Office strives to make clear, namely, it does not grant patents to natural phenomena, such as human beings or animals or body parts in any ordinary sense. It grants patents to human inventions that are novel, non-obvious and useful.

The theology presupposed here is clearly at odds with those religious traditions such as Christianity and Judaism which believe in a transcendent and holy God who created the natural world, loves it and asks that the human race created in the divine image strive to make the world a better place. These traditions hold that the creator God is sacred, not the creation. The 18 May theology reflects rather the point of view of Jeremy Rifkin, famed for his outspoken resistance to progress in biological research and medical technology. This is a tacit naturalism of sorts. In his book, *Algeny*, he describes his own mission as a 'resacralization of nature'.[25]

Sweeping over the difference between these respectively different metaphysical positions could have ethical ramifications. Jews and Christians hold that we humans should be good stewards of our God-given creativity and out of love for neighbor pursue, among other things, the development of better ways to relieve human suffering and improve the human experience with life. The Rifkin position implies that nature prior to human creative intervention is sacred and should be left alone. This severs the warrant for pursuing medical research and development of therapies that could relieve human suffering and improve the health of the human race. Here is the issue on which I believe the patent debate should focus: how can patents help or retard the development of genetically based therapy for cancer, heart disease, cystic fibrosis, Alzheimer's, Huntington's chorea, Williams Syndrome and countless others? In effect, the religious leaders have unnecessarily cut themselves off from making a contribution to this central concern. We will take up this concern later when we address the question: should we play God?

Cloning

The world woke up on 23 February 1997 to the fact that the era of cloning had dawned. At the Roslin Institute near Edinburgh, Scotland, embryologist Ian Wilmut produced a live adult lamb from cells originating in a sheep mammary gland. The method was simple, technologically speaking. Wilmut took a mammary cell from an adult sheep and placed its DNA into the egg of another sheep. He removed the egg's DNA and fused the adult DNA to the egg. The fused cell began to grow and divide, just like a normal fertilized egg. It became an embryo, was planted in the womb of a ewe, and at the time of publication was already a seven-month old lamb, named Dolly. DNA tests show that Dolly contains only the genes of the adult ewe who provided her DNA.

What are the implications? Although concerns for animal cloning are important, the overriding ethical issue is this: should we clone human beings? Former President William Clinton's National Bioethics Advisory Commission has said 'no' by placing a ban on cloning for the purposes of creating human beings. In a press conference, the US president said that replicating ourselves by this method would violate our individual identity and that we should not 'play God'. The Church of Scotland would agree. Donald Bruce, who directs the Church's Society, Religion and Technology Project – a committee on which Ian Wilmut serves – described human cloning as a 'perversity'. To use technology to replicate a human being is against the basic dignity of our uniqueness in God's sight, Bruce told the press. Cloning would be ethically unacceptable as a matter of principle, because it violates the uniqueness of our lives which God has given to each of us and to no one else.

It is my own considered judgment that, in principle, no distinctively theological affirmations would make cloning humans unethical. Though not unethical, it might be unwise. I support the attempt to effect a temporary ban against human cloning until good reasons can be brought forth and considered. I do not favor an absolute ban that eliminates all future consideration.

The argument raised by the former US president and the Church of Scotland fits with fears enunciated by many, namely, that cloning would compromise human identity and violate human dignity. This is an unfounded fear. It is based on the *gene myth* (which we will discuss later) according to which we believe 'it's all in the genes'. Widespread is the assumption that who we are is determined by our genetic code, that our DNA is our destiny. With this assumption we can see why some might feel their identity would be compromised when another person shares the same genome.

Yet, neither science nor common sense support this assumption. Scientifically, the genes alone do not determine our identity. Who we are is influenced by our DNA, to be sure; but how the genes behave is influenced by environmental factors. These environmental factors include the cytoplasm in the host egg as well as our nutrition and socialization while growing up. In addition, common sense gained from everyday observation reveals that no matter how much two people share in common they still differ. Who we are as individual persons is determined by three things: our genome, our environmental influences and the appearance of a subjective self with free will and the ability to engage in self-definition. Even if we were to grant that God loves diversity and also grant that individual identity is important, cloning would be at most only a partial threat.

The experience of identical twins is informative. For siblings to be identical means they have the same genome. Yet, each twin grows up with his or her own subjectivity and own sense of identity, and he or she can claim his or her own individual rights. The experience of a cloned person would be similar. The clone would be aware that another person shares the same genetic code and might even find this fascinating; yet he or she would be just as much an individual as any of the rest of us.

It would be society's moral obligation to treat cloned persons as individuals as well. I hold theologically that God loves each of us regardless of our genetic make-up, and that we should do likewise. In secular language, this means that each of us should be treated with dignity. I would not like to see the fear that cloned persons have less identity become translated by society into a stigma in which such persons are denied dignity.

Genetic Determinism, Human Freedom and the Gene Myth

The fifth issue deals with the problem of myth and reality, of public perception and laboratory truth. It has to do with the growing popular image of the almighty gene as the all-determining factor in the human condition. It begins innocently with the thought that, if we could only find the gene for a certain disease, we could find the cure by simply manipulating this gene. We then continue with the logic. Why stop with diseases? Do genes also determine behavior? If so, should we blame persons for their anti-social behavior or judge them as innocent? Should we try to alter the genes of anti-social individuals or groups? 'It's all in the genes,' we say.

This line of thinking belongs to what I call the *gene myth*, namely, a widespread cultural thought form that says, 'it's all in the genes'. The gene myth is deterministic in two senses. The first is puppet determinism, wherein we assume the DNA acts like a puppeteer, and we dance on genetic strings like a puppet. If the DNA determines our hair color and what diseases we will have, perhaps the DNA determines how we will behave and may even control our virtues and vices. The second is Promethean determinism, wherein we assume that, once our scientists have learned how DNA works, we can then take charge – that is, we can get into the DNA with our wrenches and screwdrivers and modify it so as to guide our own evolutionary future. Puppet determinism presumes that we are victims of our genes, whereas Promethean determinism presumes that we can take charge of our genes. Both belong to the gene myth. Both may be misleading even while they provoke theological, ethical and even legal questions.

The big question here is this: does genetic determinism threaten human free will? The assumption of the Western philosophy coming down to us from Augustine that underlies our understanding of law is that guilt can only be assigned to a human agent who acts freely. Will the concept of genetic determinism (might we call it genetic predestination?) compromise our confidence in free agency? The specter on the genetic horizon is that confirmable genetic predispositions to certain forms of behavior will constitute compulsion, and this will take us to a fork in the ethical and legal road: either we will declare the person with a genetic predisposition to crime innocent and set him or her free, or we will declare him or her so constitutionally impaired as to justify incarceration and isolation from the rest of society. The first fork would jeopardize the welfare of society; the second fork would violate individual rights.

Does the science of molecular biology support the deterministic assumptions of the gene myth that might lead us to this dramatic fork in the social road? No. For the most part, laboratory scientists see little or no evidence supporting a philosophy of genetic determinism that would alter our understanding of human freedom. At minimum, nurture remains as important as nature. In opposing what he calls 'genetic predestination', John Maddox draws us back to the basics: genotype underdetermines phenotype.

> The link between genotype and phenotype is not always unambiguous. A genotype may be a necessary, but not a sufficient, condition for the phenotype; the individual concerned inherits only a susceptibility for the phenotype ... it would be rash to deny that the missing ingredients may be aspects of nurture. ... Is it likely that some of the most labile aspects of the human phenotype, those constituting personality, will be exempt from similar and more subtle influences?[26]

Such deliberation leads molecular biologist R. David Cole to write against genetic predestination.

> There is no reason for the non-scientist to be intimidated by the success of the deterministic approach in elucidating the biological role of genes in human nature, and certainly no reason to be intimidated by any scientist who might try to convince us that determinism is all that is. Although the case for free will cannot be rigorously proven, those of us who believe in it need feel no threat from the findings of the Human Genome Initiative.[27]

No, genetic determinism does not erase free will at the human level. Yet, there is reason to worry on another but related front: the misconception of gene power may have deleterious social consequences.

Included among possible deleterious social consequences could be an exacerbation of racial prejudice and discrimination. The controversy over the widely read book, *The Bell Curve*, by Charles Murray and Richard Herrnstein, is a case in point.[28] On the basis of IQ tests, this book suggested that public policy should shuttle greater financial resources toward certain racial groups designated as the cognitive elites – Jews, orientals, whites – and remove support from those designated as cognitively challenged: Latinos and African Americans. Sociologist Troy Duster is worried about such racial repercussions. If we identify genes with race, genes with social status, or genes with crime, then we may inadvertently provide a biological support for prejudice and discrimination. He sounds the alarm: 'Today, the United States is heading down a road of parallel false precision in this faith in the connection between genes and social outcomes. This is being played out on a stage with converging preoccupations and tangled webs that interlace crime, race, and genetic explanations.'[29]

The Gay Gene: is Original Sin Back Again?

In the summer of 1993, a scientific bomb exploded that is still causing considerable ethical fallout. Dean H. Hamer and his research team at the National Cancer Institute announced that they had discovered evidence that male homosexuality – at least some male homosexuality – is genetic. Constructing family trees in instances where two or more brothers are gay combined with actual laboratory testing of homosexual DNA, Hamer located a region near the end of the long arm of the X chromosome that likely contains a gene influencing sexual orientation. Because men receive an X chromosome from their mother and a Y from their father (women receive two Xs, one from each parent), this means that the possible gay gene is inherited maternally. Mothers can pass on the gay gene without themselves or their daughters being homosexual. A parallel study of lesbian genetics is as yet incomplete, and the present study of gay men will certainly require replication and confirmation. Scientists do not yet have undisputable proof. Nevertheless, Hamer was ready to write an article making the dramatic announcement, 'We have now produced evidence that one form of male homosexuality is preferentially transmitted through the maternal side and is genetically linked to chromosome region Xq28.'[30]

What are the implications of this? *Time* magazine projected an ethical and political forecast: 'If homosexuals are deemed to have a foreordained nature, many of the arguments now used to block equal rights would lose force.' *Time* cited a gay attorney saying, 'I can't imagine rational people, presented with the evidence that homosexuality is biological and not a choice, would continue to discriminate.'[31] The logic seems to be this: if male homosexuality is genetically inherited, then those with this inheritance can claim rights based on this inheritance. If sexual orientation is genetically determined and not a choice, gay men can claim the ethical high ground to justify the gay life style. Yet, I ask, might such ethical logic be buying too quickly into the gene myth? Would it be worth our time to pause and project the various directions that ethical reasoning might take us? Are there other possible directions?

I would suggest here that, if we eventually accept as fact that male homosexuality is genetically inherited, the ethical logic that follows could go in a number of different directions. *The scientific fact does not itself determine the direction of the ethical interpretation of that fact.* To demonstrate this I would like to begin with a basic question: does the genetic disposition toward homosexuality make the bearer of that gene victimized or responsible, innocent or guilty? Two answers are logically possible. On the one hand, a homosexual man could claim that, because he inherited the gay gene and did not choose a gay orientation by his own free will, he is innocent. He could claim this innocence either because homosexuality cannot be judged to be immoral on the grounds that it is natural or, even if society believes homosexuality to be immoral, he is innocent because he is a victim of his birth and cannot help the fact that he has inherited his particular genome. On the other hand, society could take the opposite road and identify the gay gene with the disposition to sin. Society could claim that the body inherited by each of us belongs to who we are – who I am as a self is determined at least in part by what my parents bequeathed me – and that an inherited disposition to homosexual behavior is just like other innate dispositions such as lust or greed or similar forms of concupiscence which are shared with the human race generally; all this constitutes the state of original sin into which we are born.[32] Signposts point in both ethical directions.

The science and the ethical reflection on the science here may jolt some theologians into remembering that nearly forgotten doctrine, namely, original sin. Setting aside for a moment any judgment as to whether homosexual behavior is moral or immoral, let us ask more generally: does our biological predisposition toward a specific behavior in itself make that behavior moral or immoral? If it is natural, is it automatically good? Not necessarily, according to the concept of original sin. To my observation, religious groups and their theologians have not yet placed this issue on their agenda.

Yet, the current scientific situation – actually the current culture with its gene myth picturing science as deterministic – is compelling us to pose such questions and to open up once again the case for original sin. The popularity of Richard Dawkins' book, *The Selfish Gene*, along with the controversy created by sociobiologists, demonstrate a growing interest in the prospect that scientists will be able to explain more and more of human behavior in biological terms.[33] Edward Wilson defines sociobiology as 'the systematic study of the biological basis of all social behavior', and he has staked out the biological claim rather forcefully: 'The genes hold culture on a leash. The leash is very long, but inevitably values will be constrained in accordance with their effects on the human gene pool.'[34] The point here is that the debate over the gay gene is taking place within a wider cultural debate – the nature versus nurture debate – regarding the primary influence on human belief and behavior. 'In the long debate over the relative influences of nature and nurture,' write Dorothy Nelkin and Laurence Tancredi, 'the balance seems to have shifted to the biological extreme.'[35]

With nature winning over nurture in the gene myth, we will be tempted to ground our morality in nature. But, will this be as easy as it looks? What if we were to discover a genetic predisposition to homophobia that leads to gay bashing? Would both the gay gene and the homophobia gene be equally moral? Equally immoral? Would we not have to appeal to some extrabiological or extrascientific criteria to think this through?

According to the concept of original sin, our nature is fallen. As fallen, our nature can lead us toward sin. Our natural inclinations are not by definition good. What is good is determined by the leadings of God, not the leadings of our biology in any strict sense. Yet, the concept of original sin cannot by any means be reduced to a natural (read genetic) propensity to do evil. Much more is going on here.

Let us refer to Augustine for a moment. This North African bishop affirmed that God is good and that nature is created good; yet, he believed sin is something we can and should fully expect for the foreseeable future. Sin is naturally unnecessary yet historically inevitable.[36] Why? What we have since come to know as the doctrine of original sin is Augustine's answer. It goes like this. By nature, and at an early point in history, God created the first human beings good. We know our original parents as Adam and Eve. These two committed the first sin. In Lamarckian fashion, this historical incident affected their biological nature so that the propensity for sinning became henceforth an inheritable trait. Augustine likens this to a disease which we inherit congenitally and pass on to our children. Adam's original sin becomes for us inherited sin, a disposition that is not necessary by nature but for us is historically inevitable. In terms of world history, sin is the historical corruption of an originally good nature.

Augustine was led to this type of explanation because of a fundamental commitment to the unity of the human race. This is a double unity, a unity of sin and a unity of salvation. He was taking with utmost seriousness passages in the writings of Paul such as 1 Cor. 15:22: 'as all die in Adam, so all will be made alive in Christ' (see also Rom. 5:12–16). Your and my sins today do not merely imitate Adam's sin. Somehow they participate, mutually penetrate and continue to propagate. Augustine was not primarily concerned with the specific propensities each of us has for lust or envy or whatever. That was secondary. Primary was this sense that all of us in the human race are in the same boat, the same sinful boat that is sailing away from consciousness of God and love for one another. This unity in sin is the correlate of our unity in salvation. Augustine wrote, 'we have derived from Adam, in whom all have sinned, not all our actual sins, but only original sin; whereas from Christ, in whom we are all justified, we obtain the remission not merely of that original sin, but of the rest of our sins also, which we have added'.[37] For Augustine the savior, Jesus Christ, is an individual human being, to be sure; yet, he is much more. Christ is the prototypical human being, the eternal *logos* and the image of the divine – the true *imago dei* – under the conditions of humanity. The whole human race finds its definition, its identity and its rescue from inherited sin through the forgiving and resurrecting power of Christ.

If we try to apply the Augustinian notion of original sin to the present discussion, it would seem that the gay gene would find its place in the larger description of a human condition that includes all of us. The homosexual disposition and the homophobic disposition would together constitute signs of a fallen human nature, a historically specific form of human nature in which desire threatens to cause psychic and social strife. The responsible or Augustinian road would ask the bearer of the gay gene to admit what all human beings are asked to admit, namely, that we have been born with an inherited disposition toward sin and that our ethical mandate is to strive for a life of love that transcends our inborn desires. Whether a given individual has the gay gene or the homophobic gene, the ethical mandate applies to both.

One of the major weaknesses in the Augustinian solution is that we in the modern world cannot split nature and history in quite the same way he did. Augustine could begin with nature created good and then identify a point in historical time – the time of Adam and Eve in the Garden of Eden – to locate the originating sin that corrupted the nature that we today inherit in our genes. There are two reasons why this is unacceptable today. First, the current scientific world-view informed by evolutionary history makes no room in its time scheme for an Eden story: that is, we cannot go back in time to find a point prior to which nature was benign and after which it had fallen. Second, evolutionary theory combined with such things as Big Bang theory in physical cosmology are leading scientists to view nature itself as history. Nature itself is not fixed or eternal, but subject to contingency and change. So, to bifurcate reality into two discrete realms, nature and history, no longer makes sense.

In sum, the Christian understanding of original sin as bequeathed from Augustine has less to do with biological determinants of our behavior and more to do with the unity all we humans share with one another in both Adam and Christ. Nevertheless, this theological tradition will be skeptical of arguments that seek moral approval on the basis of genetic determinism. The gene myth has no automatic theological endorsement. To reiterate: the scientific fact does not itself determine the direction of the ethical interpretation of that fact.

In the meantime, what should theologians do about laboratory discoveries such as that of the gay gene? Meeting in Berkeley, California, on 17 August 1993, the geneticists, ethicists and theologians working together on a research project conducted by the Center for Theology and the Natural Sciences at the Graduate Theological Union dealing with 'Theological and Ethical Questions Raised by the Human Genome Initiative' framed the following statement:

> The recent report of an X-linked predisposition to some forms of male homosexuality has already created a furore and we think it appropriate to pause and reflect critically if briefly upon what implications may or may not be justified. Although many critics have emphasized the high quality of the researchers and of the design of the research, they also point out that the results are still preliminary. Assuming that the research is replicated and supported by additional experimental designs, the scientific fact still does not itself determine the direction of the ethical interpretation of that fact. The ethical logic could go in several directions. On the one hand, genetic predisposition may remove sexual preference from the list of behaviors that can be blamed on individual choice or on the behavior of parents. On the other hand, it may lead to a cry to develop 'cures' or eugenic measures to eliminate the predispositional gene, as have earlier studies of diversity between races lent misplaced credibility to discriminatory practices.
>
> The possible genetic predisposition to some forms of homosexuality is but one instance of a broader theme of naturally occurring human genetic diversity. The problem of how to recast notions of freedom and responsibility in light of that diversity remains a basic philosophical issue. The honest expression of diverse opinions within the lesbian and gay community to the recently publicized claims

shows the kind of maturity that we appreciate and commend to other social commentators. As theological and scientific commentators, we urge that the best of genetic research be taken seriously. There is a rich variety of theological reflection both in the religious traditions and in recent developments which leads us to affirm that the theological questions raised by this genetic research are profound and subtle. We recognize that genetic diversity requires a response of love, respect and justice.

Somatic Therapy v. Germline Enhancement

A seventh ethical issue which appears in both secular and religious discussions is the distinction between somatic therapy and enhancement. By 'somatic therapy' we refer to the treatment of a disease in the body cells of a living individual by trying to repair an existing defect. Body cells contain the full complement of 46 chromosomes. In contrast, germline cells in the reproductive process contain only 23 chromosomes, and these are passed on to the next generation. Intervention into the germline cells would influence heredity, and the possibility of significantly enhancing the quality of life of future generations through germline intervention is looming on the genetic horizon.[38]

All ethical commentators I have reviewed agree that somatic therapy is morally desirable, and they look forward to the advances HGP will bring for expanding this important work. Yet, the ethically minded stop short of endorsing genetic selection and manipulation for the purposes of enhancing the quality of biological life for otherwise normal individuals or for the human race as a whole. We can speculate that the new knowledge gained from HGP might locate genes that affect the brain's organization and structure so that careful engineering might lead to enhanced ability for abstract thinking or to other forms of physiological and mental improvement. But, such speculations are greeted with the greatest caution. Molecular hematologist W. French Anderson says,

> Somatic cell gene therapy for the treatment of severe disease is considered ethical because it can be supported by the fundamental moral principle of beneficence: It would relieve human suffering. Gene therapy would be, therefore, a moral good. Under what circumstances would human genetic engineering not be a moral good? In the broadest sense, when it detracts from, rather than contributes to, the dignity of man. ... Somatic cell enhancement engineering would threaten important human values in two ways: It could be medically hazardous.... And it would be morally precarious, in that it would require moral decisions our society is not now prepared to make, and it could lead to an increase in inequality and discriminatory practices.[39]

In short, genetic enhancement risks violating human dignity by opening up the possibility of discrimination.

Religious ethicists agree: somatic therapy should be pursued, but enhancement through germline engineering raises cautions about protecting human dignity. The World Council of Churches is representative. In a 1982 document we find:

somatic cell therapy may provide a good; however, other issues are raised if it also brings about a change in germ-line cells. The introduction of genes into the germ-line is a permanent alteration. ... Nonetheless, changes in genes that avoid the occurrence of disease are not necessarily made illicit merely because those changes also alter the genetic inheritance of future generations. ... There is no absolute distinction between eliminating 'defects' and 'improving' heredity.[40]

The primary caution raised by the WCC here has to do with our lack of knowledge regarding the possible consequences of altering the human germline. The problem is that the present generation lacks sufficient information regarding the long-term consequences of a decision today that might turn out to be irreversible tomorrow. Thus, the WCC does not forbid forever germline therapy or even enhancement; rather, it cautions us to wait and see.

Another reason for caution regarding germline enhancement, especially among the Protestants, is the specter of eugenics. The word 'eugenics' connotes the ghastly racial policies of Nazism, and this accounts for much of today's mistrust of genetic science in Germany and elsewhere.[41] No one expects a resurrection of the Nazi nightmare; yet, some critics fear a subtle form of eugenics slipping in the cultural back door.[42] The growing power to control the design of living tissue will foster the emergence of the image of the 'perfect child', and a new social value of perfection will begin to oppress all those who fall short. Although the perfect child syndrome is not yet widely discussed in the published literature, religious ethicists speaking in March 1992 at the 'Genetics, Religion and Ethics Conference' held at the Texas Medical Center in Houston saw the image of the 'perfect child' to be a clear and present danger.

Are We Asking Our Scientists to Play God?

The debate over germline intervention brings us directly to the question popularized by newspaper headlines: should we ask our scientists to play God? Should we ask them to refrain from playing God? The way the question is posed in the press is usually so superficial as to be misleading. Yet, beneath the superficiality we find a theological issue of some consequence, namely, do we as human beings share with our creator God some responsibility for the continuing creativity of our world? The concept of creation includes anthropology and the notion that the human race is created in the divine image. I will argue here that, if we understand God's creative activity as giving the world a future, and if we understand the human being as a created co-creator, then ethics begins with envisioning a better future. This suggests we should at minimum keep the door open to improving the human genetic lot. The derisive use of the phrase, 'play God', should not deter us from shouldering our responsibility for the future. To seek a better future is to 'play human' as God intends us to.[43]

The acerbic rhetoric that usually employs the phrase, 'play God', is aimed at inhibiting if not shutting down certain forms of scientific research and medical therapy. This applies particularly to the field of human genetics and, still more particularly, to the prospect of germline intervention for purposes of human enhancement – that is, the insertion of new gene segments of DNA into sperm or eggs before fertilization or into undifferentiated cells of an early embryo that will be passed on to future generations and may become part of the permanent gene pool. Some scientists and religious spokespersons are putting a chain across the gate to germline enhancement and with a posted sign reading, 'Thou shalt not play God'. A *Time*/CNN poll cites a substantial majority (58 per cent) who believe altering human genes is against the will of God.[44]

Why do critics of genetic research prescribe a new commandment, 'Thou shalt not play God'? The answer here is this: because human pride or *hubris* is dangerous. We have learned from experience that what the Bible says is true: 'pride goes before destruction' (Proverbs 16:18). And in our modern era pride among the natural scientists has taken the form of overestimating our knowledge, of arrogating for science a kind of omniscience that we do not in fact have. Or, to refine it a bit: 'playing God' means we confuse the knowledge we do have with the wisdom to decide how to use it. Frequently lacking this wisdom we falsely assume we possess, scientific knowledge leads to unforeseen consequences such as the destruction of the ecosphere. Applied to genetic therapy, the commandment against 'playing God' implies that the unpredictability of destructive effects on the human gene pool should lead to a proscription against germline intervention. In light of this, 'there is general agreement that human germ-line intervention for any purpose should always be governed by stringent criteria for safety and predictability'.[45] This 'general agreement' seeks to draw upon wisdom to mitigate pride.

A related implication of the phrase, 'playing God', is that DNA has come to function in effect as an inviolable sacred, a special province of the divine, that should be off limits to mere mortals. Robert Sinsheimer, among others, suggests that, when we see ourselves as the creators of life, we lose reverence for life.[46] It is just this lack of reverence for life as nature has bequeathed it to us that drives Jeremy Rifkin to attack the kind of genetic research that will lead to algeny – that is, to 'the upgrading of existing organisms and the design of wholly new ones with the intent of "perfecting" their performance'. The problem with algeny is that it represents excessive human pride. 'It is humanity's attempt to give metaphysical meaning to its emerging technological relationship with nature.'[47] Rifkin's message is: let nature be! Don't try to make it better! In advocating this 'hands off' policy, Rifkin does not appeal to Christian or Jewish or other theological principles. Rather, he appeals to a vague naturalism, according to which nature herself claims sacred status. He issues his own missionary's call: 'The resacralization of nature stands before us as the great mission of the coming age.'[48]

What is the warrant for treating nature in general, or DNA specifically, as sacred and therefore morally immune from technological intervention? Ronald Cole-Turner criticizes Sinsheimer and Rifkin for making an unwarranted philosophical and theological leap from the association of DNA with life to the metaphysical proscription against technical manipulation.

Is DNA the essence of life? Is it any more arrogant or sacrilegious to cut DNA than to cut living tissue, as in surgery? It is hard to imagine a scientific or philosophical argument that would successfully support the metaphysical or moral uniqueness of DNA. Even DNA's capacity to replicate does not elevate this molecule to a higher metaphysical or moral level. Replication and sexual reproduction are important capacities, crucial in biology. But they are hardly the stuff of sanctity.[49]

To nominate DNA for election into the halls of functional sacrality, says Cole-Turner, is arbitrary. Theologians in particular should avoid this pitfall. 'To think of genetic material as the exclusive realm of divine grace and creativity is to reduce God to the level of restriction enzymes, viruses, and sexual reproduction. Treating DNA as matter – complicated, awe-inspiring, and elaborately coded, but matter nonetheless – is not in itself sacrilegious.'[50]

The phrase 'playing God' raises up for us the question of the relationship between the divine creator and the human creature. We can distinguish the Christian and Jewish theism from a naturalism that reveres life from the religious belief in God as creator of all things, life included. Natural life, important as it is, is not ultimate. God is ultimate.

One can argue to this position on the basis of *creatio ex nihilo*, creation out of nothing. All that exists has been called from nothing by the voice of God and brought into existence, and at any moment could in principle return to the non-existence from which it came. Life, as everything else in existence, is finite, temporal and mortal. The natural world depends upon a divine creator who transcends it. Nature is not its own author. Nor can it claim ultimacy, sanctity, or any other status rivaling God. This leads biologist Hessel Bouma and his colleagues at the Calvin Center for Christian Scholarship to a pithy proposition: 'God is the creator. Therefore, nothing that God made is god, and all that God made is good.' This implies, among other things, that we should be careful when accusing physicians and scientists of 'playing God'. We must avoid idolatrous expectations of technology, to be sure; 'but to presume that human technological intervention violates God's rule is to worship Mother Nature, not the creator. Natural processes are not sacrosanct'.[51]

Conclusion: Theological Commitments to Human Dignity

The ethical issues just described are but a small sample drawn from a longer list that would include questions regarding the social implications of defining a 'defective' gene, equity of access to genetic services, gender justice, environmental impact, patenting knowledge of DNA sequences or new life forms, developing biological weapons, eugenics and numerous others. Some of our farsighted religious leaders have entered into serious conversation with conscientious scientists so that cooperative thinking about our response and responsibility for the future can be anticipated.[52] 'Science and studies in genetics and biology have given us a fascinating insight into our world,' writes ethicist Thomas Shannon, and only through a careful examination of this insight 'can we be responsible to ourselves, to our ancestors, and to our environment'.[53]

It is worth noting that virtually all Roman Catholics and Protestants who take up the challenge of the new genetic knowledge seem to agree on a handful of theological axioms. First, they affirm that God is the creator of the world and, further, that God's creative work is continuous.[54] God continues to create in and through natural genetic selection and even through human intervention in the natural processes. Second, the human race is created in God's image. In this context, the divine image in humanity is tied to creativity. God creates. So do we. With surprising frequency, we humans are described by theologians as 'co-creators' with God, making our contribution to the evolutionary process.[55] In order to avoid the arrogance of thinking that we humans are equal to the God who created us in the first place, we must add the term 'created' to make the phrase 'created co-creators'. This emphasizes our dependency upon God while pointing to our human opportunity and responsibility. Third, these religious documents place a high value on human dignity.

By 'dignity' they mean what philosopher Immanuel Kant meant, namely, that we treat each human being as an end, not merely as a means to some further end. The United Church of Canada eloquently voices the dominant view: 'In non-theological terms it [dignity] means that every human being is a person of ultimate worth, to be treated always as an end and not as a means to someone else's ends. When we acknowledge and live by that principle our relationship to all others changes.'[56] Pope John Paul II begins to appropriate the dignity principle in an elocution where he condemns 'in the most explicit and formal way experimental manipulations of the human embryo, since the human being, from conception to death, cannot be exploited for any purpose whatsoever'.[57] As church leaders respond responsibly to new developments in the HGP, we can confidently forecast one thing: this affirmation of dignity will become decisive for thinking through the ethical implications of genetic engineering. Promoting dignity is a way of drawing an ethical implication from what the theologian can safely say, namely, that God loves each human being regardless of our genetic make-up and, therefore, we should love one another according to this model.

Yet, there is more. The theology of co-creation leads Ronald Cole-Turner to a beneficent vision: 'For the church, it is not enough to avoid the risks. Genetic engineering must contribute in a positive way to make the world more just and more ecologically sustainable, and it must contribute to the health and nutrition of all humanity.'[58]

Notes

1   The material for this study was drawn from the CTNS research project funded by the Ethical, Legal and Social Issues Division of the National Institutes of Health, grant HG00487, and appears in greater detail in a Ted Peters, ed., *Genetics: Issues of Social Justice* (Cleveland: Pilgrim 1998).

2   HGI has been criticized because (1) as 'big science' with top-down administration it seems to squeeze out local initiative by smaller laboratories and (2) the large financial investment in genome mapping and sequencing leaves few funds left over for other worthy research projects. 'The genome project has been overhyped and oversold,' complains Boston University School of Medicine health law professor George J. Annas, who then adds, 'it is the obligation of those who take legal and ethical issues seriously to insure that the dangers, as well as the opportunities, are rigorously and publicly explored,' 'Who's Afraid of the Human Genome?', *Hastings Center Report*, 19:4 (July–August, 1989), 21.

3   James D. Watson contends that 'the more important reward is satisfying one's curiosity about how nature operates, and for biologists this means a deeper understanding of the nature of living organisms,' 'The Human Genome Project: Past, Present, and Future', *Science*, 248 (6 April 1990), 48.

4   Ibid., 46.

5   See Ann Lammers and Ted Peters, 'Genethics: Implications of the Human Genome Project', *The Christian Century*, 107:27 (3 October 1990), 868–72; *Genethics: The Clash Between The New Genetics and Human Values*, ed. by David Suzuki and Peter Knudtson (Cambridge: Harvard University Press, rev. edn, 1990); and David Heyd, *Genethics: Moral Issues in the Creation of People* (Berkeley: University of California Press, 1992).

6   'The task of the theologians is to bring their discipline to bear on the fundamental questions posed by ethics,' writes Trutz Rendtorff: *Ethics*, 2 volumes (Minneapolis: Fortress, 1986–9), I, 10.

7   'Genetic discrimination is defined as discrimination against an individual or against members of that individual's family solely because of real or perceived differences from the normal genome of that individual,' Paul R. Billings, Mel A. Kohn, Margaret de Cuevas, Jonathan Beckwith, Joseph S. Alper and Marvin R. Natowicz, 'Discrimination as a Consequence of Genetic Testing', *American Journal of Human Genetics*, 50 (1992), 481.

8   See Thomas H. Murray, 'Ethical Issues in Human Genome Research', *FASEB Journal*, 5 (January 1991), 55–60.

9   Mitchel L. Zoler, 'Genetic Tests', *Medical World News* (January 1991), 1–4. 'It is clear that unfair and discriminatory uses of genetic data already occur under current conditions. Enacted state and federal laws are inadequate to prevent some forms of genetic discrimination particularly that due to the health insurance industry'; Billings, et al., 'Discrimination as a Consequence of Genetic Testing', 481. A *Time*/CNN poll on 2 December 1993 asked, 'Do you think it should be legal for employers to use genetic tests in deciding whom to hire?' 87 per cent answered no; nine per cent answered yes. See Philip Elmer-DeWitt, 'The Genetic Revolution', *Time*, 143:3 (17 January 1994), 46–53.

10 Reporting on the Working Group on Ethical, Legal and Social Issues (ELSI) jointly sponsored by the National Institutes of Health (NIH) and the Department of Energy (DOE), Elinor J. Langfelder and Eric T. Juengst write, 'The Americans with Disabilities Act prohibits discriminatory actions based on a person's genotype, including the possibility of having affected children' and argue that pre-employment medical tests should be limited to those necessary to assess job-related physical and mental conditions: 'Social Policy Issues in Genome Research', *Forum for Applied Research and Public Policy*, 8:3 (Fall 1993), 15. The insurance industry tends to oppose restrictions in favor of regulations. 'Genetic testing restrictions may not adequately protect a person's access to insurance,' argues Ami S. Jaeger, because current use of medical histories already yield considerable

genetic information. It is better to have the genetic information and to use it 'within a regulatory framework that provides universal access and adequately protects the rights of individuals', 'An Insurance View on Genetic Testing', *Forum for Applied Research and Public Policy*, 8:3 (Fall 1993), 25. As of this writing eight states have laws limiting insurer use of or access to genetic information: Alabama, Arizona, Florida, Louisiana, Montana, North Carolina, Washington and Wisconsin.

11 Invoking the principle of confidentiality in order to avoid job discrimmination is seriously considered by the Joint NIH-DOE Working Group on Ethical, Legal and Social Issues (ELSI) of human genome research. Yet, more importantly, ELSI supports 'universal access to … basic health services' and states that 'information about past, present or future health status, including genetic information, should not be used to deny health care coverage or services to anyone'. Rather than relying simply on protection of privacy, the point here is that genetic information, whether available or not available, should not affect access to basic health care. See *Genetic Information and Health Insurance* (Washington, DC: National Institutes of Health, National Center for Human Genome Research, Publication No. 93-3686, 10 May 1993), 2.

12 'Biotechnology: Its Challenges to the Churches and the World' (August 1989), World Council of Churches, P.O. Box 2100, 1211 Geneva 2, Switzerland, 2 (hereinafter: WCC).

13 'United Methodist Church Genetic Task Force Report to the 1992 General Conference', 118 (hereinafter: Methodist).

14 'The Church and Genetic Engineering', Pronouncement of the Seventeenth General Synod, United Church of Christ, Fort Worth, Texas, 1989, 4 (hereinafter: UCC). See the interpretation and commentary of this Pronouncement by Ron Cole-Turner, 'Genetics and the Church', *Prism*, 6:1 (Spring 1991), 53–61.

15 In December 1993, China announced a program of abortions, forced sterilization and marriage restrictions to 'avoid new births of inferior quality and heighten the standards' of the Chinese people. See *Time*, 143:3 (17 January 1994), 53. This is eugenics old fashion style as practiced earlier in the twentieth century in England, the United States and Nazi Germany. The genetics revolution may make eugenics more efficient.

16 '*Gaudium et Spes*', in *Renewing the Earth: Catholic Documents on Peace, Justice and Liberation*, ed. by David O'Brien and Thomas A. Shannon (New York: Image Books, 1977), 229.

17 *Human Genetics: Ethical Issues in Genetic Testing, Counseling, and Therapy*, The Catholic Health Association of the United States, 4455 Woodson Road, St. Louis, MO 63134-0889 (1990), 21.

18 Cited by Christopher Anderson, 'NIH Drops Bid for Gene Patents', *Science*, 263 (18 February 1994), 909.

19 Venter and his colleague, William A. Haseltine, CEO of Human Genome Sciences, made the cover of *Business Week*, 3423 (8 May 1995) with an article by John Carey, 'The Gene Kings', 72–8.

20 33 US 130 (1948); cited by Rebecca Eisenberg, 'Genes, Patents, and Product Development', *Science*, 257 (14 August 1992), 904.

21 Daniel J. Kevles and Leroy Hood, eds, *The Code of Codes: Scientific and Social Issues in the Human Genome Project* (Cambridge, MA: Harvard University Press, 1982), 313, 314.

22 'HUGO Statement on Patenting of DNA Sequences', HUGO Americas, 7986-D Old Georgetown Road, Bethesda MD 20814, USA; report in *Human Genome News*, 6:6 (March–April 1995), 5.

23 General Board of Church and Society of the United Methodist Church, 100 Maryland Avenue, N.E., Washington, DC, 20002.

24 Battle imagery was used in the front page coverage of the *New York Times*, CXLIV:50:060, National Edition: 'Religious Leaders Prepare to Fight Patents on Genes', page 1.

25 Jeremy Rifkin, *Algeny* (New York: Viking, 1983), 252.

26 John Maddox, 'Has Nature Overwhelmed Nurture?' *Nature*, 366 (11 November 1993), 107.

27 R. David Cole, 'Genetic Predestination?', *Dialog*, 33:1 (Winter 1994), 21.

28 Charles Murray and Richard Herrnstein, *The Bell Curve: Intelligence and Class Structure in American Life* (New York: Free Press, 1994).

29 Troy Duster, 'Genetics, Race, and Crime: Recurring Seduction to a False Precision', *DNA on Trial: Genetic Information and Criminal Justice* (Plainview, NY: Cold Spring Harbor Press, 1992), 132.

30 Dean H. Hamer, Stella Hu, Victoria L. Magnuson, Nan Hu and Angela M.L. Pattatucci, 'A Linkage Between DNA Markers on the X Chromosome and Male Sexual Orientation', *Science*, 261:5119 (16 July 1993), 321–7.

31 William Henry, based on reports by Ellen Germain and Alice Park, 'Born Gay?', *Time*, 142:4 (26 July 1993), 36–9.

32 The question of whether homosexuality is sinful is a matter of dispute. We are not able to settle the dispute here. Rather, we are mapping different directions in which the ethical logic might take us. Pertaining to one side of the dispute, however, we note that Christian ethics has traditionally relied upon the Levitical Holiness Code which prescribes the death penalty for homosexual acts (Lev. 18:22; 20:13). New Testament passages denounce homosexual relationships as idolatrous (Rom. 1:26–7) and indicate that certain kinds of same sex practices preclude entry into the kingdom of God (1 Cor. 6:9–10; 1 Tim. 1:9–10). We also note how today The Federation of Parents and Friends of Lesbians and Gays (FLAG) answers 'no' to the question of their pamphlet title, 'Is Homosexuality a Sin?', published in 1992 by P-FLAG, P.O. Box 27605, Washington, DC 20038–7605. The pamphlet quotes former Lutheran Bishop Stanley E. Olson saying that 'Diversity is beautiful in creation. How we live our lives in either affirming or destructive ways is God's concern, but being either homosexually oriented or heterosexually oriented is neither a divine plus nor minus' (ibid., 9). Ethicist Karen Lebacqz associates sin not with homosexuality but with 'homophobia, gay-bashing, discriminatory legislation toward lesbians and gays, refusal to include lesbian/gay bisexual people into our churches and communities' (ibid., 11). James B. Nelson identifies four distinct positions within Christian ethics regarding homosexuality: (1) the rejecting-punitive position, (2) the rejecting–non-punitive position, (3) the qualified acceptance position, and (4) the full acceptance position. See 'Ethics' in *The Westminster Dictionary of Christian Ethics*, ed. by James F. Childress and John Macquarrie (Louisville: Westminster/John Knox Press, 1967, 1986), 273.

33 Richard Dawkins, *The Selfish Gene* (New York: Oxford, 1976, rev. 1989).

34 Edward O. Wilson, *Sociobiology: The New Synthesis* (Cambridge: Harvard University Press, 1975), 4; *On Human Nature* (New York: Bantam, 1978), 175, respectively.

35 Dorothy Nelkin and Laurence Tancredi, *Dangerous Diagnostics: The Social Power of Biological Information* (New York: Harper Collins, Basic Books, 1989), 12.

36 On the teaching of the Augustinian tradition that sin is universal though not necessary, see Reinhold Niebuhr, *The Nature and Destiny of Man*, 2 volumes (New York: Charles Scribner's Sons, 1941), 1,242. Robert John Russell helpfully

delineates the Manichaean, Pelagian and Augustinian systems. He introduced the term 'universal contingent' to describe sin as inevitable but not necessary. See his 'The Thermodynamics of Natural Evil', *CTNS Bulletin*, 10:2 (Spring 1990), 20–35.

37   Augustine, 'On the Merits and Remission of Sins' (*De Peccatorum Meritis et Remissione, et de Baptismo Parvulorum*) I:16. The key to Augustine's interpretation of Paul is the unity the whole human race has both in Adam and in Christ. Once this unity is affirmed, the question becomes one of explaining it. Biological inheritance seems to serve this purpose. Yet, Paul himself did not go this far. 'He developed no theory of a biologically inherited original sin.' See Brevard S. Childs, *Biblical Theology of the Old and New Testaments* (Minneapolis: Fortress, 1993), 583.

38   Gregory Fowler, Eric T. Juengst and Burke K. Zimmerman identify three types of germline intervention: (1) pre-implantation screening and selection of early stage embryos, which is not technically genetic engineering; (2) directly injecting normal genes into the DNA of pre-embryos conceived *in vitro*; and (3) gametocyte therapy – that is, genetic modification of gametes prior to conception. See 'Germ-Line Gene Therapy and the Clinical Ethos of Medical Genetics', *Theoretical Medicine*, 10 (1989), 151–65. See also Burke K. Zimmerman, 'Human Germ-Line Therapy: The Case for its Development and Use', *Journal of Medicine and Philosophy*, 16:6 (December 1991), 594–5.

39   W. French Anderson, 'Genetics and Human Malleability', *Hastings Center Report*, 20:1 (January/February, 1990), 23. W. French Anderson, in a more recent work with John C. Fletcher, argues that the situation is changing. Whereas in the 1970s and 1980s there was a strong taboo against germline modification, in the 1990s that taboo was lifting. 'Searches for cure and prevention of genetic disorders by germ-line therapy arise from principles of beneficence and non-maleficence, which create imperatives to relieve and prevent basic causes of human suffering. It follows from this ethical imperative that society ought not to draw a moral line between intentional germ-line therapy and somatic cell therapy,' 'Germ-Line Gene Therapy: A New Stage of Debate', *Law, Medicine, and Health Care*, 20:1/2 (Spring/Summer, 1992), 31.

40   *Manipulating Life: Ethical Issues in Genetic Engineering* (Geneva: World Council of Churches, 1982), 6–7. The 1989 document reiterates this position more strongly by proposing 'a ban on experiments involving genetic engineering of the human germline at the present time' (WCC, 2). Eric T. Juengst finds that the arguments for a present ban on germline intervention are convincing, but he also argues that the risks of genetic accidents – even multigenerational ones – can be overcome with new knowledge. Germline alteration ought not to be proscribed simply on the grounds that enhancement engineering might magnify current social inequalities. He writes, 'the social risks of enhancement engineering, like its clinical risks, still only provides contingent barriers to the technique. In a society structured to allow the realization of our moral commitment to social equality in the face of biological diversity – that is, for a society in which there was both open access to this technology and no particular social advantage to its use – these problems would show themselves to be the side issues they really are,' 'The NIH "Points to Consider" and the Limits of Human Gene Therapy', *Human Gene Therapy*, 1 (1990), 431.

41   Peter Meyer, 'Biotechnology: History Shapes German Opinion', *Forum for Applied Research and Public Policy*, 6:4 (Winter 1991), 92–7.

42   See Troy Duster, *Backdoor to Eugenics* (New York and London: Routledge, 1990) and Jeremy Rifkin, *Algeny* (New York: Viking, 1983), esp. pp.230–34. Not all are

opposed to eugenics, especially if eugenics means better human health. John Harris, for example, writes, 'where gene therapy will effect improvements to human beings or to human nature that provide protections from harm or the protection of life itself in the form of increases in life expectancy... then call it what you will, eugenics or not, we ought to favor it,' 'Is Gene Therapy a Form of Eugenics?', *Bioethics*, 7:2/3 (April 1993), 184.

43 Paul Ramsey writes, 'Men ought not to play God before they learn to be men, and after they have learned to be men they will not play God' (*Fabricated Man: The Ethics of Genetic Control*, New Haven: Yale University Press, 1970, 138). Israeli philosopher David Heyd sees playing God more positively in terms of shared creativity: 'if indeed the capacity to invest the world with value *is* God's image, it elevates human beings to a unique (godly) status, which is not shared by any other creature in the world. This is playing God in a creative, "human-specific" way' (*Genethics* (Berkeley and Los Angeles: University of California Press, 1992), 4, italics in original.

44 See Philip Elmer-DeWitt, 'The Genetic Revolution', *Time*, 143:3 (17 January 1994), 48.

45 Zimmerman, 'Human Germ-Line Therapy', 606.

46 Robert L. Sinsheimer, 'Genetic Engineering: Life as a Plaything', *Technology Review*, 86:14 (1983), 14–70.

47 Rifkin, *Algeny*, 17.

48 Ibid., 252.

49 Ronald Cole-Turner, *The New Genesis: Theology and the Genetic Revolution* (Louisville: Westminster/John Knox Press, 1993), 45.

50 Ibid.

51 Hessell Bouma, *Christian Faith, Health, and Medical Practice* (Grand Rapids: William B. Eerdmans, 1989), 4–5.

52 In addition to ethical responsibility, church leaders also anticipate a broader pastoral responsibility. Ethicist Karen Lebacqz recommends that congregations respond to new developments in genetic therapy through (1) *support* for persons and families facing illness and death; (2) *education* of and by the clergy to help all church members interpret genetic illness and its accompanying hopes and tragedies; and (3) *advocacy* in public policy debate that will support legislation to aid disabled persons and others needing social protection. See Karen Lebacqz (ed.), *Genetics, Ethics, and Parenthood* (New York: Pilgrim Press, 1983).

53 Thomas A. Shannon, *What Are They Saying About Genetic Engineering?* (New York: Paulist Press, 1985), 94.

54 UCC, 2; WCC, 31; Methodist, 114; Church of the Brethren, 453; United Church of Canada, 14.

55 United Church of Canada, 14.

56 United Church of Canada, 13. See *Human Life and the New Genetics: A Report of a Task Force Commissioned by the National Council of Churches of Christ in the USA*, 1980, 43; 'A Social Statement on Abortion', adopted by the second biennial Churchwide Assembly of the Evangelical Lutheran Church in America (ELCA) meeting in Orlando, Florida, 28 August – 4 September 1991, 2; *Manipulating Life*, 7–8.

57 Pope John Paul II, 'Biological Experimentation', 23 October 1982, *The Pope Speaks*, 1983.

58 Cole-Turner, 'Genetics and the Church', 55.

Chapter 8

Cloning Shock:
A Theological Reaction

Science Shocks, Religion Reacts

The moment cloning was announced, immediately and intuitively the world
recognized this as a theological issue. It is more than just science. It is more
than just a new technological discovery. It is more than just an occasion for
jokes about the name 'Dolly' or, as found in the announcement appearing with
the picture of two sheep on the cover of *Time*, 'Will There Ever Be Another
You?' (read ewe). This science raises religious questions, and the ambient
anxiety raises ethical ire.

Within hours of the release of news regarding Ian Wilmut's cloning
achievement of producing a live lamb from cells originating from a sheep
mammary gland, the Church of Scotland released its theological analysis and
rebuttal. The *Time* magazine coverage spoke of 'soulquakes' and asked
theological questions of readers such as 'Can souls be xeroxed?'[1] The 3 March
1997 cover of *Der Spiegel* pictured multiple copies of Adolph Hitler, Albert
Einstein and Claudia Schiffer, along with a caption in large capital letters, '*Der
Sündenfall*' (the fall into sin).

Radio, television and the printed press interviewed theologians and ethicists
of many religious persuasions. The media was looking for ethical outrage,
looking for someone to report a desecration of something sacred or to shriek
fear that human individuals would lose their individuality. When a *Time*
magazine poll asked, 'Is it against God's will to clone human beings?' 74 per
cent answered 'yes', 19 per cent answered 'no'.[2] 'Stop Cloning Around' was the
title of a *Christianity Today* editorial, and a *Christian Century* editorial said
that 'cloning a person would violate that person's freedom to establish her own
identity'.[3] The Christian Life Commission of the Southern Baptist Convention
issued a resolution on 6 March 1997 entitled, 'Against Human Cloning'. The
United Methodist Genetic Science Task Force followed suit on 9 May 1997,
recommending that the US president ban the practice before it gets started.
Martin Marty assessed the situation by observing, 'Crossing the new scientific
horizon produces intuitions that science now possesses the key to a door most
would rather have locked forever. The folk language draws on clichés: "Don't
fool with Mother Nature" and "You shouldn't play God".'[4]

Not every theologian or ethicist was outraged, to be sure. Philip Hefner at
the Chicago Center for Religion and Science (CCRS) told the press that we
should be stewards of this new cloning capability and that we are accountable
to God for what we do.[5] The Center for Theology and the Natural Sciences

(CTNS) at the Graduate Theological Union told the press that cloning is potentially good, because 'God could be seen as continuing to create through human agency'. CTNS went on to caution: if cloning becomes used in human reproduction, we as a society need to guard the dignity of children against possible commodification and merchandising.[6] Whether in a mood of outrage or a mood of cautionary stewardship, the secular media and the theological community immediately agreed: human cloning is a religious issue.

In what follows, I plan to look at the scientific shock – that is, to look briefly at just what was accomplished by the cloning experiment at the Roslin Institute in Edinburgh, Scotland. From the scientific point of view, the breakthrough consists in showing that we can begin with an already differentiated adult cell and return it to the predifferentiated state to initiate normal development in a cloned mammal. Then, I will turn to the religious and ethical reaction, giving particular attention to the fear that somehow human individuality and identity might be threatened as we think about cloning human beings. Against what appears to be the emerging widespread presumption, I will argue on scientific and theological grounds that we can safely say that no serious threat to human individuality or identity exists here. I will then proceed to assert that on distinctively theological grounds, no good reason for proscribing human cloning can be mustered. However, this does not preclude other grounds for caution. I will caution us to guard against misuse of cloning as a 'for sale' service in human reproduction on the grounds that it risks commodifying children – that is, cloning along with some other reproductive high tech services could risk treating children with quality control standards that might reduce them to merchandise. I would argue that, theologically and culturally, this is a moment in time when we need to be ethically alert and take steps to protect the dignity of future children.

What was the Science at Roslin?

Along with colleagues at Roslin, embryologist Ian Wilmut devised a cloning procedure, patented it, announced it to the press on 22 February 1997 and then published the details in the 27 February 1997 issue of *Nature*. The Roslin team removed cells from the udder of a pregnant Finn Dorset ewe, placed them in a culture, and starved them of serum nutrients for a week until the cells became quiescent – that is, they arrested the normal cycle of cell division, inviting a state akin to hibernation. Second, they took an unfertilized egg, or oocyte, from a Scottish Blackface ewe and removed the nucleus. When removing the nucleus with the DNA, they left the remaining cytoplasm intact. Third, the scientists placed the quiescent cell next to the oocyte and then introduced pulses of electric current. The gentle electric shock caused the cells to fuse, and the oocyte cytoplasm accepted the quiescent DNA. A second electric pulse initiated normal cell division. Fourth, after six days of cell division, the merged embryo was implanted into the uterus of another Blackface ewe and brought through pregnancy to birth on 5 July 1996. The newborn lamb was named Dolly. The procedure was called *somatic cell nuclear transfer*.

A key question has apparently been answered with this experiment: is cell differentiation reversible? The answer seems to be 'yes'. Embryonic cells are predifferentiated. Adult cells are normally differentiated in order to perform the particular tasks of particular parts of the body. For example, genes for hair are turned on in the hair while genes for toenails are turned off in hair but on where the toenails belong. In theory, cloning could be accomplished by employing embryonic cells in their predifferentiated state. The trick here was to make an adult differentiated cell function as an undifferentiated embryonic cell. 'The fact that a lamb was derived from an adult cell confirms that differentiation of that cell did not involve the irreversible modification of genetic material required for development to term.'[7]

In 1993, at the George Washington Medical Center in Washington, DC, Robert J. Stillman and Jerry Hall cloned 17 human embryos. These clones were made by splitting other pre-embryos after a few cell divisions, but prior to cell differentiation. The embryos were allowed to develop for six days. Because the pre-embryos selected for the experiment contained identifiable genetic defects, they were not expected to survive pregnancy. They did not. Similarly, shortly after the Roslin story broke, Don Wolf at the Oregon Regional Primate Research Center reported cloning monkeys – that is, making twins from embryos. The significant advance of the Roslin team over the Washington and Oregon experiments is that Dolly's DNA was taken from an already differentiated adult cell and, in the host oocyte, began division again at the predifferentiated stage. The scientific breakthrough is that we know now that future cloning could begin with the cells of adult animals, perhaps even adult human beings.

The procedure was not clean and easy. The successful cloning of Dolly was accompanied by numerous misfires. Out of 277 tries, the Roslin scientists were able to make only 29 embryos survive beyond six days. At 14 days, 62 per cent of the fetuses in ewe wombs were lost, a significantly greater proportion than the estimate of six per cent after natural mating. Eight ewes gave birth to five lambs, with all but one dying shortly thereafter. Dolly is the only one to survive. Triumph is accompanied by loss.

Does Cloning Violate the Uniqueness of Human Life?

The development of a successful cloning procedure by the Scottish researchers raises many crucial issues of an ethical, if not aesthetic or religious, character. When considering the ethical implications of cloning animals on a mass scale, for example, we must ask: would cloning technology applied to the most marketable cows in order to enhance meat production further commodify animals and deny them any respect beyond mere instrumental value for human consumption? Would cloning, like other genetic manipulations of research animals intended to make them into medicine factories, be further evidence of human speciesism and tyrannous dominion over the natural world?[8]

Nevertheless, despite the critical importance of these issues, the overriding ethical issue for most people seems to be this: should we clone human beings?[9]

This question sends an electrical charge into our religious sensibilities. It shocks us into theological reflection. It may not be immediately clear what we ought to think, but we know we need to think something. When receiving a shock from an electrical outlet, we immediately withdraw our hand to safety. So also, it appears, *cloning shock* causes us to withdraw immediately into what we hope will be safety: namely, a theologically grounded opposition. We say, 'No to the new procedure.' And we add, 'We say "no" because God says, "No".' But, I ask: does God really say 'No'?

Back in 1971, James Watson predicted this debate. Watson, along with Francis Crick, won the Nobel Prize for the discovery of the double helix structure of DNA. Writing on cloning for the *Atlantic*, he said, 'The first reaction of most people to the arrival of these asexually produced children, I suspect, would be one of despair.' He then went on to suggest that people with strong religious backgrounds would want to 'de-emphasize all those forms of research which would circumvent the normal sexual reproductive process'.[10] He seems to have been correct, or at least partially correct.

In a 22 February 1997 press release, Donald Bruce, Director of the Society, Religion and Technology Project of the Church of Scotland, said that cloning human beings would be 'ethically unacceptable as a matter of principle'. According to Christian belief, he said, cloning would be a 'violation of the uniqueness of human life, which God has given to each of us and to no one else'.[11] This argument, that each individual person has a unique identity that would be violated by cloning, has been repeated in religious and secular circles with great frequency since the 'Dolly' announcement.

What kind of an argument might this be? The first assumption here is that for a human person to have an individual identity he or she must have a unique genome. The second assumption is that God has ordained that each person have a genome differing from every other person. The third assumption holds that, through this genetic technology, we human beings could accidentally produce two persons with the same identity and, thereby, violate the Divine Creator's intention. On the basis of these scientific and theological assumptions, the ethical conclusion drawn here rules out human cloning.

However, the first assumption is empirically false. What distinguishes a clone is that he or she would have the same genome as the person from whom the DNA was originally taken. Both the original DNA donor and the clone would have identical genotypes. But, we might ask, does this mean they would have identical phenotypes? No, not necessarily. DNA does not always express itself in predictable fashion. There are variations in expression and spontaneous mutations. In addition, environmental factors are frequently decisive; that is, food, exercise, health care and countless other environmental factors influence gene activity. If the DNA donor and clone are reared a generation apart in time, let alone in separate locations, similarities will certainly be noticeable, but differences will also abound.

In addition, we have the experience of twins. Like clones, identical twins are born with identical genomes. Despite parents who may occasionally dress them alike and treat them alike, they grow up as separate and distinct individuals. Each has his or her own interior consciousness, sense of self, thought processes and ethical responsibility. Even if studies in behavioral genetics eventually show strong DNA influence on predispositions to certain forms of behavior or even an uncanny affinity for one another, they remain two separate individuals with separate lives to lead. A clone would be, in essence, a delayed twin and, because of the delay, would probably experience even more independence than twins born at the same time. A clone would be similar to a monozygotic twin in that he or she would share an exact genome with another person. However, a clone whose DNA was placed in an enucleated oocyte from none other than the mother of the nuclear donor would have different cytoplasm and different mitochondrial DNA – that is, the immediate cell environment would be different and might trigger slightly different patterns of genetic expression.

No reputable theological position has ever held that twins share a single soul. Each has his or her own soul, his or her own connection to God. The human soul, theologically speaking, is not formed from DNA as the phenotype is formed from the genotype. The soul is not a metaphysical appendage to the physical. To the question asked by *Time* magazine, 'Can souls be xeroxed?', we might answer, 'no'. Or, perhaps we might answer: 'If yes, then the result is two souls, not one.'

The key to understanding the soul theologically is not its emergence beyond the physical as psyche or mind. Rather, the key is understanding the soul in terms of our relationship to God. The unique relation of a person to God is not determined by DNA. It is determined by God's active grace, by God's desire to love us as we are.

Karen Lebacqz, developing the concept of soul in the work of Helmut Thielicke and applying it to the cloning issue, contends that the soul is not an attribute of our own but rather constitutes an 'alien dignity'. Neither our individuality nor our soul is threatened by cloning. 'My value or dignity is given by God; it derives from the fact that God loves me. In such an understanding, "soul" is not an individual possession but a statement about relationship. Soul has to do with our standing before God.'[12]

It would seem to me that no sound theological argument against cloning could be raised on the grounds that it violates an alleged God-given identity. Our identities in society come from growing up in society. Our identities before God come from God's continuing grace and from our desire or lack of desire to live in close communion with God. Souls do not come in any final form with our DNA.

Should We Ban Human Cloning?

At a press conference in the Oval Office at the White House on 4 March 1997, US President Bill Clinton described cloning as more than mere science: 'It is a matter of morality and spirituality as well.' He said, 'Each human life is unique, born of a miracle that reaches beyond laboratory science. I believe we must respect this profound gift and resist the temptation to replicate ourselves.' With this introduction he proceeded to issue a directive that 'bans the use of any federal funds for any cloning of human beings' and asked the scientific community in the private sector for a 'voluntary moratorium on the cloning of human beings'. He then asked the National Bioethics Advisory Commission (NBAC) to study the matter and come up with policy recommendations. During the question–answer period he described people who might want to replicate themselves as 'trying to play God'. Politics can be as religious as science is religious.

The NBAC returned its report on 6 June 1997 with the following conclusion: 'At this time it is morally unacceptable for anyone in the public or private sector, whether in a research or clinical setting, to attempt to create a child using somatic cell nuclear transfer cloning.' The report went on to ask the US Congress to pass legislation, setting a three- to five-year moratorium on the use of federal funding in support of human cloning, and it asked non-federally funded private sectors to comply voluntarily with this moratorium. The NBAC further recommended that religious groups carry on a discussion of the ethics of cloning.[13] On 9 June, President Clinton sent a bill to Congress, the 'Cloning Prohibition Act of 1997', that would prohibit somatic cell nuclear transfer for the purpose of creating a child while permitting cloning of animals and cloning experiments to produce human therapies.

Washington is not the only capital in which the question of banning human cloning has been asked.[14] The California Senate Select Committee on Genetics and Public Policy in Sacramento held hearings on 9 April 1997. On behalf of the American Society for Reproductive Medicine, Ryszard Chetowski, MD, testified that 'the practice of cloning an existing human being by nuclear transfer – that is, replicating an existing or previously existing person by transferring the nucleus of an adult, differentiated cell into an oocyte in which the nucleus has been removed (an enucleated egg) – is unacceptable'.[15] He continued by distinguishing between the use of cloning to produce a human being and the use of the same technique to produce beneficial medical therapies. Chetowski supports embryo research that will likely lead to improving the success of bone marrow transplants, repairing spinal cord injuries and replacing the skin of burn victims. A ban on cloning human beings should leave embryo research intact.

Francis C.J. Pizzulli offered to the California Senate what he thought was an avowedly secular and non-religious argument for a ban on cloning, namely, that each human being has the right to a unique genome. What he considered 'valid secular state interests' are found 'in the protection of individuality, autonomy, and privacy. ... protecting a citizen's right to a uniquely undetermined genotype'.[16] The concept of human right is here applied to the uniqueness of genotype, and he asks for a policy to protect that right by prohibiting the design or determination of a genotype in advance by cloning.

This proposed protection of strictly unique genotypes raises a logical question: would monozygotic twins be in violation of each other's right to a unique genotype? If a set of twins were judged to be in violation, which one would go to jail? Or would both go to jail? Although Pizzulli himself was less than fully clear on this, others who hold this view typically argue that twins are naturally determined, but clones are determined by choice. Whereas nature dictates shared genomes in the case of twins, clones would be the result of intentional human decision. The argument, finally, is an argument against human choice in determining genotype. In short, this argument against human cloning represents the kind of religious opposition forecasted by Watson, only here it is proposed as a secular rights argument.

To repeat, individual identity is not at stake when cloning is the mode of a person's conception. And, even if it were, the assumption that each of us has a right to genotypical uniqueness would require some supporting evidence. The burden of proof would fall on the shoulders of the one making the assertion. I, for one, cannot anticipate a convincing argument. Along the way, such an argument would have to take into account a potential threat towards twins.

This kind of argument betrays a veiled naturalism, a variant on the alleged 'thou shalt not play God' commandment. It presupposes that what nature bequeaths us prior to human choice has a higher moral status than what happens when we influence nature through technological intervention. Since most people by nature have unique genomes, it morally privileges unique genomes over what could be accomplished through cloning. Twins are seen here as exceptions to natural law and now moral law. Twins can be excused because they could not help it. Cloners cannot be excused, because they could. The fact that clones are predetermined by human decision is allegedly what makes cloning immoral and warrants legislation to ban the practice. What nature does is legal, and what we do will be moral if we copy nature. The argument commits the 'genetic fallacy': it tries to base an 'ought' on an 'is' – that is, it argues that, because nature has behaved in a certain way in the past, we ought to behave the same way in the future. This is a fallacy, because moral judgments are intended to pull us forward toward a reality better than the one we have inherited. The situation as it is does not necessarily describe how it ought to be.

Dignity for Children: the Real Risk Posed by Human Cloning

The idea of a ban against human cloning may be a good idea, even if supported to date by bad arguments. What other kinds of arguments should be brought to bear on the discussion leading toward public policy formulation? Specifically, what theological concerns are relevant to understanding the ethical implications of human cloning? My chief concern – and I grant that a long list of other concerns could rightly be introduced here – is the risk cloning might pose to the dignity of children. My concern for dignity is not based on a perceived threat to the individuality or identity of the child. Rather, it is based on the potential that cloning, along with other genetic technologies, may play into the hands of economic forces that will tend to commodify newborn children. Our dignity as imputed to us by God cannot be eliminated or even diminished by unethical actions, but it can be violated. The NBAC report, *Cloning Human Beings*, notes that 'Even for absolute opponents, the process of cloning humans only violates human dignity; it does not diminish human dignity.'[17] The NBAC also registers its fear of commodification by citing Rabbi R.E.N. Dorff's testimony before the Commission on 14 March 1997: commodification would deny 'the sacred character of human life depicted in the Jewish tradition, transforming it instead to fungible commodities on the human marketplace to be judged by a given person's worth to others'.[18] Whether this threat is sufficient to warrant an outright ban, I am unable to judge with certainty; yet, I wish to raise up the warning in such a way that it contributes to the public discussion.

As a theologian reading the New Testament, I interpret 1 John 4:19, 'We love because [God] first loved us', with the following maxim: God loves each of us regardless of our genetic makeup, and we should do likewise. This religious commitment has an Enlightenment or secular companion principle, namely, we should treat each person as an end and not merely as a means for something more valuable. These two together are the heartbeat of what I mean by dignity.[19]

Significant here is that dignity is a relational concept. Earlier, I said that the soul should be understood theologically as referring to our relationship to God. Similarly, dignity is relational, even though we might not normally think so. Ordinarily, we think of dignity as something inborn, something innate, an endowment by nature or by God that we as a body politic must revere in morality and law. That it is, at least philosophically speaking. Yet dignity, as we actually experience it, is relational. It is the experience of being treated as worthy, and then incorporating into ourselves the sense of self-worth. When other people, or when the law, treat us, individually, as an end – and not merely as a means to some further end – then we gain a sense of our own fundamental value as a human being. Our ethical task is to impute dignity to those who may not already experience it so that they might rise up and claim dignity for themselves. To treat a person as a person of worth is to love. In complementary fashion, love is a relational force that enhances an individual's sense of self-worth.

It is not individuality or identity per se that constitutes a person's dignity. Uniqueness does not determine dignity. Rather, it is the sense of value or worth that trumps all other claims to value or worth. Our value as a person comes exponentially from the people who love us and, ultimately, if not ontologically, from God's love for us.

Certainly I am not alone in sensing that human cloning could pose a risk to the dignity of future children. But just what is the nature of that risk? Under which bridge do we locate the troll who might come up and snatch away dignity? Just where is cloning shock going to hurt us?

Some theological ethicists fear that cloning, along with the advance of reproductive choice, will undermine the procreative unity of the family, and this in turn will harm children. Writing in an editorial for *Dialog*, Gilbert Meilaender registers this kind of concern for protecting the dignity of the child. What a child needs, he presumes, are two, loving parents who procreated sexually.

To say that a child ought to spring from the sexual union of a man and a woman (indeed, more precisely but unnecessarily for our purposes here, from the union of husband and wife) is not just to utter a moral rule. It is to see the child not simply as a project at which we aim in order to meet our needs and desires but as a gift. The child replicates neither father nor mother – and that genetic independence is a sign that parental nurture is ordered toward the independence of the next generation. Cloning would alter that mystery of our humanity in incalculable and irreparable ways.[20]

Protective of the child's individuality and of the child's prerogative of being born to parents who will respect individuality by cultivating independence for future generations, Meilaender supports sexual rather than asexual procreation. With two sexes, we guard against duplicating one or another parent. With two sexes giving birth to a child who is other to both parents, the parents are more likely to give room for developing independence. Asexual procreation through cloning would disadvantage the child's status in the family.

In contrast to Meilaender, I do not think that the location of cloning shock will be in the sex life of mothers and fathers in families. The risk to children is not found in the replacement of sexual with asexual conception. Rather, where it is found is in thinking of children as products, as the outcome of technological reproduction with quality control standards. Alien Verhey warns us:

> If we see children as achievements, as products, then the 'quality control' approach appropriate to technology will gradually limit our options to choosing either a perfect child or a dead child. Our capacity as parents to provide the sort of uncalculating care and nurture that evokes the trust of children will be diminished. If we would cherish children as begotten, not made, as gifts, not products, then we will not be hospitable to cloning.[21]

What Meilaender and Verhey share is the notion that we should see children as gifts, as gifts from God to be treasured and honored for who they are in themselves. 'Gift' here does not in any way imply possession on the part of the parents; rather, by hinting that a gift comes to us from beyond and may even have a mysterious dimension to it, they intend to say that each child deserves to be revered. I agree.

Cloning as a method of conception could, in the medium-range future, join artificial insemination, donor semen and donor eggs, *in vitro* fertilization and surrogate motherhood in expanding the range of choice in procreation. We can forecast that reproductive clinics would market cloning along with these other services to potential parents. Although advertising typically cloaks the reproductive business in medical and health care language, genetic and related technologies are finding a market with buyers.

We all know of infertile couples who strive and struggle to create a warm family, and we know that, when a new baby comes into their world, it is given love and devotion. How joyful they are when infertility therapy is successful. The fulfillment of the deep need many of us feel to create a family becomes translated into authentic love for children. Self-fulfillment for the parents and treating children with dignity are not necessarily competitors; they can be complementary.

The new element with cloning and related genetic advances is 'quality control'. The motives for a clone conception are likely to include the desire to replicate a favorite relative or perhaps to borrow DNA from someone known for good health, intelligence or athletic prowess. Genetic advances in general – and cloning procedures in particular – will increase the prospects of 'designer babies'. Reproduction will come to look more and more like production. Babies will come to look more and more like products.

We can imagine the megalomaniac who might want to clone himself or herself. Such a person, out of pride perhaps, might seek a form of immortality through children akin to the way wealthy benefactors have buildings named after them. The risk that such a child's dignity would be jeopardized is found in the prospect that role expectations might be so strong as to snuff out individual initiative. Christians like to think of our dignity as deriving in part from our being created in the image of God, the *imago dei*. In addition to the *imago dei*, the cloned child of a megalomaniac would bear a superimposed image of the cloner, the *imago mei*. We intuitively want to avoid putting a child in such a position. Yet, it is a likely scenario when cloning services go on sale.

What is more likely is the following. We can imagine a future couple sitting in the reception room of a reproductive clinic looking at an album. This album would contain pages of pictures of children with special DNA formulas, clones whose genotypes this clinic has paid royalties for and is licenced to sell. The parents-to-be begin with choice, begin with choosing the DNA profile of their future child. No doubt they will use quality criteria. If the technology fails – as technology frequently does – will they abort? If the baby is born and fails to meet expectations, will it be sent back to the factory? Will the parents ask for a refund? A discount? To what extent will such children be treated as commodities?[22]

Red, Green or Amber Light?

Is this risk sufficient to warrant a total ban on human cloning? Perhaps not. But warning sirens should alert us to potential harm to the dignity of cloned children. Ethical thinking leading to public policy should be the order of the day. Rather than a green light or a permanent red light, I endorse the amber light of a temporary ban until safety and ethical issues can be sorted out.[23]

I welcome the new world of expanded choice. I do not believe the way forward lies in curtailing scientific development so that people will be forced to procreate children the old-fashioned way. I do not believe the way forward is through denying choice. We cannot allow our ethics to derive from our fears of scientific advance. Rather, we need to construct ethical visions that take expanded choice into consideration. We need to construct visions of just what it means to treat children with dignity when they are the product – that is, when they are the gift – of advanced reproductive technology. For cloned children as well as children conceived the old-fashioned way, we need to be reminded that

God loves each of us regardless of our genetic makeup, and we should do likewise.

Notes

1   Jeffrey Kluger, 'Will We Follow the Sheep?', *Time*, 149:10 (10 March 1997), 67–73.
2   Ibid., 71.
3   Alien Verhey, 'Theology after Dolly', *The Christian Century*, 114:10 (19–26 March 1997), 285; see John F. Kilner, 'Stop Cloning Around', *Christianity Today*, 41:5 (28 April 1997), 10–11. An Associated Press report on Pope John Paul II's Sunday morning homily, 2 March 1997, at St Peter's Square suggested that the pontiff opposed cloning when he used the phrase 'dangerous experiments' that harm human dignity (*The Washington Post*, 3 March 1997, A16). To be consistent with previous commitments made by the pope in his *The Gospel of Life* (*Evangelium Vitae*) (New York: Random House, Times Books 1995) and with statements by the Congregation for the Doctrine of the Faith, the Vatican would necessarily take a stand against human cloning on the grounds that it constitutes asexual reproduction; whereas it is the Vatican's view that conception via sexual procreation is the point at which the human soul and hence human dignity come together.
4   Martin E. Marty, 'A Wolf in Sheep's Clothing', *The Lutheran*, 10:5 (May 1997), 27.
5   See Philip Hefner, 'Cloning as the Quintessential Human Act', editorial in *Dialog* (Summer 1997).
6   Robert Russell, Richard Randolph and Ted Peters, 'CTNS Press Release: Regarding the Successful Cloning of an Adult Sheep in Scotland', *CTNS Bulletin*, 17:2 (Spring 1997), 23–4.
7   I. Wilmut, A.E. Schnieke, J. McWhir, A.J. Kind and K.H.S. Campbell, 'Viable Offspring Derived From Fetal and Adult Mammalian Cells', *Nature*, 385 (27 February 1997), 810–13.
8   A non-issue has been plant cloning. Currently, genetically identical copies of organisms are commonplace in the plant-breeding world, but they are referred to as 'varieties' rather than 'clones'. Plant cloning and animal cloning have not elicited the ethical outrage that human cloning has.
9   Actually, the core genetics issue is gene transfer in germline intervention wherein a given genome is altered – that is, where a genotype is engineered – and then perpetuated in future generations. Cloning is a comparatively milder issue because it at least keeps a given genome intact.
10 James D. Watson, 'Moving Toward The Clonal Man: Is This What We Want?', *Atlantic*, 227:5 (May 1971), 50–53. Watson did not initiate religious speculation on cloning. The Princeton bioethicist Paul Ramsey had previously lectured and written against cloning in response to Nobel Prize winner Joshua Lederberg, who advocated such experiments. See Paul Ramsey, *Fabricated Man: The Ethics of Genetic Control* (New Haven: Yale University Press, 1970).
11 'Cloning Animals – A Suitable Case for Concern', *Glasgow Herald*, 25 February 1997.
12 Karen Lebacqz, 'Cloning: Asking the Right Questions', *Ethics and Policy*, newsletter of the Center for Ethics and Social Policy at the Graduate Theological Union (Winter 1997), 4.
13 *Cloning Human Beings*, Report and Recommendations of the National Bioethics Advisory Commission. Rockville, Maryland, June 1997 (iii). The NBAC spoke to

the president's fear that we might 'replicate ourselves' by observing that such 'fears stemmed from the incorrect idea that an exact copy, although much younger, of an existing person could be made. This fear reflects an erroneous belief that one's genes bear a simple relationship to the physical and psychological traits that make up a person. Although genes provide the building blocks for each individual, it is the interaction among a person's genetic inheritance, the physical and cultural environment, and the process of learning that result in the uniqueness of each individual human. Thus the idea that nuclear transplantation cloning could be used to re-create exemplary or evil people has no scientific basis and is simply false' (2).

14   Other nations that have already enacted laws banning the cloning of human beings include Argentina, Australia, Great Britain, Denmark, Germany and Spain.

15   'Testimony Before the Senate Select Committee on Genetics and Public Policy', American Society for Reproductive Medicine, Office of Government and Media Relations, 409 12th Street SW, Washington, DC 20024.

16   Francis C.J. Pizzulli, 'Statement on Human Cloning', California Senate Select Committee on Genetics and Public Policy', 9 April 1997.

17   *Cloning Human Beings*, 46.

18   Ibid., 47.

19   This is the theme of my book, published before the cloning controversy broke, *For the Love of Children: Genetic Technology and the Future of the Family* (Louisville: Westminster/John Knox, 1996).

20   Gilbert C. Meilaender, 'Hello Dolly', *Dialog*, 36:2 (Summer 1997). Elsewhere, Meilaender makes it clear that he believes it is God who gives us our individuality: *Faith and Faithfulness: Basic Themes in Christian Ethics* (Notre Dame: University of Notre Dame Press, 1991), 160, 'Individuality is not individually produced; it is a gift resulting from our relationship to God.'

21   Alien Verhey, 'Theology after Dolly', 286.

22   The primary reason for the NBAC's recommending a ban on cloning human beings is that it poses a threat to safety. 'It is important to recognize that the technique that produced Dolly the sheep was successful in only 1 of 277 attempts. If attempted in humans, it would pose the risk of hormonal manipulation in the egg donor; multiple miscarriages in the birth mother; and possibly severe developmental abnormalities in any resulting child' (*Cloning Human Beings*, 60). Secondarily, the NBAC registered fear of objectification and commodification of children resulting in a threat to personhood (ibid., 67–9).

23   This means I support the presidential commission's recommendation for a ban with a sunset clause: that is, a review and reconsideration after five years. I find helpful the stand taken by the 'Statement from the United Methodist Genetic Science Task Force' of 9 May 1997: 'As people of faith, we believe that our identity as humans is more than our genetic inheritance, our social environment, or the sum of the two. ... We do not know all the consequences of cloning (psychological, social, or genetic). It is important that the limits of human knowledge be considered as policy is made. ... At this time, we call for a ban on human cloning. ... If humans were ever cloned, they, along with all other human beings, would have inherent value, dignity and moral status and should have the same civil rights. ... There must be no discrimination against any person because of reproductive origin.' To obtain the full statement, contact the General Board of Church and Society of the United Methodist Church, 100 Maryland Avenue N.E., Washington, DC 20002.

Chapter 9

The Stem Cell Debate:
Ethical Questions

The story for the year 1997 was the cloning controversy, the public debate over cloning human beings. Ian Wilmut, the laboratory midwife to the world famous sheep, Dolly, never intended to clone a human being. He still opposes the idea.[1] Almost everyone opposes the idea. Yet, the cultural explosion ignited by this new scientific achievement continues to spread fallout. The prospect of gaining too much control – too much choice – over our own evolutionary future elicits anxiety, fear, suspicion. Genetic science seems to be igniting fires previously smoldering in our primordial sensibilities. Science is secular. And when secular science enters our DNA, we fear it is entering a realm of the sacred. We fear a Promethean blunder. We fear that our own human *hubris* will violate something sacred in our nature, and we fear that nature will retaliate with disaster. To protect ourselves from a possible Promethean blunder by science, we are tempted to stop further research with the commandment: 'thou shalt not play God!'[2]

Then, during 1999, we opened the first few pages of chapter two of the cloning controversy story. I will refer to this chapter as 'the stem cell debate'. The debate has only begun. What is not yet clear is just what needs to be debated. Perhaps nothing. Perhaps everything. What is clear is that the fallout from the cloning explosion is still lighting fires here and there. Whether or not the public will add stem cells to the fuel to make those fires burn hotter remains to be seen.

Stem cells have become front page news in Australia, as well as in the United States and other countries. On 4 February 1999, the Australian National Academy of Science issued a position statement. Note the structure of Recommendation 1.

> Council considers that reproductive cloning to produce human fetuses is unethical and unsafe and should be prohibited. ... However, human cells derived from cloning techniques, from ES cell lines, or from primordial germ cells should not be precluded from use in approved research activities in cellular and developmental biology.[3]

Here two things are put together. First, disapproval of reproductive cloning for the purposes of making children. Second approval of research on human embryonic stem cells, approval even in the face of ethical squeamishness regarding embryo research. If this Australian statement is a barometer, we need to ask: what is the cultural weather forecast? What might be coming?

177

In what follows it will be my task to report on the fast moving frontier of stem cell research within the field of genetics. I will try to identify the ethical questions that are relevant to what could turn out to be one of the most dramatic new chapters in medical history, a chapter just beginning and expected to continue over the next decade or longer. Then I will try to formulate questions regarding theological anthropology, agenda questions raised by science that need addressing by systematic theologians and public policy makers. I will ask more questions than I am ready to answer, yet I believe that such work invested in trying to formulate the relevant question (*die Fragestellung*) takes us more than just half way toward a helpful answer.

What are the New Discoveries?

Human embryonic stem cells (hES cells) are cells that are self-renewing – virtually immortal – and have the capacity to develop into any or all tissue types in the human body. If medical scientists could gain the ability to turn on selected genes to grow selected tissues and organs for transplantation, hES cell based therapies would revolutionize treatment of degenerative age-related diseases such as Parkinson's disease, diabetes and congestive heart failure.

Two recent claims of laboratory triumph are relevant. First is the isolation of hES cells by James Thomson, an associate veterinarian in the University of Wisconsin's Regional Primate Research Center. Thomson began with fertilized ova – spare embryos from *in vitro* fertilization (IVF) not placed in a uterus – and cultured them to the blastocyst stage, about four to six days. At this point he removed the outer shell of the blastocyst, separated out the individual cells and placed them on a feeder tray. The cells divided. They reproduced themselves. Because these cells are as yet undifferentiated – that is, they are pluripotent and able to make any part of a human body – they are the cells from which other cells stem. Because they replicate themselves indefinitely, Thomson in effect created an immortal line of embryonic stem cells.[4]

Second, John Gearhart, a professor of gynecology and obstetrics at Johns Hopkins University School of Medicine, drew human embryonic germ cells (hEG cells) from fetal gonadal tissue. These cells, when taken from an aborted fetus, resemble in nearly all respects the pluripotent stem cells described by Thomson.[5] I will provide more detail on the Gearhart discovery in the description that follows.

Stem Cells: What are They?

Many types of stem cells exist in the human body. All have the capacity to replicate and to self-renew, and they have the capacity to differentiate in order to produce specific body parts such as muscle cells, skin cells, nerve cells and such. Yet scientists believe they are organized in a hierarchy according to a scale of specialization. Please watch carefully as I label the steps on the hierarchical staircase.

On the top we find *totipotent* (totally potent) stem cells, which are capable of forming every type of body cell. Each totipotent cell may replicate, differentiate and become a human being. All cells within the early embryo are totipotent until roughly the 16-cell stage.

Next are the *pluripotent* stem cells which can develop into any of the three major tissue types: endoderm (interior gut lining), mesoderm (muscle, bone, blood) and ectoderm (epidermal tissues and nervous system). Pluripotent stem cells can eventually specialize in any bodily tissue, but they cannot themselves develop into a human being.

Finally, we have tissue-*specific* stem cells committed to making blood, muscle, nerve, bone or other tissues. Hematopoietic stem cells, for example, are responsible for all types of blood cells, but no other tissue types. These renew themselves, yet they specialize in the tissue they produce. Their continued presence in an adult person gives the body its repairing and healing ability.

We have just made the point that tissue-specific stem cells, such as those we find in the hematopoietic, intestinal and epidermal systems, are valuable to the body because they continue to replace themselves. Yet, curiously enough, they may turn out to be even more valuable. They may be transferable. Recent experiments with mice have successfully transferred neural stems cells from the brain to the bone marrow, resulting in the production of blood. Once transplanted from the brain into the bone marrow, the neural stem cells produced a variety of blood cell types including myeloid and lymphoid cells as well as early hematopoietic cells. This shows two things. First, the neural stem cells appear to have a wider differentiation potential than what is required to produce brain tissue.[6] Second, some kind of triggering mechanism must be present in the blood system that can instruct the stem cell genes to produce blood. Thinking ahead medically, this brightens the prospect that neural cell transplants might be able to treat human blood cell disorders such as aplastic anemia and severe combined immunodeficiency.[7]

Regardless of how interesting this might be, our focus here is on pluripotent cells. What Thomson and Gearhart have done is isolate pluripotent hES cells. The Thomson method takes a human egg fertilized *in vitro*, which itself is a totipotent stem cell. Thomson then nurtures it to the blastocyst stage, about four to six days. He then removes the trophectoderm, the outer shell, thereby exposing the inner cell mass. He separates the cells and places them on a feeder tray and cultures them. Each cell is now pluripotent, capable of making any bodily tissue. This is because they no longer constitute an embryo, nor can they become a whole embryo. They are not thought of as potential human beings.

Gearhart arrives at pluripotent stem cells, but he takes another route. He begins with an aborted fetus at about the five to eight week stage. He removes the primordial germ cells, which at this stage still have the full complement of 46 chromosomes. Later in fetal development the gonads would otherwise become distinguished either as ova with 23 chromosomes or sperm with 23 chromosomes. Prior to this stage, still at the five to eight week period after conception, the germ cells are migrating toward the genital ridge with 46 chromosomes. The Gearhart procedure catches them in this early migratory movement. Once the primordial germ cells are separated and placed on a feeder tray, they become cultured pluripotent hEG cells.

It is not yet clear whether or not hES cells are identical to hEG. Both are pluripotent and appear to be equivalent in function. Yet, it may be discovered that different alleles appear in different hES, because hES cells could be imprinted by either the male or female source. The blastocyst stage of embryogenesis is a stage that avoids the gender imprint. What is not yet known is whether original gender imprint will matter. For the foreseeable future the two types of stem cells will be treated the same.

The Enormous Potential Value of Stem Cell Research

Stem cell research is a step to be taken toward the improvement of transplantation therapy and toward lengthening a person's life.[8] We will postpone discussion of life extension, noting here the relevance to transplantation medicine. Specifically, rejuvenation through transplantation of tissue grown in a laboratory from stem cells would be of enormous value for *cardiomyocytes* to renew heart muscle to prevent congestive heart failure; replacement of *hematopoietic stem cells* for producing healthy blood in bone marrow to resist infection by the HIV virus and to treat AIDS and possibly sickle cell anemia; cultivating *endothelial cells* to reline blood vessels as treatment for atherosclerosis, angina and stroke due to arterial insufficiency; rejuvenating *islet cells* in the pancreas to produce natural insulin to fight diabetes; renewal of *neurons* in the brain to treat Parkinson's disease and victims of stroke; *fibroblast and keratinocyte cells* to heal skin in the treatment of burns; and *chondrocytes* or cartilage cells to treat osteoarthritis or rheumatoid arthritis.[9]

The key will be to discover just what turns which genes on and off. Once scientists have gained the knowledge of triggering gene expression, they can apply that knowledge to pluripotent stem cells and direct the growth of selected bodily tissue. Particular organs could be grown in culture. Heart tissue or entire organs such as the pancreas or liver could be grown in the laboratory. These would be healthy rejuvenating organs ready for transplantation.

In order to transplant the laboratory grown organs, however, we need to override our immune system in order to avoid organ rejection. Two scenarios lie before us. One would be to create a 'universal donor' cell that would be compatible with any organ recipient. The task here would be to disrupt or alter the genes within the cell responsible for the proteins on the cell's outer surface that label them as foreign to the recipient's immune system. This approach would be difficult. It would involve disrupting genes within the same DNA in which we are trying to express certain other genes. Exposing such cells to harsh conditions with rounds of different drugs may damage more than just the target surface proteins.

A preferable second scenario would be to make cells that are genetically compatible (histocompatible) with the organ recipient – that is, to make cells with an identical genotype. If the organ genotype matches that of the recipient, no immune system rejection will take place.[10]

Enter cloning: that is, somatic cell nuclear transfer. We can imagine the following scenario for customizing organ growth and transplantation. We could begin with an enucleated human oocyte, an egg with the DNA nucleus removed. Via somatic nuclear transplantation – cloning – we could insert the DNA nucleus of the future transplant recipient. We could then turn on selected genes; that is, we could cause the stem cell to differentiate into cardiomyocytes to produce heart tissue. The heart tissue could be grown *ex vivo*, outside the body, and then through surgery placed within the recipient. Because the implanted heart tissue has the same genetic code as the recipient, no rejection would occur. This is in part the Dolly scenario. It differs in part because it grows only organ tissue and not an entire fetus.

Another variant on the second scenario that distinguishes it from Dolly would be one that eliminates the use of the oocyte. Instead of an oocyte, the recipient's DNA nucleus might be placed within a non-egg cell. The goal would be to accomplish laboratory organ growth in a stem cell that is not an egg. To accomplish this, we need further research on cytoplasm's role in gene expression.

What is there in the cytoplasm that programs the DNA? Could we discover this? If so, we could begin not with an oocyte, but rather with an hES cell. We could enucleate a non-egg stem cell and insert the specific DNA nucleus, then reprogram the cytoplasm to cause the desired differentiation.

Asking the Ethical Questions

Whether we like it or not, the growing ethical debate over stem cell research draws much of its energy from the abortion debate. The new science demands new formulations of the issues, but it is not yet clear just what form these new formulations should take. In the meantime, voices are being lifted up in defense of the helpless embryo threatened with death at the hands of the laboratory executioner. The use of blastocysts and aborted fetuses leads Frank E. Young to write, 'The devaluation of humans at the very commencement of life encourages a policy of sacrificing the vulnerable that could ultimately put other humans at risk, such as those with disabilities and the aged, through a new eugenics of euthanasia.'[11]

In this context of ethical concern, the variant on the second scenario described above appears to have a slight ethical advantage. The removal of the DNA nucleus from the donated oocyte might be considered the destruction of a potential human life; the insertion of a DNA nucleus appears to be an asexual creation of a human embryo. We suddenly find ourselves in the middle of the abortion debate. By beginning with hES cells, scientists think this debate could be avoided. However, the use of hES cells does not avoid the embryo problem completely. The Thomson method relies on destroyed blastocysts as the source for hES cells; and the Gearhart method relies on aborted fetuses. Much needs to be cleared up here.

As we ferret our way through the ethical debate, one important task, as I see it, will be for scientists and ethicists to agree on the relevant vocabulary. In particular, the distinction between totipotent and pluripotent stem cells must be stipulated with sufficient clarity to permit ethical analysis. Right now, it appears that only one attribute distinguishes them: a totipotent stem cell has the potential for becoming an embryo and hence a human being, whereas a pluripotent stem cell does not. Yet, we must ask, why is this the case? Is it because totipotent cells have a genetic potential lacking in pluripotent cells? No. What distinguishes them is that totipotent cells have access to a placenta making them available for implantation, whereas pluripotent stem cells lack placenta access. Will this distinction hold? We will see.

Question: What is in the Petri Dish, Property or Person?

One inescapable ethical question to be confronted has been formulated by Glenn McGee and Arthur Caplan: 'What's in the dish?'[12] Is an oocyte hosting a transferred DNA nucleus a person or a potential person? Is a fertilized ovum from an IVF clinic that has been borrowed in order to make a blastocyst a potential person, or is it merely a piece of property to be donated for destruction in medical research? If the blastocyst is a potential person because its trophechtoderm makes it totipotent, is each interior pluripotent hES cell less of a person just because it no longer has access to a trophoblast? Would the pluripotent hES cell be a person if we could discover how to turn on its trophoblast genes and make a placenta? Would these questions apply as well to hEG cells taken from an aborted fetus? Even if pluripotent hES and hEG cells could be removed from the list of potential persons, would their respective sources in destroyed blastocysts and aborted fetuses render their utilization unethical?

These questions are essential to evangelical Right-to-Life advocates and Roman Catholics who borrow categories from earlier stages in the abortion debate. Richard Land, who heads the Ethics and Religious Liberty Commission of the Southern Baptist Convention, objects to treating stem cells as property: 'Human cells, tissues, and organs should not be commodities to be bought and sold in a biotech slave market.' He adds, 'Some researchers have established in their own minds an arbitrary lesser moral status for human beings in their embryonic stage of development.'[13]

The Roman Pontiff and the Congregation for the Doctrine of the Faith attribute full human personhood, dignity and moral status to the embryo from the moment of fertilization on. In order to avoid any sleight of ethical hand that might compromise this firm position, the Vatican uses interchangeably terms such as 'zygote', 'pre-embryo', 'embryo' and 'foetus'.[14]

What is of indispensable value here for our ethical deliberation is the Vatican's unflinching resolve to protect the dignity of human personhood. However, the questions raised by stem cell research are more than this line of ethical deliberation is currently ready to handle. The Vatican's approach is like an ethical spray gun, whereas what we need in this instance is to paint with a fine pencil brush. We need to color within the lines, so that we avoid accidently blotting out advances in the quality of human health and flourishing.

Question: Will Stem Cell Research Encourage Increased Embryo Destruction and Abortions?

Although this is a quantitative question applied to a qualitative ethical concern, we intuitively sense that the public impact of such science is morally relevant. We rightly fear that, if such science and its resulting technology proceed, this might encourage couples to fertilize ova for the purposes of sale or donation and that it might encourage abortions for harvesting hEG cells. At this point, however, it appears that this would be an unfounded fear.

More fertilized ova are already being generated by reproductive technology clinics than will ever be implanted. It is known well in advance that many will be destroyed as a matter of course. Therefore, diverting some for scientific research purposes constitutes a potential beneficial use for tissue that would otherwise be discarded. Scientific research is not in effect preventing human births.

Let us press the question: would stem cell research lead to increased demand for fetal tissue or for IVF embryos? Probably not. Over the last four or five years of research, relatively few fetuses, less than 100, have actually been harvested for experimentation. Experiments at the University of San Francisco and the University of Wisconsin use less than two dozen IVF embryos per year. The hope is that eventually laboratories could generate enough stem cells in culture to preclude constant demand for more and more tissue. In sum, stem cell research as at present understood should have a negligible impact on IVF or abortion practices.

The Ethics Advisory Board of the Geron Corporation, for a case in point, has taken a position against deliberately fertilizing ova for the purpose of selling or even donating them to make hES cells. Stem cell research of this type should proceed on the assumption that it would have a sufficient supply of discarded fertilized ova that would never have had the opportunity for implantation. The Ethics Advisory Board strongly recommends that the donating women or couples provide fully informed consent, and this consent would be based on the knowledge of potential commercial uses and profits that might result from this research.[15] The donating woman or couple may not be included in the profit making. The reduction or removal of the profit motive at this stage of harvesting would be ethically helpful, because it avoids treating fertilized ova and fetuses as property.

The practice of using aborted fetuses as a source of hEG cells would pass a strict Roman Catholic moral test if it meets one condition. If the fetuses are the result of spontaneous or natural abortion, then harvesting hEG cells would be licit, from the Roman Catholic point of view. If they are the result of elective abortion, it would be illicit. Similarly, Jewish ethical principles are likely to yield approval on the grounds that medical science is drawing something good out of an otherwise tragic situation, drawing good out of a respectful use of a dead body. Apart from the question of when life begins in or beyond the womb, the appeal here is to the moral value of the dead providing something life-giving for those who come later.

No matter how relevant such traditional deliberations might be, many more questions remain to be formulated and addressed.

Question: What is the Status of Totipotent and Pluripotent Stem Cells?

Does it help us ethically to distinguish scientifically between totipotency and pluripotency? Is it accurate to attribute the status of embryo to totipotent stem cells and deny it to pluripotent stem cells? Even if we are successful at removing pluripotent stem cells from the category of embryos – and, thereby, exempting them from legal restrictions on embryo research – have we really dealt sufficiently with the ethical issues?

Let us review the proposed scientific distinction. Why is it that pluripotent stem cells are one step down the embryonic staircase?[16] Totipotent stem cells are capable of producing all tissue, including the trophoblast necessary for implantation. Totipotent stem cells have the potential of becoming embryos. Pluripotent stem cells have every capability of the totipotent stem cells except one: they have no trophoblast. Without the trophoblast, pluripotent cells cannot for this reason develop into a full human being. In this limited sense, pluripotent cells are not potential embryos.

However, it may turn out that the difference between totipotency and pluripotency is little more than a verbal distinction. The genetic code remains the same. The potency for making all bodily tissues remains the same. When using the blastocyst as source, the trophechtoderm is removed, and this denies to the internal hES cells access to what is necessary for implantation. What distinguishes the pluripotent stem cells is their loss of the blastocyst environment and the potential for sharing in the benefits of implantation. In sum, it is not nature but rather the laboratory procedure that demotes cells from totipotency to pluripotency.

Relevant here is the following question: would a pluripotent stem cell under optimum conditions be able to produce a trophoblast and eventually a placenta for implantation? Why not, if the genetic code is complete and if it has the potential for making any tissue? Already experiments with mice have successfully shown that it is possible to form a fetus from a stem cell.[17] It is the pre-differentiated state of the embryonic stem (ES) cell that, in principle, makes it capable not only of producing any bodily tissue, but also of becoming an embryo.

This forces us to ask: would all ethical concerns previously pertaining to the use of embryos in research now apply to pluripotent hES cells? It would seem that this is the case. But, there is more. We now need to ask just what is being covered up by the totipotent–pluripotent distinction and also to ask about the implications of possible totipotency in normal somatic cells.

Question: Why is 'Derivation' Important?

The distinction between totipotency and pluripotency covers over the question of derivation. Those who advocate US government funding to support stem cell research wish to avoid the problems associated with restrictions on embryo research, so they exempt stem cells through definition. If stem cells are pluripotent and not totipotent, they escape prohibitions against the destruction of the embryo for purposes of research. The term 'derivation' is brought in to re-enforce this move.

In a December 1999 draft of the National Institutes of Health (NIH), 'Guidelines for Research Involving Human Pluripotent Stem Cells', the Department of Health and Human Services (DHHS) is reported to have concluded that 'the Congressional prohibition does not prohibit the funding of research utilizing human pluripotent stem cells because they are not embryos'. It further reports that appropriations law (P.L. 105-277, section 511,112 STAT, 2681-386) prohibits funds 'for the creation of a human embryo or embryos for research purposes; or research in which a human embryo or embryos are destroyed, discarded or knowingly subjected to risk of injury or death'. The problem, of course, is that the human embryonic stem cells are derived from early embryos. So, what to do? The proposed NIH answer, approved by DHHS, is to permit funding for pluripotent stem cell research, but deny it for deriving these stem cells from embryos. 'DHHS funds may not be used for the derivation of human pluripotent stem cells from early human embryos.'

What, then, should be the source of hES cells? Laboratory-created embryos? No. They should come from IVF clinics, where the original intent was to fertilize ova for implantation. US government funds can be used 'only if the cells were derived from early human embryos that were created for the purposes of infertility treatment and were in excess of clinical need of the individuals seeking such treatment'.

With regard to hEG cells, the NIH is more lenient. 'Unlike pluripotent stem cells derived from early human embryos, DHHS funds may be used to support research to *derive* pluripotent stem cells from fetal tissue, as well as for research *utilizing* such cells.'[18]

Reading between the lines, perhaps we can see Roman Catholic or right-to-life logic at work here. The use of fetal tissue for research is licit when the fetuses result from spontaneous abortions, but it is not licit when elective abortions are involved. Roman Catholics want to avoid any direct or indirect support for elective abortion. Yet, a hint of moral wiggle room seems to exist when deriving stem cells from fetal sources. No wiggle room seems to exist at present in right-to-life thinking regarding the deliberate destruction of embryos. One might surmise that, without saying it, these proposed government guidelines are responding to such concerns regarding the moral inviolability of what is perceived to be the integrity of the embryo, an integrity that goes as far back as the fertilized zygote. Governmental response to this is most appropriate, and welcomed. My only plea is that, if this is the operative thinking, it should be stated clearly as an ethical concern and not hidden under an alleged scientific distinction between totipotency and pluripotency.

Question: is there a Potential Baby in Every Body Cell?

Now, though still quite hypothetically, we might engage in further ethical speculation regarding the possible totipotency inherent in any pre-differentiated pluripotent cell. Recall the yet-to-be-discovered role that cytoplasm and other non-nuclear factors play in gene expression. One significant research task lying before molecular biologists is to determine just how the cytoplasm interacts with the DNA nucleus and to gain the ability to reprogram cytoplasm to make specific tissue. Once this ability to reprogram is achieved, in principle it could apply to any cell. We would not necessarily at that point have to rely on oocytes or fertilized ova or, perhaps, even blastocysts as the source. Somatic cells might become the source of pluripotent cells.

Then, we would experience a shift in ethical ground tantamount to an earthquake. Initially and naïvely, we could breathe a sigh of relief. If laboratory scientists are no longer tempted to harvest stem cells from IVF products or aborted fetuses, it appears that our fears are over. Human dignity is no longer threatened, because potential babies will no longer lose their potential lives in laboratory procedures. After all, nature (or God) has given us one source for making babies – fertilized ova – and this source will be protected. We could brush off our hands and thank the alliance of scientists and ethicists for solving this sticky problem.

However, the relief will be only momentary. At this point we will begin to feel the ground under our feet starting to shift. The needles on our ethical seismograph will begin to dance furiously. Would we begin to think of each cell in our body as an embryo? Would this mean that, in principle, we could make a baby from any cell in our body? Here is what we need: (1) the full genetic code to make every tissue available in every somatic cell; (2) the ability to return our DNA nucleus to quiescence and then to its pre-differentiated state, as in the case of Dolly; and (3) the ability to reprogram the cytoplasm to cause selected genetic expression and, along with this, to initiate embryonic development. This is all it takes. The first two are already in the well bag. Nature has given us a full complement of genes in every somatic cell. The cloning experiments at the Roslin Institute have given us the technology of quiescence for returning an already differentiated somatic nucleus to its pre-differentiated state and, hence, pluripotency. Only the third scientific task remains to be accomplished, and this would demonstrate the principle that babies can come from anywhere.

Now, we find ourselves in a most fascinating ethical situation. Let us ask: does every cell in our existing body have the same moral status as that of a pluripotent hES cell or the same status as a totipotent fertilized ovum or blastocyst? What have we done? Have we sent the moral status of common somatic cells up the ethical staircase? Or have we brought pluripotent hES cells down a few steps? Or have we done both?

We have little remorse at going to the barber for a haircut or clipping our finger nails. Nor do we feel immoral at donating blood or even a kidney to save the life of someone who might die without our bodily gifts. We tend not to think of our cells, limbs or body parts as themselves potentially whole persons with full dignity. Our body parts have a level of dignity, to be sure, but it is a dignity borrowed from ourselves as whole persons.

Nor do we feel compelled morally to exhaust our potential for reproduction. Despite the millions of ova in a woman and sperm in a man, we do not feel a compulsion to see every one individually contribute to the making of a new human person. Despite the Onan incident (Genesis 38:8–10), we recognize that God's creation begins with an excess of ova and sperm in the reservoir of potentiality within which some individual persons become an actuality. In natural sexual processes, only a fraction of ova become fertilized by only a fraction of sperm. And, of the resulting zygotes, the majority are flushed naturally out of the mother's body before implantation. If this natural parsimony is already operative with germ cells, might it relieve us of moral pressure to treat every pluripotent stem cell as an embryo, as a potential individual person?

What is in the petri dish? A person? No, I do not think so. Even if we can say in principle that what is in the petri dish is genetically a potential person, this does not in itself warrant putting an end to stem cell research. The genetic potential for making persons is virtually ubiquitous. In principle, it lies in every cell of every human body. Yet, we have no ethical warrant to actualize all this potential. No warrant exists to make babies out of every available germ cell, let alone every already differentiated somatic cell, nor do I think it is required of every pluripotent stem cell.

This is a safety-in-numbers argument. In itself, it may not be persuasive in ethical deliberation. This I grant. Yet it gains persuasive strength when combined with the argument from beneficence. What I find decisive is the related argument from beneficence: stem cell research carries with it promise of significant advances in medicine. The potential for reducing human suffering and improving human health and well-being is enormous. If it cannot be shown conclusively that individual human dignity is violated at the source of stem cells, then it seems to me that the argument from beneficence should be decisive in providing ethical encouragement to proceed with such research.

Notes

1 'The Roslin Institute and PPL Therapeutics have made it clear that they regard the idea [of human reproductive cloning] as ethically unacceptable' (Ian Wilmut and Donald Bruce, 'Dolly Mixture', in *Engineering Genesis: The Ethics of Genetic Engineering*, ed. by Donald Bruce and Ann Bruce, London: Earthscan Publications, 1998, 75). See also Ian Wilmut, 'Cloning for Medicine', *Scientific American*, 279:6 (December 1998), 58–63; and Ian Wilmut and Keith Campbell, *The Second Creation* (London: Headline, 2000). For a theological discussion, see *Human Cloning: Religious Responses*, ed. by Ronald Cole-Turner (Louisville: Westminster/ John Knox Press, 1997).

2 'Dolly's public fame emerged not from what she really is, but from what she represents. She is a metaphor for the Promethean power that scientists now have to create and control life, and her innocent image drives fear into the hearts of those

who think man has wrongly crossed into God's domain,' Lee M. Silver, 'A Sheep and a Metaphor', *Science*, 287:5457 (25 February 2000), 1405.

3   *On Human Cloning*, A Position Statement, 4 February 1999, Australian Academy of Science, GPO Box 783, Canberra, ACT 2601, Australia.

4   James A. Thomson, Joseph Itskovitz-Eldor, Sander S. Shapiro, Michelle A. Waknitz, Jennifer J. Swiergiel, Vivienne S. Marshall and Jeffrey M. Jones, 'Embryonic Stem Cell Lines Derived from Human Blastocysts', *Science*, 282: S391 (6 November 1998), 1145–7.

5   Michael J. Shamblott, Joyce Axelman, Shunping Wang, Elizabeth M. Bugg, John W. Littlefield, Peter J. Donovan, Paul D. Blumenthal, George R. Huggins and John D. Gearhart, 'Deriviation of Pluripotent Stem Cells from Cultured Human Primordial Germ Cells', *Proceedings of the National Academy of Sciences*, 95 (November 1998), 13726–31.

6   Christopher R.R. Bjornson, Rodney L. Rietze, Brent A. Reynolds, M. Cristina Magli and Angelo L. Vescovi, 'Turning Brain into Blood: A Hematopoietic Fate Adopted by Adult Neural Stem Cells in Vivo', *Science* 283:5401 (22 January 1999), 534–6. 'Evidence is mounting that the findings are not aberrations but may signal the unexpected power of adult stem cells'; see Gretchen Vogel, 'Can Old Cells Learn New Tricks?', *Science*, 287:5457 (25 February 2000), 1419.

7   Evelyn Strauss, 'Brain Stem Cells Show Their Potential', *Science*, 283:5401 (22 January 1999), 471.

8   'Carrying the potential to allow the repair of any failing organ by the injection of healthy youthful cells, this breakthrough may ultimately impact health care more broadly than the discovery of anesthesia or the development of antibiotics,' Thomas B. Okarma, 'Human Primordial Stem Cells', *Hastings Center Report*, 29:2 (March–April 1999), 30.

9   This is the published research agenda of the Geron Corporation, Menlo Park, California.

10 Roger A. Pedersen, 'Embryonic Stem Cells for Medicine', *Scientific American*, 280:4 (April 1999), 68–75.

11 Frank E. Young, 'A Time for Restraint', *Science*, 287:5457 (25 February 2000), 1424.

12 Glenn McGee and Arthur L. Caplan, 'What's in the Dish?', *Hastings Center Report*, 29:2 (March–April 1999), 36–8. One insightful point made by these two authors which we will not take up thoroughly here has to do with context. Whether protoplasm is in the dish or in the womb matters. Is its moral status different when in the womb where it can be brought through pregnancy to term than when it is in the petri dish? Is the interaction between an hES cell and its environment morally decisive?

13 Cited in 'Embryo Research Contested', by Denyse O'Leary, *Christianity Today*, 43:6 (24 May 2999), 27.

14 '*Donum Vitae* or "Instruction on Respect for Human Life in Its Origin and on the Dignity of Procreation; Replies to Certain Questions of the Day"', in *Bioethics*, 3rd edn, ed. by Thomas A. Shannon (Mahwah, NJ: Paulist Press, 1987), 591.

15 Karen Lebacqz, Michael M. Mendiola, Ted Peters, Ernlé W.D. Young and Laurie Zoloth-Dorfman, 'Research with Human Embryonic Stem Cells: Ethical Considerations', *Hastings Center Report*, 29:2 (March–April 1999), 31–6.

16 The National Bioethics Advisory Commission employs the distinction as introduced by Harold Varmus, then NIH director, at a hearing in January 1999. *Totipotent* cells have 'unlimited capacity. Totipotent cells have the capacity to differentiate into the embryo and into extra-embryonic membranes and tissues'.

Pluripotent cells 'can generate all of the cell types in a fetus and in the adult that are capable of self-renewal. Pluripotent cells are not capable of developing into an entire organism', *Ethical Issues in Human Stem Cell Research*, September 1999, by NBAC, 6100 Executive Boulevard, Suite 5B01, Rockville, Maryland 20892–7508; *www.bioethics.gov.*

17   Andràs Nagy, Janet Rossant, Rèka Nagy, Wanda Abramov-Newerly and John C. Roder, 'Derivation of completely cell culture-derived mice from early-passage embryonic stem cells', *Proceedings of the National Academy of Sciences*, 90 (September 1994), 8424–8.

18   US Department of Health and Human Services, 'National Institutes of Health Guidelines for Research Using Human Pluripotent Stem Cells' (November 2000), *www.nih.gov/news/stemcell/stemcellguidelines.htm* (emphasis added). The American Association for the Advancement of Science supports both public and private funding for stem cell research derived from all sources; yet, the AAAS recognizes that many religious traditions which take a developmentalist view of personhood will be at odds with those opposing use of embryos for anything other than pregnancy. Despite such unsettled religious differences, says the AAAS, these concerns need not exclude publicly funded research activities on cell lines that have already been established. See Audrey R. Chapman, Mark S. Frankel and Michele S. Garfinkel, *Stem Cell Research and Applications* (November 1999), *http://www.aaas.org/spp/dspp/sfrl/projects/stem/main.htm.*

Chapter 10

Designer Children: The Market World of Reproductive Choice

The storm clouds of a new form of discrimination loom on the horizon, a cultural weather front that could lead to a return of the now defunct eugenics movement. I call the newer version *free market eugenics*. Selective abortion will be the method.

During the first quarter of the 20th century, political activity in England and the United States included advocates of eugenics – that is, a movement to use family planning to improve the health, intelligence and productivity of the human race. By encouraging the so-called 'proper' people to breed and by discouraging the 'wrong' people from making babies, eugenicists sought to prepare the way for future generations of superior people. Positive eugenics encouraged intelligent men and women to meet, marry and propagate in order to provide civic leaders for the future. The negative eugenics platform lobbied for legislation to discourage baby making among the mentally retarded, feebleminded, physically disabled, alcoholics and petty thieves. This led to the forced sterilization of thousands of inmates in America's prisons, on the grounds that convicted felons should not propagate children who might also become felons and cost the state corrections system further expenses.

The idea of eugenics was abandoned in America during the 1930s because it was based on faulty science. When it became clear that two mentally retarded persons could give birth to a child with normal intelligence, the assumptions on which eugenics were based dissolved.

This was too late to stop the Nazis, however. By the mid-1920s, the National Socialist Party in Germany brought together eugenics with Anti-Semitism, and 'racial hygiene' (today: ethnic cleansing) became party policy. Nazis sought and received advice from California officials on ways to implement eugenics measures in state-run institutions. Eugenics became the means for enhancing the interests of the so-called 'Aryan race'. This led to the development of the Superman (*Übermensch*). Adolf Hitler's SS was charged with the mission of racial hygiene that led to the gas chambers and other extermination procedures used on children who were physically disabled or mentally handicapped. Eventually, the gas chambers were used on political dissidents and Jews.

Nazi Germany was a fascist dictatorship. Eugenics was imposed from the top down. This top-down approach is not likely to repeat itself in the near or medium-range future. The political climate has changed. However, the idea of neo-eugenics may sweep over us quite soon; if it comes, it will blow in on the winds of a free market economy.

191

Like a single leaf from an oak in October, the Herman J. Muller Repository for Germinal Choice floats on the winds of the times. This sperm bank, established by Robert K. Graham in the late 1970s, collects sperm from Nobel prize winners and offers insemination to women under 35 with high IQs. The goal: to help guide nature into producing more intelligent children. This overt eugenic program is singular and small, hardly worth including in a weather report about things to come.

Still, I forecast that a new form of eugenics may eventually come upon us at gale speed. As moving air is invisible to the eye, at first we will feel but not see eugenic winds blowing from two directions: discrimination in health insurance and personal tastes for designer children. I forecast that these breezes will advance to gale or hurricane force, and future children will walk in the debris of the coming storm over selective abortion.

The advance of genetic research is leading to the advance of medical diagnosis, and this in turn is leading toward possible discrimination against people diagnosed with bad genes. Why? Because bad genes are thought to be expensive, and private insurance carriers would like to save the money.

The triumphs of the Human Genome Project thus far can be measured in part by the discoveries of disease-related genes. The gene for cystic fibrosis has been found on chromosome seven. Huntington's chorea was discovered lurking on the end of chromosome four. In 1994, inherited breast cancer was traced to a defective gene on chromosome 17. In 1995, scientists found that early onset Alzheimer's disease is due to a gene mutation on chromosome 14. Colon cancer has been associated with a gene on chromosome two. Disposition to muscular dystrophy, sickle-cell anemia, Tay Sachs disease, late onset diabetes, certain cancers and numerous other diseases are being tracked to locatable genetic origins. The search goes on for disease-causing alleles leading to 5000 or more genetically based diseases. The search goes on as well to find the DNA switches that turn such genes on and off, and the search includes the creation of genetic therapies to turn the bad genes off and keep the good genes on.

Such discoveries should fill us with cheer and hope because this new knowledge could be used in medical care for diagnosis, prevention and therapy. It could advance the quality of health for everyone. Yet, this apparent good news comes as bad news to people born with genetic susceptibilities to disease when medical care is funded by private insurance companies and when medical insurance is tied to employment. An identifiable genetic predisposition to disease counts as an existing condition, and the pressure is on to deny coverage to people with existing conditions. Just as new techniques for prevention and therapy become available, the very people who could benefit may be denied access to these medical services.

Paul Billings, a genetics researcher and ethicist at the Stanford University Medical School, has begun collecting anecdotal evidence that genetic discrimination has already begun. Testifying before Congress, Billings said he found one woman who, during a routine gynecological check, spoke to her physician about the possibility of her mother having Huntington's disease. She subsequently lost all insurance when she applied for life insurance and her medical records were reviewed.

Phenylketonuria (PKU) experiences today may become routine genetic experiences tomorrow. Billings reports on an eight-year-old girl who had been diagnosed with PKU 14 days after her birth through a newborn screening program. A low phenylalanine diet was prescribed at the time, and her parents effectively followed the diet rules. The child has grown to be a normal and healthy person. Her health care at birth was covered by her father's group insurance policy associated with his employment. When he changed jobs, however, the carrier associated with his new employer declared her ineligible for coverage. Once a genetic predisposition for an expensive disease becomes part of one's medical record, insurance carriers and employers connected to them will find it in their best financial interest to minimize or outrightly deny health care coverage.

Loss of health care and perhaps loss of employment opportunities may, if left unchecked, create a whole new underclass. After hearing from Paul Billings and others, Congressman John Conyers said,

> Like discrimination based on race, genetic discrimination is wrong because it is based on hereditary characteristics we are powerless to change. The fear in the minds of many people is that genetic information will be used to identify those with 'weak' or 'inferior' genes, who will then be treated as a 'biological underclass'.[1]

For the most part, Uncle Sam in Washington has not been willing to listen to prophetic voices raised on behalf of the genetically poor and oppressed who may appear in the next generation. In order to make the point that this is a serious matter, researchers in the Working Group on Ethical, Legal and Social Issues (ELSI) of the Human Genome Project at the National Institutes of Health (NIH) and at the Department of Energy (DOE) created a task force and produced a 1993 report calling for action. The task force included geneticists, ethicists and representatives from the insurance industry. The central message here is this: information about past, present or future health status – especially health status due to genetic predispositions – should not be used to deny health care coverage or services to anyone.

Some listening is taking place. The recent court martial of two US Marines, John Mayfield and Joseph Vlacovsky, for refusing to allow their DNA to be deposited in a Pentagon data bank led to a modification of policy. Out of fear that genetic information could be used to discriminate, the Pentagon restricts the use of DNA for the identification of human remains on the battlefield. It dropped its original plan to keep DNA information for 75 years. Donors may now request destruction of their gene samples upon leaving Defense Department service.

In late 1995, the Genetic Privacy Act was introduced in the federal legislature, as well as six state legislatures. It is a proposal governing collection, analysis, storage and use of DNA samples and the genetic information obtained from them. The act would require explicit authorization to collect DNA samples for genetic analysis and limit the use of information gained from them. The aim here is to protect individual privacy by giving the individual the right to authorize who may have access to his or her genetic information.

This is a good start, but in my judgment it is not enough. Laws to protect genetic privacy would appeal to our sense of autonomy, to our desire to take control of what appears to be our own possession, our genome. But, privacy protection will not in itself eliminate the threat of genetic discrimination. This for two reasons. First, it probably will not work. Genetic information as well as medical records are computerized. Computers are linked. In the world of computech, someone who really wants to penetrate the system to gain information will eventually find a way to do so. An attempt to maintain control over genetic information is likely to fail.

Second, privacy regarding one's genome is undesirable. Knowledge of one's genome could be of enormous value to preventative health care. The more our physician knows about our genetic predispositions the more she or he can plan to head off difficulties before they arise. Rather than privacy, it seems to me that we want *genetic information without discrimination.*

A few years ago our 23-year-old godson, Matthew, was rushed to the hospital for emergency surgery. Without warning, he was suddenly diagnosed as suffering from familial polyposis, a colon cancer already in quite an advanced stage. The surgeon's team worked for a number of hours in a heroic effort to remove all malignancy. The operation was successful. The surgeon, fatigued after his Herculean achievement, flopped down in a chair next to Matthew's nervously waiting parents. 'Are there any cases of colon cancer in Matthew's grandparents?' asked the doctor.

'We don't know,' answered Matthew's mother and father. They went on to explain that Matthew had been adopted as an infant and the records closed. My wife, Jenny, and I had been present at the baptism two decades prior.

'Well,' said the doctor, 'on the day Matthew was admitted to the hospital I read in a British medical journal that a marker has been found for this kind of cancer. It's genetic. It runs in families. Had we known that Matthew had a predisposition, we could have been monitoring him from age ten or so on, removing pre-cancerous polyps, and he never would have come to this crisis situation.'

This case shows the potential value of computerized and sharable genomic information. At some point in the future, when a simple blood test will reveal each of our individual genomes, this knowledge could be used to great benefit. I advocate laws to promote genetic information without discrimination so that what we learn about our genomes will contribute to better health care rather than deny it.

A number of states currently have laws requiring that genetic information be secured from birth parents and made available to adopting parents. This genetic information has been coming from family histories: that is, learning the frequency of a disorder in a family without revealing the identity of the family. As genetic testing becomes more sophisticated, DNA tests themselves will likely suffice.

If adoptable children become viewed as commodities to be consumed by adopting parents, however, such genetic testing could inadvertently lead to discrimination. If the child tests positively for a genetic defect, the adopting parents may think of the child as defective and refuse to adopt the child. This refusal could be due to two reasons. First, the adoptive parents may simply be engaged in the *perfect child syndrome* and be willing to accept nothing less than a perfectly healthy infant or toddler. Second, they may turn down the adoption fearing that they might lose their family health care insurance and become stuck with unpayable medical bills. The first reason is cultural or ethical, the second economic.

Can we forecast a connection between genetic discrimination and selective abortion? Yes. The following case will make the connection. A couple living in Louisiana had a child with cystic fibrosis, a genetic disorder leading to chronic lung infections and excruciating discomfort. When the wife became pregnant with the second child, a prenatal genetic test revealed that the fetus carried the mutant gene for cystic fibrosis. The couple's health maintenance organization demanded that they abort. If they refused to abort, the HMO threatened to withdraw coverage from the newborn and to withdraw coverage from the first child as well. The couple threatened to sue. Only then did the HMO back down and grant coverage for the child coming to birth.

This incident may be a harbinger of things to come. With the advance of prenatal genetic testing, both parents and insurance carriers can tell in advance that a given child might be prone to having a debilitating and expensive disease. Pressure to abort may emerge from the financial interests of the insurance industry. It would not be unrealistic to imagine a decade from now a published list of genetic predispositions that, if found in a fetus, would mandate an abortion under penalty of loss of coverage. This would outrage pro-life parents. Even those who may have taken a pro-choice position on abortion would find this financial pressure to be the equivalent of a compromise on choice.

We are moving step by step toward the selective abortion scenario. In addition to pressure from the privately funded insurance industry, parents themselves will likely develop criteria for deciding which fetuses will be brought to term and which will be aborted. Genetic criteria will play a major role. Prenatal testing to identify disease-related genes will likely become routine, and eventually tests for perhaps hundreds of deleterious genes may become part of the prenatal arsenal. Parents wanting what they believe to be a perfectly healthy child may abort repeatedly at each hint of a genetic disorder. Parents willing to accept some degree of malady may abort only the most ominous cases. What we can fully expect is that choice and selection will enter the enterprise of baby making at a magnitude unheard of in previous history.

The point at which most families will confront the issue we are identifying here is when they find themselves in a clinic office talking with a genetic counselor. Preferably before pregnancy or even before marriage, a genetic analysis of heritable family traits can help immensely in planning for future children. However, talking with the genetic counselor too often begins with a pregnancy already in progress. The task of the genetic counselor is quite specific: to provide information regarding the degree of risk that a given child might be born with a genetic disorder and to impart this information objectively, impartially and confidentially (when possible) so that the autonomy of the parents is protected. What is surprising and disconcerting to mothers or couples in this situation is that genetic risk is usually given statistically, in percentages. The assumption that medical science is an exact science is immediately challenged, and the parents find themselves confronted with difficult to interpret information while facing an unknown future. Conflicting values between marital partners or even within each of them increase the difficulty. Anxiety can rise.

The statistical unknown comes in two forms. First, for an autosomal recessive defective gene such as that for cystic fibrosis, when both parents are carriers, the risk is 50 per cent that their child will also be a carrier and 25 per cent that the child will actually contract the disease. Upon receiving information regarding this risk, the parents decide to proceed toward birth or terminate the pregnancy. Second, via amniocentesis and other testing procedures being developed, the specific genetic makeup of a fetus can be discerned. In cases of Down's Syndrome, for example, which is associated with trisomy (three copies of chromosome 21), we know from experience that eight out of every ten negative prenatal diagnoses lead to the decision to abort. Even though the genetic predisposition can be clearly identified in this way, what remains unknown is the degree of mental retardation that will result. Mild cases mean near-average intelligence, and such individuals are pleasant members of families. Yet the choice to abort has become the virtual norm. The population of Down's Syndrome people in our society is dropping, making this a form of eugenics by popular choice.

In only three to five per cent of cases does a positive prenatal diagnosis reveal the presence of a genetic disorder so severe that the probable level of suffering on the part of the child warrants consideration of abortion. In making this judgment, I am invoking a principle of compassion, what bioethicists dub the principle of *nonmaleficence* aimed at reducing human suffering whenever possible. In situations where such a diagnosis is rendered and where the prospective parents strongly desire to bring a child into the world as an expression of their love, a number of things happen. First, genetic counselors report that parents, without thinking about it, refer to the child as a 'baby', never a 'fetus'. They clearly think of the life growing in the womb as a person. Second, when confronted with the bad news, they experience turmoil. The turmoil leads more often than not to a decision to terminate the pregnancy, but certainly not always. It is not the job of the genetic counselor to encourage abortion, and advocates of procreative liberty stand firm in protecting the right of parents to decide to bring such a child to birth. Third, even when the decision to terminate is made, these grieving parents see their decision as an expression of their love, not a denial of love. It is an act of compassion.

Ethically significant here is the distinction between convenience and compassion. As the practice of prenatal genetic testing expands and the principle of autonomy – that is, the responsibility for choice – is applied to the parents and not to the unborn child, we can forecast that the total number of abortions will increase, perhaps increase dramatically. Each pregnancy will be thought to be tentative until the fetus has taken and passed dozens, perhaps hundreds, of genetic tests. A culturally reinforced image of the desirable child – the perfect child syndrome – may eventually lead couples to try repeated pregnancies, terminating the undesirables and giving birth to only the best test passers. Those finally born in this fashion risk being commodified by their parents. In addition, those who might be born with a disability but still with the potential for leading a productive and fulfilling life might never see the light of day.

A social by-product of the embracing of selective abortion might be increased discrimination against living people with disabilities. The assumption could grow that to live with a disability is to have a life not worth living. Persons with disabilities find this fearsome. They fear that the medical establishment and its supportive social policies will seek to prevent 'future people like me' from ever being born. This translates as 'I am worthless to society'. The imputation of dignity to handicapped persons may be quietly withdrawn as they are increasingly viewed as unnecessary and perhaps expensive appendages to an otherwise healthy society. This would be a tragedy of the first order. Disabled persons are persons who deserve dignity and, furthermore, deserve encouragement. Marsha Saxton, a disabled rights advocate who herself suffers from spina bifida, reports that such people can gain victory in their difficult life struggles. Most disabled people report how the disability, the pain, the need for compensatory devices and assistance can produce considerable inconvenience; but, they go on to say that very often these become minimal or are forgotten once individuals make the transition to living their everyday lives.

Given the precedent set by Jesus, who spent so much of his time with the disabled – whether born blind or having contracted diseases such as leprosy – it seems that no disciple of Jesus could lightly acquiesce to the wholesale aborting of this group of people. One could easily imagine Jesus' disciples today organizing social services and advertising: 'Don't abort! Send us your genetically defective babies.' No medical insurance company is likely to cover such an enterprise, of course.

Whether we asked for it or not, the advancing frontier of genetics and its impact on reproductive technology thrusts us back once again into the abortion debate. I cannot resolve the abortion controversy here. I can point out, however, that *Roe* v. *Wade* in 1973 did not answer some of the questions we will be asking in 2003. The question the Supreme Court has already answered is whether a woman has a choice to abort during the first trimester. Genetic discrimination will raise for us the additional question: by what criteria might a fetus be considered abortable? Whereas for *Roe* v. *Wade* the issue focused on the woman's right to decide what to do with her body, here we focus on the fetuses and the criteria by which some will live and others will not. A skeptic might say that, as long as the woman has the right to choose, it is a moot point to talk of criteria of choice; yet, I believe it is worth pressing on. A woman's right to choose is a legal matter. The criteria for choosing is an ethical matter.

Even though abortion on request is legal, not all grounds for requesting it are ethical. In the case of selective abortion, a decision based solely on the desires of the parents without regard for the child's well-being is unethical. Recall Martin Luther's words, 'Even if a child is unattractive when it is born, we nevertheless love it.'

As we approach the era of selective abortion for purposes of sorting out desirable from undesirable genes, most Christians are not ethically ready. Despite the fact that massive intellectual resources of a theological and ethical type have been invested in thinking through the abortion controversy, we are unprepared for the kind of decisions large numbers of prospective parents will be confronting. Much thought has been given to the issue of abortion on request and to the question of when human dignity begins; but, what we need now are middle axioms to guide the choices that will inevitably confront the next generation of parents-to-be. At this point, certain minimalist middle axioms present themselves.

First, selecting out defective or undesirable genes is better done prior to conception than after. Whether or not the conceptus has full personhood and full dignity comparable to living adults, ethicists certainly agree that the fertilized zygote has already achieved a moral status deserving a certain level of respect and honor that resists brute manipulation or irreverent discarding. Genetic selection in the sperm or ovum prior to fertilization, prior to the DNA blueprint of a potential person, seems obviously more defensible.

Second, the choice of selective abortion should be the last resort. Pre-fertilization selection, when possible, should be given priority. Prenatal fetal gene therapy should also be given priority.

Third, the motive of compassion that seeks to minimize suffering on the part of children coming into the world should hold relative sway when choosing for or against selective abortion. Compassion, taken up as the principle of nonmaleficence in bioethics, constitutes the way that parents show love toward children-to-be. In those rare cases, three to five per cent of prenatal diagnoses, the genetic disorder is so severe that no approximation to a fulfilling life is possible. Here, the decision to abort can be understood as a form of caring for the baby, as well as self-care for the parents. Yet, we must acknowledge that this is a judgment call. No clear rule tells us exactly when the imputed dignity of the unborn child may be trumped by a compassionate decision to abort.

Fourth, we should distinguish between eugenic purposes and compassion purposes when engaged in genetic selection. The goal of eugenics is to reduce in the population the incidence of a certain genetic trait, usually an undesirable trait. Eugenics is social in scope and derives from some social philosophy. At this point, bioethicists tend to oppose eugenic policies because if practiced on a large scale it could reduce biodiversity and, more importantly, eugenics connotes the political totalitarianism of the Third Reich. The compassion or nonmaleficence principle, when limited to the concrete situation of a family making a decision regarding a particular child, is much more acceptable. The line between eugenics and compassion is not a clear one, however, because we may eventually argue, on the basis of the principle of compassion, that the attempt to rid future branches on a family tree of an autosomal recessive gene such as cystic fibrosis makes good eugenic sense.

Fifth, we should distinguish between preventing suffering and enhancing genetic potential. Genetic selection based on the compassion principle to help reduce suffering is understandably an act that, in at least a minimal sense, is directed toward the well-being of the child. In the future, when genetic selection and perhaps even genetic engineering make possible designer babies that may have higher than average intelligence, good looks or athletic prowess, we will move closer to the perfect child syndrome. The risk of commodifying children and evaluating them according to standards of quality control when being sold to paying parents goes up. That there is risk of commodification does not in itself provide sufficient warrant for prohibiting enhancement, but it will call forth attention to what I believe to be a sound biblically defensible principle: *God loves us regardless of our genetic makeup, and we should do likewise.*

Note

1 'Designing Genetic Information Policy', Sixteenth Report by the Committee on Government Operations, US Government Printing Office (2 April 1992), 15, 19.

Chapter 11

Multiple Choice in Baby Making

Like the Mississippi River following the spring snow melt, the family landscape is being flooded with new technologies having to do with baby making or not making. The explosion of progress in reproductive technologies is creating choice in a dimension of life we previously consigned to destiny, namely, procreating children. Fertile women can stop baby making with Norplant, RU486 or abortion. Infertile couples can still make babies with the help of artificial insemination, *in vitro* fertilization (IVF), donor semen, donor eggs, frozen embryos and surrogate motherhood. Soon, we will be able to exact quality control regarding the health and perhaps the genetic makeup of future children with the aid of genetic screening, genetic engineering, nuclear transplantation, egg fusion, cloning, selective abortion and *in utero* fetal surgery. A woman can become a mother at age 62. And, if experiments in ectogenesis and interspecies gestation prove successful, a woman will be able to become a mother without herself becoming pregnant.

Technology and choice quickly translate into markets. The already nascent reproductive industry is likely to expand as new technologies open up new possibilities for baby stopping, baby making and baby selecting. Infertility clinics will soon expand the range of services they offer, and this may increase the clientele to include fertile couples and perhaps even individuals who are willing to pay for designer babies.

Under market conditions, will babies become commodities? The issue is less that they might be bought and sold, in my judgment; rather, what is at stake is the value children will have for us when they are the result of engineering or selection in order to manufacture a superior product. Of course, parents want their children to enjoy good health. But, choice at the level of reproductive technology means selecting the healthy baby and discarding the unhealthy. Parents may yearn for a child with certain genetic traits, talents or abilities. But, choice at the level of genetic screening for acceptable embryos or engineering for superior genetic configurations may lead to the *perfect child syndrome*, wherein the neighborhood children born the ol' fashioned way may be led to feel inferior. Or, worse, something might go wrong – technology is seldom perfect – and something less than the perfect child will be produced, causing the parents to deprive the child of unconditional affection.

The possibility of treating children as commodities raises the specter that human dignity will be threatened. So, on the basis of observations of the way Jesus behaved with poor and diseased outcasts and of the theology of the incarnation wherein God loves the imperfect world enough to become a part of it, I submit the following as a fundamental principle: *God loves each of us regardless of our genetic makeup, and we should do likewise.*

Even those less interested than I in basing an ethic upon Jesus might hold some reverence for the Enlightenment commitment to human dignity, to Immanuel Kant's dictum that we treat each person as an end and not merely as a means. My central concern here is that children – perfect or imperfect, by choice or by destiny – receive unconditional love from their parents and equal opportunities in society. I cede a certain presumptive primacy to the babies being made by reproductive technology, so that they are treated as ends in themselves and not merely as means for attaining some other social or parental values. I want an ethic that successfully places the love of children first and foremost and that orients all secondary concerns for parental fulfillment and technological means toward this end.

The Children of Martha and Phil

One of the salient characteristics of the new situation being created by options in baby making is the increase in choice, the increased sense that people can take control of their family destiny. The advances in reproductive technology provide a sense of empowerment in the face of a biological destiny that in previous generations was a brute given. Science is providing hope. Yet, with increased choice comes increased responsibility for new and delicate ethical concerns. I have found the experience of my friends Martha Maier and Phil Isensee to be paradigmatic for many of the ethical issues surrounding reproductive technology. Their story will be instructive. So, I tell it here.

'I was shooting blanks,' Phil told me, meaning that the active half of his sperm seemed to be unable to penetrate and fertilize his wife's ovum. He had had a vasectomy reversal in order to ready the family for bringing children into the world. But it was not working. After a year of attempts with sperm concentration, AIH (Artificial Insemination by Husband) and other measures to assist impregnation, Phil was judged to be infertile. It was the mid-1980s and the Midwest clinic helping the couple suggested alternative birth technologies.

Martha reports experiencing some confusion and even anger when realizing that she and her husband would not become parents the old-fashioned way. 'I'd always wanted to have children,' she says, so the infertility news came as a serious disappointment. It was comparatively less disappointing for Phil, since he had undergone a vasectomy before marrying Martha and had not been planning on becoming a father. Yet, he and Martha are a very close couple, so he shared her initial grief and sought with enthusiasm to jump the hurdles necessary to create a family.

Martha and Phil moved to Berkeley, where for a period Martha was a student of mine. Now, on the west coast, they began to pursue adoption and attend meetings of Resolve, a national organization offering referral, education and support services for people dealing with infertility.[1] Discussions at Resolve regarding ethical issues surrounding adoption, especially private adoption, began to stir up doubts. Private adoption requires searching for a pregnant woman who might consider giving up her baby and then convincing her that these are the people with whom she should place the child. 'Is this right,' quizzed Phil, 'to be in a position where you want a mother to give up a child?' Then, typically the adopting parents provide the birth mother with financial support for four to seven months, paying medical expenses and such. 'Am I buying a baby?' Phil asked himself. Martha and Phil are highly reflective people and investigated the ethical ramifications of what they were doing while doing it; the adoption process as they understood it left them feeling uneasy.

Compared to adoption, it seemed to this conscientious couple that AID (Artificial Insemination with Donor sperm) had no greater ethical risk. The East Bay Fertility Clinic in Berkeley provided the reproductive services that led ultimately to the birth of two children by artificial insemination. The sperm donors for both Emily and Jeffrey are anonymous. I asked Phil if he had any feelings of jealousy regarding the presence of another man's sperm in his wife's body. 'For me it was no big deal,' he said. 'In my mind I'd already separated sexual intercourse from procreation back when I got my vasectomy. I look on the donated sperm as a gift, a gift that made my family possible.'

Martha told me that at first she thought nearly daily about the connection between her egg and the sperm of a strange man, wondering whether or not this might have a dramatic impact down the road. Now, with two youngsters romping around the home, she says she almost never thinks about it any more. Attending to the needs of growing children is totally occupying. She agrees with Phil: the donated sperm is a 'gift'.

The two of them went together for the insemination appointment. 'Everything was ready,' Phil reported and, without pausing, went on to say, 'I held her hand and then they inseminated her.' This matter-of-fact remark deeply impressed me. 'Why did you hold her hand?' I asked. 'Because we needed to show it was the two of us doing this together,' he said. The technology could be impersonal, he went on to explain, but these children are 'the product of our relationship' regardless of the means of fertilization.

While a seminary student in Berkeley, Martha read widely in feminist literature, being influenced in particular by the relational epistemology and ethics of Carol Gilligan.[2] I asked whether the coldness or impersonalness of the reproductive technology was disruptive to the relational dimension of her life. The answer was quite to the contrary. She stressed that she and Phil had employed the technology as a means whereby the existing marital relationship could be enhanced by incorporating a relationship to children.

So far, so good. Now, the story gets considerably more complicated. Emily, the first born, is a healthy happy child, who could be the apple of any parent's eye. Jeffrey, equally loved and treasured by his parents, is finding life somewhat more difficult to negotiate. He has a genetic disorder known as Williams Syndrome.

Affecting perhaps one in 20 000 newborns, Williams Syndrome is a genetic defect due to a missing piece of chromosome seven. Missing here is the gene producing the protein elastin that gives strength and elasticity to vessel walls. This condition is the result of a spontaneous mutation. Symptoms typically include congenital heart defects, slow physical development, mild mental retardation (IQ around 70), shortness of stature, propensity for high blood pressure, and loose joints. It is difficult for three-year-old Jeffrey to run straight down the hall without falling to one side or the other. Because knowledge of Williams Syndrome is relatively new – it was only identified in 1961 – not enough is known to predict life span. What is known is that some persons with Williams Syndrome are currently in their sixties. Very few persons with Williams, it is assumed, will ever develop to where they can live and support themselves independently. Jeffrey is likely to be dependent upon his parents for support for his entire life. Now, we might ask, who will live longer?

A century or two ago, a child born with Williams Syndrome, then unidentified as such, might have simply appeared as the weakling in the family. Many such children might not have survived beyond the postnatal period, and those who did certainly would not outlive their parents. They probably did not live long enough to procreate and pass the mutated chromosome seven on to another generation. But, with the aid of recent advances in medical technology, Jeffrey may outlive the parents upon whom he depends for support. Who will care for Jeffrey in his old age? What if Jeffrey as a young man decides to procreate, and what if he passes his defective chromosome seven on to another generation? He would have a 50/50 chance of doing so. Who will care for the two generations of dependants?

I probed Phil to see if he might be holding a grudge against the man who donated the sperm. 'No,' he said. He could not resent the donor. Because Williams Syndrome results from a spontaneous mutation, it is not necessarily the case that the donor actually passed the defective DNA on to Jeffrey. Nevertheless, the geneticist reported the problem to the clinic, asking that the donor be told what had happened in the event that this news might influence decisions to donate in the future.

When Martha was pregnant with Jeffrey, she underwent prenatal genetic screening. The test showed no known genetic defects in the fetus. At that time, no test for Williams Syndrome existed, so prenatal knowledge of this disease was impossible. I asked the couple a speculative question, 'If you had known at the time of genetic screening that Jeffrey would be born with Williams Syndrome, would you have seriously considered an abortion?'

This was a disturbing question, which Martha acknowledged. 'Maybe,' she conceded, 'but I'm really glad that I did not have to face that decision at that time. Now that we have Jeffrey and love him, I could not conceive of not having him in our family. If I could decide now what to do back then, I would not have an abortion.'

'Did you make the right decision to pursue your family through reproductive technology?' I asked as a global question. Martha answered affirmatively and confidently. Phil too was affirmative. Then, he added a piece of philosophical wisdom he had gained from theologian Joseph Sittler that he thought applied to their situation: 'Make a decision and then offer up a prayer.'

Libertarian Choice v. Egalitarian Values

The reproductive adventure of this family is packed with fascinating ethical issues, but our focus here is on one: choice. Advancing technology opened up new possibilities for Martha and Phil to create a family. Had they decided not to avail themselves of AID, this would have been a choice to frustrate a strong desire and commitment. Fully cognizant of what they were getting into, they decided to follow through with AID and accept the puzzling risks by committing themselves unconditionally to loving the children that would come into their family. Whether sitting still or taking action, they had choice. This situation leads University of Texas law professor John A. Robertson to exclaim:

> Like Caesar crossing the Rubicon, there is no turning back from the technical control that we now have over human reproduction. The decision to have or not have children is, at some important level, no longer a matter of God or nature, but has been made subject to human will and technical expertise. It is now a matter of choice whether persons reproduce now or later, whether they overcome infertility, whether their children have certain genetic characteristics, or whether they use their reproductive capacity to produce tissue for transplant or embryos and fetuses for research.[3]

Thrilled with the opportunities provided by technological advance, Robertson exhibits a touch of *hubris* in taking what used to be 'a matter of God or nature' and subjecting it to 'human will and technical expertise'. Robertson's colossal mistake, in my judgment, is to ignore the fact that technology in the modern world has a life and a power of its own; so it is unlikely that we humans will subject it completely to 'human will'. Nevertheless, he is right when he says that the flooding of new reproductive technology inundates us with choice. We are becoming overwhelmed by choice. We have no choice but to swim in a sea of choice.

When it comes to issues of choice, the American ethical psyche is schizoid. Like two house cats who sometimes hiss competitively and at other times nap together in a single ball of fur, Americans operate out of two ethical visions – the libertarian and the egalitarian – that sometimes compete and at other times complement. On the one hand, American culture is deeply committed to the libertarian vision which maximizes individual liberty, which assumes that each of us is born free and that the ethical or political task is to prevent criminals or government from eclipsing this freedom. Despite the fact that these values derive from the liberal vision of the 18th-century Enlightenment, many today call this the conservative position. In complementary contrast, the egalitarian vision assumes that, regardless of how we are born, we are imprisoned by cultural prejudices, economic forces or political structures, so that the ethical and political task of government is to liberate, to set us free. Legislation and law enforcement on behalf of equal opportunity or equal access to resources is the primary method for the egalitarians. Also, deriving from the Enlightenment vision of a better world, today we dub this the liberal position. It is my judgment that both the conservative–libertarian and the liberal–egalitarian camps need to attend to the threat of commodification and to defend the dignity of children.

Procreative Liberty: the Libertarian View

Robertson, mentioned above, belongs squarely in the libertarian camp. He advocates a comprehensive philosophy he calls *procreative liberty*. At its most general level, procreative liberty refers to the freedom either to have children or to avoid having them. Even though the freedom to choose whether or not to have a child is most frequently exercised by couples, Robertson is well aware that he is cultivating a rights-based political philosophy rooted in modern individualism. It follows that procreative liberty belongs not just to traditional married couples, but also to gay and lesbian couples or even individuals.

What about the risk of commodification? He notes that the Human Genome Initiative will increase the capacity to screen out undesirable traits 'by identifying new genes for carrier and prenatal testing, including, potentially, genes for alcoholism, homosexuality, and depression'.[4] We already test fetuses *in utero* for such things as cystic fibrosis or Down's syndrome and screen out the unhealthy ones by aborting those with defective genes. This method is also used to discriminate between genders, usually resulting in the aborting of female fetuses. In the future, through selective abortion or the more sophisticated selection of embryos *in vitro*, couples will be able to engage in quality control by screening out potential children with undesirable genes. Past experience teaches clearly that 'most affected fetuses will be discarded based on a judgment of fitness, worth, or parental convenience'.[5] Because abortion is currently the most simple method of selection, these developments will make all pregnancies 'tentative' until prenatal screening certifies that the fetus is acceptable.

The question of commodification arises at this point. Parental choice may mean that criteria such as fitness, worth and convenience will determine which, if any, children will see the light of day. 'The danger is that selection methods will commodify children in a way ultimately harmful to their welfare. Carried to an extreme, parents will discard less than "perfect" children and engineer embryos and fetuses for enhanced qualities. A worst-case scenario envisages repressive political regimes using these techniques to create a government-controlled Brave New World of genetically engineered social classes.'[6]

Yet, after alerting us to the dangers of commodification, Robertson returns to his defense of individual liberty: 'The perceived dangers of "quality control" appear to be insufficient to remove these choices from the discretion of persons planning to reproduce.'[7] Unless we can establish on a case-by-case basis that harm will be done to someone other than the planning parents, the presumptive right to procreative choice requires social and legal protection. It is Robertson's view that no religious ideals or cultural norms regarding family life are sufficient to justify restricting procreative liberty.

This doctrine of procreative liberty also seeks to protect the right to refuse to use the new technologies. Public action to prevent the birth of genetically defective or disabled offspring by mandatory means – a potential public threat, as the current debate over community rating of health care insurance reveals – is not justified. Families should be permitted to have children the old-fashioned way, relying on the luck of the genetic draw, and still retain their rightful place in the communal health care system. The result will be some couples employing the new reproductive technologies to the maximum, with others continuing to accept the roll of the procreative dice.

The Relational Challenge to Individual Choice: the Egalitarian View

Robertson represents the libertarian side of the current values debate. On the egalitarian side we find the nuanced position of Lisa Sowle Cahill. A feminist and a Roman Catholic ethicist at Boston College, Cahill challenges the ideology of choice because it isolates the individual from society. Reproductive libertarianism leaves decisions about whether and how to combine intentional meanings with biological ones strictly to individuals and protects them with policies of informed consent. Cahill's own position is that a family ethic based on biological kinship ought not to be replaced by an ethic based solely on choice.[8]

Cahill charges that practices such as donor insemination, *in vitro* fertilization with donor gametes and surrogate motherhood depend upon questionable assumptions: that choice is a universal and nearly absolute value; that individuals alone have the right to choose whether and how to recognize other moral values, such as the value of a biological relation to one's child; that trading with a donor who may be uninterested in a social relation to a child to which he or she is a co-parent is legitimized solely by its instrumental value; and that a biological asymmetry of the family parents' relation to the child will normally make no difference in family ecology. 'The end result socially and morally,' she fears, 'is a dearth of resistance to patriarchal socializations of embodiment, including men's need for guarantees of biological paternity; women's social and self-definition through motherhood; the sale of gametes, embryos, and, in surrogacy, children; as well as the services of economically disadvantaged women.'[9]

What is needed to redress this situation? Cahill recommends a re-evaluation of intersubjectivity and biology as together normative for sex, marriage, parenthood and family, a re-evaluation in which biology is a subordinate but important and protected meaning in these social relations. The challenge she sees is one of reinstating the connection between the unitive and procreative dimensions of sexuality, to affirm embodiment of sexuality through the bodies of mother and father as well as children, and to make this affirmation in the context of gender equality. What she advocates here places us in the middle of the argument being pressed by the Vatican, a conversation we will return to following some observations about the dignity of children.

Dignity Conferred and Dignity Claimed

It is not my intention here to resolve the dispute between the libertarians and the egalitarians; yet, the dispute is instructive for two reasons. First, both represent deeply held ethical convictions in American culture and, in the case

of Lisa Cahill, theological convictions as well. Second, both disputing parties
are responding to one thing: choice. Whether we like it or not, choice has
arrived on our doorstep.

Whether we want to invite choice to come further into our family home or
whether we try to keep it outside, my message to both libertarians and
egalitarians is this: *God loves each of us regardless of our genetic makeup, and we
should do likewise.* This is my proposed application of 1 John 4:11: 'Beloved,
since God loved us so much, we also ought to love one another.' Among the
ways God has manifested divine love toward us is the ministry of the incarnate
Son that took him to the most humble of persons in first-century Israel, the
beggars, the lepers, those crippled or blind from birth, and to social outcasts
such as adulterers or traitorous tax collectors. In addition, Jesus spoke over the
stern objections of his disciples when he uttered the words, 'Let the little
children come to me, and do not stop them; for it is to such as these that the
kingdom of heaven belongs' (Matt. 19:14).

Among its many benefits, love creates dignity in the beloved. To be the
object of someone's love is to be made to feel valuable, to feel worth. Once you
or I feel this sense of worth imputed to us by the one who loves us, we may then
begin to own it. We may begin to claim self-worth. Worth is first imputed, then
it is claimed.

It is often assumed that human dignity is innate, that it is inborn. Legally,
this makes sense, because such a dignity doctrine permits us in court to defend
the rights of every individual regardless of how humble he or she might be. But
phenomenologically, this view is mistaken. Dignity, at least the sense of dignity
understood as self-worth, is not simply inborn. Rather, it is the fruit of a
relationship, a continuing loving relationship. A newborn welcomed into the
world by a mother and father who provide attention and affection develops a
self-consciousness that incorporates this attention and affection as evidence of
self-worth. As consciousness becomes constituted, this sense of worth can be
claimed for oneself, and individual dignity develops.

Dignity has a proleptic as well as a relational structure – that is, it is
fundamentally future-oriented. The conferring of dignity on someone who does
not yet in fact experience or claim it is a gesture of hope, an act that anticipates
what we hope will be a future actuality. Martha and Phil conferred dignity
upon their children-to-be through the loving devotion that motivated the
extraordinary means they took to bring them into the world. They continue to
confer dignity daily by treating their children, regardless of their children's
health, with a love that says: 'You're very valuable!' What Martha and Phil
hope is that, in the future, when Emily and Jeffrey become more mature, these
two will claim that sense of dignity for themselves.

Our final dignity, from the point of view of the Christian faith, is
eschatological; it accompanies our fulfillment of the image of God. Rather
than something with which we are born that may or may not become socially
manifest, dignity is the future end product of God's saving activity which we
anticipate socially when we confer dignity on those who do not yet claim it. The
ethics of God's kingdom in our time and in our place consists of conferring
dignity and inviting persons to claim dignity as a prolepsis of its future fulfillment.

How does dignity function ethically? By 'dignity' here I mean the Enlightenment notion that a human person should be treated as an end and not merely as a means to some further end. There is nothing in this world we may value more highly than the existence and welfare of a human person. Yet human dignity understood this way may be under threat. The threat arises from the commodification of children owing to the commodification of so many things surrounding the making of children. As the industry of reproductive technology expands in the free market, are we likely to treat the products – the babies being born – like other products we purchase, namely, as commodities we choose by taste and then consume if they please us? Or, will we be able to differentiate between products and persons, consuming the former and loving the latter?

Dignity for Persons or Dignity for Sex?

Perhaps it is a curiosity, but at this point in history it is the Vatican that champions the cause of human dignity for the world. I suggest that it is a curiosity because we normally identify the Enlightenment as the torch bearer for dignity, noting that Enlightenment humanism precipitated a vigorous conservative reaction by the Roman Catholic Church during the late 19th and early 20th centuries. But, now the baton has been passed, and it is the church who sees herself struggling to keep the dignity lamp lit as the fierce winds of impersonal technology and postmodernist relativism threaten to blow it out. Pope John Paul II warns us that in the world today 'the criterion of dignity – which demands respect, generosity and service – is replaced by the criterion of efficiency, functionality and usefulness [and this amounts to] the supremacy of the strong over the weak'.[10]

Perhaps, at this point, I should make clear where I stand regarding the forceful positions taken recently by the Vatican. In *Donum vitae*, otherwise known as *Instruction on Respect for Human Life in Its Origin and on the Dignity of Procreation*, the Vatican's Congregation for the Doctrine of the Faith appeals to dignity as its fundamental anthropological principle.[11] Our dignity is established because we are persons who are 'endowed with a spiritual soul and with moral responsibility, and who are called to beatific communion with God'. Dignity elicits an ethic of 'respect, defense and promotion' of human being. On this basis, argues *Donum Vitae*, each person has a 'primary and fundamental right' to life.

The distinctively theological foundation for positing human dignity here is an assumed doctrine of creationism. This term, 'creationism', ought not to be confused here with the fundamentalist Protestant school arguing for a six-day creation in opposition to standard theories of evolution. Rather, in the context of *Instruction*, it is the doctrine that God creates *de nihilo* a fresh soul for each human person at conception.[12] The document is clear: the 'spiritual soul' of each person is 'immediately created' by God.[13] Human life is sacred because from the beginning – that is, from conception – it involves the creative action of God and remains forever in special relation to God. God is Lord from beginning to end, even to the end that never ends. It follows that no one can claim the right to destroy what God has created for eternity.

It follows further from this affirmation of human dignity that science and technology must be oriented toward serving human dignity. Science and technology are valuable resources, to be sure. But, when it comes to values, they are dumb. In themselves they cannot show us the meaning of existence or call us to moral responsibility. 'Thus science and technology require, for their own intrinsic meaning, an unconditional respect for the fundamental criteria of the moral law; that is to say, they must be at the service of the human person, of his inalienable rights and his true and integral good according to the design and will of God.'[14] Such an assertion is more than a mere philosophical observation. Revealing the foreboding anxiety that must have led to the writing of this document, its authors announce that 'science without conscience' will only lead to our ruin. The task of the church becomes, then, one of providing science with a conscience.

From the Vatican's point of view, not only does the human person as an individual have dignity, so also does the act of sexual intercourse have dignity. I find this to be a non sequitur. Yet, the Vatican argues that the event in which God intervenes in human affairs to deposit a soul in the fertilized zygote imputes dignity not only to the zygote, but also to the act of sexual intercourse that brought sperm and ovum into proximity. This is important to note: not only do persons have dignity, so also do certain acts have dignity, in this instance the act of sexual intercourse. This is the assumption that comes to the fore when *Donum vitae* prohibits the most innocent of the possible reproductive techniques, homologous techniques such as artificial insemination with the husband's sperm (AIH) or embryo transfer to the mother of her egg fertilized *in vitro* (ET).

> A homologous IVF and ET procedure that is free of any compromise with the abortive practice of destroying embryos and with masturbation, remains a technique which is morally illicit because it deprives human procreation of the dignity which is proper and connatural to it.[15]

Because the conjugal sex act retains its own independent dignity, it takes on moral valiance going in two directions. In one direction, if a married couple engages in sexual intercourse then they must avoid contraception and embrace openness to forces that transcend them that determine if they will procreate a child. In the other direction, a married couple ought not to pursue bringing a child into their family by any means other than sexual intercourse. I find it notable that through some slippage in logic the understandable dignity that should accrue to a human person suddenly applies not to a person but to an act.

Returning to the dignity of the child conceived, the Vatican combines the forces of grace and exhortation in support of the love of children.

> Although the manner in which human conception is achieved with IVF and ET cannot be approved, every child which comes into the world must in any case be accepted as a living gift of the divine Goodness and must be brought up with love.[16]

Although I am grateful to the Vatican for including this final exhortation to love children regardless of their procreative origin, I believe the unquestioned connection between the sex act and the making of a baby needs to be questioned. With the advent of improved birth control methods in the 1960s and now the exploding frontier of advancing reproductive technologies, increased choice means increased separation between sex and baby making. That the quality of sexual love enjoyed by two parents might indirectly affect the atmosphere of love in a child's household is a connection that will perdure, to be sure. But the connection between a specific sex act and the bringing of a child into the world is becoming less and less necessary. To make an ethical argument that borrows moral capital from the rich idea of human dignity and tries to make it pay duty on the moral purchase of the sex act is a form of ethical embezzlement.

It seems to me that, if we press the notion of human dignity as an ethical principle to help us forage through the jungle of reproductive technology and if we acknowledge that the connection between sexual intercourse and baby making will in the future lose its sense of necessity, then we will have to find another basis for establishing the value of sexual bonding. Sexual intercourse is not justifiable solely on the grounds that it makes babies. It must have some other more independent value. Perhaps this other value is intuitively obvious; but those of us afflicted with ethical minds find we must try to spell out what is obvious, noting that we then discover that it may not have been so obvious after all. The obvious value of sex is that it is fun. But many things are fun, and fun all by itself is insufficient to justify such a complicated phenomenon as sexual relationship. Love is involved too, and love elicits the interest of theologians.

Sexual Love and the Love of Children

Theologically, the Vatican does not have a patent on justifying ethically the value of sexual relationship. The turn of the century Russian Orthodox theologian Vladimir Solovyev offers an alternative. He emphasized that human loving has the capacity to lift the self up and go beyond itself. Love, especially sexual love, has the power to overcome egoism and self-centeredness. 'Love is of importance,' he writes, 'not only as one of our feelings, but as the transfer of all our interest in life from ourselves to another, as the shifting of the very center of our personal life. This is characteristic of every kind of love, but *par excellence* of sex-love; it is distinguished from other kinds of love by greater intensity, by a more engrossing character, and by the possibility of more complete all-around reciprocity.'[17]

What is the relation of such love to the begetting of children? Because sexual love has a beauty and value in and of itself, the making of babies, as important as it is, is by no means entailed in the love relationship of a man and a woman. 'The coincidence of a strong passion of love with the successful begetting of children is merely fortuitous,' says Solovyev, 'and even so is sufficiently rare; historical and everyday experience proves beyond doubt that children may be successfully begotten, ardently loved, and excellently brought up by their parents, though these latter should never have been in love with each other.'[18] What Solovyev wants to demonstrate here is that love between parents is a most valuable thing, and its value is intrinsic, independent of its connection to giving birth to children. I appreciate this point, and I would like to go on to stress the other side of the equation, namely, that our love for children is independent of its connection to sexual love and even to such things as biological inheritance or reproductive technology.

Notes

1   Resolve, Inc., P.O. Box 474, Belmont, MA 02178.
2   Carol Gilligan, *In a Different Voice: Psychological Theory and Women's Development* (Cambridge: Harvard University Press, 1982).
3   John A. Robertson, *Children of Choice: Freedom and the New Reproductive Technologies* (Princeton: Princeton University Press, 1994), 5.
4   Ibid., 150.
5   Ibid., 151.
6   Ibid., 150.
7   Ibid., 151.
8   Lisa Sowle Cahill, *Sex, and Gender, and Christian Ethics* (Cambridge: Cambridge University Press, 1996), chapter VIII.
9   Ibid.
10 Pope John Paul II, *The Gospel of Life* (New York: Random House, Times Books, 1995), 42.
11 Congregation for the Doctrine of the Faith, *Instruction on Respect for Human Life in Its Origin and on the Dignity of Procreation: Replies to Certain Questions of the Day*, Introduction: 1–2; in Thomas A. Shannon, *Bioethics* (New York: Paulist, 3rd edn, 1987). See also Thomas A. Shannon and Lisa Sowle Cahill, *Religion and Artificial Reproduction* (New York: Crossroad, 1988).
12 Creationism, referring to the creation of the soul at conception (or, according to some views, at birth), has been upheld since the days of Jerome in opposition to two alternative views, pre-existence and traducianism (sometimes called generationism). Origen and others held that each soul pre-exists and becomes incarnate at birth. Traducianists such as Tertullian and Gregory of Nyssa held that the human soul is transmitted by parents to children, usually through the physical act of generation. Pope John Paul II is a creationist in this sense of the term.
13 *Instruction*, Introduction: 5, in Shannon, *Bioethics*, 3rd edn, 595.
14 *Instruction*, Introduction 1–2, in Shannon, *Bioethics*, 3rd edn, 591–2.
15 *Instruction* II, A, 5; in Shannon, *Bioethics*, 3rd edn, 609.
16 Ibid.
17 Vladimir Solovyev, *The Meaning of Love*, tr. by Jane Marshall (London: Geoffrey Bles, The Centenary Press, 1945), 30.
18 Ibid., 31.

Chapter 12

Playing God and Germline Intervention

Should we 'play God' with the human germline? Should we intervene in human germ cells so as to alter the genetic makeup of future generations not yet born? Does such intervention into the future of DNA betray excessive human confidence – pride or *hubris* – and constitute a violation of the sacred? Some scientists and religious spokespersons say 'yes' and are trying to shut the door to germline enhancement and tack up a sign reading, 'Thou shalt not play God'.

Our task here will be to examine arguments regarding germline therapy and enhancement, especially the arguments raised by the Council for Responsible Genetics in its 'Position Paper on Human Germ Line Manipulation'.[1] We will also look briefly at the Christian theology of creation, including anthropology and the notion that the human race is created in the divine image. I will argue that, if we understand God's creative activity as giving the world a future, and if we understand the human being as a created co-creator, ethics begins with envisioning a better future. This suggests we should at minimum keep the door open to improving the human genetic lot. The derisive use of the phrase, 'play God', should not deter us from shouldering our responsibility for the future.[2] To seek a better future is to 'play human' as God intends us to.[3]

My position is not that of a strong advocate for germline intervention. I take the much more modest position of holding the door open to the prospect of intervening in the germline on the grounds that the arguments against it to date are unconvincing. This chapter argues for an *open door* rather than a *closed door* policy.

The Human Genome Project and Germline Intervention

The issue of 'playing God' for good or ill comes to the forefront of discussion in our time owing in large part to the enormous impact of the Human Genome Project on the biological and even the social sciences. Descriptively, we know the stated purposes directing the Human Genome Project as currently conceived. First, its aim is knowledge. The simple goal that drives all pure science is present here, namely, the desire to know. In this case, it is the desire to know the sequence of the base pairs and the location of the genes in the human genome. Second, its aim is better human health. The avowed ethical goal is to employ the newly acquired knowledge in further research to provide therapy for the many genetically caused diseases that plague the human family.

John Fletcher and W. French Anderson put it eloquently: 'Human gene therapy is a symbol of hope in a vast sea of human suffering due to heredity.'[4] As this second health-oriented purpose is pursued, the technology for manipulating genes will be developed and questions regarding human creativity will arise. How should this creativity be directed?

Virtually no one contests the principle that new genetic knowledge should be used to improve human health and relieve suffering. Yet a serious debate has arisen that distinguishes sharply between therapy for suffering persons who already exist and the health of future persons who do not yet exist. It is the debate between somatic therapy and germline therapy. By 'somatic therapy' we refer to the treatment of a disease in the body cells of a living individual by trying to repair an existing defect. It consists of inserting new segments of DNA into already differentiated cells such as are found in the liver, muscle or blood. Clinical trials are underway to use somatic modification as therapy for people suffering from diabetes, hypertension and Adenosine Deaminase Deficiency. By 'germline therapy', however, we refer to intervention into the germ cells that would influence heredity and, it is hoped, improve the quality of life for future generations.[5] Negatively, germline intervention might help to eliminate deleterious genes that dispose us to disease. Positively, though at present well beyond our technical capacity, such intervention might actually enhance human health, intelligence or strength.

Two issues overlap here and should be sifted out for clarity. One is the issue of somatic intervention versus germline intervention. The other is the issue of therapy versus enhancement. Although somatic treatment is usually identified with therapy and germline treatment with enhancement, there are occasions where somatic treatment enhances, such as injecting growth hormones to enhance height for playing basketball. And germline intervention, at least in its initial stages of development, will aim at preventive medicine. The science of enhancement, if it comes at all, will only come later.

Every ethical interpreter I have reviewed agrees that somatic therapy is morally desirable and looks forward to the advances gene research will bring for expanding this important medical work. Yet, many who reflect on the ethical implications of the new genetic research stop short of germline intervention for therapeutic purposes and especially oppose genetic selection and manipulation for the purposes of improving the human species.[6] Enhancement implies eugenics. The growing power to control the human genetic makeup could foster the emergence of the image of the 'perfect child' or a 'super strain' of humanity. Some religious leaders worry that the impact of the social value of perfection will begin to oppress all those who fall short. Ethicists at the March 1992 conference on 'Genetics, Religion and Ethics' held at the Texas Medical Center in Houston held the following:

> Because the Jewish and Christian religious world-view is grounded in the equality and dignity of individual persons, genetic diversity is respected. Any move to eliminate or reduce human diversity in the interest of eugenics or creating a 'super strain' of human being will meet with resistance.[7]

In sum, recent ethical thinking tends to be conservative in the sense that it seeks to conserve the present pool of genes in the human genome for the indefinite future.

Now the question of 'playing God' begins to take on concrete form. The risk of exerting human creativity through germline intervention is in part that the end may not justify the means. Though we begin with the best of intentions – a beneficent goal of reducing human suffering or enhancing the quality of life – the means to achieve that goal may include negative repercussions that escape our control. Physically, our genetic engineering may disturb the strength-giving qualities of biodiversity that supposedly contributes to human health. Owing to our inability to see the whole range of interconnected factors, we may inadvertently disturb some sort of existing balance in nature and this disturbance could rebound deleteriously. If this were the only objection to germline intervention, we could simply postpone it until scientific knowledge grows sufficiently to account for what today is unforeseen.[8]

Those opposed to 'playing God' do not just question the means, but implicitly doubt the end. They assume that, by bettering the human genome through preventive intervention or especially through enhancement, we would create an unacceptable social situation. Germline alteration to eliminate defective genes or to enhance human potential would contribute to stigma and discrimination. The very proffering of criteria to determine just what counts as a 'defective' gene may lead to stigmatizing all those persons who carry that gene. The very proffering of the image of the ideal child or a super strain of humanity may cultivate a sense of inferiority in those who do not measure up. To embark on a large-scale program of germline therapy or enhancement may create physical and social problems, and then we would blame the human race for its pride, its *hubris*, its stepping beyond its alleged God-defined limits. The result of such thinking is a prematurely closed door to the prospect of germline intervention.

One of my concerns is to ask: just how might theological considerations be brought to bear? The fact that the phrase 'playing God' is frequently used seems to warrant pursuing this question.

Relevant to germline intervention is the following. The correlate concepts of God as the creator and the human as the created co-creator orient us toward the future, a future that should be better than the past or present. One of the problems with conservative arguments is that they implicitly assume that the present state of affairs is adequate. These arguments tacitly bless the status quo. The problem with the status quo is that it is filled with human misery, some of which is genetically caused. The present time is characterized as a 'vast sea of human suffering due to heredity'. Granting that opponents of germline intervention may be guided by non-maleficence and beneficence regarding the welfare of the human race, their premature door closing constitutes an inadvertent acceptance of a present reality that is in need of transformation.

What we should emphasize, I believe, is that it is possible for us to envision a better future in therapeutic categories: a future in which individuals would not have to suffer the consequences of genes such as those for cystic fibrosis, Alzheimer's or Huntington's disease. It is even possible for us to envision a future in which human potential is enhanced. That we should be cautious and prudent to recognize the threat of human *hubris*, I fully grant. However, our ethical vision cannot acquiesce with present reality; it must press on to a still better future and employ human creativity with its accompanying genetic technology to move us toward that end.

Germline Enhancement: a Closer Look

Let us take a closer look at the arguments involved. In 1991, *The Journal of Medicine and Philosophy* took up the concerns surrounding germline intervention, and Eric Juengst summarized five arguments in favor of germline modification for the purposes of therapy.

> (1) *Medical utility*: germline gene therapy offers a true cure for many genetic diseases.
> (2) *Medical necessity*: such therapy is the only effective way to address some diseases.
> (3) *Prophylactic efficiency*: prevention is less costly and less risky than cure.
> (4) *Respect for parental autonomy* when parents request germline intervention.
> (5) *Scientific freedom* to engage in germline inquiry.

Juengst also summarized five arguments opposing germline intervention.

> (1) *Scientific uncertainty and risks* to future generations.
> (2) *Slippery slope to enhancement* that could exacerbate social discrimination.
> (3) *Consent of future generations* is impossible to get.
> (4) *Allocation of resources*: germline therapy may never be cost-effective.
> (5) *Integrity of genetic patrimony*: future generations have the right to inherit a genetic endowment that has not been intentionally modified.[9]

In order to engage the issue in some detail and to test the above-mentioned theological commitment, I turn our attention to a representative case in point, namely, the position paper drafted by the Council for Responsible Genetics (CRG) in the Fall of 1992.[10] The CRG proffers three types of argument in opposition to germline modification in humans: a technical argument, a slanderous argument and an ethical argument.

The first argument against germline manipulation is technical. Although the motive for modifying germ genes may be the enhancement of human well-being for future generations, unexpected deleterious consequences may result. Removal of an unwanted disease gene may not eliminate the possibility that other gene combinations will be created that will be harmful. Inadvertent damage could result from biologists' inability to predict just how genes or their products interact with one another and with the environment.

> Inserting new segments of DNA into the germ line could have major, unpredictable consequences for both the individual and the future of the species that include the introduction of susceptibilities to cancer and other disease into the human gene pool.

It would seem to the prudent observer that we should take a wait-and-see attitude, that we move cautiously as the technology develops. The problem of unexpected consequences is one that confronts all long-term planning and in itself should not deter research and experimentation guided by a vision of a healthier humanity.[11]

The second argument appeals to guilt by association and is thereby slanderous. The CRG Human Genetics Committee says, 'the doctrine of social advancement through biological perfectibility underlying the new eugenics is almost indistinguishable from the older version so avidly embraced by the Nazis'. The structure of this argument is that, because germline modification can be associated with eugenics and because eugenics can be associated with Nazism, therefore, we can associate proponents of germline enhancement with the Nazis and, on this ground, should reject it. The argument borders on the *ad hominem* (circumstantial) fallacy.

One problem is that the CRG argument is too glib, failing to discern the complexities here. The eugenics movement of the late 19th and early 20th centuries was originally a socially progressive movement that embraced the ideals of a better society. In England and America, it became tied to ethnocentrism and the blindness of class interests, leading to forced sterilization of feeble-minded prisoners. It was eventually discarded because advances in genetics proved it unscientific.[12] In Germany, the eugenics movement became tied to anti-Semitism, resulting in the racial hygiene (*Rassenhygiene*) program of the Nazi SS and the atrocities of the so-called 'final solution'.[13] With this history in mind, the present generation must assuredly be on guard against future programs of 'ethnic hygiene' which seem to plague the human species in one form or another every century. Yet, we must observe that ethnocentric bias in England and America and the rise of Nazism in Germany were social phenomena that employed eugenics for their respective ends. Eugenics was not the source of injustice, even if it was a weapon in the service of injustice. The CRG's use of the volatile word 'Nazi' in this discussion of germline enhancement is an attempt to paint their opponents in such a repulsive color that no one will view the matter open-mindedly.

The third CRG argument, the ethical argument, is much more worthy of serious consideration. The central thesis here is that germline modification will reinforce existing social discrimination. The position paper declares,

> The cultural impact of treating humans as biologically perfectible artifacts would be entirely negative. People who fall short of some technically achievable ideal would increasingly be seen as 'damaged goods'. And it is clear that the standards for what is genetically desirable will be those of the society's economically and politically dominant groups. This will only reinforce prejudices and discrimination in a society where they already exist.[14]

Let us look at this argument in terms of its component parts. The assumption in the first sentence is that germline intervention implies biological perfectibility and, on account of this, that human persons will be treated as artifacts. It is of course plausible that a social construction of the perfect child or the perfected human strain might appear in Saturday morning cartoons and other cultural forms. Yet, this does not seem to apply to the actual situation in which genetic scientists currently find themselves. They are occupied with much more modest aspirations such as protection from monogenetic diseases such as cystic fibrosis. The medical technology here is not much beyond infancy. At this point in technological history we do not find ourselves on the brink of designer children or the advent of a super strain. What is 'genetically desirable' is by no means scientifically attainable. Thus Hessel Bouma and his colleagues are less worried than the CRG because they recognize that the technological possibility of creating a genetically perfect human race is still very remote.

> Things like intelligence and strength are not inherited through single genes but through multifactorial conditions, combinations of inherited genes and numerous environmental factors. Our ability to control and to design is limited by the complexity of many traits, so there are seemingly insurmountable technological and economic barriers that weaken the empirical slippery-slope argument that we are sliding into the genetic engineering of our children.[15]

Continuing our analysis of the ethical argument, the CRG rightly alerts us to the social psychology of feeling like 'damaged goods' and being treated like 'damaged goods'. If a 'technically achievable ideal' should become a cultural norm, then those who fail to meet the norm would understandably feel inferior.[16] Furthermore, the economically and politically advantaged groups will help to steer the definition of the ideal norm to serve their own class interests.[17] Here, the CRG should be applauded for alerting us to a possible loss of human dignity.

At this point a reaffirmation of human dignity is called for, I believe, wherein each individual person is treated as having the full complement of rights regardless of his or her genes. Ethical support here comes from the Christian doctrine of creation, wherein God made men and women in the divine image and pronounced them 'good' (Genesis 1:26–31). It also comes from the ministry of Jesus, wherein the Son of God sought out the outcasts, the lame, the infirm, the possessed – surely those who were considered the 'damaged goods' of first-century Palestine – for divine favor and healing.[18] Each human being, regardless of health or social location or genetic endowment, is loved by God, and this recognition should translate into social equality and mutual appreciation. There is no theological justification for thinking of some persons as inferior to others, and new technical possibilities in genetics ought not to change this.

We also note the CRG's prognostication for the future: germline modification 'will only reinforce prejudices and discrimination in a society where they already exist'. Prejudices and discrimination exist in the present, says the CRG. This is an obvious fact I readily concede. Does it follow, however, that germline intervention 'will only reinforce' them? No, for two reasons. The word 'only' ignores the obvious physical benefits to those whose lives are made better by this technique. In addition, we must note that prejudice and discrimination seem to flourish quite well without germline manipulation. The existence of the former cannot simply count as an argument against the latter.

If the argument rests on the premise that germline enhancement will create a technical ideal achievable by some but not others, it fails on the grounds of triviality. This could apply to countless ideals in our society. We daily confront innumerable ideals that are met by some but not all, whether they be athletic achievements, beauty trophies, professional promotions or lottery winnings. These may elicit temporary feelings of inferiority on the part of those who come in second or further behind, but they are widely ignored by those who did not compete. Given the realistic prospects for germline intervention, the new situation would not alter the present situation in this respect. If it is technically possible to relieve some individuals from suffering the consequences of diabetes through the regular use of insulin, the achievement of this ideal by those afflicted by diabetes leads to only gratitude on their part and on the part of those who love them. Somatic cell therapy or even germline modification for diabetes will only extend this gratitude. To those who are not afflicted or likely to be afflicted by diabetes, this achievement may be applauded from a distance, or perhaps ignored.

One could envision a next step, of course, where germline intervention could, if made universally available, eliminate the likes of diabetes from the human gene pool. We would then have a future wiped clean of genetically based diabetes. If this constituted an achieved ideal for the whole human race, and if the unexpected consequences were less harmful than diabetes, many will have been spared the suffering diabetes could have caused and no reinforcement of prejudice and discrimination will have occurred.

What if we were to falter somewhere along the way? Suppose we began a worldwide program to eliminate the disposition to diabetes from the human gene pool, achieved success in some family, ethnic or class groups, and then, owing to lack of funding, support or other factors, had to abandon the project. What would happen to those individuals who still carried the deleterious gene? Would they suffer stigma or discrimination? Perhaps. The CRG rightly alerts us to such a possibility. Yet, we might ask, does this prospect provide sufficient warrant to shut down the research and prohibit embarking on such a plan? I do not believe so.

Intergenerational Genethics

The CRG buttresses the central ethical argument with two subarguments. One is that the present generation, presumably the one engaging in germline modification, cannot be held accountable by future generations for the wrongful damage we inflict on them. We, our progeny's ancestors, will not be around any more to be accountable. There may be an equivocation at work here. On the one hand, the present generation will be absent in the future and, therefore, we cannot be held accountable in the sense that we cannot be punished by imprisonment. On the other hand, though absent, we can be held accountable in the sense that future fingers could be waved and fists thrown into the air as our progeny express anger at our failure to assume responsibility. Just because we cannot be punished does not mean we are not accountable in a moral sense.

Yet, for the CRG, somehow the concept of accountability is supposed to count against germline enhancement. Again, the argument fails on account of triviality, because our responsibility to our progeny applies across the board to all departments of life. There is nothing special about genes. One might even make a case that environmental responsibility is of graver ethical concern. The excessive depletion of non-renewable natural resources and pollution of the biosphere is due to the hedonism of the present generation, to present selfishness that is willing to sacrifice the welfare of future generations for the prosperity of our own. Germline intervention, in contrast, could be motivated only by seeking benefit for future generations whom we may not live to see. With or without accountability, the latter at least has the virtue of altruism going for it.

The other subargument raises an interesting issue worth pondering. The CRG says: 'Germline modification is not needed in order to save the lives or alleviate suffering of existing people. Its target population are "future people" who have not yet even been conceived.'[19] On the face of it, this argument looks like another brand of defense for the ecological hedonists just mentioned, whose interest is limited to only the present generation without any regard for future progeny. But, this may be a misreading. The CRG is not eliminating completely our responsibility for future generations. Yet, for some unexplained reason, the CRG makes central the distinction between people who exist and people who do not yet exist. The assumption is that moral priority is given to those who exist over against those who have 'not yet even been conceived'. The interesting puzzle is the relative moral status of present and future, existents and not-yets.

Suppose we draw up the previous concern for accountability and combine it with the concepts of rights and wrongful birth. Might future generations blame us today for their wrongful birth by damaging them through germline intervention? Or, in contrast, might they blame us for not intervening in the germline, thereby leaving them to suffer from diseases we could have prevented? We are on the verge of an ethical crisis – that is, on the verge of an ethical challenge where creative action is demanded – because, whether we engage in germline intervention or not, if we are technically capable, we will be morally accountable.

Here the contrast with the environmental crisis is illuminating. We can imagine our great-grandchildren living on a deforested earth, mines depleted of their minerals, lakes dead from acid rain, food supply contaminated by chemicals, skin cancerous owing to excessive ozone exposure, raising their fists in anger at us. They will claim we violated their right to a life-giving environment and, despite what the CRG says, they will claim we are accountable as they burn us in effigy.

Does this apply by analogy to germline modification? We can certainly imagine a future person asserting, 'My parents, grandparents and the genetic scientists of their generation violated my rights by giving me a bad genetic endowment.' It would be a variant on the wrongful birth accusation. Yet, not everyone sees the sense this makes. Hardy Jones, for example, would argue: had this individual's progenitors taken successful steps toward enhancing the genetic endowment of their offspring, this would not be the child they actually had. Having a child with defective genes cannot be a violation of that child's right, because it is not possible to respect that right by not having the child or by bequeathing a different genetic constitution. The only child who can claim a right is one that exists, and the particular configuration of genes is definitional to the person who exists. 'Genetically defective persons are not analogous to existing individuals who subsequently acquire biologically bad qualities.'[20]

John Robertson makes a similar argument when asking about the consent or lack of consent on the part of future generations as to what we do today to affect their germline. If no harm occurs, he argues, this is a mere theoretical objection. If harm does occur, the question of identity arises. 'Later generations allegedly harmed without their consent may not have existed at all. Different individuals would then exist than if the germline gene therapy had not occurred.'[21]

Perhaps the CRG position paper writers presumed this kind of distinction between existing and not yet existing persons, and this permitted them to give qualified approval of somatic modification for living persons while proscribing germline manipulation.[22] What this means for us here, then, is that, if we are to affirm ethical responsibility for the genetic inheritance we bequeath our progeny, the framework of rights and accountability might be inadequate. As long as the CRG works strictly within this framework, perhaps its conclusions are understandable. I submit that a broader framework, a framework provided by a theologically inspired vision of a better future, will respectfully request that the door to germline intervention remain open. An open door will keep the beneficent end in view until it becomes convincingly clear that negative repercussions resulting from the technological means require us to then close the door.

The Not-Yet-Future and the Ethics of Creativity

This theological framework begins with the idea of God as creator, the world as creation, and the act of creating conceived both as creation out of nothing *(creatio ex nihilo)* and continuous creation *(creatio continua)*. My own way of conceiving of *creatio ex nihilo* together with *creatio continua* is as follows. The first thing God did was to give the world a future.[23] The act of drawing the world into existence from nothing is the act of giving the world a future. As long as we have a future, we exist. When we lose our future, we cease to exist. God continues moment by moment to bestow futurity, and this establishes continuity while opening reality up to newness. Future giving is the way in which God is creative. It is also the way God redeems. God's grace comes to the creation through creative and redemptive future giving.

God creates new things. The biblical description of divine activity in the world includes promises and fulfillments of promises. This implies two divine qualities. First, that God is not restricted to the old, not confined by the status quo. God may promise new realities and then bring them to pass. The most important of the still outstanding divine promises is that of the 'new creation' yet to come. Second, this God is faithful, trustworthy. On the basis of the past record, the God of Israel can be trusted to keep a promise. For us this means that we can trust God's creative and redemptive activity to continue in the future.

The next step in the argument is to conceive of the human being as the created co-creator. The term, 'created co-creator', comes from the work of Philip Hefner.[24] The term does a couple of important things. First, the word 'created' reminds us that the way God creates differs from the way we human beings create. God creates *ex nihilo*. We are created by God. We are creatures. So, whatever creativity we manifest cannot rank on the same level as creation out of nothing, on the same level with our creator. Yet, secondly, the term 'co-creator' signifies what we all know, namely, that creation does not stand still. It moves, it changes. So do we. And, furthermore, we have partial influence over the direction in which it moves and the kind of changes that take place. We are creative in the transformatory sense. Might we then think of the *imago dei* – the image of God embedded in the human race – in terms of creativity? Might we think of ourselves as co-creators, sharing in the transforming work of God's ongoing creation?

Human creativity is ambiguous. We are condemned to be creative. We cannot avoid it. The human being is a tool maker and a tool user. We are *homo faber*. We cannot be human without being technological, and technology changes things for good or ill. Technology is normally designed for good reasons such as service to human health and welfare, but we know all too well how shortsightedness in technological advance does damage. This is indirect evil. Direct evil is also possible. Technology can be pressed into the service of violence and war, as in the making of weapons. It is by no means an unmitigated good. Yet, despite its occasional deleterious consequences, we humans have no choice but to continue to express ourselves technologically and, hence, creatively.

We cannot not be creative. The ethical mandate, then, has to do with the purposes toward which our creativity is directed and the degree of zeal with which we approach our creative tasks.

There are advantages to such a future-oriented theology of creation for dealing with the question of germline intervention. First, a future-oriented theology of creation is not stymied by giving priority to existing persons over against future persons who do not yet exist. A theology of continuing creation looks forward to the new, to those who are yet to come into existence as part of the moral community to which we belong. Second, such a theology is realistic about the dynamic nature of our situation. Everything changes. There is no standing still. What we do affects and is affected by the future. We are condemned to be creative for good or ill. Third, the future is built into this ethical vision. Once we apprehend that God intends a future, our task is to discern as best we can the direction of divine purpose and employ that as an ethical guide. When we invoke the apocalyptic symbol of the New Jerusalem where 'crying and pain will be no more' (Revelation 21:4), this will inspire and guide the decisions we make today that will affect our progeny tomorrow.

The creative component to a future-oriented ethic denies that the status quo defines what is good, denies that the present situation has an automatic moral claim to perpetuity. Take social equality as a relevant case in point, a matter of serious CRG concern. As one can plainly see, social equality does not exist at present, nor has it ever existed in universal form. We daily confront the frustrations of economic inequality and political oppression right along with the more subtle forms of prejudice and discrimination that the CRG rightly opposes. Human equality, then, is something we are striving for, something that does not yet exist but ought to exist. Equality needs to be created, and it will take human creativity under divine guidance to establish it, plus vigilance to maintain it when and where it has been achieved. Wolfhart Pannenberg puts it this way: 'The Christian concept of equality does not mean that everyone is to be reduced to an average where every voice is equal to every other, but equality in the Christian sense means that everyone should be raised up through participation in the highest human possibilities. Such equality must always be created; it is not already there.'[25] An ethic that seeks to raise us to the 'highest human possibilities' cannot accept the status quo as normative, but presses on creatively toward a new and better future. With regard to the issue at hand, Ronald Cole-Turner makes the bold affirmation: 'I argue that genetic engineering opens new possibilities for the future of God's creative work.'[26]

Conclusion

The health and well-being of future generations not yet born is a matter of ethical concern when viewed within the scope of a theology of creation that emphasizes God's continuing creative work and that pictures the human being as the created co-creator. A vision of future possibilities, not the present status quo, orients and directs ethical activity. When applied to the issue of germline intervention for the purpose of therapy and even for enhancing the quality of human life, the door must be kept open so that we can look through, squint and focus our eyes to see just what possibilities loom before us. This will include a realistic review of the limits and risks of genetic technology.[27] But, realism about technological limits and risks is insufficient warrant for prematurely shutting the door against possibilities for an improved human future.

Notes

1 Council for Responsible Genetics, 'Position paper on Human Germ Line Manipulation', 19 Garden Street, Cambridge, MA 02138, (1992).

2   Although the phrase, 'play God', has been with us for some decades as a reference
    to the prospect of scientific creation or manipulation of life, Jeremy Rifkin thrust it
    before the public with his 1977 book title, *Who Should Play God?* (New York: Dell,
    Laurel edition, 1977); cf. J. Rifkin, *Algeny* (New York: Viking, 1983); 'Playing God
    with the Genetic Code', *Threshold*, 6:3 (January 1994), 17–18. Rifkin has garnered
    his share of critics. Walter Truett Anderson dubs Rifkin's hysterical attack against
    genetic engineering 'biological McCarthyism'. Anderson's own position is that the
    human race should become deliberate about the future of its own evolution: 'This is
    the project of the coming era: to create a social and political order – a global one –
    commensurate to human power in nature. The project requires a shift from
    evolutionary meddling to evolutionary governance, informed by an ethic of
    responsibility – an evolutionary ethic, not merely an environmental ethic – and it
    requires appropriate ways of thinking about new issues and making decisions'
    (W.T. Anderson, *To Govern Evolution*, New York: Harcourt Brace Jovanovich,
    1987, 9, 135).
3   Paul Ramsey writes, 'Men ought not to play God before they learn to be men, and
    after they have learned to be men they will not play God.' See P. Ramsey,
    Fabricated Man: The Ethics of Genetic Control (New Haven: Yale University Press,
    1979), 138. The question of playing God in genetic intervention is only one of many
    reasons for inviting theological attention into this field. M. Therese Lysaught at the
    Park Ridge Center for the Study of Health, Faith, and Ethics writes, 'a Christian
    theological analysis of the Human Genome Project and genetics needs to examine a
    host of questions in addition to the question of human intervention into nature –
    for example, questions of theodicy, of divine agency, of theological anthropology,
    of social justice, of the meaning of suffering within a Christian theological
    framework, of the meaning of Christian community, as well as methodological
    questions surrounding the science/religion dialogue'. See M.T. Lysaught, 'Map,
    Myth, or Medium of Redemption: How do we Interpret the Human Genome
    Project?', *Second Opinion*, 19:4 (1994), 83.
4   J.C. Fletcher and W.F. Anderson, 'Germ-line Gene Therapy: A New Stage of
    Debate', *Law, Medicine, and Health*, 20 (1992), 31.
5   Burke K. Zimmerman identifies 'three strategies' for germline intervention: (1)
    screening and selection of early-stage embryos; (2) direct modification of the DNA
    of early-stage embryos coupled with IVF; and (3) genetic modification of gametes
    prior to conception. Although screening is not usually included in germline
    discussion, it along with the other two strategies would affect the future human
    gene pool. See Burke Zimmerman, 'Human Germ-line Therapy: The Case for its
    Development and Use', *Journal of Medicine and Philosophy*, 16:6 (1991), 594–5; cf.
    G. Fowler, E. Juengst and B.K. Zimmerman, 'Germ-line Therapy and the Clinical
    Ethos of Medical Genetics', *Theoretical Medicine*, 10 (1989), 151–65. At this
    writing, Ralph Brinster of the University of Pennsylvania has successfully altered
    early-stage stem cells residing in the testes of mice, alterations that would be passed
    on to subsequent generations.
6   On 30 June 1994, the Steering Committee on Bioethics for the Conseil de l'Europe
    (CDBI) approved somatic therapy but recommended a ban on germline alteration.
    W. French Anderson writes, 'Somatic cell gene therapy for the treatment of severe
    disease is considered ethical because it can be supported by the fundamental moral
    principle of beneficence: It would relieve human suffering. ... [But] enhancement
    engineering would threaten important human values in two ways: It could be
    medically hazardous in that the risks could exceed the potential benefits and the
    procedure therefore cause harm. And it would be morally precarious in that ... it

could lead to an increase in inequality and discriminatory practices.' See W.F. Anderson, 'Genetics and Human Malleability', *Hastings Center Report*, 20 (January–February 1990), 23. David Suzuki and Peter Knudtson draw a sharp ethical distinction between somatic gene therapy, which can be seen as the equivalent of an organ-transplant operation that modifies a patient's phenotype without changing the genotype, and germline gene therapy, which modifies 'cells belonging to lineages that are potentially immortal'. See D. Suzuki and P. Knudston, *The Clash Between the New Genetics and Human Values* (Cambridge: Harvard University Press, 1990, rev. edn), 183–4. However, because the technical distinction between these two is becoming more difficult to discern, some can say 'the bright ethical line separating somatic and germline therapy has begun to erode'. See K. Nolan, 'How do we Think About the Ethics of Human Germ-line Genetic Therapy?', *Journal of Medicine and Philosophy*, 16:6 (1991), 613. French Anderson, in a more recent work with John Fletcher, argues that the situation is changing. Whereas in the 1970s and 1980s there was a strong taboo against germline modification, in the 1990s that taboo is lifting: 'Searches for cure and prevention of genetic disorders by germline therapy arise from principles of beneficence and non-maleficence, which create imperatives to relieve and prevent basic causes of human suffering. It follows from this ethical imperative that society ought not to draw a moral line between intentional germline therapy and somatic cell therapy,' J.C. Fletcher and W.F. Anderson, 'Germ-line Gene Therapy: A New Stage of Debate', *Law, Medicine, and Health Care*, 20 (1992), 31.

7   J.R. Nelson (ed.), 'Summary Reflection Statement of the Genetics, Religion, and Ethics Project', paper presented at The Institute of Religion and Baylor College of Medicine, The Texas Medical Center, PO Box 20569, Houston, Texas, 77225, 1992. This follows the precedent of the World Council of Churches: 'somatic cell therapy may provide a good; however, other issues are raised if it also brings about a change in germline cells. The introduction of genes into the germline is a permanent alteration ... Nonetheless, changes in genes that avoid the occurrence of disease are not necessarily made illicit merely because those changes also alter the genetic inheritance of future generations. ... There is no absolute distinction between eliminating "defects" and "improving heredity".' World Council of Churches, *Manipulating Life: Ethical Issues in Genetic Engineering*, World Council of Churches: Geneva, 1982. A 1989 document reiterates this position more strongly by proposing 'a ban on experiments involving genetic engineering of the human germline at the present time,' World Council of Churches, 'Biotechnology: Its Challenges to the Churches and the World', World Council of Churches: Geneva, 1989, 2.

8   Eric T. Juengst argues that the arguments for a present ban on germline intervention are convincing, but he argues that the risks of genetic accidents – even multigenerational ones – can be overcome with new knowledge. Germline alteration ought not to be proscribed simply on the grounds that enhancement engineering might magnify current social inequalities. He writes, 'the social risks of enhancement engineering, like its clinical risks, still only provide contingent barriers to the technique. In a society structured to allow the realization of our moral commitment to social equality in the face of biological diversity – that is, for a society in which there was both open access to this technology and no particular social advantage to its use – these problems would show themselves to be the side issues they really are'. See E.T. Juengst, 'The NIH Points to Consider and the Limits of Human Gene Therapy', *Human Gene Therapy*, 1 (1990), 431.

9   E.T. Juengst, 'Germ-line Therapy: Back to Basics', *Journal of Medicine and Philosophy*, 16:6 (1991), 589–90. For more on this, see M.A.M. De Wachter, 'Ethical Aspects of Human Germ-line Therapy', *Bioethics*, 7 (1993), 166–77. Nelson A. Wivel and LeRoy Walters list four arguments against germline modification: (1) it is an expensive intervention that would affect relatively few patients; (2) alternative strategies for avoiding genetic disease exist, namely, somatic cell therapy; (3) the risks of multigenerational genetic mistakes will never be eliminated, and these mistakes would be irreversible; and (4) germline modification for therapy puts us on a slippery slope leading inevitably to enhancement. They also list four arguments favoring germline modification: (1) health professionals have a moral obligation to use the best available methods in preventing or treating genetic disorders, and this may include germline alterations; (2) the principle of respect for parental autonomy should permit parents to use this technology to increase the likelihood of having a healthy child; (3) it is more efficient than the repeated use of somatic cell therapy over successive generations; and (4) the prevailing ethic of science and medicine operates on the assumption that knowledge has intrinsic value, and this means that promising areas of research should be pursued. See N.A. Wivel and L. Walters, 'Germ-line Gene Modification and Disease Prevention: Some Medical and Ethical Perspectives', *Science*, 262:5133 (22 October 1993), 533–8. Arthur Caplan believes HGI scientists may have sold their research souls too soon by promising to refrain from germline intervention just to appease the hysteria over potential eugenic uses. There is no moral reason to refrain from eliminating a lethal gene from the human population; and there is no slippery slope from germline therapy to eugenics: 'It is simply a confusion to equate eugenics with any discussion of germline therapy.' See A.L. Caplan, 'If Gene Therapy is the Cure, What is the Disease?', in G.J. Annas and S. Elias (eds), *Gene Mapping* (Oxford and New York: Oxford University Press, 1992), 139.
10 See note 1.
11 C. Thomas Casky, like the CRG, believes that germline correction has little practical appeal while generating considerable ethical apprehension. Yet he leaves the door open: 'I would reserve one area for consideration of germline manipulation … It is conceivable that at some point in the future genetic manipulation of an individual's germline may be undertaken to introduce or reintroduce disease resistance.' See C.T. Casky, 'DNA-based Medicine: Prevention and Therapy', in D.J. Kevles and L. Hood (eds), *The Code of Codes: Scientific and Social Issues in the Human Genome Project* (Cambridge: Harvard University Press, 1992), 129. John A. Robertson takes a position that would oppose the CRG, saying that 'these fears appear too speculative to justify denying use of a therapeutic technique that will protect more immediate generations of offspring,' J.A. Robertson, *Children of Choice: Freedom and the New Reproductive Technologies*, (Princeton, NJ: Princeton University Press, 1994), 162.
12 D.J. Kevles, *In the Name of Eugenics* (Berkeley and Los Angeles: University of California Press, 1985).
13 R.N. Proctor, *Racial Hygiene: Medicine Under the Nazis* (Cambridge: Harvard University Press, 1988).
14 This statement comes directly from the position paper. It fits appropriately what one of the drafters, R.C. Lewontin, elsewhere says critically about science and class interests: '"Science" is the ultimate legitimator of bourgeoisie ideology', Steven Rose, (R.C. Lewontin and Leon J. Kamin, *Not in Our Genes*, New York: Pantheon Books, 1984), 31.

15 H. Bouma, *Christian Faith, Health and Medical Practice* (Grand Rapids: W.B. Eerdmans, 1989), 264.

16 'Why does the notion that medical technology might give some children an advantage elicit such a strong negative reaction?' asks Zimmerman. 'Perhaps it is because the notion of fairness is well embedded in Western culture.' He goes on to note that we already accept randomized differences between people and the inevitability that some individuals will excel over others. Then in support of germline enhancement he adds: 'What about the positive side, of increasing the number of talented people. Wouldn't society be better off in the long run?,' Zimmerman, 'Human Germ-line Therapy', 606–7.

17 We must be clear that genetic prejudice would be a cultural or social phenomenon, not a scientific one. 'It is society, not biology, that turns some genetic characteristics into liabilities,' writes Roger L. Shinn, *Forced Options: Social Decisions for the 21st Century*, 2nd edn, (New York: Pilgrim, 1985), 140. If our society is serious about the fairness or justice dimension here, we could institute a sort of 'affirmative action' public policy in which the underprivileged classes would be given privileged access to germline enhancement technology.

18 Cole-Turner makes much of Jesus' healing ministry as a directive toward inspiring modern science and technology to continue healing and to think of this as continuing the divine work of redemption. See Ron Cole-Turner, *The New Genesis: Theology and the Genetic Revolution* (Louisville: Westminster/John Knox, 1993), 80–86.

19 See note 1.

20 H. Jones, 'Genetic Endowment and Obligations to Future Generations', in E. Partridge (ed.), *Responsibilities to Future Generations* (Buffalo: Prometheus, 1981), 249.

21 Robertson, *Children of Choice*, 162.

22 David Suzuki and Peter Knudtson promulgate a 'genetic principle' that parallels the CRG: 'While genetic manipulation of human somatic cells may lie in the realm of personal choice, tinkering with human germ cells does not. Germ-cell therapy, without the consent of all members of society, ought to be explicitly forbidden.' (David Suzuki and P. Knudston, *Genethics*, St Leonards, Australia: Allen and Unwin, 163). The Suzuki and Knudtson position is obviously based upon a libertarian ethic so, to be more precise, they should be seeking the consent of those individuals involved rather than the vague 'all members of society'.

23 Ted Peters, *God – The World's Future: Systematic Theology for a Postmodern Era* (Minneapolis: Fortress, 1992).

24 P. Hefner, 'The Evolution of the Created Co-Creator', in Ted Peters (ed.), *Cosmos as Creation: Science and Theology in Consonance* (Nashville: Abingdon, 1989) 212; P. Hefner, *The Human Factor: Evolution, Culture, and Religion* (Minneapolis: Fortress, 1993), 35–42. Cf. K. Rahner, *Theological Investigations*, trans. C. Ernst, vol. 5 (Baltimore, Helicon), 137–8; J.M. Gustafson, 'Where Theologians and Geneticists Meet', *Dialog: A Journal of Theology*, 33 (Winter 1994), 10. Pope John Paul II places anthropology within creation when speaking of the humans among us as 'products, knowers, and stewards of creation', R.J. Russell (ed.), *John Paul II on Science and Religion* (Vatican City and Notre Dame, Indiana: Vatican Observatory Publications and University of Notre Dame Press, 1990) M5. With reference to women in ministry, Lynn Rhodes speaks of us human beings as 'co-creating the Christian vision for the future'. See L.N. Rhodes, *Co-Creating: A Feminist Vision of Ministry* (Philadelphia: Westminster, 1987), 40.

25 W. Pannenberg, *Ethics* (Louisville: Westminster/John Knox, 1981), 140.

26 Cole-Turner, *The New Genesis*, 98.
27 Roger Shinn's advice is salutary here: 'I know of no way of drawing a line and saying: thus far, scientific direction and control is beneficial; beyond this line they become destructive manipulation. I think it more important to keep raising the question, to keep confronting the technological society with the issue.' See R.L. Shinn, (1985, 142). Deborah Blake says it eloquently: 'The risk of the nineties is the seduction of a technological fix. The challenge for the nineties is to find the moral courage necessary to guide and realize the promises made by this new genetics so that our moral wisdom is not outpaced by our technological cleverness.' Deborah Blake, 'Ethics of Possibility: Medical Biotechnology for the Nineties', *The Catholic World*, 234 (September–October 1991), 237.

Chapter 13

Coevolution: Pain or Promise?

How can we as members of the human race live at peace in a world with 600 or more known viruses, many of which spell suffering and death to persons among us? Viruses look like predators and we their prey. Though tiny (we need an electron microscope to see them) viruses seem like monsters on the prowl, threatening to devour and destroy us. Fiercely they infect us, cause disease, fill our bodies with pain, and with merciless apathy leave us to suffer and, in some cases, to die.

Might the concept of coevolution hold out some promise for living at peace with viruses? If we think of individual selves as but statistical parts of the much larger human race, and if we think of the human race as so interconnected with the rest of nature as to be coevolving in the direction of a symbiotic equilibrium, will that bring comfort and peace of mind? Could a scientific theory descriptive of the role of viruses in the process of evolution enable us to embrace the virus as our sister, our friend, our comrade, our walking partner up the pathway of evolution? Could we go so far as to identify God with a virus, a virus we accept as part of our evolutionary past, to be jettisoned as we advance in scientific understanding of how nature works?

In my judgment, the concept of coevolution is intrinsically fascinating and provides us with a valuable perspective regarding the human race as an aggregate. Through the lenses of coevolution we can see just how thoroughly we *homo sapiens* are enmeshed and bound up with nature and nature's history. We can forecast changes in the human genome, viewing continuing human development in concert with changes in the rest of nature in and around us. But, this provides only a statistical picture of who we are, a picture of ourselves as a species. What is left out of this picture is the individual person, an individual person who may be victimized by an infectious disease and may undergo pain, suffering, loneliness and premature loss of life.[1] No broad picture of the epic of evolution can provide physical healing to a body racked with pain or comfort to a soul tormented by a sense of cosmic injustice.

My argument in what follows will be that the concept of coevolution, no matter how fascinating or fruitful, is philosophically trivial. Though important scientifically perhaps, the concept of coevolution is philosophically, and thereby theologically, trivial.[2] It is trivial in the sense that it can *describe* how nature works, yet cannot *prescribe* how we ought to think or act as human persons. As individual human persons we are more than our nature, more than what our genetic history has bequeathed us. We can embrace this 'more than' by affirming our freedom. It is by affirming our freedom in the midst of pain that we can find promise.

This freedom comes in two forms, Promethean freedom and spiritual freedom. Promethean freedom sees the virus as a predator, an enemy to be defeated. Like a military intelligence operation, we ask our scientists to infiltrate the world of the virus to learn its inner workings, locate its weaknesses and plan a strategy for human victory or, if this be impossible, to invent a way for us to live with viruses in a state of peaceful coexistence. Promethean freedom is ambitious and creative. It transforms nature and consciously contributes to coevolution.

As important as Promethean freedom is to the scientific enterprise and to the forward movement of modern medicine, I would like to turn our attention more toward spiritual freedom. By introducing spiritual freedom I am not endorsing escapism. I am not opening up an escape hatch so that we can flee this world of physical woe into one of disembodied bliss. Quite the contrary. By spiritual freedom I mean the fullest possible acknowledgment of our material reality, the existential acceptance of ourselves as inescapably natural creatures subject to finitude in a world we share with viruses.

In what follows, I plan to outline two types of coevolutionary thinking. The first is gene–gene coevolution: the notion that the virus and the human interact genetically and that the genomes of each are undergoing complementary change through time. The second is gene–culture coevolution: a notion promulgated by sociobiologists that attempts to explain the morphology of culture on the model of genetic evolution. I will suggest that this argument is fallacious, that it has yet to be proved that human culture is evolutionary in the same sense that the human genome is. This discussion will have theological relevance, because some scholars have suggested that God is a virus, meaning that God is a genetically determined cultural construct. In opposition, I will argue that thinking of God as a virus is an unfounded notion.

I will point out that some theologians are more than merely comfortable with the concept of coevolution; in fact, they warmly embrace the idea. One outcome is the belief that our biocultural evolutionary past witnessed the emergence of human freedom. More than that, our biocultural evolution has determined that we will be free.

This idea of determined freedom will provide the open door for us to walk through into a discussion of human freedom, especially spiritual freedom. I will argue that, for individuals among us who become victims of infectious disease and who undergo suffering in the face of death, some genuine peace of mind is achievable through the constitution of the self via an act of courageous acceptance. I will look at the suffering and faith of Job and argue in specifically Christian terms that in the incarnation, God has experienced the limits of finitude and subjugation to suffering and death; if we surrender our self to this gracious God, we will regain a full self that is truly in touch with all of creation. The paradox is this: in death there is life.

Gene–Gene Coevolution: Viruses and Humans

The term *coevolution* was first introduced by P.R. Ehrlich and P.H. Raven in 1964 to describe the parallel and interactive evolution of butterflies and their host plants. Since then, 'this concept has been a growing wonder to biologists, including virologists'.[3] Others, in addition to virologists, have found the concept of coevolution suggestive and fruitful, and philosophical adaptions have begun to proliferate. Here we will look at two uses of the term. We will look initially at gene–gene coevolution characteristic of the virus–human interaction. Then, we will turn to the field of sociobiology to look at gene–culture coevolution.

A virus appears to be a ruthless predator, attacking and destroying its prey. Yet, curiously enough, it is totally dependent upon its apparent prey for its own life as such. And, in order to sustain its own existence, it genetically adapts to its prey while, in some cases, the prey in turn genetically adapts to the virus. Adaptation may take the form of simple genetic selection, actual mutation, or a combination of both. The result is a parallel if not interactive evolutionary dynamic.

It may help here to distinguish a virus from a bacterium. Both are microbes. Both are tiny, although typically viruses are by orders of magnitude much smaller than bacteria, perhaps a 100th to a 1000th the size of bacteria. Yet, they differ markedly. Bacteria are free-standing life forms. They take in their own nourishment and reproduce independently. They are not, for the most part, parasitic.

A virus, in contrast, is a total parasite. A virus cannot imbibe nourishment, cannot grow, cannot reproduce, cannot do anything on its own. To live, a virus must take up residence in the cell of a host life form. Viral capsules have differing shapes. An arenavirus is a roughly surfaced ball. A filovirus is a long sickle-shaped thread that curves around itself. The rabies virus is shaped like a bullet. They all lodge in a living cell and spill their half-dozen or so genes into the host cell.

The virus cycle begins when it penetrates a host cell. Once inside the cell, the virus sheds its own protective protein coat. This exposes the viral genes to the cell nucleus, lodging in the cell's own DNA. The virus then employs the host DNA to replicate the viral genes. Finally, the virus dons a new protein coat, escapes the cell, and proceeds to infect another host.

Viruses are aggressive, infectious. When the cells of human beings are penetrated by viruses such as influenza or ebola, they become ill and sometimes die. Yet, illness is not always the result. We can distinguish between infection and disease. Infection occurs when an agent such as a virus invades and takes up residence in a host and multiplies within the host. The infection may, or may not, result in outward signs of a disease affecting the entire organism.[4]

Individual persons or individual organisms may die, but not necessarily the entire population. The Australian rabbit story illustrates the coevolutionary principle. In the 1850s, a British gentleman introduced a few dozen rabbits from England to the Australian continent for sport, for the rabbit hunt. In its Australian environment, however, the English rabbit found virtually no natural predators. It multiplied. Eventually, Australians complained of being overrun by rabbits. To remedy the overpopulation, in 1950 a highly virulent strain of a rabbit virus – *myxoma*, which leads to *myxomatosis* – was deliberately brought from Brazil and introduced to Australia. Borne by mosquitoes as vectors, within three months the myxomatosis decimated the Australian rabbits, killing 99.8 per cent of the population.

What about the remaining 0.2 per cent? Rapid evolution took place, many think. The mixing of the genomes of both the rabbits and the myxoma led to genetic alterations in both. Each adapted to the other. By 1958, the fatality rate dropped to only 25 per cent. The majority of Australian rabbits soon carried myxoma in their genome but had become unaffected by the disease.[5]

The virus cycle may be accompanied by a population cycle. The individual organisms not killed in the first wave of infection are either genetically resistant to begin with or become resistant after developing antibodies. The principle of natural selection permits the resistant individuals to survive to reproduce themselves, thereby leading to future resistant generations. This applies to the viruses as well. The most lethal strains kill all their hosts, causing themselves to die out. The more moderate strains permit their hosts to live, thereby insuring that they will have hosts into the next generation. The virus strains that kill more slowly have the advantage. After six generations or so, an equilibrium is reached: a less virulent virus that permits its host to live, married to an animal host healthy enough to pass the virus on. In short, host and virus evolve together.

The coevolutionary population cycle can be accounted for in terms of simple selection; yet, genetic alteration can also be a factor. Viruses come in two types: DNA viruses and RNA viruses. The larger and more stable are the DNA type, which includes variola (the smallpox virus) and the herpes viruses (genital herpes, cytomegalovirus and Epstein–Barr virus). The more stable DNA viruses tend to keep their genomes intact from one generation to the next, with only rare mutations. RNA viruses, on the other hand, are a million times more likely to undergo mutations than their host. Influenza is an RNA virus with a wide variety of mutant strands. The predominant strain reflects centuries of evolutionary adaptation, showing genetic flexibility so as to take advantage of ever new environmental niches.

This fear of flexibility led to the ordered slaughter of chickens throughout Hong Kong on 28 December 1997. The order was given to protect the human population from the 'bird flu', an avian virus known now as H5N1 that infected 18 people, eight of whom died. The virus entered the respiratory tract and then spread to every tissue throughout the body, causing hemorrhage and death. Evidently, the 18 persons contracted this strain by handling infected poultry. They did not pass it from person to person. However, virologists were concerned that the bird flu might mutate, taking a form that would encourage human-to-human transmission. The chicken slaughter was ordered as a preventative measure.[6]

Retroviruses are an important subset within the genetically flexible RNA type. In this category we find HIV and a number of other human viruses. Retroviruses possess reverse transcriptase, an enzyme that utilizes the viral RNA as a template to make a DNA copy, and this DNA copy is then incorporated into the DNA of the infected cell. The term *retrovirus* reflects the Latin word for 'backward', *retro*, because it begins with RNA and then moves toward forming a DNA genome, rather than the other way around. Some retroviruses seek out the germ cells – the eggs in the ovaries and the sperm cells in the testes – where they place their own genome into the host germline. The virus genome is then passed along to future generations of the host genome, thereby insuring its own future.[7]

Why do viruses behave this way? To accomplish a single focused end, such as survival? Biologists of our era speak of the 'life strategy' in Darwinian selection in terms of a striving for 'evolutionary fitness'. Reproductivity is the key: if a life form, a particular genome, for example, can reproduce itself, it will survive beyond the death of the individual. What we find in the virus–human coevolution is a competitive race to establish greater evolutionary fitness.

Richard Dawkins proposed in 1976 the explanatory concept of the 'selfish gene', according to which the gene becomes the actor and the reproducing organism becomes the means whereby the gene insures its own immortality.[8] Sociobiologist Edward O. Wilson, borrowing from Samuel Butler's observation about eggs and chickens, said it this way: As 'the chicken is only an egg's way of making another egg ... [so] the organism is only DNA's way of making more DNA'.[9] According to the model of the selfish gene, the virus has one and only one purpose, namely, to perpetuate its own genetic code, no matter what the cost. Or, from a strictly genetic perspective, the virus is itself a very effective way for its particular DNA to make more DNA.

'A virus has only one mission, one goal, and that is to replicate itself,' says C.J. Peters. 'Viruses get into a host cell and use that cell's machinery to put their DNA or RNA to use making more virus. Darwin would have loved them: they exist only to make more of themselves and they are highly interactive in the natural selection process.'[10]

Frank Ryan believes that viruses are directed by what he calls 'genomic executive intelligence'. Viruses are devoid of mind, to be sure; yet, they possess a means of control, a quasi-single-minded pursuit of the only goal that matters from an evolutionary standpoint, namely, the creation of more viruses like themselves. This genomic intelligence enables the virus to be both receptive and responsive to new host situations, provoking the adaptation necessary to attain this goal.[11]

Genomic intelligence benefits not only the virus but also the host, according to Ryan, because after the initial aggressive attack by the virus it eventually makes possible a 'mutualistic symbiosis'. Ryan uses the term *coevolution* to refer to the dynamic process of change, whereby two very different species evolve parallel to each other. He then uses the term *symbiosis* to refer to the state of equilibrium that results from this coevolution. Symbiosis is the meeting point, when virus and host arrive at a stable and mutually interdependent relationship. 'A virus begins as a lethal attacker, yet, given time, it ameliorates its behavior through coevolution until, after many generations of both virus and host, a totally new modus vivendi emerges – a true symbiosis in place of what was formerly a predator-and-prey relationship.'[12]

Those who work with a virus–human coevolutionary scheme frequently accompany their observations with a pair of moral maxims. The first is the decentering maxim: thou shalt not think of the human race as the center of creation. 'Humans by no means occupy center stage in the biosphere,' writes C.J. Peters.[13] We are but one of 4000 species of mammals on earth. We are outnumbered by insects, of which there are 750 000 species. These are outnumbered by microorganisms. We can find 100 000 bacteria on a square inch of skin, and 100 000 000 million in a teaspoon of soil. Bacteria predated the human race by two million years, and bacteria have the evolutionary adaptability to outlast us. If nature were to take a poll, the human race would be outvoted. So, when thinking about the 600 or so viruses, Joshua Lederberg contends that the single biggest threat to the continued dominance of the human race on our planet is the virus: 'The survival of humanity is not preordained.'[14]

The second maxim is this: thou shalt not think of the virus in moral terms. Frank Ryan puts it this way: viruses 'are amoral, in the true sense – a complete absence of morality'.[15] Why are viruses amoral? Because they have one and only one single-minded purpose, namely, survival. Evidently, the selfish gene or any other natural entity which seeks solely its own survival makes it into the amoral category.

These two maxims combined with the larger concept of coevolution suggest a possible route for philosophical reflection: perhaps we human beings should let go of our fear of being the prey for the predator virus. Perhaps we human beings should see our victimization by the virus as part of a larger symbiotic whole that is nature. Perhaps we human beings should subsume our own desire for survival into something more inclusive. Perhaps we should find the sacrifice of members of our race meaningful in the grand epic that is evolution.[16] This is not the route I intend to follow.

The route of philosophical reflection I choose to follow is brute realism. It begins with acknowledging the scientific observations that contribute to the notion of virus–human coevolution. It then acknowledges that this is the way nature works. The way nature works may be fascinating, it may be marvelous, it may be baffling at times. Yet it simply is the way nature works. This renders the concept of coevolution trivial, in the philosophical sense of being trivial. It is merely descriptive of how nature works. Nature must work in one way or another. Coevolution seems to be the way that nature on planet earth works. Once this is observed and conceptually established, we move on. There is no warrant to think that the coevolutionary process is inherently sacred, worthy of awe, or the ground of human values.

Gene–Culture Coevolution: is God a Virus?

The question has been posed: Is God a virus? The question's ridiculous; yet it arises out of a coevolutionary scheme of thinking, thereby warranting comment here.

The virus–human coevolutionary scheme is part of a larger scheme, the gene–culture coevolutionary theory of the sociobiologists and evolutionary psychologists. Edward O. Wilson, for example, says that 'to genetic evolution the human lineage has added the parallel track of cultural evolution'.[17] The two are more than parallel. They are inextricably linked, it is argued; culture evolves just as our genome evolves. As our genome has evolving chemical units known as genes, so does culture have evolving conceptual units, what Wilson calls 'culturgens'. A culturgen (from the Latin *cultura*, culture, and *geno*, create) is a 'relatively homogeneous group of mental constructions or their products' passed on from generation to generation.[18] Here are Wilson's coevolutionary principles:

> Culture is created by the communal mind, and each mind in turn is the product of the genetically structured human brain. Genes and culture are therefore inseverably linked. But the linkage is flexible, to a degree still mostly unmeasured. The linkage is also tortuous: genes prescribe epigenetic rules, which are the neural pathways and regularities in cognitive development by which the individual mind assembles itself. The mind grows from birth to death by absorbing parts of the existing culture available to it, with selections guided through epigenetic rules inherited by the individual brain.[19]

The theory as here stated is based on an obvious fallacy. We might dub it the fallacy of equivocation, a fallacy committed when one term is used in two different ways. In this case, the term 'mind' is used in two different ways, one that includes a brain and another that does not. The first way is to speak of the individual mind which, according to Wilson as well as many contemporary neuroscientists, is the product of a genetically structured human brain. The structure comes in the form of epigenetic rules, according to Wilson. These rules are gene-determined preferences in the brain for one cultural decision rather than another. Wilson makes it clear that it is the individual mind that is structured by the physical brain, which in turn is directed by the genes according to epigenetic rules. Yet, he then proceeds to use the word 'mind' in a second way to refer to what causes a culture, namely a 'communal mind'. There is no physical brain structuring the communal mind. The communal mind is not the product of a communal brain, as an individual mind is the product of an individual brain. Be that as it may, Wilson still thinks he can identify communal culturgens that correspond to an individual's genes.

If Wilson wants to rely upon the physical brains producing individual minds which then in turn produce a shared communal mind, this would make sense. But, then he could not logically apply the same evolutionary principles to culture that he applies to the human brain without committing the fallacy of composition. This fallacy is committed whenever one argues from the properties of the parts to the properties of the whole. I could not legitimately argue, for example, that because my particular office and those of my colleagues are small the whole building of which my office is a part is also small. The smallness of the offices does not translate into smallness of the building as a composite whole. It is logically possible to have a small office in a very large building. So also, to presume that a 'communal mind' would have the same properties as epigenically ruled and brain-structured individual minds risks such fallacious reasoning. And, even though one could on the basis of evidence reasonably theorize about the genetic evolution of the human brain, what is learned here would not necessarily apply to a communal mind, let alone to the culture that is allegedly produced by this communal mind. What we learn about biological evolution may or may not apply to society or culture. Cultures may or may not evolve in tandem with our genetic code. This subject has yet to be empirically studied and scientifically analyzed.

Despite such fallacies at the foundations, sociobiologists and evolutionary psychologists plunge on with their theorizing. Wilson believes that as a scientist he must abandon now outdated religious beliefs, especially belief in the God of theism who acts in nature and history to create and redeem. Deism or atheism are the theological alternatives best fitted for the scientific understanding of biology and culture. However, he admits that religion has influenced our culture, and the communal mind is stuck with this outdated belief in an active God. 'The human mind evolved to believe in the gods,' he writes. 'It did not evolve to believe in biology.'[20] Biology gives us the truth, he contends, and religion misleads us. 'The essence of humanity's spiritual dilemma is that we evolved genetically to accept one truth and discovered another.'[21] Evidently, the epigenetic rules in our brains led the communal mind to believe in divine realities that Wilson doubts exist; now, Wilson has the mission of trying to create culturgens based on the truths found in biology.

Richard Dawkins' variant on this thesis depicts God as a virus. He identifies belief in God with idea-memes, ideas that can be passed on from one brain to another. Memes are Dawkins' equivalent to Wilson's culturgens. The God-meme is one such idea. Even if the God-meme may have served some beneficial purpose for our ancestors, it no longer has value for us today. We no longer have a need to believe in God, and the theory of evolution has helped some of us to get rid of this outdated idea. 'God exists, if only in the form of a meme with high survival value, or infective power, in the environment provided by human culture.'[22] It is this infective power coming from the cultural environment into our minds that places the God-meme in the category of the virus.

John Bowker reacts to the challenge of the sociobiologists. 'Is, then, God a virus?' Bowker asks. 'No, because the analogy between genes and memes is too imprecise to be of any help in understanding the transmission of cultural items or information.'[23] He adds, 'It becomes clear that we cannot eliminate God from inclusion. ... The Christian doctrine of creation is one of relationship and of God's continuing sustenance ... adequate explanations of particular phenomena or events will clearly not need to specify God, even if God is a constant constraint over all eventualities without exception.'[24] Even though Bowker says Dawkins is 'unequivocally wrong' about memes and describing God as a virus, he is somewhat sympathetic to a concern Dawkins has, a concern voiced by Wilson as well, that religions have in the past endorsed tribalism and contributed to the history of human violence.[25] Christian

Bowker, and his atheist and deist opponents, unite in opposition to religion that divides the human race.

It appears to me that the claim that God is a virus – an idea-meme or culturgen – merely begs the ideological question. That ideas about God exist, no one doubts. The only question of philosophical or theological importance, however, is whether God exists. To identify the reality of God strictly with the cultural idea of God is simply an ideological superimposition. It is not warranted by anything studied in biology or even in culture for that matter. The burden of proof for God's non-existence remains unaddressed in the sociobiological scheme. It is assumed, not proven.

It is quite possible in our era to think coherently of an interaction between biological evolution and cultural development without rejecting the God of theism. Philip Hefner, for example, understands 'evolution as the work of God to allow for the emergence of that which is necessary for the fulfillment of God's intentions'.[26] Hefner presupposes that we *homo sapiens* are two-natured creatures, 'a symbiosis of genes and culture'. Within this symbiosis that constitutes our biocultural evolution, we human beings have developed freedom; in fact, our biocultural evolution has bequeathed freedom to the human race. Our freedom is the emergent product of gene–culture coevolution. Freedom is the gift nature has given us. At our stage in the evolutionary story, we as free creatures are now in a position to act creatively in the evolutionary process. We are created co-creators, according to Hefner: '*The freedom that marks the created co-creator and its culture is an instrumentality of God for enabling the creation (consisting of the evolutionary past of genetic inheritance and culture, as well as the contemporary ecosystem) to participate in the intentional fulfillment of God's purposes.*'[27] For Hefner, God would not be a virus coevolving for the sole purpose of its own survival. Nor would God be a culturgen or idea-meme, the now outdated purpose of which is to provide human survival value. Rather, God is seen as the creator over time imparting purpose to the whole of creation. In seeking fulfillment of this purpose, God makes possible the freedom and responsibility of created co-creators within evolutionary history.

Evolution and Freedom

Biocultural evolution itself has led to the emergence of what we know to be human freedom, as Philip Hefner has observed. Evolution has determined that we would be free. Yet, we might ask: where does human freedom fit within the evolutionary scheme? Karl Rahner would go so far as to say that evolution has a purpose, and that purpose is the production of human freedom. The human being, 'together with other beings possessing self-consciousness, freedom and dynamic transcendent orientation towards God, appears as the goal of cosmic evolution'.[28] This is an extreme position. Scientists tend to dismiss the idea of purpose in evolution completely, and theologians who affirm purpose in evolution tend to think in terms of a creation-wide fulfillment.[29] To focus all of a postulated evolutionary *telos* on human freedom and its concomitant God-consciousness may be excessive, yet instructive.

Where does human freedom connect to our concern with virus–human coevolution? One possibility would be the Promethean one. Like Prometheus stealing fire from the gods in heaven in order to light candles on earth, we could enthusiastically support our scientists – the virus hunters – to work night and day, uncovering the secrets of nature and producing the therapies that would protect the human race from the perils of virus infection. Bug sprays, rodent poisons and vaccines would all conspire to influence the direction of virus–human coevolution. It is freedom and its sister, transcendence – transcendence over the world of nature of which we are otherwise thoroughly a part – that would enable us to become created co-creators on behalf of our own evolutionary future. If our past evolution has bequeathed to us this freedom, then this freedom could itself become a factor in our future evolution. The Promethean enterprise of medical research is an expression of that freedom and will inescapably have a coevolutionary impact.

As fruitful a discussion as Prometheanism might be, this is not the route I wish to travel next. Rather, I would like to look at another dimension of freedom, a more subtle dimension belonging to the human person in relation to God. It is the freedom to live as centered whole persons, a freedom that may at first look like it will be sacrificed to the survival of an unconquerable virus.

Freedom is a dynamic characteristic belonging to who we are as whole persons. The orienting and organizing focus of freedom is the centered self, the person. Every part and every function of what constitutes us as personal selves participate in our freedom. Paul Tillich says this 'includes even the cells' of our bodies.[30] Almost anticipating a discussion of virus infection, Tillich writes,

> That which is not centered, that which is isolated from the total process of the self, either by natural or by artificial separation (disease or laboratory situations, for instance), is determined by the mechanism of stimulus and response or by the relation between the unconscious and the conscious. However, it is impossible to derive the determinacy of the whole, including the separated parts, from the determinacy of the isolated parts. Ontologically the whole precedes the parts and gives them their character as parts of this special whole.[31]

Infection by a virus would initially stimulate a cellular response by a part of our body. Our pre-conscious cellular response is not yet an act of freedom, however. An act of freedom is an act of the whole person, an act characterized by 'deliberation, decision and responsibility'.[32] A response to the virus at the level of personal decision constitutes the act of freedom.

The mention of decision reminds us that freedom is commonly understood in terms of making choices – the idea of the human subject arbitrarily deciding between alternatives. Yet, the idea of making choices has never been sufficient for theologians. A theological understanding of freedom must include a component of liberation, a setting free of the self to realize its true nature and to embrace authentically the goals of its source and end, God. Marjorie Hewitt Suchocki speaks of 'the freedom to develop according to one's highest potential'.[33] Karl Rahner identifies 'liberty in the theological sense' with the 'self-determination of the total subject in the direction of finality'. To this finality 'liberty chooses to be related in its act of choice, though of course in order to establish its own real nature, which is the self-fulfillment of the person or subject'.[34] Such definitions emphasize that human freedom or liberty requires a realization or actualization of one's essential nature, a nature that is itself formed through self-constitution in light of a vision of God's grace and purpose for our lives.

Freedom, Pain and Suffering

What about human freedom, theologically understood, in the face of pain and suffering? Despite the optimistic prospect that coevolution might eventually bring about a symbiotic equilibrium between the human population and ebola or HIV, in the meantime individual persons will suffer great pain and great loss.

When a predator virus at the aggressive stage infects a person and precipitates a disease, it looks as though what we previously knew as human freedom is eclipsed. The victims of ebola in the Sudan come down with temperatures of 103 degrees. An angry rash of raised red papules proliferates over their chests, arms and groins. Stools become bloody. Victims become bedridden, emaciated, unable to swallow. Half of those infected die. An unwanted and premature death is a serious eclipse of human freedom. When we are ill our body becomes a prison of pain, locking our spirit into a chamber of abject loneliness.

The biblical Job is a victim of an infectious disease. What the Bible describes as skin ulcers or 'loathsome sores' (Job 2:7) indicate that he was beset with leprosy, or Hansen's disease.[35] Leprosy is caused by a bacillus (bacterium), not a virus. Yet this disease, accompanied by his other troubles – loss of children, loss of estate, loss of social respect – leave him in the pit of loneliness and despair.[36] Out of the pit of human anguish, the voice of Job speaks for the victims of ebola, HIV or the Black Death.

My flesh is clothed with worms and dirt; my skin hardens, then breaks out again. (Job 7:5)

Like a slave who longs for the shadow, and like laborers who look for their wages, So I am allotted months of emptiness, and nights of misery are apportioned to me. (Job 7:2–3)

So overwhelming is the constriction caused by suffering that Job sees death as liberation, the grave as freedom.

I would choose strangling and death rather than this body.
I loathe my life; I would not live forever. Let me alone, for my days are a breath. (Job 7:15–16)

Why did I not die at birth, come forth from the womb and expire? (Job 3:11)

Or why was I not buried like a stillborn child, like an infant that never sees the light?
There the wicked cease from troubling, and there the weary are at rest.
There the prisoners are at ease together; they do not hear the voice of the taskmaster.
The small and the great are there, and the slaves are free from their masters. (Job
3:16–19)

Infectious disease can cut down the wicked and the righteous alike. There is no
apparent justice. Victimization is not repayment, not a punishment that fits any
known crime. The pain is physical. The suffering is spiritual. It is unjust,
cosmically unjust. And who is responsible for cosmic justice? God is.
Enslavement to suffering leads to questioning heaven, to interrogating the
ultimate.

I loathe my life; I will give free utterance to my complaint; I will speak in the
bitterness of my soul.
I will say to God, Do not condemn me; let me know why you contend against me.
(Job 10:1–2)

Job provides us with the classic question of theodicy (from *theos*, God, and
dike, justice): how can we think of the God of creation as just when we are
innocent victims of injustice?

Job's wife, so angry about the injustice, admonishes him: 'Curse God, and
die.' Yet Job cannot quite bring himself to do this, saying, 'Shall we receive the
good at the hand of God, and not the bad?' (Job 2:9–10).[37] The bad is so
overwhelming that Job's faith is locked in a mortal struggle for the sanity of his
soul. Though the struggle be harsh, Job's faith remains inexplicably strong:
'Naked I came from my mother's womb, and naked I shall return there; the
Lord gave, and the Lord has taken away; blessed be the name of the Lord' (Job
1:21).[38]

At one level, Job, like all those who suffer from an infectious disease, loses
his freedom. Yet, at another level, he affirms his freedom ever more strongly in
the face of adversity. He affirms himself in the face of weakness and thereby
becomes an even stronger self. The key that unlocks the prison gates of
infirmity is his trust in that which is beyond himself, his trust in God.

Job loves God. And he loves God for Godself, not simply because God gives
him good things such as health or prosperity. Job does not treat God as we
treat Santa Claus, remembering the North Pole only at the time of year when
we are on the take. God, in Job's eyes, is not reduced to a set of attributes such
as justice, mercy or power. Job loves God even in the midst of confusion,
dismay and disappointment over what is happening. This love in spite of
adversity constitutes Job as a self with integrity, as a free person regardless of
his fate.

At the heart of the matter is a paradox, a paradox that cannot make sense
until it is experienced. Jesus lays the paradox before us: 'Those who find their
life will lose it, and those who lose their life for my sake will find it' (Matthew

10:39). Similarly, when we surrender our self wholly and completely to God, we receive back a full and robust self that is liberated, free and in touch with all of reality. This is an inexplicable yet powerful truth. C.S. Lewis puts it this way: 'We must remember that the soul is but a hollow which God fills. Its union with God is, almost by definition, a continual self-abandonment – an opening, an unveiling, a surrender, of itself. ... For in self-giving, if anywhere, we touch a rhythm not only of all creation but of all being.'[39]

We are calling this spiritual freedom. By 'spiritual' here I am not suggesting a metaphysical entity, spirit, that is disembodied. Quite the opposite. By 'spiritual', I am referring to the total conscious acceptance of ourselves as embodied, as finite creatures completely and inextricably at one with the natural world that is our reality. The spiritual dimension is found in the conscious act of fully accepting this reality.[40]

Paul Tillich identifies this as an act of courage, the courage to be in the face of unmovable finitude. Awareness of our finitude includes awareness of our own future death. Suffering from sickness provokes within us awareness of our impending death, whether that death be near or yet far off.[41] It is an awareness of the possibility of our ceasing to be, of dropping from being into non-being. Thoughts about our own death elicit anxiety, the sense of dread as non-existence knocks at our door. To take this anxiety up into oneself while affirming oneself constitutes the freedom of the spirit; it is an act of courage: 'Courage is the self-affirmation of being in spite of the fact of nonbeing.'[42]

This is what Karl Rahner means by 'liberty of the sick', namely, the freedom experienced by a person who confronts death in this self-constituting way. It is best for us to die consciously, argues Rahner, insofar as it is possible. More than merely *suffer* our death, we should paradoxically *suffer it actively* as an act of freedom. And because death has a way of stopping time, of marking the end of our own finite existence, it functions to define us. Death is the final point at which we, in our personal history on earth, are finished. It is an achievement of freedom if we, in advance, consciously take this finality up into ourselves and affirm ourselves ahead of time. This describes 'the Christian conviction that in death a person's free history assumes its final form. This means that the final "Judgment" of the person takes place'.[43] To die is to live, to live freely.

Cross and Resurrection

In despair, Job shakes his fist at heaven, castigating the apparent unfeelingness of the infinite for his finite plight. When God finally answers Job, the divine voice sounds through a whirlwind.

> Where were you when I laid the foundation of the earth? Tell me, if you have understanding. (Job 38:4)

> Do you know the ordinances of the heavens? Can you establish their rule on the earth? (Job 38:33)

Without a flinch or an apology, God trumpets that the divine master of the cosmic mysteries is beyond human understanding, unsearchable and ineffable. The creation is a wondrous and enigmatic place that baffles human assumptions and expectations. Why? Jon Levenson says that the creation is built by God. It is theocentric, not anthropocentric. The voice from the whirlwind admonishes us to adjust to a world not designed for our benefit. Trusting God means to let go of our claims – even our just claims – against reality's incomprehensible designer and master.[44]

The New Testament gospel adds something to what is revealed to Job in the whirlwind. In the incarnation in Jesus Christ, the infinite becomes finite; the incomprehensible becomes ordinary; and heaven experiences life on earth. Although there is no record of Jesus contracting an infectious disease, he comes to know first-hand pain and torment. Like Job, Jesus loses his freedom. He becomes a prisoner to suffering and death. And, like Job, he reaffirmes his freedom by an act of courage, by trusting God and taking his own death up into his personal integrity.[45]

What is revealed about God in the cross is that God has come to know first-hand the sufferings of our finite and estranged life.[46] Martin Luther flirts with the edges of Chalcedonian orthodoxy by emphasizing that the divine itself is fully present in the lowest of the low, that God is self-subjugated to the pit of dread, despair and even death. 'It is correct to talk about God's death,' he argues. 'It could be said: God dead, God's passion, God's blood, God's death.'[47] Jürgen Moltmann adds: 'In Jesus' suffering God suffers; in his death, God himself tastes of damnation and death. ... In this way, the old image of God, the image of fatherly or cold authority against which the question of theodicy rebels, is transformed in the cross.'[48] The message of the cross is that we among the human race are not left alone to our suffering, that God is Emmanuel, God with us. Suffering may still be enigmatic, frustrating and unjust; but, no longer can we limit God to unfeeling and apathetic transcendence.

As decisive as the cross is, the gospel story does not end there. It is followed by the resurrection. Good Friday is followed by Easter. 'Jesus' resurrection is the answer to the cry of the forsaken and the glorious beginning of the resolution of the question of theodicy in the world,' says Moltmann. 'The cross of Jesus has lasting meaning only as the conquered, dark past which is on its way toward a glorious future.'[49] As Jesus rose from the dead on the first Easter, the gospel promise is that we too will rise into the everlasting new creation of God, where 'mourning and crying and pain will be no more' (Revelation 21:4).

Job had no assurance of resurrection (Job 14:10–12). He could at best envision death as a realm of peace, as a sleep separating him from the unbearable sufferings of this life (Job 3:16–19). Yet, he did not consider suicide an option. His faith in the unfathomable God was life-preserving.

The message of the cross is that God knows first-hand our most profound sufferings. This means, among other things, that we are not alone in our sufferings. The divine presence within our pain is complemented by the divine promise that suffering and death will give way to a new reality, resurrection and new creation.

Emillie Townes trusts the message of the resurrection to such a degree that she believes the message itself can remove suffering. We may still be victimized by pain, to be sure, but suffering as the distinctively human agony over the meaninglessness or injustice of pain is overcome by living life out of the resurrection. 'True suffering has been removed through the event of the resurrection,' she writes.[50] 'The roots of this stance are grounded in the liberating message of the empty cross and the resurrection. ... The resurrection moves the oppressed past suffering to pain and struggle and from pain and struggle to new life and wholeness.'[51] Resurrection is the promise amidst the pain.

Conclusion

We ask an existential question here: how can we live at peace in a world threatening to infect us with viral diseases? Infection leads to pain. Pain evokes suffering. Pain and suffering remind us of our finitude, of our death. In some cases, actual death prematurely robs us of the freedom to live a healthy life. We puff up with rage, shaking our fist at heaven for the injustice. Where amidst the pain can promise be found?

Will it be found in the doctrine of coevolution? No. Any philosophy built on a coevolutionary naturalism will dismiss the intensity of pain and loneliness of suffering for individual victims of virus infection on behalf of a statistical equilibrium that will benefit only future generations. Any romanticized vision of virus–human coevolution will provide small comfort to an individual overwhelmed by influenza or dying of AIDS. The concept of coevolution may be intellectually satisfying. It may be suggestive of further scientific research. It may even lead to a holistic picture of mutual symbiosis between the human and the virus. Yet, it has a limit. It simply cannot speak adequately to the profound existential need for us as individuals to confront the loneliness and injustice of pain, suffering and death.

Is there promise of peace somewhere else? Perhaps. Some promise can be found in human freedom. But, what kind of freedom? Promethean freedom holds out its own form of promise. For the human race as a collective, our research virologists and medical doctors and health care delivery institutions hold out promise that new vaccines and new therapies will save lives. Such past and projected medical achievements represent the triumphs of human freedom; they represent transcendence of our natural history and human co-creative power for influencing our evolutionary future.

Yet, as respectable and glorious as Promethean freedom can be, I want to point out a counterbalancing freedom that only individual sufferers can enjoy, namely, spiritual freedom.[52] Spiritual freedom places promise squarely within the pain, and draws life from it. The promise within the pain is God in Godself, incarnate in Christ and spiritually present to us in our courage to affirm our true selves in the face of the worst of adversity.

Notes

1   Can we distinguish pain and suffering? C.S. Lewis distinguishes *pain a*, a physical ache, from *pain b*, a higher-level pain that includes suffering, anguish, tribulation, adversity and trouble: *The Problem of Pain* (New York: Simon & Schuster, Touchstone, 1940, 1996), 80. John Hick modifies the vocabulary slightly to define *pain* as 'a physical sensation with its own nerve structure' and *suffering* as a human reaction to pain plus other circumstances that leads to fear, anxiety, remorse, envy, humiliation, a sense of injustice, estrangement, frustration, boredom and so on: *Evil and the God of Love* (New York: Harper, 1966, 1978), 292–3.

2   'In no case can scientific experience as such produce a foundation and source of systematic theology,' Paul Tillich, *Systematic Theology*, 3 volumes, (Chicago: University of Chicago Press, 1951–1963), I, 44.

3   Frank Ryan, *Virus X* (Boston: Little, Brown, and Co., 1997), 238. See P.R. Ehrlich and P.H. Raven, 'Butterflies and Plants: A Study in Coevolution?', *Evolution*, 18 (1964), 586–608; D.H. Janzen, 'When is it Coevolution?', *Evolution*, 34 (1992), 611–12.

4   Joshua Lederberg, Robert E. Shope and Stanley C. Oaks, Jr. (eds), *Emerging Infections: Microbial Threats to Health in the United States*, a study by the Institute of Medicine (Washington, DC: National Academy Press, 1992), vii, 42.

5   See Robin Marantz Henig, *A Dancing Matrix: How Science Confronts Emerging Viruses* (New York: Random House, Vintage 1993), 6–7.

6   'Investigators Present Latest Findings on Hong Kong "Bird Flu" to the FDA', *JAMA*, 279 (4 March 1998), 643–4.

7   Robert Gallo, *Virus Hunting: AIDS, Cancer, and the Human Retrovirus* (New York: Basic Books, 1991), 4–5.

8   Richard Dawkins, *The Selfish Gene* (Oxford: Oxford University Press, 1976, 1989).

9   Edward O. Wilson, *Sociobiology: The New Synthesis* (Cambridge, MA: Harvard University Press, 1975), 3.

10 C.J. Peters, with Mark Olshaker, *Virus Hunter* (New York: Doubleday, Anchor 1997), 28.

11 Ryan, *Virus X*, 53, 303.

12 Ibid., 308.

13 Peters, *Virus Hunter*, 308.

14 Cited in Henig, *A Dancing Matrix*, xvi.

15 Ryan, *Virus X*, 53.

16 'Determining the morality of human actions on the basis of natural selection or the course of evolution leads, moreover, to paradoxes. Evolution has produced the smallpox and AIDS viruses. But, it would seem unreasonable to accuse the World Health Organization of immorality because of its campaign for total eradication of the smallpox virus or to label unethical the efforts to control the galloping spread of the AIDS virus,' Francisco Ayala, 'So Human an Animal: Evolution and Ethics', *Science and Theology: The New Consonance*, ed. by Ted Peters (Boulder: Westview Press, 1998), 132.

17 Edward O. Wilson, *Consilience* (New York: Alfred A. Knopf, 1998), 127.

18 C.J. Lumdsen and E.O. Wilson, *Genes, Mind, and Culture* (Cambridge: Harvard University Press, 1981), 121.

19 Wilson, *Consilience*, 127.

20 Ibid., 262.

21 Ibid., 264.

22 Dawkins, *Selfish Gene*, 193.

23 John Bowker, *Is God a Virus? Genes, Culture, and Religion* (London: SPCK, 1995), 115.
24 Ibid., 116.
25 Ibid., 118.
26 Philip Hefner, *The Human Factor: Evolution, Culture, and Religion* (Minneapolis: Fortress Press, 1993), 45.
27 Ibid., italics in original.
28 Karl Rahner, 'Evolution', in *Encyclopedia of Theology: The Concise Sacramentum Mundi* (New York: Searbury, Crossroad, 1975), 481.
29 Gordon D. Kaufman recognizes that 'there is no reason (from a biological standpoint) to suppose that the process of evolution has actually been directed ... toward any goal whatsoever,' *God, Mystery, Diversity* (Minneapolis: Fortress Press, 1996), 103. Stopping short of creation-wide fulfillment, Kaufman sees past evolution as preparatory for the present stage of humanly formulated directionality. The history of our cosmos 'gradually developed increasing directionality, ultimately creating a context within which deliberate purposive action could emerge' (ibid).
30 Tillich, *Systematic Theology*, I, 183.
31 Ibid., I, 183–4.
32 Ibid., I, 184. 'Freedom is nothing more than the possibility of centered personal acts,' Tillich, *Dynamics of Faith* (New York: Harper, 1957), 5.
33 Marjorie Hewitt Suchocki, *The Fall to Violence* (New York: Continuum, 1994), 130.
34 Karl Rahner, 'The Liberty of the Sick, Theologically Considered', in *Theological Investigations*, 22 volumes (New York: Crossroad, 1961–88), XVII, 102.
35 Job's medical diagnosis is a matter of speculation and debate. A combination of scurvy and pellagra has been suggested, a condition that arises from chronic malnutrition and vitamin deficiency. But because Job was originally a man of means, it is unlikely he was underfed. Others suggest 'Baghdad Button' or 'Jericho Rose', a boil which becomes ulcerous and leaves a deep scar. See Marvin H. Pope, *Job*, volume 15 of the *Anchor Bible* (New York: Doubleday, 1965, 1973), 21.
36 Gustavo Gutierrez connects illness with poverty. Job 'is henceforth a sick as well as a poor man. To the death that is at work in his flesh there is added social death, for in the opinion of that time persons suffering from uncurable illnesses were to some extent outcasts from society. A factor contributing to this attitude was the conviction that poverty and sickness were a punishment for the sins of the individual or the family. In the eyes of his contemporaries, therefore, Job is a sinner and, because he had been a rich and important person, a great sinner,' *On Job*, (Maryknoll, NY: Orbis, 1987), 6. René Girard gives only scant attention to Job's disease, emphasizing rather the social discrimination against a once powerful man who has fallen into disgrace. 'He is ostracized and persecuted by the people around him ... He is the scapegoat of his community,' *Job: The Victim of His People* (Stanford: Stanford University Press, 1987), 4.
37 'God would not be God if He were not free both to give and to take away,' writes Karl Barth. See *Church Dogmatics*, 4 volumes (Edinburgh: T.&T. Clark, 1936–62), IV, iii/i/387. What is decisive for Barth is that 'the relationship between Yahweh and Job has the character of freedom' (ibid., 386). And Job loves God as God, not just for what God can give. 'Job would not be Job if he were not free to receive both evil and good from God. This implies that he fears and loves the free God as such, that in his conduct towards Him he has regard to His free disposing ... grounded

in a fear and love of God which are decisively concerned about God Himself and not His gifts' (ibid., 388).

38 J. Gerald Janzen calls our attention to Job's imagery here: Job finds himself emotionally and existentially in a state like that of a newborn infant, helpless. Janzen builds a case for seeing family imagery as more basic to Job than justice imagery. 'I propose that God does not address justice issues directly because ... God focuses on the deeper domain of experience in which Job's bitterness is most deeply rooted – the domain of birth, life, primal nurture, and care. ... This world is shot through with signs of God's creative care and providential nurture.' See 'Lust for Life and the Bitterness of Job', *Theology Today*, 55:2 (July 1998), 158. Janzen fails to speak to the dramatic question of theodicy: are viruses and the suffering they lead to part of God's nurture?

39 Lewis, *Problem of Pain*, 136. Elsewhere he writes: 'When we act from ourselves alone – that is, from God *in* ourselves – we are collaborators in, or live instruments of, creation' (ibid., 91).

40 Elsewhere I use the term 'soil' in the dialectic of 'soil and spirit' to refer to the inextricably physical nature that we are. See *GOD – The World's Future* (Minneapolis: Fortress, 1992), 141–3.

41 'Suffering, like death, is an element of finitude. ... In Christianity the demand is made to accept suffering as an element of finitude with an ultimate courage and thereby to overcome that suffering which is dependent on existential estrangement, which is mere destruction,' Tillich, *Systematic Theology*, II, 70.

42 Paul Tillich, *The Courage to Be* (New Haven: Yale University Press, 1952), 155.

43 Rahner, *Theological Investigations*, XVII, 104.

44 'Open and unconditional submission to the God of creation grants humanity a reprieve from the cold inhumanity of the radically theocentric world. The recognition of God's inscrutable yet unimpugnable mastery is always painfully difficult – God has made things that way – but it does result in the good life in which God reinstates his justice and renews his generosity. Such is the comforting conclusion of this most disturbing book,' Jon D. Levenson, *Creation and the Persistence of Evil: The Jewish Drama of Divine Omnipotence* (San Francisco: Harper, 1988), 156.

45 Tillich first affirms Job, then Jesus. He first affirms divine mystery, then divine participation in human suffering. He writes, 'The question of theodicy finds its final answer in the mystery of the creative ground.' Then, after rejecting patripassianism while affirming Christology, he adds, 'it is meaningful to speak of a participation of the divine life in the negativities of creaturely life. This is the ultimate answer to the question of theodicy,' *Systematic Theology*, I, 270.

46 Marilyn McCord Adams sees suffering as redemptive because it begins with God's suffering in Jesus Christ. In Christ God 'unites himself to a human consciousness and takes the suffering to himself. Thus, he knows from experience what it is like for pain to drive everything else from a finite consciousness and to press it to the limits of endurance'. We, in turn, are inspired to remain faithful to the limit of endurance. Adams uses the term 'martyr' to describe the faithful person. 'The religious martyr who perseveres at the cost of his life wins the highest good. For in loving God more than any temporal good and trusting God to see his good in the face of death, he is rightly related to God. He is also freed from the power of evil, because evil controls us only by bribing us with temporal goods,' 'Redemptive Suffering: A Christian Solution to the Problem of Evil', in *The Problem of Evil: Selected Readings*, ed. by Michael L. Peterson (Notre Dame: University of Notre Dame Press, 1992), 180–81.

47 Cited in the 'Formula of Concord', *The Book of Concord*, ed. by Theodore G. Tappert (Minneapolis: Fortress, 1959), 599.

48 Jürgen Moltmann, 'God and Resurrection', *Hope and Planning* (New York: Harper, 1971), 43.

49 Ibid., 42.

50 Emillie M. Townes, 'Living in the New Jerusalem', in *A Troubling in My Soul: Womanist Perspectives on Evil Suffering*, ed. by Emillie M. Townes (Maryknoll, NY: Orbis, 1993), 84.

51 Ibid., 85.

52 Elswhere, what I call here 'spiritual freedom' I dub 'moral freedom', as gained from orienting the self toward the good, or 'Christian freedom', as gained from orienting the self toward a gracious God and defining the good in terms of charity, meaning love for God and love for neighbor. See *Playing God? Genetic Determinism and Human Freedom* (New York: Routledge, 1997), 18–25.

IV

NUCLEAR WASTE AND EARTH ETHICS

Chapter 14

Whole and Part: The Tension between the Common Good and Individual Freedom

Our task here is to identify ethical issues pertinent to the siting and management of hazardous waste facilities. Yet ethics, like whales and dirigibles, come only in large packages. The type of ethical issue which is likely to arise over the siting of a hazardous waste facility may very well be part and parcel of a much greater complex of competing cultural and moral values. It is this greater complex of competing values which will be the primary concern of this chapter, especially the tension between the common good and our reverence for individual freedom.

Introduction

We will begin the chapter by identifying the ethical challenge posed by the siting of dangerous waste, namely, the need to think in terms of the good of the whole of society. We will then turn to the broad cultural context in which we in America currently find ourselves. Where we find ourselves is in the midst of an erosion of the mores and ideals, which a century ago united our people around a sense of the common good. What seems to be developing is a view of politics as a naked arena to be filled only with competing personal preferences and special interests. This cultural setting may make it difficult to assess the genuine ethical implications inherent in proposals for siting hazardous waste facilities.

Because the proper management of hazardous waste has to do with the health of the environment and the safety of society as a whole, the issue of the common good comes immediately to the fore. In the third section of the chapter we will give our attention to ethical theory proper. Here, we will note how the idea of the common good is supported in our philosophical tradition by Plato's notion of the transcendent good and, also, how it is supported in the Judeo-Christian religious tradition by the symbol of the Kingdom of God. What is key here is that the good is something which transcends individual preference; that is, the good belongs to the human race as a whole. It is only out of such a vision of the good that we can discern the genuinely ethical dimensions to siting and managing hazardous waste. Thus, there is a reciprocity. Our concern over handling hazardous waste prompts questions of the common good, and our vision of the common good helps define the ethical dimensions of hazardous waste handling.

In the fourth section we will look at a relevant attempt at application of such ethical thinking, the 1987 report of the World Commission on Environment and Development of the United Nations. This Commission makes specific recommendations regarding the handling of hazardous waste within the context of a broad ecological ethic which argues, among other things, that the overall health of the planet depends upon the elimination of poverty.

Finally, we will suggest some ethically conscious principles aimed at directing planning for disposal of hazardous waste. These principles belong in the category of middle axioms, guides which try to bridge the gap from the overall ethical vision of the common good and the practical problem of making concrete decisions regarding siting and management of waste facilities.

The Ethical Challenge of Hazardous Waste

Defining Hazardous Waste

The term 'hazardous waste' can be interpreted broadly or narrowly. Broadly it refers to every kind of waste which needs careful management. This refers to any discarded substance whose chemical or biological nature makes it potentially dangerous to people or to the environment. More narrowly speaking, the Environmental Protection Agency has identified as 'hazardous' those substances which are explosive, corrosive or toxic. By 1985, 200 such substances found their way onto the EPA list and became subject to regulation. Not included in the EPA list are two important items: radioactive waste and infectious substances such as sewage or hospital waste. Legally, these last two are not 'hazardous waste', which simply means that they are regulated by agencies other than the EPA. Despite the limits of legal nomenclature, infectious and radioactive substances certainly fit under the broad concern to protect people and the environment from contamination, and this broader understanding of dangerous waste is the one most relevant to ethical discussion.

One of the nation's occupying concerns at this point in time is the question of how to dispose of dangerous wastes: through incineration, dumping at sea, or the development of safe long-term landfills. The siting question arises primarily with the landfill option. The key concern in hazardous waste landfill development is to prevent leachate – the liquid which trickles down through the waste and picks up contaminants – from escaping into ground water. Designs usually include non-porous bottom liners, drainage sumps, a sorting of waste according to type and constant monitoring. These will be considerably more expensive and require much more sophisticated management than the sanitary landfills with which most of our people are familiar. The increased risk and the increased expense associated with hazardous waste landfills pose a social challenge, to which the easiest response is denial. Almost no one wants such a facility to be located in their own community, giving rise to the NIMBY problem: 'not in my backyard!'[1] Unfortunately, of course, there is no place that is not somebody's backyard.

The problems associated with hazardous waste landfills increase in their drama when we tackle high-level nuclear waste respository siting. The term 'high-level wastes' (HLWs) refers to post-fission products of commercial reactors such as the aqueous solution from the first cycle solvent extraction and spent fuel. HLWs have high-intensity, penetrating radioactivity. Also involved here are transuranic wastes (TRUs). TRUs deserve special attention because they contain alpha partical-emitting nuclides that have long half-lives and tenacious retention if incorporated into the human body. Alpha radiation has a greater carcinogenic potential than do beta or gamma radiation. HLWs and TRUs are currently being stored at reactor sites or in away-from-reactor (AFR) facilities awaiting terminal disposition.

Justice, Compensation and Bribery

The siting of chemical waste landfills and nuclear waste repositories will undoubtedly raise questions of justice. For precedents we may look to past experience with public works projects in general, such as dam construction. Here we assume that justice may be done even if a given project causes certain individuals the inconvenience of having to move their residence. The ethics of justice normally requires that two criteria be met: (1) the negative impact on the environment and on certain people will be offset by a clear good accruing to the larger society, and (2) those individuals and communities incurring the adverse impact are offered a means of redress and are duly compensated.[2] We are likely to carry over these criteria of justice into waste siting mitigation.

Such a carryover will not be easy, however, because current political discussion tends to focus only on the second criterion involving redress and compensation. The means of redress available in a democratic society may permit endless debate and court contests which work in favor of those groups who wish to deny site placement in their respective communities. Good reasons can always be given as to why one geographical segment of the society should not have to bear greater inconvenience or, more importantly, greater health risk than the populace in general. It is a matter of equality versus inequality. The host community of a waste site may suffer inequality by being subjected to greater risk, and we will all sympathize with this plight. In each particular case, it is difficult if not impossible to justify imposing such an inequality on a given community. This observation helps focus the problem at hand: if we treat the matter on a case-by-case basis, the actual siting may be stalled forever because no one is expected to step forward and freely invite into their community a hazardous chemical landfill or radioactive repository.

Our inclination then will be to turn toward compensation as a method for locating a site. We may even define 'mitigation' as coming to terms with a given community to accept everyone else's dangerous refuse.[3] We will want to buy compliance. What is at stake here is not merely appropriate or just compensation to make up for the adverse impact. Rather, our temptation will be to go well beyond. We may offer a host community a superfluity of funds to build a new town swimming pool, rebuild roads and in general to infuse the economy with outside wealth. This supercompensation becomes an ethical problem: if it is demanded by the host community, it is extortion; if it is offered by the authorities, it is bribery.

Part and Whole

Extortion and bribery may be practical and perhaps even effective, but it is not ethical. What will bring mitigation into the ethical sphere is conscious consideration of the first criterion mentioned above, namely, the projected good accruing to the society as a whole. There is a mutuality or reciprocity which characterizes the relationship of part and whole: the good of the whole society benefits the individual person or community, whereas the achievements of the individual or community accrue to the increased benefit of the whole. It is this which places the issue of siting and its concomitant management responsibilities in the ethical sphere.

We might wish to avoid consideration of the ethical dimensions, of course. Yet the very logic of establishing waste facilities prompts us to think about the good of the whole. Whatever toxic or otherwise dangerous substances are involved come from a variety of geographical locations. The whole of our nation witnesses the constant transport of hazardous materials from one place to another. In Europe there is even transnational movement. The linkage and interdependence of various regions quickly becomes obvious here. Waste unites us geographically.

Not only is there a geographical connectedness here, there is also a temporal tie with future generations yet unborn. Once a landfill has finished its reception cycle and has been covered over with lawn, it remains dangerous for decades. HLWs are extremely long-lasting in their toxicity. Repositories may remain dangerous for thousands of years. The DOE estimates that it generally takes 1500 years for the relative biohazard index of HLWs to arrive at that of the ore from which it was made. For spent fuel it takes 10 000 years. A site which contains plutonium 239 will be a threat for 250 000 or even 500 000 years.[4] Our planet and our progeny who will live on it in the centuries which follow us will inherit certain risks and, unless we plan for it, they will inherit none of the benefits. In sum, we cannot reduce the ethical dimensions of the hazardous waste problem to the amount of compensation given to a community hosting a landfill or repository site. To consider the matter ethically, we need to take into consideration the good of the whole of society, both geographically and temporally.

Yet to think in terms of the good of the whole is difficult in our time and place. This is because the concept of the commonweal is evaporating from the values which guide the course of American deliberation. The disappearance of the habit of valuing the good of the whole easily escapes our attention because of our cultural preoccupation with individual freedom. It is to this background situation that we now turn.

Freedom and Individualism in America

'Freedom' is functionally the most sacred word in our modern vocabulary. If we wish to sanctify a program or persuade others to endorse it, we must show how it contributes to freedom. It justifies what we do. We appeal to it. We strive for it. All other enterprises serve it. Freedom functions uncritically as an end in itself, never a means to a further end.

Freedom as Individual Autonomy

What we in the modern world mean by freedom is tacitly, but consistently tied to the autonomy of the individual. The modern world took form in the 18th century with two closely allied rebellions against external authority: we rebelled against having kings and queens tell us what to do, and we rebelled against having religious leaders tell us what to think. We sought to replace these external authorities with internal ones. This is what the word 'autonomy' literally means, namely, we become a law (*nomos*) unto our self (*auto*). Freedom in America and in the West generally has come to be associated with the autonomy of the individual to think and decide without external constraint.

The problem this eventually leads to is the loss of a common bond, the loss of a glue which will mold and hold the social order. In his famous book of the 1830s, *Democracy in America*, the French social philosopher Alexis de Tocqueville alerted us to our coming destiny. He described rugged individualism in America with a mixture of admiration and anxiety. Its revolutionary and free spirit is admirable. Yet it creates anxiety, because if each individual were to unbridle completely his or her passions and seek bald self-interest, American society would dissolve into anarchy. It would destroy itself in a mad orgy of selfish competition.

Habits of the Heart

What could save us from this fate? Tocqueville answers: our values, our mores. The French observer conjectured that the success of America was found in its establishing free institutions which were inspired by high ideals. Such ideals were widely shared. They had to be widely shared if they were to have the power to shape an image of the common good and enlist institutional cooperation on the part of free individuals. These mores Tocqueville called 'habits of the heart', and by this phrase he referred to notions, opinions and ideas that 'shape mental habits'. They are the 'sum of moral and intellectual dispostions of men in society'.[5] What this means is that, if individualism is complemented by cultural mores which embrace a vision of what is the good, then the dynamics of freedom will contribute to the health of the social whole. It is the high value we place on the commonweal which maintains a healthy and progressive balance between the centrifugal forces of individualism and the centripetal forces of social unity.

The Loss of our Habits of the Heart

As we begin a new century, however, anxiety is growing. The acids of modern individualism seem to cut deeper with each generation. What is gradually lost is the habits of the heart, the shared mores which nurture and cultivate a vision of the common good. This is the theme of an important study by a team of sociologists organized by Robert Bellah at the University of California in Berkeley. This group is concerned that American individualism may have grown so cancerous that it could be destroying those social integuments that Tocqueville saw as moderating its more destructive potentialities, that it may be threatening the survival of freedom itself.[6] Our very concept of freedom sows the seeds of its own destruction.

> Freedom is perhaps the most resonant, deeply held American value. In some ways, it defines the good in both personal and political life. Yet freedom turns out to mean being left alone by others, not having other people's values, ideas, or styles of life forced upon one, being free of arbitrary authority in work, family, and political life. What it is that one might do with that freedom is much more difficult for Americans to define. And if the entire social world is made up of individuals, each endowed with the right to be free of others' demands, it becomes hard to forge bonds of attachment to, or cooperation with, other people, since such bonds would imply obligations that necessarily impinge on one's freedom.[7]

What complicates the matter in the 20th century is the segmentation, if not outright fragmentation, of daily life. We divide life into a number of functional sectors: home and workplace, work and leisure, white collar and blue collar, public and private. Such sectoring suits well the needs of large corporations which operate bureaucratically and impersonally. We cannot live all day long in an impersonal atmosphere, of course. So, for our own mental health, we find we have to secure a domain for the personal. To do so we draw a line between the impersonal atmosphere of the work or public sector, on the one hand, and the personal domain of home, family and private leisure, on the other. This leads to two forms of individualism: utilitarian individualism appropriate in the economic and occupational spheres and an expressive individualism appropriate to the private life.[8]

The colossal mistake we in America currently make is that we are relegating values and morality to the personal or private sector. What is good, we meekly assert, is what the individual thinks is good. Goodness is being reduced to personal preference. When translated into political action, the best we can do is have people band together who share the same personal preference, that is, produce self-interest lobbies. The result is a naked arena of competing interest groups. Gone is a vision of the commonweal. We no longer answer to a clarion of virtue which calls and enlists us to support the social whole. Modern America works with the assumption that goodness is restricted to the sphere of expressive individualism.

What we need, argues Robert Bellah and company, is a transformation of modern life which will be based upon a vision of the common good. The source for such a vision lies in the fallow soil of our existing traditions. If we cultivate and nurture seeds which have already been sown, we may bring a 'social ecology' into blossom. Bellah notes how the current ecology movement unites science with ethics. Every ecological fact has an ethical significance.[9] Hence the social ecology for which we strive will be based upon a more basic 'moral ecology'. It will be based upon a commitment to the common good, the seeds of which we can find buried within our existing philosophical and religious traditions.

The Common Good

Let us turn from this cultural overview to the domain of ethics proper.[10] Thinking about Robert Bellah's suggestive advice, we will look briefly at the idea of the common good as we find it first in our philosophical heritage and then in theological tradition.

Plato and the Good

Philosophy in the West originated in ancient Greece with Plato, for whom the desired society oriented itself around the good, what he called the Agathon. In his important vision of the well-governed social order found in *The Republic*, Plato tells us that 'the idea of the good (*tou agathou* idea) is the highest knowledge, and that all other things become useful and advantageous only by their use of this'.[11] Even justice is subordinate to this good. What we need to do is fix our gaze upon the Agathon and use it for the right ordering (*kosmein*) of the city and its citizens.

It is significant to note that for Plato the good is 'beyond being', which means it is something after which we strive but do not yet possess conclusively. We pursue what is good while at the same time it continues to elude us in its completeness. There is a transcendent dimension to the good, which means it comes to us from beyond us. It is by no means the product of individual human preference. It enters our personal existence from the very ground of our existence, that is, from eternal being. The late Eric Voegelin, a political philosopher at Stanford's Hoover Institute until his death and a modern disciple of Plato on these matters, believed this means two things: that there is a oneness to the whole of the human race and that the order of society is more than the sum of the interests of its individual members. He contends that we become fully human by virtue of our 'participation in a whole which transcends' our 'particular existence'.[12]

The Kingdom of God

When we turn to the history of theology in the West, we turn to the symbol of the Kingdom of God. It was to God's kingly rule that the people of Israel were called when liberated from their enslavement to the kingly rule of the Egyptian pharaoh. It was to God's kingdom of grace and everlasting life to which Jesus called the peoples of the world. The followers of Jesus began to look forward to the future, to the advent of the new creation, when the kingdom of God will be consummated and the divine will will be done 'on earth as it is in heaven'. The fifth-century saint from North Africa, Augustine, saw God as the author and guarantor of the good and, recognizing this, he said we should operate politically out of our vision of the future city of God, the *civitas dei*. Hence, as with Plato's Agathon, the good as envisioned in the symbol of the kingdom of God is transcendent to present society. Its source comes from beyond ourselves. It is that which we desire and after which we strive, but we do not yet possess it completely.

A modern theologian and ethicist, Wolfhart Pannenberg, of the University of Munich, defines the current ethical problem as one of establishing values independently of the arbitrariness of individual subjectivity or personal preference. Plato's notion of the Agathon or the Christian symbol of God's kingdom point us toward a transcendent ground for the good. The good can only come from a reality which draws the human race beyond its present situation toward something new and better. It is this which inspires us to improve upon what is, to transform existing realities in the name of a good which is constantly stretching us to go beyond. Ethics becomes active. He writes, 'the striving for God as the ultimate good beyond the world is turned into concern for the world'.[13] In short, a vision of a transcendent good is potentially revolutionary; that is, the idea of the common good is a change agent.

The Commonweal

It is on the basis of the coming kingdom of God that we formulate our vision of the commonweal. What is the commonweal? Beginning with the original hope among the people of Israel, its key terms are peace and justice. And, further, such peace and justice are possible only as expressions of a deep human unity, only as expressions of an underlying wholeness. Pannenberg says that 'the unity of mankind corresponds to the universality of the one God. There can be no peace unless the community of mankind is given priority over national interests'.[14] What this means, among other things, is that, when political decisions are made which give expression to such an anticipated unity, the vision of the good is being made effective in the here and now. The symbol of God's kingdom comes to secular expression whenever we think of ourselves as world citizens, as parts of a greater whole.[15]

What we need to gain from the above discussion is the following set of observations: (1) the common good exists, and it is transcendent to present social reality; (2) the common good is greater than the sum of our individual preferences; (3) the idea of the common good implies a unity to the whole of the human race, to a sense of world citizenship; (4) this wholeness is temporal or intergenerational as well as geographical; and, finally, (5) the rightness of our actions must take into account the risks and benefits accruing to persons and communities apparently removed from ourselves.

Poverty and our Common Future

The issue of the good of the whole presses its way into our consciousness when we take our ecological and economic futures into serious consideration. The World Commission on Environment and Development, established by the United Nations in 1983, issued a 1987 report which says that the future of life on the earth is in jeopardy. We are being threatened on many fronts: deterioration of the ozone layer; the greenouse effect; acidification, deforestation and desertification; and, most pertinent to our discussion here, the disposal of toxic wastes. The bad judgment and poor planning of the present generation is gravely threatening the habitat of future generations. Today's industrial orgy will leave such a mess that our children will not only have to clean up but also bear the expense of protecting themselves for countless decades. World population expert Lester Brown pines: 'we have not inherited the earth from our fathers; we are borrowing it from our children'.[16]

Economic Pluralism as an Ecological Danger

In order to meet the threat to our common destiny posed by these ecological trends, we must deal first with the economic pluralism which fosters if not creates them. The commission concludes that the split between the poor and the rich is the decisive factor contributing to the loss of planetary health.

> The earth is one but the world is not. We all depend on one biosphere for sustaining our lives. Yet each community, each country, strives for survival and prosperity with little regard for its impact on others. Some consume the earth's resources at a rate that would leave little for future generations. Others, many more in number, consume far too little and live with the prospect of hunger, squalor, disease, and early death ...
> The failures that we need to correct arise both from poverty and from the short-sighted way in which we have often pursued prosperity.[17]

What is significant here is the point that poverty is both a cause and an effect of environmental deterioration. Unless we attack the problem of poverty in our world, we will not be able to thwart the threats to our environment or work toward a healthier planet.

Poverty as both Cause and Effect

Poverty is a cause. Poor people cannot afford the added expense entailed in a disciplined use of the environment. Whatever is necessary for immediate survival dictates what is done. Deforestation provides a definitive example. The burning of wood for boiling water to make it drinkable, for cooking and for heating is wreaking havoc on the world's forests. As the population of the poorest of the poor in the third world continues to grow at 2 to 3.5 per cent per year, the stress on the environment accelerates. The conjunction of poverty and industrial pollution are devastating our forests at unprecedented rates. We lose forests roughly the equivalent of half the state of California every year.

Poverty is also an effect. Short-sighted economic development can be damaging. In Brazil, there is a deliberate and massive program to burn large portions of the Amazon rain forest in order to make room for cattle ranching and crop production. Such a great forest as the Amazon region actually helps shape continental climate patterns. Unrestrained destruction of trees is likely to adversely affect rainfall and temperature for the agricultural regions in the southern hemisphere. In the not very long run, such deforestation leads to erosion and, eventually, desertification. Farmers right now are losing 3.1 billion tons of topsoil annually from water and wind erosion, which is two billion tons in excess of an acceptable level of soil loss. Without topsoil, the land no longer produces food. People leave the land and swarm into the cities, increasing the size of barrios and slums.

What the UN commission recommends is an internationally endorsed program of sustainable development. It operates with the premise that growth is necessary if the poor peoples of the world are to improve their own lot and to be in a position to work for ecological health. Yet unlimited growth in the industrialized first and second worlds could devastate the global ecology. Therefore, we need to work on greater efficiency in fuel use while sharply reducing our production of pollution. On behalf of the long-term, the commission recommends limited and controlled growth for the short and intermediate futures. What is absolutely necessary to carry out such a recommendation, of course, is widespread acknowledgment that we need worldwide cooperation to stamp out poverty.

> Humanity has the ability to make development sustainable – to ensure that it meets the needs of the present without compromising the ability of future generations to meet their own needs. ... The Commission believes that widespread poverty is no longer inevitable. Poverty is not only an evil in itself, but sustainable development requires meeting the basic needs of all and extending to all the opportunity to fulfill their aspirations for a better life. A world in which poverty is endemic will always be prone to ecological and other catastrophes.[18]

Any move toward sustainable development will have to be based, whether consciously or unconsciously, on a holistic vision. Our common future is dependent upon a vision of the common good, and the good of the whole requires combating poverty of the part.

UN Commission Recommendations on Hazardous Waste

Within the context of this vision, the Commission makes some specific recommendations regarding the handling of hazardous waste. First, 'the overriding policy objective must be to reduce the amount of waste generated and to transform an increasing amount into resources for use and reuse'.[19] This will reduce the total volume that otherwise must be treated or disposed of through incineration, landfill disposal or dumping at sea. Note that there is no suggestion of a moratorium or an elimination of the production of hazardous wastes. Production of such wastes is assumed to be necessary for industrial growth. The assumption here is that industrial growth is required to combat poverty, and victory over poverty is required if we are to have a healthy planet. In short, greater industrial efficiency in the production and recycling of hazardous waste is called for by the policy of sustainable development.

Its second recommendation has to do with the transport of hazardous wastes across national borders. Between 1982 and 1983, wastes in western Europe transported for disposal in another country virtually doubled, to a level of 250 000 to 425 000 tons. The Netherlands sends 4000 shipments and West Germany sends 20 000 shipments of hazardous wastes per year to East Germany. What we need, argues the Commission, is strict controls on international shipments which would include standards for adequate disposal facilities as well as prior notification to and consent from the recipient countries. Unfortunately, there does not yet exist an effective mechanism either to monitor or to control hazardous waste trade and dumping. The Commission says that 'governments and international organizations must more actively support efforts to achieve an effective international regime to control the transfrontier movement of hazardous wastes'.[20]

Thirdly, 'the Commission would urge all states to continue to refrain from disposing of either low- or high-level [radioactive] wastes at sea or in the sea-bed. Moreover, it would seem prudent to anticipate continuing opposition to sea dumping and to actively pursue the siting and development of environmentally safe, land-based methods of disposal'.[21] Disposal at sea, either by incineration or by straight dumping, amounted to 1.8 million tons in 1983. There are too many long-term uncertainties regarding the safety of our oceans to permit continuation of this practice. The 1985 London Dumping Convention extended a previous moratorium against dumping with the effect of placing the burden of proof upon those who would argue that it is a safe procedure. The UN Commission encourages this direction of policy making and, until safety can be guaranteed, recommends retrievable landfill methods of disposal.

Ethical Principles for Siting and Management

The UN Commission has provided us with an example of an attempt to move from a vision of the common good – in this case a vision of our common future understood as the health of the planet – toward a general policy proposal termed 'sustainable development'. Here, in the concluding section of our chapter, we will make a parallel move. Beginning from a basic commitment to the commonweal, we will move toward formulating some middle axioms which can serve as guides for directing siting and management of hazardous waste facilities.

Principle 1: our basic criteria should be safety and permanence[22]

To determine the satisfactoriness or unsatisfactoriness of any waste management proposal, we need to ask: is it safe; is it permanently safe? This was certainly the underlying assumption of President Jimmy Carter in his adddress to Congress on 12 February 1980: 'My paramount objective in managing nuclear wastes is to protect the health and safety of all Americans, both now and in the future.' It is also the assumption behind the UN Commission's recommendation against continued sea dumping.

By 'safety' we refer primarily to the protection of those people who reside in the vicinity of a hazardous waste disposal site. We refer as well to the protection of the biosphere by keeping the level of chemical toxicity or radioactivity as low as reasonably achievable (ALARA).[23] This will require sophisticated attention. Management of hazardous waste ought not to be relegated to a mere afterthought. It should be treated as a matter of importance because safety is at stake. Hence a corollary to this first principle is that we should employ the best application of available technology and management to reduce the degree of risk to ALARA.

The term 'permanence' calls to mind the October 1980 DOE Environmental Impact Statement: 'the principal objective of waste disposal is to provide reasonable assurance that these wastes, in biologically significant concentrations, will be permanently isolated from the human environment'.[24] It is this quality of permanent isolation which defines 'disposal' or, especially in the case of radioactive wastes, 'terminal storage'.

The point here is that we need to be confident that future generations will enjoy the same protections we wish for our own generation. These basic criteria imply that we are responsible for developing the technology to secure permanent safety. Or, failing to do so, we refrain from disposal and keep our waste in monitored and retrievable form.

Principle 2: the siting of hazardous waste facilities should be determined primarily by the technical criteria appropriate to safety and permanence

The choosing of a site is the point where accidents of geography and the common good converge. Some geographical locations make better hosts for a waste facility than others. For a chemical waste landfill, the area chosen should not experience a flood more often than once a century. The soil beneath should be heavy so as to resist the flow of water. The best sites have a thick natural layer of clay. Although such sites must be carefully chosen, they exist in large number around the country.

Much more care needs to be taken with regard to the proposed deep mine repositories for high-level radioactive waste. A suitable site for mined geologic disposal must include the following characteristics: the rock mass' previous geologic history should indicate probable stability for the next 10 000 years or more; it should be relatively isolated from circulating ground water; it must be capable of containing waste without losing its desirable properties; it must be amenable to technical analysis; and the technological feasibility to develop a repository within it must exist.[25] Under consideration are formations of granite, salt, basalt, shale, alluvium, tuff and argillite. Included here have been the salt domes of Deaf Smith County, Texas, and the basalt host near Hanford, Washington. The present first choice is Yucca Mountain in Nevada. Because the number of factors is so large, relatively fewer sites are available.[26]

Other things being equal, sites in rural areas apart from population centers will be chosen. No doubt politically minded interest groups will attempt to divert or direct siting decisions. Such influences, however, should remain secondary to the technically interpreted criteria of safety and permanence. Only after these criteria have been met equally at a number of optional sites should other criteria become factors in decision making.[27]

Principle 3: we may justly site a waste facility if (a) it can be reasonably expected to contribute to the good of the whole society and (b) those persons and communities incurring adverse direct impacts are offered a means of redress and are duly compensated

These are the two criteria of justice mentioned above.[28] It is the first of these two, the vision of the good of the whole, which risks being forgotten. The adverse impact upon a local community of siting a waste facility may be regrettable, to be sure, but in itself, this is insufficient grounds for prohibiting its establishment. Once it is clear that the advantage of everyone is being served, then we can justify both the siting and appropriate compensation for those individuals adversely affected.

At this point we need to discriminate between compensation and bribes. Justified would be compensation (to the degree that it could be accurately calculated) as payment for actual damages or loss incurred as a result of waste facility siting. A loss in property value or loss of environmental beauty and tranquility would fit here. Not justified ethically would be excessive overpayment or bribes that amount to windfall profits based solely on accident of geography. The difference between these two, obviously, will be very difficult to determine. The disruption of a host community's quality of life cannot be easily quantified and measured in terms of dollars and cents. Because of this, any known error should tip toward the side of overpayment rather than toward inequity.

Principle 4: we should not ask residents near a disposal site to do anything we ourselves would not be willing to do if we were in their situation

This is a form of the golden rule. It was taught by Confucius in ancient China and appears among the religious beliefs of many traditions. Jesus put it this way: 'as you would have others do unto you, do so also unto them'. Philosopher Immanuel Kant's version is known as the categorical imperative: act on maxims which can be considered a universal law.

Once a siting location has been determined, not all community residents will wish to sell their property and relocate. Many will want to stay. In doing so, the criterion of safety will become significant. During siting mitigation discussions and redress, no doubt local residents will say to government and industry officials: 'Well, if it's so safe, why don't you put it in your own back yard?' Those in charge of siting hazardous substances, if they want to be ethical, will simply have to affirm that in all honesty they are not asking others to shoulder risks they themselves are unwilling to shoulder. This means that landfills and repositories should be made as safe as possible. One test of such safety would be the willingness of those most in the know to live on-site.

Principle 5: we owe our progeny knowledge of the hazard

In addition to host communities at our point in time, we need to think of host communities in the future. We should not hide our toxic garbage. The withholding of knowledge from future generations would effectively eliminate them from membership in our ethical community. At minimum we owe them an on-site warning monument with an explanation of the dump's contents. The availability of a complete description of landfill or repository holdings would maximize future options. In addition to a warning, we should take all measures possible to help insure the site against vandalism or sabotage.

Principle 6: the protection of future generations may require site management expense sharing and accident indemnification

This is another way of saying: the user should pay. The generation enjoying the benefits of chemical and radioactive waste production should consider investing a portion of today's profits in an endowment fund, gathered perhaps from a pollution tax. This endowment fund would be set up to support site management for decades, if not centuries. Some of the interest could be drawn for maintenance expenses, while the bulk of the principal would compound to create an accident insurance fund. Of course, interest over a 100- or 1000-year period might grow to quite a sum. Should there be continuity of financial insitutions over a long period of time with a minimum of expensive repository emergencies, the eventual dispersal of accrued wealth could be dubbed a fortuitous compensation of the present generation to the welfare of the future.

Principle 7: we need to develop an implementation ethic which requires vigilance in employing our best technology and our best management

If we grant that all parties concerned embrace the vision of the commonweal and make plans accordingly, we would still confront another more practical problem, namely, the potential gap between design and implementation. No matter how ethically conscientious our vision, there is risk that its execution may fail to provide the greatest safety and permanence possible. What is called for is a code of moral practice which will encourage the highest quality workmanship over the long haul.

What the public rightly fears are accidents or abnormal occurrences (AOs) which endanger people or the biosphere. The 1984 explosion of liquid gas storage tanks in Mexico City killed 1000 people; the Bhopal tragedy in India killed 2000, while injuring another 200 000 people. Such endangerment is a daily affair. From 1980 to 1985, the US Environmental Protection Agency logged 6928 accidents involving toxic chemicals and radioactive materials at US plants. This is an average of five per day. With regard to waste storage in particular, we note that, over a 20-year period, 430 000 gallons of HLWs have leaked into the the soil adjacent to the Columbia River at the Hanford project in the state of Washington. At the Maxey Flats storage area near Morehead, Kentucky, plutonium traces have seeped from their burial plots through the soil and into nearby streams.

Leaks, errors, accidents, bad judgment and careless implementation policies have potentially devastating consequences. On the one hand, we must acknowledge our finitude and admit that AOs are impossible to eliminate completely. On the other hand, because of the severity of the endangerment, we must admit waste facility management (along with other phases of toxic substance management) to the ethical sphere. Because of financial constraints we may be tempted to cut corners on quality. Because of the long-term and perhaps even boring nature of the work, we may be tempted to slacken our concentration. Nevertheless, commitment to safety requires that we muster our best technology and commitment to permanence requires that we be vigilant in establishing effective long-term management policies and oversight.

Conclusion

Our task in this chapter has been to uncover the ethical dimensions of siting and managing hazardous waste facilities. We have been assuming a distinction between the question of ethics and the question of public acceptance. Ethics is the discipline which asks about what is good or bad, right or wrong. It is not concerned primarily with public acceptability. At a given point in time the public may be prone to act ethically, at another point perhaps not. Yet, the ethical task remains constant. In short, the ethical task can be distinguished from the purely practical task of persuading the populace to accept governmental or industry programs.

We have concluded that what brings our concern for handling hazardous waste into the ethical sphere is, first of all, that it prompts questions regarding the common good. We saw how the vision of the common good, whether growing from our philosophical or our religious roots, is dependent upon our apprehension of a reality which is transcendent. It transcends the present by calling us to a future which can be better. It transcends the personal preference of individual people, because it presumes that the good of the individual is dependent upon the good of the whole. To think ethically, then, is to begin with a vision of the unity of the whole human race united over time as well as space. It is to live as a world citizen.

The problem we in America now face is that our public morality decreasingly relies upon a vision of the commonweal. By relegating values to the private domain of personal freedom, we end up with a naked public arena filled only with competing self-interests. The potential for moral anarchy is high. If, in this context, we seek to solve the issues arising from siting toxic chemical and radioactive wastes, the moral anarchy may prove dangerous to human health and to ecological sustainability. What this leads to is the strong suggestion that we take serious cognizance of the common good when considering the siting of waste facilities. This is imperative from an ethical point of view. It may even have the practical value of preserving for the long term the individual freedom which we in our culture so tenaciously hold on to.

Notes

1 Elizabeth Peelle and Richard Ellis, 'Beyond the "Not-In-My-Backyard" Impasse', Forum for Applied Research and Public Policy (Fall 1987), 68–77.

2 Such criteria are enunciated by Harvard professor John Rawls, who advances the understanding of 'justice as fairness'. After he has established that each person has an equal right to basic liberty, Rawls says that 'social and economic inequalities are to be arranged so that they are both (a) reasonably expected to be to everyone's advantage, and (b) attached to positions and offices open to all': *A Theory of Justice* (Cambridge: Harvard University Press, Belknap edn, 1971), 60. When unavoidable unequalities occur, they call for redress and compensation ibid., 100–102.

3 Some sort of risk–benefit analysis is likely to be invoked to give a semblance of justice. 'Risk' can be defined technically as the probability that an event with adverse effects will occur, multiplied by the magnitude of expected adversity. The probability that a person might become a victim of an automobile accident is relatively high, although, because one is far more likely to receive injury and not death, the magnitude of the consequences for society is relatively low. With regard to a HLW repository, in complementary contrast, the magnitude of a disaster could be great, killing perhaps tens of thousands; nevertheless, the expected probability of such an accident at a well-managed site would, one hopes, be very low. The risk, then, for either automobile or HLW repository accidents is very low. At least, so it seems to technical people who are making siting plans. To the public, however, the magnitude of a hazardous or radioactive waste accident is more likely to become the focus of fear and outrage, regardless of the technical definition of 'risk'. Cf. J.A. Hébert, W.L. Rankin, P.G. Brown, C.R. Schuller, R.F. Smith, V.A. Goodnight and H.E. Lippek, 'Nontechnical Issues in Waste Management: Ethical, Institutional and Political Concerns', unpublished paper of the Human Affairs Research Centers, Batelle Pacific Northwest Division, Seattle, Washington 98105, May 1978. The public fear and outrage which comes to expression during the process of redress will tempt us to think that the ethical answer is to be found by granting greater benefits, that is, greater compensation. This constitutes a bribe and will not be an ethical solution, however.

4 *Management of Commercially Generated Radioactive Waste, Final Environmental Impact Statement of the US Department of Energy*, volume I of three (October 1980) DOE/EIS-0046F, 3.37; hereinafter abbreviated: DOE/MCGRW. G.I. Rochlin, using 4 per cent uranium ore as his base, says the long-lived components which emit alpha radiation may have to be kept contained and isolated for up to 10^6 years: 'Nuclear Waste Disposal: Two Social Criteria', *Science*, 195:4273 (7 January 1977), 25.

5   Alexis de Tocqueville, *Democracy in America*, trans. George Lawrence, ed. by J.P. Mayer (New York: Doubleday, Anchor Books, 1969), 287.

6   Robert N. Bellah, Richard Madsen, William M. Sullivan, Ann Swidler and Steven M. Tipton, *Habits of the Heart: Individualism and commitment in American Life* (San Francisco: Harper & Row, 1985), vii; hereinafter abbreviated: *HH*.

7   *HH*, 23.

8   Ibid., 43–6.

9   Cf., Stephen Toulmin, *Return to Cosmology: Postmodern Science and the Theology of Nature* (Berkeley and Los Angeles: University of California Press, 1982), 265–8; cf. *HH*, 284.

10 James M. Wall, editor of *The Christian Century*, served on a panel examining the US government's effort to identify permanent storage sites for nuclear waste. In a recent editorial he wrote, 'What to do with nuclear waste is a problem that requires a moral examination precisely because it is so filled with uncertainty that we dare not resolve it without some sense of a higher purpose at stake' (*The Christian Century*, 105:33, 9 November 1988), 1004. It is this higher purpose which we are here exploring in terms of a transcendent ground for the commonweal.

11 Plato, *The Republic*, Book VI; S.505.

12 Eric Voegelin, *The New Science of Politics* (Chicago: University of Chicago Press, 1952), 27; cf. 156. Cf. also by Voegelin, *Plato and Aristotle, in Order and History*, 5 volumes: (Baton Rouge, LA: Louisiana State University Press, 1956–1987), III, 112. That the good is transcendent is important here. In a democratic society we assume that justice depends upon the active participation of all concerned. But participation alone cannot guarantee invocation of the common good, because it is possible for all participants to divide into self-interest groups and simply compete for their own advantage. In addition, in the case of storing hazardous wastes, future generations cannot actively participate in the decision making of the present generation. Therefore justice, if it is to be invoked authentically, must derive from a vision of a transcendent good of the whole of society, regardless of who is in charge of the decision making.

13 Wolfhart Pannenberg, 'The Kingdom of God and the Foundation of Ethics', in *Theology and the Kingdom of God* (Philadelphia: Westminster Press, 1969), 111.

14 Ibid., 125.

15 This means to Pannenberg, among other things, that participatory democracy is the form of government most consistent with the symbol of God's kingdom. 'The universal nature of the Christian hope for a political order of peace and justice that would unite all humanity has the closest connection with democratic ideals. This is true first of all of the democratic principles. They are based on humans as humans, on all humans, not on the people of this or that nation. Thus from the outset the concept of world citizenship is a vital part of democratic thought.' See Wolfhart Pannenberg, *Ethics* (Philadelphia: Westminster Press, 1981), 138f.

16 Lester R. Brown, *Building a Sustainable Society* (New York & London: W.W. Norton, 1981).

17 *Our Common Future*, by the World Commission on Environment and Development (Oxford & New York: Oxford University Press, 1987), 27. Hereinafter abbreviated: *OCF*. One of the central themes is that we can no longer compartmentalize our crises. They cannot be limited to one nation or one sector of life. 'These are not separate crises: an environmental crisis, a developmental crisis, an energy crisis. They are all one' (ibid., 4).

18 *OCF*, 8. At the 1979 MIT Conference on 'Faith, Science, and the Future', the World Council of Churches began developing an ethical vision similar to that of the

UN Commission, but it is rather more robust. The key term is a 'Just, Participatory and Sustainable Society'. See *Faith and Science in an Unjust World*, 2 volumes (Philadelphia: Fortress Press, 1980), I,4. In this line, ethicist C. Dean Freudenberger offers us a definition of 'sustainability': 'A sustainable society and a sustainable agriculture is one where the idea of permanent carrying capacity is maintained, where yields (agriculture, forestry, energy production, industrial activity, water use) are measured on a sustainable basis rather than by the conventional criteria of the maximization of yields per acre or profit from investment. A sustainable agriculture is one in which waste products can be absorbed back into the ecosystem without damage,' *Food for Tomorrow?* (Minneapolis: Augsburg Publishing House, 1984), 103f.

19 *OCF*, 227.
20 Ibid., 228.
21 Ibid., 271f.
22 In an earlier paper I argued that safety and permanence are the already assumed criteria of those considering policy 'Ethical Considerations Surrounding Nuclear Waste Repository Siting and Mitigation', prepared for the project on 'The Socioeconomic Analysis of Repository Siting', Battelle Memorial Institute, Columbus, Ohio, December 1981. A summary appeared in *Nuclear Waste: Socioeconomic Dimensions of Long-Term Storage*, ed. by Steve H. Murdock, F. Larry Leistritz and Rita R. Hamm (Boulder, Colorado: Westview Press, 1983), chap. 2. An even more brief rendering appears in my article, 'Nuclear Waste: The Ethics of Disposal', *The Christian Century*, 99:8 (10 March 1982), 271–3.
23 I employ the qualifier ALARA (as low as reasonably achievable) to avoid the incoherences of such phrases as 'absolute safety'. It is taken from the insightful work of Margaret M. Maxey, 'Radwastes and Public Ethics: Issues and Imperatives', *Health Physics*, 34 (February 1978), 130.
24 DOE/MCGRW, 1.1.
25 'Statement of Position of the U.S. Department of Energy in the Matter of Proposed Rulemaking on the Storage and Disposal of Nuclear Waste' (15 April 1980) PR-50, 51 (44 FR61372) II-28.
26 We need to note that the question as to whether at present it is technologically feasible to guarantee safety and permanence is debatable. Many fear that we are not yet ready for final disposal. Until such confidence in our technology is established, monitored retrievable storage (MRS) is appropriate.
27 On this point there may exist a mild disagreement between myself and Clark Bullard, chairman of the Central Midwest Compact Commission for Low-Level Radioactive Waste Management. Bullard's position is that site location is negotiable and that the idea of a 'best site' inhibits negotiations. He writes, 'if one believes there is only one best site, it becomes impossible to negotiate compensation for perceived risks. If compensation is offered by the government or industry, it is seen as bribery. If it is demanded by the local community, it is extortion. The approach we are taking is to define a basic level of safety acceptable to the state, and leave communities and industries free to propose any combination of site and technology that exceeds state standards', 'Issues in Low-Level Radioactive Waste Management', *The International Journal of Air Pollution Control and Hazardous Waste Management*, 37:11 (November 1987), 1340. The logic of Bullard's position presumes that there exist multiple sites which meet minimum standards, that we are working with engineered rather than natural barriers to provide safety, and that public participation is essential to decision making. These are sound assumptions, especially when dealing with retrievable

storage of low-level radioactive waste. My principle of giving primacy to the technical criteria pertaining to a site's natural safety increases in importance when we deal with permanent disposal of high-level radioactive waste, because there are fewer sites available and because permanent storage is the target.

28 Here we wish to make application of John Rawls's 'difference principle', according to which 'all social values – liberty and opportunity, income and wealth, and the bases of self-respect – are to be distributed equally unless an unequal distribution of any, or all, of these values is to everyone's advantage. Injustice, then, is simply inequalities that are not to the benefit of all,' *A Theory of Justice*, 62. We may add to this Rawls's notion of reciprocity, 'the principle of mutual benefit', to see how compensation contributes to 'everyone's advantage' (ibid., 102).

Chapter 15

Not in My Backyard!
the Waste-Disposal Crisis

In government circles it is called the 'NIMBY problem'. Whether the proposal is for AIDS clinics, halfway houses for prison parolees or dumps for toxic and nuclear waste, it is usually met by the opposition of citizens, groups who shout 'Not in my backyard!'

Yet these components of modern life must exist in somebody's backyard. As James Wall pointed out in 'Storing Nuclear Waste: My Backyard or Yours?', 'What to do with nuclear waste is a problem that requires a moral examination precisely because it is so filled with uncertainty that we dare not resolve it without some sense of a higher purpose at stake.'[1] Without determining a higher purpose, we will never overcome the NIMBY obstacle.

NIMBY expresses our desire for self-preservation. People perceive the location of hazardous-waste landfill in their neighborhoods as a threat to their own and their families' health. Also, most people do not trust industrial or governmental leaders. History supports this suspicion. From 1980 to 1985, the US Environmental Protection Agency recorded 6928 accidents – an average of five per day – involving toxic chemicals and radioactive materials at American plants. A congressional research team in April 1985 concluded that nearly half of the 1246 hazardous-waste dumps it surveyed showed signs of polluting nearby ground water. The Office of Technology Assessment estimates that at least 10 000 hazardous waste sites in the United States now pose a serious threat to public health and are in dire need of cleaning up. During the 1970s, leakage from steel drums holding low-level nuclear waste brought about the closing of disposal sites in West Valley, New York, Sheffield, Illinois and Maxey Flats, Kentucky. One could recite a lengthy litany of foul-ups, safety violations and instances of mismanagement, stupidity and cost cutting. All this has diminished public confidence in government and business leaders. Motivated by fear and distrust, people join citizens' action campaigns, hire lawyers to file class-action suits, and even take to the streets to protest the apparent threat to their safety and health. This seems the democratic thing to do, the right thing to do.

But is it? Our perspective changes quickly when we try to view NIMBY in light of the needs of society as a whole. We need waste dumps just as we need prisons and halfway houses. Our society as a whole needs somebody's backyard. Yet, in an age in which public participation is becoming integral to decision making, we find that virtually no one wants to make a backyard available. NIMBY is becoming NIABY – 'not in anybody's backyard!'

Over the next decade, our nation will face increased pressure to find a home for toxic refuse. The people's mood, however, is one of refusal. Many states will run out of landfill sites in the early 1990s, but voter referendums are turning down new site proposals. Standards have now been set for disposal of hazardous wastes, but local citizens' groups have petitioned to block the construction even of sites that would meet those standards. The Federal Nuclear Waste Policy Act mandated that deep-mine disposal of high-level radioactive effluent and spent fuel rods from nuclear reactors commence by 1998, but states with proposed geological sites are screaming foul. What we have is a standoff: government agencies are instructed to establish dumpsites, while local citizens' groups prevent those agencies from performing their task.

We need ethical reflection on the situation. There have been two approaches to NIMBY that could be dubbed 'ethical'. In the case of the already alluded to defend-the-underdog approach, we assume that government agencies and associated industries conspire to exploit citizens by dumping toxic garbage on a community to the financial benefit of some power elite. The local citizens are the underdogs. The ethical thing to do seems to be championing the underdogs' cause against the monolith of governmental and industrial power.

Although defending the defenseless is laudable, as a general rule this policy has two weaknesses. First, government and industry are not always marshaled against the people. Quite frequently, government agency employees who set and enforce policy are very conscientious and are simply doing the best they can, given their mandate from the legislature. Second, the defend-the-underdog approach looks after the interests of only a particular community; it does not take into account the good of the whole society.

A second approach concerns the wider issue of environmental protection. I call it the 'constipate-the-system' strategy. This approach assumes that, if all communities take the NIMBY attitude, government agencies will not be able to find any backyard in which to dump toxic chemicals and nuclear waste, and the system will become plugged. To relieve this constipation, we must consume less – and to that end, nuclear power generators must shut down. This would force that industry out of business and perhaps even reduce our dependence on non-biodegradable petrochemicals. However, regardless of one's position on the desirability of nuclear power or of petrochemicals, the toxic and radioactive waste cannot be wished out of existence. We still must find a place for waste that has already been generated, and the longer we postpone dealing with it directly, the more we increase the danger of contamination.

Let me suggest a third ethical approach to NIMBY that would not supplant as much as supplement the defend-the-underdog and constipate-the-system proposals: whole–part ethics. Whole–part ethics assumes a built-in connection between individuals and the global human community, between the present generation and our future progeny. It attempts to discern the good of the whole society, the commonweal, and to establish constructive reciprocity between the individual person or individual community and the society as a whole. We must acknowledge that our society has produced toxic waste and will continue to do so into the foreseeable future, and that it is in the best interests of the commonweal to handle that waste properly so as to protect human health and the natural environment. This means that, when all is said and done, it will have to go in somebody's backyard.

The process of determining just whose backyard will play host will undoubtedly raise questions of justice. For precedents we may look to past experience with public works projects in general, such as dam construction. Here we can borrow a little from John Rawls's *A Theory of Justice* and assume that justice may be done even if the dam's location causes some individuals the inconvenience of having to move their residence. In these cases, the ethics of justice make two demands: that the negative impact on the environment and certain people will be offset by a clear benefit to the larger society, and that individuals and communities suffering adverse effects are offered a means of redress and are duly compensated. These criteria of justice can also apply to waste-dumping disputes.

The goal of redress and compensation will be impossible to achieve completely, however, because future generations, though among those to be affected by toxic waste storage, obviously cannot take part in negotiations about where to place that waste today. Once a hazardous-waste landfill has been filled and covered, it remains dangerous for decades. Certain nuclear wastes are extremely long lasting in their toxicity. Some repositories may remain dangerous for thousands of years. The Department of Energy estimates that it generally takes 1500 years for the relative biohazard index of high-level wastes to arrive at that of the ore from which it was made. For spent fuel, it takes 10 000 years and a site that contains plutonium 239 will be a threat for 250 000 to 500 000 years. Our planet and its life-forms will inherit certain risks and, unless we make plans, they will inherit none of the benefits of waste disposal. A responsible ethic demands that we consider the good of the whole of society, temporally as well as geographically.

With this in mind, I propose some principles to help us translate the abstract whole–part dialectic into public policy regarding waste disposal. First, our basic criteria should be safety and permanence. Waste disposal methods should not threaten the safety of those who live near disposal sites. Chemical toxicity and radioactivity levels should be kept as low as reasonably achievable in order to protect the biosphere. And we need to be confident that future generations will enjoy the same protections we wish for ourselves. These two criteria imply that we are responsible for developing the technology to secure permanent safety, or at least keep our waste in monitored retrievable storage.

Second, locations for hazardous-waste facilities should be determined primarily by technical ability to preserve safety and permanence. Some places make better hosts for waste facilities than others. For example, a chemical-waste landfill should be placed in an area that does not flood more often than once a century. The soil beneath should be heavy so as to resist the flow of water. The best sites have a thick natural layer of clay. Much more care needs to be taken in choosing locations for deep-mine repositories for high-level radioactive waste. A suitable disposal site for mined geologic waste must include the following characteristics: the rock mass' previous geologic history should indicate probable stability for the next 10 000 years or more; it should be relatively isolated from circulating ground water; it must be capable of containing waste without losing its desirable properties; and it must be amenable to technical analysis.

Third, as mentioned above, the location of a waste facility is just if the repository can be reasonably expected to contribute to the good of the whole society, and if those persons and communities suffering adverse effects have a means of redress and are duly compensated. Sometimes businesses or the government attempt to buy a community's compliance by offering more than appropriate or just compensation. They may offer a host community money to build a new town swimming pool or rebuild roads, and in general infuse the economy with outside wealth. The DOE, for example, offered the state of Nevada $10 million per year to relinquish its legal right to object to hosting a high-level nuclear repository and $20 million per year if the site were to be chosen. Such overcompensation is extortion if demanded by the host community and bribery if offered by the authorities.

Extortion and bribery neglect two important considerations. Such a practice reduces the government's motivation to apply its best technology and most vigilant management to the safekeeping of waste; it assumes that the right to increase the risks to public health and the environment can be purchased. Second, it contracts only with the present generation and ignores the future. Those living today increase their wealth, but those who come after us inherit only the toxic threat.

Compensation could be ethical if it addressed the first criterion mentioned above, namely, the projected benefit to the commonweal. This requires a mutual relationship between part and whole: the good of the whole society benefits the individual person or community, while the achievements of the individual or community benefit the whole. Justifiable compensation (to the degree that it could be accurately calculated) would pay for actual damages or loss, including decreased property value or loss of environmental beauty and tranquility. The difference between overpayment or bribes and ethical compensation will be very difficult to determine. The disruption of a host community's quality of life cannot be easily measured in terms of dollars and cents; therefore rectification of known error should lean toward overpayment rather than underpayment.

In some cases the roles are reversed, which clouds the issue of redress. The EPA is now offering $50 000 grants to citizens' groups that commission evaluations from experts of their own choice. Some communities, seeking financial income to offset high unemployment, decide on the basis of their findings to invite waste facilities into their backyard. The Alabama-Coushatta tribe of Native Americans in East Texas, for example, has proposed building a waste incinerator on its land. The people of Chenois, Missouri, have asked for a hazardous-waste dump and received a permit, leading surrounding communities to lodge a legal protest. We may in the distant future have to reassess the ethics of this kind of practice, because we might wake up some day to find that we have dumped all our toxic refuse in poorer communities – that the rich have exploited the poor once again.

Fourth, we should not ask residents near a disposal site to do anything we would not be willing to do if we were in their situation. Not all community residents will wish to sell their property and relocate if a waste facility is planned for their area. The repositories should be made as safe as possible for those remaining in the neighborhood. One test of such safety would be the willingness of those most in the know to live on-site.

Fifth, we owe our progeny knowledge of the hazard. Withholding knowledge from future generations excludes them from our ethical community. At minimum we owe them an on-site warning that explains the dump's contents. If possible, we should compile and make available a complete description of the landfill or repository holdings. We should also take all feasible measures to insure the site against vandalism or sabotage.

This leads directly to a sixth principle: the user should plan for future facility management and accident indemnification. The generation enjoying the benefits of producing chemical and radioactive waste should consider investing a portion of today's profits in an endowment fund, gathered perhaps from a pollution tax. This endowment fund could support site management for decades, if not centuries. Some of the interest could be drawn for maintenance expenses, while the bulk of the principal would create an accident insurance fund. Interest over a 100- or 1000-year period might grow to quite a sum. Barring unforeseeable circumstances, the fund could eventually provide a fortuitous compensation for the welfare of the future.

Finally, we need to employ our best technology and best management with painstaking care. No matter how ethically conscientious our vision, execution may fail to provide the greatest safety and permanence possible. We must encourage the highest quality of workmanship over the long haul. Financial constraints may tempt us to cut corners on quality. Because of the long-term and perhaps even boring nature of the work, we may slacken our concentration. But commitment to safety requires that we muster our best technology, and commitment to permanence requires that we be vigilant in establishing long-term management policies. All of us have an interest in solving the NIMBY problem. We should solve it justly. We will not be able to move beyond our current impasse until individual communities begin to work together with government agencies while sharing a vision of the good society as a whole.

Note

1   James M. Wall, 'Storing Nuclear Waste: My Backyard or Yours', *The Christian Century*, 105:33 (9 November 1988), 1003–4.

V

THE HUMAN BODY: A THEOLOGICAL PROGNOSIS

Chapter 16

Wholeness in Salvation and Healing

We in the Church of Jesus Christ have a message to deliver, namely, God is our savior, and if we place our faith and confidence in God we can experience in this temporal life a foretaste of the eternal well-being which awaits us in the new creation yet to come. Health now is a sign of future salvation. It is this that makes it a blessing from God. It is this which makes it a significant concern for the ministry of the church. If we are to deliver this message with its full power, one of its manifestations will doubtless take the form of a ministry of healing.

Our task in this chapter will be to examine the New Testament understanding of salvation and our present-day ministry of healing. What we will find in the process is that the concept of wholeness helps us to connect the two in a most suggestive fashion. This will lead to recommendations for theological curriculum and congregational caring which will emphasize proclamation of God's gift of tranformatory wholeness plus our own ministry which seeks to embody and share this transformatory power in people's lives. En route to this conclusion, we will make three assumptions.

Our first assumption is that wholeness, health and salvation are concepts which belong together. Our English word 'health' derives from the Old Anglo-Saxon word 'hale' which means uninjured, that is, 'whole'. To be healthy is to be whole. If we greet a friend by saying, 'hail!', we mean 'be thou healthy or whole!' Our word 'hello' shares the same root. So does 'hallow', meaning holy or saintly. In short, health, wholeness and holiness belong together.

A parallel etymology makes the same point with regard to biblical language. The New Testament word for salvation, σωτήρια, is rendered *salus* in Latin, and comes into English with derivatives such as 'salve' as well as 'salvation'.[1] It is very appropriate, then, to ask how this combination of health–wholeness–holiness might give direction to our theological reflection as well as planning for effective congregational ministry.

Our second assumption is that we should think of God's saving work as a making whole. Salvation is the healing of the wounds wrought by estrangement. It is the establishment of communion where previously there had been alienation. It signifies a renewal of creation. It is the transformation of something broken into something whole.

Our third assumption is the cardinal principle of holism, namely, the whole is greater than the sum of the parts.[2] This means that the whole of anything cannot be reducible to the collection of parts which make it up. There is a qualitative jump from an aggregate to a whole. This is pertinent to the current discussion because individual physical healing is a part of something greater, namely, God's saving work on behalf of the whole of creation. This evokes a caution: we dare not reduce salvation to personal healing. Although healing is an authentic and necessary part of the work of salvation, salvation itself is a broader and more inclusive whole.

Salvation and Healing in the New Testament

The episodes of healing in the New Testament constitute proleptic anticipations of the eschatological healing which will come with the advent of the new creation. Hence, the miracle stories of Jesus are much more than mere accounts of someone diseased regaining health. They are part of something much larger. They fit into a much bigger picture, and the bigger picture provides the context for interpreting their meaning. In the miracles especially we witness the same saving power of God *within* history which will ultimately *transform* history into the everlasting kingdom of God. On this count, the healing episodes play a role parallel to the Exodus, namely, they constitute historical events which serve typologically to communicate the nature of eschatological salvation, to communicate the transformatory power of the new creation to us within the confines of the old creation.

The essence of salvation in the Old Testament is deliverance into safety. From the root *yesha*, the two most frequently used forms are *yeshuah* and *yesha*. 'God is my salvation' (Isa. 12:2); and out of gratitude we 'make a joyful noise to the rock of our salvation' (Ps. 95:1). The most significant proper name deriving from this root is *yesus*, which is rendered Ιησοῦς in the Septuagint and the New Testament (Matt. 1:21,25). When combined with *gâ'al*, 'to redeem', meaning to purchase back property or slaves which had fallen into alien hands, salvation came to mean deliverance from slavery, that is, liberation. This provides the typological background for envisioning the new creation for which the old creation is groaning in travail, as Paul puts it, when the creation will be liberated from slavery to corruption, ἡ κτίσις ἐλευθερωθήσεται ἀπὸ της δουλείας της φθοας (Rom. 8:21). This salvation is grounded in hope, γὰρ ελπίδι εσωθημεν, a hope in a divine act which we do not yet see but which we await expectantly (Rom. 8:23).

Salvation has to do with justification and new creation. With regard to justification, it is important to note that in the Old Testament, God saves Israel because God is righteous. It is presumptuous for Israel to imagine that God saves her because she herself is righteous (Deut. 9:4–6; Ezek. 36:22–32). God remains faithful even if Israel violates the covenant. The Holy One of Israel will cover the people's sins and justify them, so that they may stand in his presence in righteousness (Isa. 43:24–6). This means, among other things, that salvation is a gift of divine grace.

With regard to new creation, Deutero (and Tritto) Isaiah combine the models of the Exodus with God's original act of creating the world. The redemption from slavery in Egypt could be performed only by the one who wrought safety and order from the chaotic waters of Leviathan (Rahab) and established the dry firmament (Isa. 43:14–16; 51:9–11). Thus the next act of salvation begins to take on eschatological dimensions as the language breaks out into visions of a new order of existence, a gift from God which spells the end of disease, suffering and degeneration.

> For behold, I create new heavens and a new earth ... no more shall be heard in it the sound of weeping and the cry of distress.
>   No more shall there be in it an infant that lives but a few days, or an old man who does not fill out his days. (Isa. 65:17a,20)

The vision is extended in the apocalyptic writings of the intertestamental period, so that the new creation is pictured as the bringer of health and fulfillment. The energies of nature will cooperate with human labor in the cultivation of a productive economy, and our well being will be guaranteed because 'health will be distilled in the dew, and sickness will be removed' (II Baruch 73:1).

All the various Old Testament words for salvation are rendered by the Septuagint as τὸ σωτήριον or the neuter plural, τα σωτήρια, meaning deliverance, safety, soundness or wholeness. 'Savior' is rendered σωτήρ and is applied either to God (Luke 1:47; Jude 25) or to Christ (Luke 2:11; John 4:42). As mentioned above, its Latin rendering as *salus* as well as English derivatives such as *salve* demonstrate its intrinsic connection with healing. Although 'salvation' in the gospels normally refers to rescue from peril or death, there are 14 instances in which salvation refers to deliverance from disease or demon possession. This is made all the more interesting because the Septuagint never ties σώζειν to healing. What seems to be going on in the ministry of Jesus is that instances of individual healing are being purposely connected to God's promised salvation for Israel and the whole of creation.

Jesus' healing ministry was sometimes tied to the forgiveness of sins, just as new creation is tied closely to justification. Perhaps the most forceful example is the healing of the paralytic in Mark 2:1–12. Here, Jesus first grants forgiveness. Then, only after the onlooking scribes murmured ironically that God alone can forgive sins, Jesus tells the crippled man to take up his pallet and walk. Both acts, the forgiveness of sins and the making of one's body whole, come from the power of God in the saving work of Jesus (cf. John 9:32–3).

The exact nature of the tie between forgiveness and healing is less than fully clear, however. For one thing, forgiveness is not normally the cause of healing. When Jesus said to the paralytic, 'My son, your sins are forgiven,' this did not immediately produce wholeness of body (Mark 2:5). Only when Jesus gave the specific command to 'rise' did healing take place. Forgiveness and therapy are distinct.

Relevant here perhaps is Jesus' disavowal of the widespread belief that one's infirmities are the result of one's sins. In biblical times as well as today, it seems that people tend to associate their physical pain with their guilt. If it were the case that a specific sin would produce a specific illness, then forgiveness alone would constitute therapy. Yet Jesus seems to repudiate this line of thinking (Luke 13:1–5; John 9:2–3). It is too simplistic and even misleading to assume there is a direct correlation between one's sins and one's ill-health. Sins need to be met by forgiveness and infirmity by healing, and the two belong together, to be sure, but the precise nature of their relationship is not exactly clear.

The accounts of Jesus' miraculous healing function very much like the parables. They are signs of God's eschatological salvation. Important in this regard is the report sent to John the Baptist while in prison regarding the fulfillment of prophecy: 'the blind receive their sight and the lame walk, lepers are cleansed and the deaf hear, and the dead are raised up, and the poor have good news preached to them' (Isa. 35:5–6; 61:1; Matt. 11:5).The healings are signs. They participate in, as well as represent, the coming salvation.

The parabolic or revelatory role of the miracles is especially vivid in the exorcism accounts. Here the issue is somewhat different from that of healing infirmity. As we noted above, in Jesus' time the popular view was that ill-health was the result of one's own sin. In the case of demon possession, however, the popular assumption was that demons are the emissaries of Satan and invade us from the outside. A person can be invaded by alien spirits regardless of whether he or she is sinful. The framework is one of God's good creation being attacked and subjected to domination by the evil one. To be demon possessed is to be enslaved and in need of deliverance. In this case Jesus is described as the mighty man, ὁ ἰσχυρός, who conquers the demons of Satan, delivers the victim of possession and reasserts the reign of the living God (Mark 3:22–7).

The significance of all this is that Jesus' healing miracles are part of a larger class of intrahistorical events which point beyond themselves to the grand event of salvation, the advent of the eschatological new creation. Alan Richardson makes the point that it was the actual historical experience of God's deliverance of Israel from Egyptian bondage at the Red Sea which formed the basis of the belief that God was the Savior of Israel. Similarly, we might add, it was in part the experience of miraculous healing and exorcism which led to the affirmation that Jesus is in fact the Christ, the one designated by God to be the savior.

However, it is important to note that the scope of salvation goes well beyond that of individual good health. Salvation is as broad as all of creation. In fact, it portends a renewal of creation. The historical becomes transmuted into a prototype of the eschatological, an advance revelation of what God's future will bring.[3] Or, to say it more fully, the deliverance from Egyptian slavery in the Exodus and deliverance from paralysis in Mark 2:1–12 are proleptic events; that is, they represent the impact the new creation is having upon us amidst the context of the old aeon. The key element is fulfillment: the quenching of our thirst, the deliverance for which we yearn. The new does not cancel, but rather fulfills the present creation. Karl Barth puts it this way:

> Salvation is more than being. Salvation is fulfillment, the supreme, sufficient, definitive and indestructible fulfillment of being. Salvation is the perfect being which is not proper to created being as such but is still future. Created being as such needs salvation, but does not have it: it can only look forward to it. To that extent salvation is its *eschaton*.[4]

Spirit and Body

It is significant that in many cases what Jesus heals are physical infirmities. This means the body is important, that it is valuable in the scheme of salvation. The embodiment of God in the human Jesus – the incarnation – reminds us that the whole of creation, the physical dimension included, is beloved by God.

This became one of the issues in the Protestant Reformation. Martin Luther found it necessary to dramatize how fully human and therefore how fully physical God became in Jesus Christ in order to express the completeness of the work of salvation. Luther did not work with a hierarchy of being, according to which the body is on the bottom and the spirit on the top. Others, such as the Zwinglians who did work with such a hierarchy, held that our higher nature is our spiritual nature. Somehow, they believed, our human spirit would combine with heaven's spiritual nature, and then our spirits would run off to live in a strictly spiritual paradise. This suggests the image of a commuter helicopter landing atop a downtown skyscraper and whisking business executives away, a pickup in which the vehicle never touches the ground. For Luther, in contrast, the vehicle touches the ground and even goes down into the basement. The incarnate God entered the lowest of the low, even entering the depths of sin, in order that the whole of creation might be delivered from sin, death and the power of the devil. Baptist theologian Bernard Ramm observes that 'no other theologian of the Reformation as much as Luther stressed the incarnation and the enhumanization of God'.[5] So, when Luther confronted the spiritualization of the faith as enunciated by Ulrich Zwingli and his disciples at Marburg in 1529, he could but utter, '*Ihr habt einen anderen Geist*'.

This could mean that Lutherans and other Christians who have a strong emphasis on incarnation would make physical well-being a high priority. It might provide impetus for sponsoring the construction of hospitals and sending out medical missionaries. It might be the motivation for pastoral care, the daily visits to the bedsides of the sick and the recovering. It might inspire an ecological and global ethic which would include stewardship of the earth's resources. It might eventually lead to the creation of a deaconate, a select group of professionals who would spearhead the church's work in meeting the needs of the poor and hungry in our world.

Nevertheless, as much as we may love what is bodily, we cannot collapse the entire Christian mission into meeting physical needs.[6] We dare not be reductionistic. It is an observable fact that often a person may be physically infirm yet spiritually healthy. On some occasions, spiritual health can be measured by a person's ability to accept the inevitability of his or her incurable disease and inevitable death. In addition, Jesus reminds us repeatedly of the difference between what is earthly and what is heavenly, advising us not to sacrifice the latter for the former (Matt. 5:11–12; Luke 12:33). In short, there is some independence and even priority of the spirit.

What this means, I think, is that we should see the physical healings performed by Jesus as well as our own experience of good health as blessings, but as blessings which are part and parcel of a much greater whole. The greater whole is God's saving work on behalf of the creation in its entirety.

Wholeness-hunger

There seems to be built right into human nature a drive toward wholeness, or, perhaps better, a competitive dialectic between the thrust toward wholeness and that toward destruction. It is in the context of deprivation or destruction that our desire for wholeness becomes vivid and takes on its redemptive or transformatory qualities. It is in the conflict with disease that wellness can be recognized as a consuming goal.

Martin Marty refers to this drive as 'wholeness-hunger' and he uses the term particularly to emphasize our disgruntlement with the modern mind.[7] The modern mind fragments life. It divides human knowledge up into separate disciplines, so that scientists and theologians have a difficult time speaking to one another. It divides our concept of healing into physical and spiritual. The hunger for wholeness signals that we have had enough of this divisiveness and that we want to put things back together again.

What the concept of wholeness can do for us at this moment is provide a conceptual vehicle whereby we can bring both medical science and Christian theology to bear on a common concern, namely, human health. What both rely upon here is faith in our innate drive toward well-being. If we were to cut our hand on a kitchen knife, for example, the physician might stitch it up. The stitching and subsequent dressing of the wound is but a scientifically devised technique for harnessing and directing the power of healing which comes from a source well beyond the doctor or nurse. Our own bodies bear the forces which heal the wound and seek to restore wholeness.

There are also psychological and spiritual versions of the same process. We may go through a period of personal depression or even a psychotic break down. This may lead to psychotherapy, a combination of counseling and prescription drugs to help us regain our true selves. Similarly, the anxious tension over a broken relationship may be destructive in numerous ways, both physical and social. Here, the ritual of saying 'I'm sorry' combined with forgiveness becomes an experience of healing, of restoration to wholeness.[8] These various dimensions intertwine, and so we should think of them together with integrating concepts such as healing and wholeness.

Pastors, theologians and church leaders are by no means the only ones doing this. In our time, wholeness-hunger is widespread and is coming to significant cultural expression. The most salient form of this expression is the holistic health movement. It will be worth our while to look briefly at this phenomenon and ask about its potential contribution to the Christian approach to human well-being.

Holistic Health

The holistic (sometimes spelled 'wholistic') health movement is on the attack against modern medicine. It recognizes the achievements of modern scientific medicine, of course. Nevertheless, holistic health advocates attack scientific medicine for its unacknowledged limitations. Scientific medicine has worked with a mechanistic model of the human being, a model that treats the body as a machine separable from one's emotional and mental nature. Thus, it cannot help but fragment the human person. This means that the model of health with which modernity works is only partial. The emerging holistic understanding seeks to be postmodern, in contrast, by treating the person as a living organism replete with body, mind and spirit. It seeks to be comprehensive, treating us as *whole persons*.

'Holism' can mean many things. The holistic approach to medicine and mental health includes three distinct, yet complementary components. First, each person is treated in context. Each of us is more than an individual with a body. We belong to families, and our family life can contribute to our becoming sick or enhance our ability to become well. Similarly, we work at a job, we embody the values of our respective ethnic group, and our daily routine involves an identifiable urban, suburban or rural environment. All of these factors need consideration when we seek to promote health, prevent illness and encourage healing.

Second, each person is treated as a living organism, not a broken machine. This represents a model change. Modern medicine has been working with the model of the human being as a machine which operates according to certain identifiable principles. Doctors go to medical school to learn how the machine works and to fix what is broken. When a patient appears in the hospital with an illness or injury, he or she is treated like a machine that needs repair. Cure comes from the outside, through medicine, surgery or guided therapy. The holistic model, in contrast, presumes that the powers of healing come first from within the so-called 'patient'.[9] We have within us the capacity to stimulate our innate healing processes and to make the changes in our lives that will promote health and prevent illness. There is a healer inside us. In a sense, New Age conspirator Marilyn Ferguson says, there is always a doctor in the house.[10]

What this means practically is that one's mental attitude is extremely important, because the assumption is made that there is a close link between body, mind and spirit. Self-healing is important. Therefore, the holistic attitude emphasizes the self-responsibility of the person in addition to any treatment that comes from the outside.

Third, treatment may include alternative medicines and therapies. The holistic approach is not limited to what is prescribed by the American Medical Association. Beyond the standard *materia medica*, we find homoeopathy, acupuncture, biofeedback, hypnosis, meditation, psychic healing, touch therapy, shamanism and root medicine. Maybe even prayer. What is being sought is a synthesis of science and spirit.[11]

Because the achievement of wellness is the objective, there is quite an emphasis on nutrition and exercise. Health food stores have become New Age centers in many communities. Jogging and aerobic exercises have become prescriptions for overcoming depression and enhancing psychological balance. Eastern practices such as the martial arts, deep breathing and Tai Chi give self-control and emotional flexibility. All capitalize on the 'wisdom of the body' which is alleged to be innate.

An important shift in basic assumption is going on here. Holistic medicine begins by thinking of health as a positive state in its own right. Health is not merely the absence of disease. It is much more. The problem with modern medicine is that it has assumed its reponsibility is basically negative: to rid people of diseases. What has not been addressed in any comprehensive way is the criteria for determining good health. The holistic approach aims at discerning just what constitutes good health and moving directly toward it.

One of the key words has become 'wellness'. Holistic health advocates are climbing a ladder that ascends from clinical disease to the absence of disease, then higher to what the World Health Organization calls 'complete physical and mental well being', to something still higher: to a state of extraordinary vigor, joy and creativity. Some call this 'super health', others 'high-level wellness'.[12]

Revisionist physicist Fritjof Capra calls health 'dynamic balance'. So understood, health is an experience of well-being that involves the physical and psychological aspects of the organism and also its interactions with the natural and social environment. This opens the door, Capra believes, to shamanism. The shamans or root doctors among American Indians and elsewhere take a systems approach to health. Human beings are assumed to be integral parts of an ordered system, especially the system we know as the cosmic order. Illness, then, is thought to result from a disharmony with the cosmic order. Even minor things such as sprains, fractures or snake bites are not simply due to misfortune; rather, they result from a disharmonious relationship with the larger world system. Accordingly, shamanistic therapies emphasize the restoration of harmony, or balance, within nature, in human relationships and in relationships with the spirit world. We can learn from the shamans, argues Capra, to see human health in this overall cosmic context.[13]

Holistic health proponents by no means advocate avoidance of doctors or the medical establishment. Rather, they seek to modify if not transform current practice. Among the modifications is the emphasis on the manner in which the physician ought to relate to the patient. The physician ought not to limit himself or herself to looking at the patient's body in isolation from psychosocioeconomic context, but rather take all of this into account. Also important is physical touch. The doctor's soft, patting touch, the careful dressing of wounds, the hand on the laboring woman's belly all function to connote intimate communication and give reassurance. Touch is therapeutic.

Holistic medicine is by no means strictly an individual affair, however. It also promotes a vigorous social ethic. It includes a strong commitment to change those social and economic conditions that perpetuate ill-health. This is an expansion of the assumption that the individual cannot be isolated from his or her social, economic and ecological context. Treatment of a lead-intoxicated child includes pressing for legislation to keep lead-based paint off babies' toys. It includes advocacy for other kinds of political activities leading toward the elimination of hunger and malnutrition, and to the elimination of the poverty and political oppression which creates hunger and malnutrition. Groups such as the Medical Committee for Human Rights and' Physicians for Social

Responsibility, for example, argue that such things as industrial pollution, nuclear development and international war are bad for our health.

Capra presents a political platform for advocacy which includes: (1) restrictions on advertising of unhealthy products; (2) 'health care taxes' levied against corporations which pollute the environment or create similar health hazards; (3) increased incentives for industry to produce more nutritious foods, including restrictions on vending machine companies so that they may sell only nutritional products in schools, hospitals, prisons and government cafeterias; (4) legislation to support organic farming; and (5) general social policies aimed at aiding impoverished people through better education, employment, civil rights, family planning and, of course, health care.[14]

Congregational Caring

Some church leaders are seeing the health in holistic health, taking cognizance especially of the reintegration of the spiritual with the physical. This was the theme of the Summer 1988 issue of *Dialog*. Among other things, editor Carl Braaten offered a wish list.

> My wish is that pastors would include in their teaching the message of the whole person and the whole earth. I wish that congregations would develop programs that give people practical concrete lifestyle alternatives that promote total health, living life to the hilt, optimum well-being – and for people of all ages.[15]

This is our challenge.

One of those who has been working to meet this challenge already for a generation now is Granger Westberg, the architect of Wholistic Health Centers which coordinate doctors, nurses and parish pastors. The first, called the 'Neighborhood Church Clinic' in southern Ohio, opened in 1969 to serve low-income people who had only limited access to otherwise costly medical services. In 1979, he opened a similar program in Hinsdale, Illinois, a wealthy Chicago suburb which has more doctors per square mile than almost every other community. When challenged on this, Westberg responds that he seeks to demonstrate the principle that the holistic approach is valid for everybody, regardless of income level. Similar centers can now be found in Minneapolis, Cleveland and Washington, DC.[16]

In Westberg's work, he has noticed two things which are potentially relevant to congregational contributions to health. First, the hospital system has never made prevention of illness a high priority. Hospitals are in the business of making sick people well, not in preventive medicine in the large sense. 'The church, on the other hand, is increasingly seeing its task as related to keeping people well.' What prevention needs is what the congregation can offer, namely, the power of group dynamics, inspirational experiences, caring fellow humans, and such. 'Science does not offer these qualities of life, but the health-giving church does.'[17]

The second relevant point is that nurses play the key role in making the bridge from congregational ministry to health care, especially prevention. His fifteen years' experience with Wholistic Health Centers demonstrates to Westberg that 'nurses have an almost uncanny ability to bring about therapeutic consultation between religion and medicine, or actually between doctors and clergy'.[18] Many Christian nurses have gone into nursing in the spirit of Christ in order to serve others. What this adds up to, finally, is that we should look to the nurses in our congregations to help move us toward preventive and holistic health care.

Inspired in part by Westberg, Rev. Jack Lundin, formerly of Chicago and now San José, has been developing a 'parish nurse' program. The way it works is for the nurses, doctors and other health professionals in a given congregation to come together and formulate their own philosophy of health in the church setting. Then, they plan ways to meet the needs of their congregation through programs which complement – not replace – the normal care given by physicians, clinics and hospitals. This may include blood pressure tests during coffee hour after worship on Sunday morning, referrals to appropriate agencies, educational programs in the church regarding nutrition or disease prevention, and such. Whatever is done integrates physical well-being with emotional health, medicine with prayer. Westberg calls this 'wholism', and by it he intends to treat each person holistically in a way that combines body, soul and spirit.

At this point we might ask: do 'wholistic ministry' and 'healing ministry' refer to the same thing? 'No,' says at least one commentator. Roland E. Miller is worried that the use of terms such as 'holism' may dilute the force of our medical work, so that it loses much of its distinctive meaning and power. We must not let the holistic vision according to which everything is linked blur our focus on health care. We still need to send doctors and nurses to work among the poor of the third world and to do so in the name of 'Christ the Healer'.[19] Miller is right in cautioning us against inflation of language so that 'wholism' comes to mean everything in general and nothing in particular. The principle of holism should by no means retard any focus of the church's ministry, especially the healing ministry.

One of the overriding themes of the present chapter is that the ministry of healing is most appropriate to congregational life. Not only does it derive from the example of Jesus who brought the kingdom of God to bear upon those burdened by infirmities, but it comes as a specific commission from Jesus to the disciples:

> preach as you go, 'the kingdom of heaven is at hand'. Heal the sick, raise the dead, cleanse lepers, cast out demons. (Matt. 10:7–8)

> And he called the twelve together and gave them power and authority over all demons and to cure diseases, and he sent them out to preach the kingdom of God and to heal. (Luke 9:1–2)

The ministry of the disciples was concentrated on preaching about the coming kingdom, to be sure; but the exorcising of demons and the healing of diseases accompanied the proclamation. If our congregations today wish to follow in the train of Jesus' disciples, perhaps we should 'go and do likewise' (Luke 10:37). The ministry of wholeness constitutes the attempt to do likewise.

The caring support of a Christian congregation can make a difference. Just what kind of a difference may not be immediately obvious. Dean Lueking says he has been searching for statistical data on the difference it makes that people carry into illness a lively faith in God as well as partnership in a congregation which shares that faith. Up to this point he has been unable to find such statistics and even believes that such could not exist, because religious matters allegedly lie beyond the researcher's poll and the computer's tally. 'The generalization still stands, however,' he says, 'that when people encounter serious disease with firm religious grounding and in the fellowship of caring people, it does make a difference for good. People are equipped to face the reality of illness ... people find strength from God in prayer, reflection upon God's Word, belief in God's promises, and support from God's people.'[20]

It just might be that the statistics for which Lueking has been searching can be found. During 1982 and 1983, Dr Randolf Byrd studied 400 patients in the coronary care unit of San Francisco General Medical Center. The task was to determine if intercessory prayer aided in the healing process. Christians outside the hospital gathered regularly to pray for the healing of patients assigned to their respective prayer lists, patients unknown personally to those offering the intercessions. The patients were divided into two blind groups with similar heart conditions. Prayers were offered for members of one group but not the other. Neither group knew whether or not it was the focus of prayers. The result was that 85 per cent of those in the group prayed for experienced recovery to health or at least did not worsen. This compares with 73 per cent of the control group who recovered or did not worsen.[21] In sum, prayer made a 12 per cent difference.

Though interesting, this may not be exactly the kind of statistic Lueking is looking for. It deals with strangers interceding for people they have never met. The Lueking approach could be dubbed 'holistic' in the sense that physical healing is combined with personal faith and interpersonal or communal support. Nevertheless, the 'good' of which he speaks and toward which all this tends is not necessarily the physical good alone. It is the good of the whole person, placing physical well-being in the context of one's whole well-being. It is to this end that the congregational ministry may make a relevant contribution.

Doctrine and Healing in Theological Education

It may be of interest to note how in the Catholic Epistles sound doctrine is described in terms of good health. We should be able to exhort others with 'healthy teaching' (εν τη διδασκαλία τη υγιαινούση) or literally 'teaching which is *hygienic*' (Titus 1:9; cf. I Tim. 1:10; II Tim. 4:3). Might we conclude from this that theological doctrine ought, among other things, to promote good health?

The way theological science and its study could promote good health is to promote health-giving congregations through the preparation of care-giving pastors. This is already being done in departments of practical theology. The pastoral care movement since World War II has revolutionized *Seelsorge* in North American Protestantism by establishing a partnership between church and hospital. What this has meant for seminarians is increased attention given to personal counseling, plus the advent of concentrated programs in Clinical Pastoral Education, most frequently in hospital settings. Thus the consciousness of the importance of the healing situation for Christian ministry is already in place.

But, the setting for pastoral care has been the hospital, nursing home, prison or residence. We must continue to support this, of course, but perhaps the time has come for us to explore the congregation – either the church building or the people assembled, or both – as a complementary setting for the healing ministry. What we need at this juncture is creative leaders, whether pastors or lay people, who will show us the way to better integrate medicine and faith into a single activity. What is effective in one location should be shared in other locations, and our theological seminaries should see themselves as conduits for such sharing. By this means the whole of the church will grow.

In addition, the theological disciplines might consider examining themselves. We need to reopen discussion on the nature of salvation, especially as it concerns the relationship of the part to the whole. This applies first to the so-called 'relationship' between body and spirit. In our formative or premodern past, we tended to think excessively of identifying salvation with spiritual transformation and excused ourselves for inattentiveness to the human body. Salvation consisted in what I call a 'soulechtomy', the extraction of the human soul from the human context. Soulechtomy refers to the attempt at spiritual ascent to heaven while leaving earth behind.

Since the advent of the modern mind and the dominance of the materialistic outlook, we have tended to subordinate as well as separate spirit from body. Since the rise of science, the physical has been considered what is real, rendering matters of the mind and spirit as epiphenomenal. Reality is objective, whereas what we think about reality amounts to only our subjective interpretation of it. Salvation now refers to the existential meaning we superimpose upon material reality. This materialism has led eventually to the reductionism of the current theological scene where salvation is sought only in terms of politicoeconomic transformation, and where traditional Christian doctrines such as spiritual salvation in heaven are repudiated as being counterrevolutionary. Thus, modern theologians like our premodern predecessors have continued the bifurcation of the human being into spirit and body, only now we have reversed our priorities.

What we need is a postmodern view which presses toward the full integration of body, soul, spirit and context. The holistic health movement sets us in the right direction by objecting to modern fragementation, by its reintroduction of spirit, by making relevant our context in a global economy and by its open experimentation with alternative medical means. Yet, we need to go further.

This leads us to the second application of the whole–part relationship. We need to recognize more fully the interdependence between the wholeness of the individual with that of the cosmos, to see that our individual well-being in the true sense participates in and is dependent upon the work of new creation. Healing in our life or in human history constitutes an anticipation of the healing which will transform the whole of the created order.

The proclamation of the gospel from our pulpits and in our lives begins with the message of salvation, with the story of Jesus as the promise of cosmic as well as personal renewal. Wellness and other similar blessings which we experience under the present conditions of brokenness and fragmentariness have a proleptic character; that is, they gain their power and their meaning from the kingdom of God which is yet to come in its fullness. Ours is a message which is both future and present, whole and part, spiritual and physical. It is a message best heard when accompanied by healing.

Notes

1   'The governing idea of salvation and healing today is holistic,' writes Carl Braaten. 'Health is wholeness. This is based on the Christian message that God was in Christ, a whole human person, that he came to bring life and salvation, to make people whole, to heal the sick, to be for every person the Great Physician': *The Apostolic Imperative* (Minneapolis: Augsburg Publishing House, 1985), 188.

2   This principle was enunciated for the contemporary discussion first by the South African philosopher, J.C. Smuts, in *Holism and Evolution* (New York: Macmillan, 1926).

3   Alan Richardson, 'Salvation, Savior', in *The Interpreter's Dictionary of the Bible*, 4 volumes (New York & Nashville: Abingdon, 1962), IV, 168–81.

4   Karl Barth, *Church Dogmatics*, 4 volumes (Edinburgh: T.&T. Clark, 1936–62), IV/1, 8; Barth's italics.

5   Bernard Ramm, 'The Sacramental Gulf', *Eternity*, 32 (July–August 1981), 36–7.

6   We need to preserve the category of spirit if we are to avoid reductionism and if we are to think holistically. 'There is a dimension of healing that goes beyond the medical and the psychotherapeutic. A person as a centered self is more than a collection of parts, more than a system of physical functions and more than a body of feelings. A person is spirit. And what is spirit? The spirit is the essential self. It is not another system of functions alongside the others. The spirit is not a fourth "thing" in addition to the physical, mental, and emotional aspects of life. The spirit is the central unity of them all' (Braaten, *Apostolic Imperative*, 186).

7   Martin E. Marty, 'The Intertwining of Religion and Health/Medicine in Culture: A View Through the Disciplines', in *Health/Medicine and the Faith Traditions*, ed. by Martin E. Marth and Kenneth L. Vaux (Philadelphia: Fortress Press, 1982), 27; cf. 20f; hereinafter abbreviated: *HMFT*. Marty borrows the phrase from John Murray Cuddihy who writes: 'Differentiation is the cutting edge of the modernization process, sundering cruelly what tradition had joined ... Differentiation slices through ancient primordial ties and identities, leaving crisis and "wholeness-hunger" in its wake,' *The Ordeal of Civility: Freud, Marx, Lévi-Strauss, and the Jewish Struggle with Modernity* (New York: Basic Books, 1974), 10.

8   Cf. Kenneth Vaux, 'Topics at the Interface of Medicine and Theology', *HMFT*, 205.

9   This is hyperbole. Modern medical practioners have never overlooked the obvious fact that the force for healing comes from the organism itself. Medicine facilitates self-healing. It is by no means a substitute for what the body does. The critique offered by the holistic health movement is more psychological and institutional than it is medical. It wants to encourage the patient to realize more fully how he or she can and should take responsibility in the healing process and, furthermore, the attending physician should encourage this.

10 Marilyn Ferguson, *The Aquarian Conspiracy* (Los Angeles: Tarcher, 1980), 246–8.

11 Arthur C. Hastings, James Fadiman and James S. Gordon, (eds), *Health for the Whole Person: The Complete Guide to Holistic Medicine* (Boulder: Westview Press, 1980); hereinafter abbreviated: *HWP*.

12 *HWP*, 17.

13 Fritjof Capra, *The Turning Point* (New York: Bantam, 1982), chap. 10; hereinafter abbreviated: *TP*.

14 Capra, *TP*, 334.

15 Carl Braaten, 'The Temple of the Holy Spirit', *Dialog*, 27:3 (Summer 1988), 173.

16 Granger Westberg, 'From Hospital Chaplaincy to Wholistic Health Center', *The Journal of Pastoral Care*, XXXIII:2 (June 1979); reprinted in *Health and Healing: Ministry of the Church*: papers presented at the Symposium sponsored by Wheat Ridge Foundation at Yahara Retreat Center, Madison, Wisconsin, 10–14 March 1980, ed. by Henry L. Lettermann, 109–16; hereinafter abbreviated: *HH*.

17 Granger E. Westberg, 'The Church as Health Place', *Dialog*, 27:3 (Summer 1988), 191.

18 Ibid., 190; cf. Granger E. Westberg, 'Parishes, Nurses, and Health Care', *Lutheran Partners*, IV:6 (November–December, 1988), 26–9.

19 Roland E. Miller, 'Christ the Healer', *HH*, 27.

20 F. Dean Lueking, 'The Congregation: Place of Healing and Sending', *HMFT*, 279.

21 Reported by Martha Sawyer, 'Study Says Prayers Can Help Healing', *Minneapolis–St. Paul Star Tribune* (6 Feb 1989).

Chapter 17

The Physical Body of Immortality

On Saturday, 26 November 1994, I did two things worth remembering. I spent the early morning reading Frank Tipler's best selling book, *The Physics of Immortality*. Later that morning, I served as lector at the funeral of Ethel Mae Jacobson.

First, the funeral. Ethel Mae was a devout Christian believer, zealous lay worker for the life of the church and beloved grandmother. Our prayers ascending before the throne of heaven sought divine solace, comfort in a time of mourning and courage to carry on. I read aloud the Twenty-Third Psalm plus other passages from Scripture that spoke of God's abiding presence and the glories of eternity that await us. The pastor led us in the following liturgical prayer that reflects the opening verses of Romans 6.

> We were buried therefore with him by Baptism into death, so that as Christ was raised from the dead by the glory of the Father, we too might live a new life. For if we have been united with him in a death like his, we shall certainly be united with him in a resurrection like his.[1]

Second, Frank Tipler's book. *The Physics of Immortality* attempts to explain scientifically what our little congregation was expressing liturgically. Tipler argues that, if we live in a closed universe that will eventually double back on itself and collapse in a big crunch, making all physical life as we know it impossible, the human race may still escape to a supraphysical dimension of reality in which conscious experiencing will go on forever. Tipler says there is a physical mechanism that leads to resurrection of living beings: it is computer simulation. By defining a living being as essentially an information processor, Tipler envisions an eschatological computing capacity in which all previously living beings will be simulated – duplicated or replicated or emulated – along with their respective environments to live in never-ending subjective time. Objective time along with its physical cosmos may self-destruct, but the supraphysical society of resurrected emulations will live on eternally at what he calls 'Point Omega'. '*We shall be emulated in the computers of the far future* ... the reality we as resurrected individuals shall inhabit in that far future is "virtual reality" or "cyberspace".'[2]

'Is this where Ethel Mae is going,' I asked myself, looking at her in the casket, 'to await the simulation of her information-processing pattern?'

Now physicist Tipler is doing more than merely trying to bring scientific thinking to bear on theological matters. 'Theology is a branch of physics,' he exclaims; 'physicists can infer by calculation the existence of God and the likelihood of the resurrection of the dead to eternal life in exactly the same way as physicists calculate the properties of the electron.'[3] Tipler's belief in God is the product of a testable physical theory, he claims. He is in effect substituting physics for theology, reducing the latter to the former. 'Reductionism is true,' he trumpets. 'Furthermore, accepting reductionism allows one to integrate fully religion and science.'[4] This integration is a reduction, make no mistake. 'Science can now offer *precisely* the consolations in facing death that religion once offered. Religion is now a part of science.'[5]

The Tipler proposal leads me to ask: theologically speaking, just what do Christians believe is at stake in the concept of resurrection? Tipler thinks he is offering a physical explanation for what Christians (along with Muslims and Jews) believe. Is he? Perhaps it would be worth combing through the list of commitments and concepts at least among Christians to see if Tipler has made a connection or simply run off to pursue an agenda of his own making.

My task in what follows is to review the concepts to which constructive Christian theology has committed itself regarding resurrection, giving special attention to the nature of the resurrected body. My task will not be to evaluate the quality of Tipler's use of science. I will leave that to other reviewers. Rather, I will use the Tipler prod as an opportunity to ask once again: just what do Christians believe when speaking about 'resurrection of the body and life everlasting'?

We will pursue this task by comparing and contrasting various aspects of the biblical view with some alternatives. We will begin by looking at four classical alternatives to the Christian commitment: (1) scientific naturalism, (2) immortality of the soul, (3) absorption into the infinite, and (4) astral projection. Included here will be a discussion of life-after-life experiences. We will then proceed to examine distinctively theological concepts such as death as the destruction of evil, the importance of the death of Jesus, the spiritual body, the interim state, para-eschatology, and the coming of the new creation. We will find that Tipler provides a moderately illuminating way to speculate on some – not all – dimensions of resurrection, but such a method would better be thought of as a complement to theology rather than as a replacement for theology.

Alternatives to the Christian View

What Christians think is not what everyone else thinks. Even within the church opinions can differ. It helps to distinguish alternative views of what might be possible beyond death's pale.

1 Scientific Naturalism

The first possibility we will dub the position of modern scientific naturalism, which in effect says, 'when you're dead you're dead!' Death is the natural conclusion to life. It is the end, pure and simple. Naturalism assumes and asserts that the natural world constitutes the whole of reality. There are no windows that open out into another reality. There is no supernature. Life is fundamentally physical in character, and there is no spiritual reality to which we can escape from the inevitable terminus that death brings. Living is only a physiological process with only a physiological meaning, argues Joseph Wood Krutch. Novelist Jack London goes on to describe our desire for immortality in terms of a delusion.

> All these baffling head-reaches after immortality are but the panics of souls frightened by the fear of death, and cursed with the thrice-cursed gift of imagination. ... [The human person] is compounded of meat and wine and sparkle, of sun-mote and world-dust, a frail mechanism made to run for a span, to be tinkered with by doctors of divinity and doctors of physic, and to be flung into the scrap-heap at the end.[6]

The naturalist position must conclude not only that individual human beings die, but knowing the scientific projections for the future of the cosmos, that all the achievements of civilization must also pass into oblivion. Moving from the personal scrap heap to the cosmic scrap heap, Bertrand Russell draws out the nihilistic consequences:

> all the labor of the ages, all the devotion, all the inspiration, all the noonday brightness of human genius is destined to extinction in the vast death of the solar system, and ... the whole temple of man's achievement must inevitably be buried beneath the debris of a universe in ruins – all these things, if not quite beyond dispute, are yet so nearly certain that no philosophy which rejects them can hope to stand.[7]

'If that's all there is,' once sang Peggy Lee on the US Hit Parade, 'then I'll just go on dancing.'

The diagnosis of this modern secular naturalism is that death is incurable. The patient will die completely and stay dead. Tipler could put himself into the naturalist category, for his diagnosis is that nothing innate to our physical makeup is immortal. The patient will die a total death.[8] Our only hope for recovery is that the information-processing pattern that constitutes our conscious experience might be duplicated at Point Omega. Without this post-mortem operation, the naturalists win the day.

2   Immortality of the Soul

In contrast to scientific naturalism, the next three alternative views all believe they can save the patient through a surgical procedure in which they extract a non-physical selfhood from the physical body. By performing what we will here call a 'soulechtomy', they believe the patient can live on even though the physical body will die.

The first soulechtomy we wish to mention is that performed by the great philosophers of the Platonic tradition in ancient Greece. The Greeks began by noticing how the ideas of the mind (*psyche*) seemed to be immune to the deteriorations of the body. Even though individuals would die, their ideas could be passed on from generation to generation unchanged. Perhaps certain ideas are eternal, the Greeks thought. If so, then the task of philosophy would be to discern which ideas are eternal and then try to train the mind to ponder only the eternal thoughts, so that the mind – which is identified with the true self apart from the body – would cut itself free from all temporal concerns. Free from temporality it could then leave the body and enter the realm of strictly disembodied and hence everlasting reality. With this scheme in mind, death became thought of positively because it would release the soul from temporal concerns and permit greater concentration on what is eternal. Thus Socrates says to Phaedo, just before drinking the hemlock that will put his body to sleep forever,

> The body and its desires are the only cause of wars and factions and battles; for all wars arise for the sake of gaining money, and we are compelled to gain money for the sake of the body. We are slaves to its service. And so, because of all these things, we have no leisure for philosophy. But worst of all is that if we do get a bit of leisure and turn to philosophy, the body is constantly breaking in upon our studies and disturbing us with noise and confusion, so that it prevents our beholding the truth, and in fact we perceive that, if we are ever to know anything absolutely, we must be free from the body and must behold the actual realities with the eye of the soul alone ... when we are dead we are likely to possess the wisdom which we desire and claim to be enamored of; but not while we are alive.[9]

What we need to notice here is the direct competition between the mind or soul, which is the suprasensible self, and the body in which it is trapped. Plato says the soul 'is imprisoned in the body like an oyster in his shell' and it seeks to escape from it through death. There is no concept here of a transformation or renewal of the physical world which would put body and soul into harmony, as one would find in Christianity. Nor does death cause Socrates to tremble with the fear of annihilation, because he seems confident that his true self is leaving a forsaken world to enter a blessed one.

Not everyone who dies becomes blessed, however. According to the Platonic scheme, human souls are confronted with a judgment beyond the grave that determines where they will spend eternity. Following the ways of God and embodying justice are the criteria. Plato writes, 'he who has lived all his life in justice and holiness shall go, when he is dead, to the Islands of the Blessed [*eis makaron nesous*], and dwell there in perfect happiness out of the reach of evil; but ... he who has lived unjustly and impiously shall go to the house of vengeance and punishment, which is called Tartarus'.[10] Then after a millennium (1000 years) the souls of both may be reincarnated and return to life on earth, the souls of those never having seen the truth returning in the form of animals while those who have sought eternal ideas will return as humans. But, the soul of the philosopher has wings with which after three millennia it can fly to the heavenly throne of God and there enjoy the eternal beatific vision.[11]

Plato's version of the soulechtomy has been partially integrated into Christian thought. The Fifth Lateran General Council of 1513 filtered Plato's view through Aristotle and then pronounced it Christian dogma, condemning and rejecting all those 'who assert that the intellectual soul is mortal or one soul common to all'.[12] The Westminster Confession combines immortality of the soul with resurrection by placing them in sequence.

Question 37: What benefits do believers receive from Christ at death?
Answer: The souls of believers are, at their death, made perfect in holiness, and do immediately pass into glory; and their bodies, being still united to Christ, do rest in their graves till the resurrection.
Question: What benefits do believers receive from Christ at the resurrection?
Answer: At the resurrection, believers being raised up in glory, shall be openly acknowledged and acquitted in the day of judgment, and made perfectly blessed in the full enjoying of God to all eternity.

John Newport is uneasy with this. He writes, 'The biblical view teaches that human persons are in no way created to be or to become immortal by their nature. Rather, persons created in the image and likeness of God live within the limits of human nature bounded by mortality and dependent upon God for the gift of immortal life through resurrection from the dead. ... Thus we see that the Greek idea of the innate immortality of the soul is alien to the teaching of the Bible, even though such ideas have become mixed in with Christian doctrine at various times in the centuries since Plato.'[13]

Does Tipler believe in a human soul? Yes, sort of. He starts with his definition of a living being as 'any entity which codes information ... – and the human soul – is a very complex computer program'.[14] Key here is the pattern of information processing. This defines an individual person as a complex machine that processes information and enjoys some independence from the body. He can 'assume that life goes on forever if machines of some sort can continue to exist forever'.[15] Following Aristotle and Thomas Aquinas, Tipler understands the soul as 'the form of activity of the body', and this is tied etymologically and ontologically to 'in*form*ation'. If the information goes on, so does the person. Point Omega will retrieve and recreate the information that now constitutes our souls.

This is not a simple scientized doctrine of the immortality of the soul, of course. As information machines, our souls have no natural power – that is, no physical power – to maintain their existence beyond physical death.[16] As computers, we will shut off. Resurrection of our souls depends totally on the grace of Point Omega which will act to simulate us in the eschatological future. And what will get simulated will be a body – soul unity in virtual reality.

3   Absorption into the Infinite

What Plato propounded is quite similar to what Brahman seers in India believed. In the ancient Asian version of the soulechtomy – the Asian version precedes Socrates and Plato by half a millennium – we find the same basic competition between what is physical and what is mental; we find a similar version of metempsychosis or reincarnation; and we find that salvation is also understood as escape from the physical realm. But a certain accent appears during the age of the Upanishads in India that distinguishes it somewhat from the Greek doctrine of body–soul separation, namely, salvation understood as absorption into the infinite. Thus, although there is considerable overlap, we will think of this as a third alternative way to view life beyond death.

In Sanskrit, one's true self, *atman*, is suprasensible or spiritual in nature and is in essence at one with the ultimate and comprehensive reality, *Brahman*. It is life amidst the cares of the body within the finite constraints of time and place that prevent ordinary human consciousness from realizing this transcendental oneness. We think of ourselves as separate and unique individual selves even though we are not. Our problem, then, is one of ignorance, of living in an illusion. To find the truth, we must transcend the cares of our physical existence by penetrating the depths of the mind until cosmic unity is apprehended. Rather than ponder a group of eternal ideas, as Plato suggested, in ancient India one seeks to get beyond all ideas whatsoever to the undifferentiated and meta-intellectual unity of all things. To do this one is not supposed to study philosophy but rather to meditate – that is, practice yoga.

Should one fail through meditative yoga to free the atman from the body before one's physical death, then *karma* – the karmic triad of desire, thought and action – will cling to the soul and force it back into rebirth. Ordinary death cannot produce the liberation which Socrates was expecting. Between death and rebirth the disembodied soul can experience great truth, but once it re-enters the new mother's womb it returns again to ignorance and must start again to walk the long path toward enlightenment. The ultimate objective of Upanishadic Hinduism is to achieve liberation, *moksha* – that is, to get off the wheel of rebirth and dwell forever in the disembodied oneness of atman and Brahman.[17] To achieve this liberation our finite consciousness must be absorbed without remainder into the infinite, into eternal oblivion.[18]

As various strands of Asian mysticism have begun to dangle amidst the loosely knit fabric of Western culture, interest has begun to grow in both meditation and reincarnation. But the connection is not regularly made. Meditation is pursued by middle-class professionals for the purpose of overcoming stress and gaining self-control, not necessarily to lose oneself in the infinite. Reincarnation, curiously enough, is often taken to be a good thing, as an opportunity to gain another chance at terrestrial living and to refute the pessimistic naturalists. In the West, it becomes an object to be sought. This is almost comical because at home in India it is something from which the truly spiritual souls seek to escape. There is a deep cleavage between European culture and Indian-based religion that often goes unnoticed. What the Eastern heirs to the Upanishads view as the equivalent to eternal life, namely, the escape from ego existence into the oblivion of the infinite, appears to those of us in the West with our strong egos and essentially materialistic disposition as eternal death.[19]

Tipler rejects the idea of reincarnation because it presupposes a formless material soul that takes multiple forms in multiple bodies. He applauds the ancient Brahmanism of the Rig-Veda, however, because its vision of a physical life is closer to his view than is the later dualistic traditions of India. 'The later

Hindu and Buddhist worldviews are inconsistent with the afterlife model in the Omega Point Theory, since these worldviews are based on the dualism of body and soul and have reincarnation back into the present world.'[20] Rather than escape the physical world or return to the physical world, the soul for Tipler presses on toward the far future in which it will be resurrected and 'angelized'.[21] This is neither reincarnation nor absorption into the infinite.

Yet, Tipler has his own version of a mental infinite, referring to it with Teilhard de Chardin's term 'Omega Point' or with the New Age notion of 'universal mind'. This eschatological state of reality takes on the attributes previous theologians ascribed to God, the key to which is infinite knowledge.

> As the Omega Point is approached, survival dictates that life collectively gain control of all matter and energy sources available near the Final State, with this control becoming total at the Omega Point. We can say that life becomes omnipotent at the instant the Omega Point is reached. Since by hypothesis the information stored becomes infinite at the Omega Point, it is reasonable to say that the Omega Point is omniscient; it knows, whatever it is possible to know about the physical universe (and hence about itself).[22]

Two more things contrasting Tipler with the mood of Eastern mysticism are noteworthy here. First, the Tipler scenario depicts life as an ambitious aggressor, taking control over its own evolutionary future to wrest the power of immortality from its dumb physicalness. This contrasts sharply with the ancient Eastern practice of accepting fate, of seeking rest in the eternal arms of Brahman. Second, Tipler's soul in the form of a resurrected body is not absorbed without remainder into the infinite; rather, individual self-consciousness and self-will remain even while participating in the universal mind. The individual does not disappear into the universal. Well, maybe not. Actually, Tipler says, 'There will be two types of afterlife: a life in a resurrected human body, followed by a literally infinite life as part of the universal mind (for those humans who choose to be uploaded).'[23]

4   The Astral Body

A third mode of conceiving life beyond death is that of the astral body or etheric double, a version of the soulechtomy employed especially in the modern occult. It may have roots in certain ancient concepts such as the Egyptian *ka*, the detached part of the personality which plans and acts for the rest of the person. The ka is born with the individual as an identical but immaterial twin, accompanies one through life as a sustaining and constructing force, and then effects existence in the world beyond death. Pictured on the walls of the early pyramids, this etheric double has one's human shape and shadows one's profile in a fashion that leads German archaeologists to dub it a *Döppelgänger*. The distinctive characteristic here is that, even though the ka is supraphysical in character, it assumes one's physical shape.

The actual name 'astral body', however, means 'star body' and connotes a form composed of light and deriving its existence from the heavens. It is an exact copy of the flesh and blood body – that is, the earthly body – but is made of a finer supraphysical material and has a shining and luminous appearance. Among the magicians of the West Indies, people of either sex called 'hags' are said to be able to release themselves from their physical bodies and travel about astrally. The release is effected through the singing of charm songs while sitting naked and alone in the woods at night.

At death, the astral body sleeps for a period of three or four days in a half-conscious state sometimes dubbed 'hades'. During this time, the cords that bind it to physical life are being cut. The astral being awakens to find itself in a world so much like the one it left that at first it may be difficult to realize that death has taken place. Sometimes, the new world appears as a beautiful land where illnesses and infirmities are healed. At other times, it is purgatorial in nature, with selfish souls mourning their loss rather than finding new delights. But this world has an illusory character to it because it still reflects memories of life on earth.

Today's occult reflects the ancient spiritualist cosmos constructed with seven planes or spheres of existence. We start out on the lowest, at the level of physical life on earth. Immediately after death, when released from the physical realm, we travel upward in our astral bodies to hades. This is followed by the world of illusion. Eventually one advances to the higher planes of supraphysical existence: the planes of color, flame, light and, finally, union with God.

Philosophers of a naturalistic bent have for some time looked upon claims regarding astral travel and spiritualist ascent with light-hearted skepticism. But recent anecdotal testimonies of involuntary out-of-the-body experiences have raised new scientific interest in the whole question of a suprasensible self and survival beyond death apart from one's body. We will return to this modern development following a brief detour through a premodern view of soulechtomy.

Is Soulechtomy Forever?

The three versions of soulechtomies just discussed – immortal soul, absorption into infinity, and astral body – all seem to presuppose not only that the self can be extracted from the body, but that in its disembodied form it is potentially if not actually eternal. Is it always the case that disembodied existence is thought to be everlasting? Not necessarily. It is conceivable that the surpraphysical self can pass out of existence.

Let us turn to the Akamba people who, like almost all traditional African religious cultures, work with a dualism. According to Akamba tradition, the human person is made up of at least two parts: the physical part which at death is put into the grave or otherwise disposed of and the non-physical part which survives and bears one's selfhood into the hereafter. Hence, physical death for the Akamba does not mean annihilation, but a departure to the world of the *Aimu*, of the departed spirits. Each human being has a spirit (*veva*): that is, he

or she has, but is not, a spirit. At death his or her personhood moves to the
spirit world where it receives another body which is identical with the body left
in the physical world. This new body belongs to the Aimu world, not ours.
There is no doctrine of reincarnation here, but we do have another case of
soulechtomy.

When someone dies to the physical world, say the Akamba, he or she begins
a process towards disintegration and disappearance into the past. The new
member of the living-dead comes back on occasion to visit former relatives,
usually appearing to one or two and asking about the welfare of the others.
The new initiates to the Aimu realm may serve as guardians in our physical
world and may even influence the birth of new children. Shamans receive
instructions on medicine and the cure of diseases from their deceased
predecessors. Some hostile disembodied souls take possession of various
individuals, causing injury and epileptic fits. Thus, there is communication
between the living-dead and their survivors, but it is not a full fellowship
because they do not share meals, chores and the joys of life.

This communication does not go on forever. It dissipates. As long as one's
name can be remembered, the living-dead may remain present. But, after three
to five generations when it is difficult for the survivors to remember, the loss
of the name signifies the loss of existence. The living-dead slip away into the
forgotten realm of non-being. 'The individual finally disappears,' writes John
Mbiti, 'melts away into the existence without personal names and hence
without personality, deprived of the totality of being. God does not enter into
the picture in this process of evaporation to reintegrate, recondense the
vapour of human being into a new whole, a new persona, a new nameable
thing.'[24]

In their own way, then, the Akamba believe there is an interim period
between physical death and final disposition. During this interim period, the
living-dead function as non-physical or spiritual beings who, as long as their
survivors remember their names, continue to bear their own identities and
personhood. The annihilation of the self does not occur at the moment of
physical death, then. As with the Greeks and Hindus, the true self disengages
itself from the physical body and continues on. Annihilation only comes later,
gradually. In contrast to Christian eschatology, there is no anticipated ultimate
future whereat the God and creator of all things will recreate us and establish
for us an everlasting life. Once the dead past is dead for the Akamba, it stays
dead.

Tipler compares his own Omega Point theory to African religious traditions
of this type, noting how the Yoruba, like the Akamba, believe the dead linger
on for a while among the living before going to the abode of the dead.

> The afterlife predicted by the Omega Point Theory is quite consistent with the
> afterlife expected in most African societies. The afterlife is similar to this life, except
> that the goods we enjoy today are magnified, and the negative aspects of the present
> life are absent. In particular, the dead in the African afterlife are as 'embodied' as the
> dead in the other religious traditions, although there is no indication that the afterlife
> bodies are identical to the bodies the dead persons had when alive. The one major

difference is that, in the Omega Point Theory, the dead are not with the living at any time after death until the Universal Resurrection. In the Omega Point Theory, when you're dead, you're dead – until the Omega Point raises you up.[25]

Life-after-Life

As one more sign that the edifice of modern naturalism and materialism is showing cracks and losing some of its mortar, the recent and widespread fascination with out-of-the-body experiences (OBEs) or near death experiences (NDEs) – sometimes dubbed near death out of body experiences or NDOBEs – reveals the double mind with which we approach natural science. On the one hand, the naturalistic philosophy that so often accompanies modernity seems too restrictive, too insensitive to our deeper feelings and aspirations, too inflexible on the question of human immortality. So, when witnesses from the beyond tell us of another reality, we are ready to listen. With a marked tone of iconoclastic relish, we like to think that the narrow restrictions of science have been exceeded, that the chains of the modern mindset have been broken. On the other hand, curiously enough, we are not ready to listen to the witness of religious faith in this matter. It is important for the public to think that 'scientists are working on this question', because we assume it can become fully believable only when it can be proved empirically. So, what we end up with is a phenomenon which commands great interest and which allows us to express a love–hate relationship with scientific truth.

Prior to the controversy stirred up by Tipler, the journalistic work and reflection of Raymond A. Moody occupied the center of discussion. During the 1970s, Moody scrupulously studied the reports of out-of-the-body experiences of three groups of people: (1) those surgical cases where the patient was pronounced 'dead' in the clinical sense of the word and then resuscitated; (2) those who came close to death but remained alive; and (3) those who died and who told others of their experience while in the process of dying. With numerous peripheral variants, a fascinating and significant core pattern has emerged. The core pattern can be discerned in this first person account of someone undergoing surgery.

> I heard the doctors say that I was dead, and that's when I began to feel as though I were tumbling, actually kind of floating through this blackness, which was some kind of enclosure. There are not really words to describe this. Everything was black, except that, way off from me, I could see this light. It was a very, very brilliant light, but not too large at first. It grew larger as I came nearer and nearer to it.
>
> I was trying to get to that light at the end, because I felt that it was Christ, and I was trying to reach that point. It was not a frightening experience. It was more or less a pleasant thing. For immediately, being a Christian, I had connected the light with Christ, who said, 'I am the light of the world.' I said to myself, 'If this is it, if I am to die, then I know who waits for me at the end, there in that light.'[26]

The core elements found in many similar reports include the darkness usually described as a tunnel, the bright light which grows larger as one approaches, the lack of fear if not feeling of well-being, the sense that the light not only symbolizes truth but is also compassionate and accepting. It is also interesting to note how, in this case, the party undergoing the OBE does not actually see the profile of Jesus. What is seen is light, obviously the light of truth. Knowing that Jesus is the truth as well as the way and the life, the patient connects the two at the level of interpretation.

People who undergo such experiences usually report that, upon return to normal day-to-day living, they now have a deeper sense of the meaning of life. Their values change. No longer do they wish to put off to tomorrow what is important today. Material possessions lose their worth and intense appreciation of human relationships and spiritual truths free them from the obsession to obtain money or status. Finally, they say they no longer have a fear of death.

The light-hearted skeptics among us have sought to identify such reports with Jungian archetypes or to explain the tunnel-light phenomenon as an imaginary recapitulation of one's birth and the emergence into the world from the mother's birth canal. Psychiatrists working at the Menninger Foundation do not believe that the souls of these people actually leave their bodies, but that we should look for some 'parapsychological explanation'. Moody himself speculates that what is being reported may look at first like Plato's immortal soul, but upon closer examination it comes closer to the idea of the 'spiritual body' reported by Paul in 1 Corinthians 15. It is my judgment that most of the cases Moody cites come closer to fitting the idea of the astral body, although not all of the testimony is easily corralled into a single theoretical idea. Regardless of which model it fits better, we have here another form of soulechtomy.

We will not tackle the scientific veracity of personal testimonies of OBEs,[27] but I believe that for the time being we must grant them hypothetical status – that is, we must grant the possibility that there is some validity to what is reported. We must note further that there seems to be continuity between these reported life-after-life experiences in our own modern world and similar reports in ancient times that may or may not have fed into the construction of religious beliefs. The tale of Er reported in the closing pages of the *Republic* has a curious or anomalous character to it, but Plato is able to refashion it to support his overall vision. Similar accounts are reported by Augustine and the Venerable Bede. In the *Tibetan Book of the Dead (Bardo Thodol)* and in Chinese *Buddhist Sutras*, we find accounts of souls passing from one incarnation to the next through darkness, experiencing light and even seeing one's future mother and father in the act of conception which will bring the soul back to the physical plane.

Now, let us simply observe a couple of things about our four options. First, there is a significant difference between modern naturalism and the various soulechtomies. The revival of soulechtomy on present-day operating tables right beneath the hands of the paradigm of the modern mind – the medical scientist – marks a point at which current consciousness challenges the modern naturalistic world-view for its narrowness. Second, none of these four positions points toward the path we should follow if we wish our evangelical explication to draw out faithfully what Christians mean by 'resurrection of the body and life everlasting'. We need now to turn to the specifically theological understanding of the significance of death and its relationship to what has been accomplished in the work of Jesus Christ. Then we will return to an analysis of soulechtomy to determine just how much – if any – complementarity there can be. We will begin by stepping back into the Garden of Eden, where all this death stuff began.

Death as the Destruction of Evil[28]

The Garden of Eden story in Genesis 2–3 introduces us to the tension between knowing that we must die, yet imagining life without dying. The fall into sin that subjects us to mortality was precipitated by the violation of God's command to avoid the knowledge of good and evil. Reacting to this disobedience, God threw Adam and Eve out of the garden and placed the cherubim at the gate with a flaming sword, preventing the man and woman from returning. Why such a dramatic reaction on God's part? Was it due to a divine temper tantrum? Could God claim temporary insanity, saying that it was blind rage that drove God to pull the trigger leading to the death of Adam and Eve? No, the expulsion from the garden expresses the same abiding love of God that leads to redemption and salvation.

Why, then, did God expel them? The answer has to do with the second special tree. Although Adam and Eve had eaten the fruit from the tree of the knowledge of good and evil, they had not yet tasted fruit from the tree of life. This is important. Had they eaten fruit from the tree of life, then they would 'live forever' (Gen. 3:22). What we know as the fall introduced into God's otherwise good creation such things as enmity between humans and wild beasts, the sweat of the brow by which a living must be wrested from nature, pain in childbirth, and all manner of suffering. None of us, not even God, wants the items on this list to go on forever. It is redemptive love, then, that motivates God to separate Adam and Eve from the tree of life. In its own way, death becomes a gift of divine grace; it marks the point at which the consequences for sin come to an end. There is no suffering in the grave. Death is the door that God slams shut on evil and suffering within his creation.

Paul says that 'the wages of sin is death' (Rom. 6:23). What does this mean? We may interpret this negatively to mean that death is the appropriate penalty for disobedience.[29] We may think that, just as serial killers should be punished in the electric chair or gas chamber, so also is eating forbidden fruit similarly punishable. Death is a sign of the deserved loss of divine grace. Yet, it may not be quite so simple. We may offer a long-range positive interpretation as well. Might we say that, in light of Genesis 3, and in light of Easter, death plays an important role in the divine plan of salvation? Is death a necessary step down the path toward resurrection and new life, to a new life immune from the sufferings of this fallen world? Perhaps, we can interpret death according to either the law or the gospel. According to the law, it is our just deserts for acting sinfully. According to the gospel, it is a gift that opens the door to an everlasting life free of the sufferings we undergo in this life.[30]

If this is the case, we need to emphasize the totality of death. The Bible really believes that we humans are mortal. We really do die and cease to exist. There is no salvation by heroic soulechtomy. The understanding of sin with which we work is that sin is a cancer which eats away at the totality of human existence, leaving no organ, whether physical or spiritual, uninfected. The resulting death means true extinction.

Does this sound like modern naturalism? It should. Death, theologically understood, puts an end to all that we are and have on this side of mortality. It puts an end to all evil. It also puts an end to all that is good, mortally good. We do not possess an intrinsically good immortal soul that is somehow exempt from the disease of sin so that it can simply shed the body like a shelled oyster and go on to a higher plane of existence in the great sea of eternal ideas. And certainly there is no room for an evil immortal soul that similarly sheds the body so that its evil existence will continue on everlastingly. Whoever and whatever we are dies totally and completely. Death symbolizes that end, the termination.

The Death and Resurrection of Jesus

This applies to Jesus. He was born a mortal, died a mortal and knew it. There are many things in common between the death of Socrates and the death of Jesus, but there are some notable differences which are relevant to our discussion here. Jesus does not live with the comfort Socrates had regarding the immortal soul and the bliss of philosophical speculation. The death of Socrates, as described by Plato, is a beautiful death. It is free of anxiety and terror. Like shedding one's coat, Socrates rids himself of his body and slips quietly off into a better existence.

This is not the case with Jesus. Death for him is the end. In Gethsemane, he is 'greatly distressed and troubled', saying to his disciples, 'my soul is sorrowful, even to death' (Mark 14:33–4). In agony Jesus prays 'with loud cries and tears' (Heb. 5:7), 'his sweat became like great drops of blood falling down upon the ground' (Luke 22:44). The contrast with Socrates is vivid. Socrates takes the cup of hemlock calmly and voluntarily, but Jesus, in contrast, petitions God: 'remove this cup from me' (Mark 14:36). 'Jesus is afraid,' writes Oscar Cullmann. 'He is afraid in the face of death itself. Death for him is not something divine; it is something dreadful. ... Here is nothing of the composure of Socrates, who met death peacefully as a friend.'[31] Note how Socrates goes out drinking the hemlock in sublime calm, whereas Jesus cries from the cross, 'my God, my God, why have you forsaken me?' (Mark 15:34). This is not a death of liberation but death in all its frightful horror. It is genuinely the 'last enemy' of God (1 Cor. 15:26).

This is by no means to picture Jesus as a coward. His courage is stalwart. Despite his petition in the Gethsemane prayer that he not have to drink the cup of death, he still concludes his prayer: 'yet not what I want, but what you want' (Mark 14:36). And despite his agonizing sense of abandonment on the cross, he still utters: 'Father, into thy hands I commit my spirit' (Luke 23:46). Death is terrible, but Jesus' faith is strong.

The death Jesus dies on Good Friday is the death of Adam, the death of us all. Yet, this is not the end of the story. On Easter, God raises the dead Jesus to new and everlasting life. Jesus dies a mortal, but God the creator of the old creation acts with the power of the new creation. God bestows new life. And this new life is different from the old life which Jesus gave up. The new life is no longer subject to sin, suffering or death. It is this that makes Jesus' resurrection salvific. In this regard, we can contrast Jesus' Easter resurrection with the resurrection miracles such as the widow's son at Nain (Luke 7:11–17), Jairus' daughter (Mark 5:21–43) and Lazarus (John 11:38–44). In these miracles, we find a resuscitation of a corpse. Three persons are raised, but they are not raised to immortality. They are simply returned to normal life. They would all have to face death again, just like the rest of us. But Jesus' corpse was not merely resuscitated, not merely restored to ordinary life. No one expected Jesus to return to Nazareth to resume his duties as a carpenter. Jesus' resurrected existence had become eschatological. Jesus will not have to die again. When those who enjoyed fellowship with the risen Jesus reported what they saw, they did not say, 'Wow, the Nazarene is back!' Rather, they reported that they had seen 'the Lord' (Luke 24:34; John 20:18).[32]

Easter opens the gate so that, as we share in Jesus' resurrection, we pass through to a new and everlasting life. As we turn and look backward, we see Jesus' death standing like the angel with the fiery sword at the Garden of Eden, preventing suffering and death from following us into the new creation.

The Spiritual Body

Now, let us ask about the nature of resurrected existence.[33] In introducing his great discussion of resurrection, Paul speaks of heavenly bodies (*somata epourania*) with their *doxa* – connoting glory or radiance or luster – and identifies them with the resurrection of the dead (1 Cor. 15:40–42). Does this indicate that he has something like the *ka* or astral body in mind? After all, does not occult thinking affirm that we have a star body, a body of light immune to the decay of more physical things? For the occultist, the body of glory simply sheds its physical body and goes on, maintaining continuity between this world and the next on the basis of some built-in radiance principle. There is no genuine death or destruction in alleged astral existence. An element of the person abides. Is this what Paul means? No. Glory here does not refer to a body with radiance or any other such quality. 'Rather, this reflects Jewish eschatological language for the future state of the righteous.'[34] For Paul, there is no abiding life force at all that perdures through death. 'Between "is sown" and "is raised" lies an infinite gulf which the body cannot span.'[35] If there is resurrection, it is new creation. Therefore the resurrected body of the New Testament must be something different from the astral body as ordinarily understood.

Total Death, Total Life

That there is total death and total new life is indicated by Paul's appeal to the image of the seed sown in the ground. The flower or tree that grows up looks quite different from what had been planted. However, in order to guard against any possible misinterpretation in terms of soulechtomy, he exploits the deadlike appearance of the typical seed to say, 'what you sow does not come to life unless it dies' (1 Cor. 15:36). This analogy is delicate. Paul wishes to affirm continuity and discontinuity between the present and future realities. Resurrection is not exactly creation out of nothing, but creation of something out of something else. A dead seed is sown, but what is harvested is new life.[36]

Paul describes this eschatological harvest in terms of four complementary contrasts.

> So it is with the resurrection of the dead. What is sown perishable [corrupt, *phthora*] is raised imperishable [incorrupt, *aphtharsia*]. It is sown in dishonor [*atimia*]; it is raised in glory [*doxa*]. It is sown in weakness [*astheneia*]; it is raised in power [*dynamei*]. It is sown a physical body [*soma psychikon*]; it is raised a spiritual body [*soma pneumatikon*]. (1 Cor. 15:42–4)

For Jesus or for us to be raised 'imperishable' is to be raised to everlasting life.[37] One's body is not resuscitated for the purpose of simply returning to one's daily toil. *Doxa*, which in reference to the heavenly bodies usually means luster, here means we are raised in honor. The power into which we will be raised, *dynamis*, is the same power by which miracles of healing are performed (1 Cor. 12:28).

Of these four antitheses, the most interesting is the contrast between the earthly and the spiritual bodies. Pertinent to our discussion here is the fact that Paul does not describe the earthly body as one of flesh (*soma sarkikon*), as one might have expected. Rather, Paul describes the earthly body as a 'psychic' body (*soma psychikon*). Literally, this is the ensouled body which we would associate with the Greek philosophical tradition.[38] For Paul, the soul dies. And as if to rub it in, Paul says it is not the *psyche* which we find in the resurrection, it is the *soma*.

The resurrected body is a 'spiritual body'. Other writings of Paul indicate that he probably intends to contrast this spiritual body with the fleshly body as well as the ensouled body. When depicting the tension which characterizes Christian existence, Paul frequently portrays it in terms of a war between the flesh (*sarx*) and the spirit (Gal. 5:13–26). Flesh is the power of sin that leads to death. The spirit is its great antagonist; it is the power of creation and new creation. Both powers attempt to invade and control us. It is important to discern here that when Paul uses these terms, he does not intend to make metaphysical statements regarding human nature – that is, flesh and spirit are not distinct ontological components of each human being. This is not another version of the Greek body–soul dualism. Rather, flesh and spirit are proclivities or forces which contend for domination of the whole person, body and soul included. Oscar Cullmann goes a bit too far when he hypostatizes them, describing flesh and spirit as 'two transcendent Powers' which can enter us from without. But he is correct in saying that 'neither is given with human existence as such'.[39] With this background, we can see why Paul might say, 'flesh and blood cannot inherit the kingdom of God' (1 Cor. 15:50).

Nevertheless, the concept of flesh as that which corrupts cannot be separated from its milder designation of the physical body which simply decays, and both meanings seem to be present in 1 Corinthians 15. Hence, there is overlap between flesh (*sarx*) and body (*soma*), although some scholars such as Cullmann try to drive a wedge between them. That there is room for some interchangeability is evidenced by the writings of the Greek fathers such as Justin Martyr, who could use the phrase 'resurrection of the flesh' and declare that because flesh was created by God it must be deemed valuable by God.[40] Early versions of the Apostles' Creed rendered part of the third article as 'I believe in the resurrection of the flesh'. This upsets Cullmann, who complains that this is 'not biblical'. Instead of 'flesh' it should read 'body', he says. Well, *contra* Cullmann, it appears quite biblical. This is clear from Luke 24:39, especially as interpreted by Augustine, who affirms that, even in our resurrected spiritual bodies, the term 'flesh' may apply just as it did to the post-Easter Jesus.[41] Perhaps Cullmann's problem is that he wants to deal with the issue strictly as a matter of word choice without looking at the conceptuality being conveyed. Paul and Luke paid less attention to vocabulary choice than Cullmann would approve of.

One attempt to get at Paul's underlying conceptuality here is to think of the *soma* as the form which can exist with one or another substance, either flesh (*sarx*) or spirit (*pneuma* or *doxa*). Following the earlier work of Lietzmann, Hans Conzelmann advocates this form–substance theory and contends that there is no such thing as a *soma* all by itself. *Soma* always exists in a specific mode of being, either as *sarx* or as *doxa*. The form is always related to its concrete mode of being. It is always either heavenly or earthly. It does not constitute the individual human being as such. It exists on its own only as an abstract concept.[42] Although Conzelmann helps us here, this theory is not careful to show just how his idea takes account of the fact that Paul's contrast is actually between a psychic body and a spiritual body, not between a fleshly and a glorified body.

It seems to me that the spirit is not simply one substance interchangeable with others. The spirit is the power of God whereby reality itself is determined. The *soma pneumatikon* is the resurrected body which is determined by the Holy Spirit. It is the reality which we will be, because God will have created us – recreated us – in this form. And because it is an eschatological reality belonging to the new creation, and because we still live amidst the old creation, we cannot expect to apprehend clearly just what this means. Now, we can only look through a mirror dimly, and Christ is that mirror reflecting the light of future glory amidst our present darkness. What we can say with confidence is that there will be a resurrection of the human self.[43] What we cannot say at this point is precisely what that resurrected mode of existence will look like.

To my reading, Paul seems to be thinking this out for the first time in his dialogue with the Corinthians.[44] He is not simply reiterating an already existing set of ideas that previously belonged to the Jews, the Gnostics, the Corinthians, or any other group we know of. He is not proposing one theory of immortality among others. Paul struggles to explicate the gospel, to apply what he knows about the resurrection of Jesus to our promised resurrection. Paul confronts the gospel and tries to represent it to an audience which probably believes the material body is inimical to the spirit. The readers of his letter in Corinth, probably heavily influenced by the Greek intellectual tradition, have misunderstood what the significance of the gospel is for human mortality and eternal life. We today do not know exactly how Paul thought of the gospel before explicating it to the Corinthians, so for us this letter serves as a primary stage of thinking through the implications of a gospel that begins with the Easter announcement, 'He is risen!'

It is interesting to note that the Easter resurrection of Christ plays no role in the Tipler eschatology. In fact, Tipler rejects the claim that Jesus Christ rose from the dead, and on the basis of this rejected claim, he declares himself to be a non-Christian and an atheist.[45] Tipler's view of resurrection is strictly eschatological, with no Christological prolepsis.

Resurrection for Tipler is solely the result of a future evolutionary event in which life understood as information processing takes hold of its own destiny and creates a supraphysical environment for its existence just prior to the moment when the physical world self-destructs.[46] Nevertheless, Tipler uses his view of our future resurrected forms to explain phenomena attached to Jesus' past resurrection appearances: how Jesus' disciples did not recognize him until he willed it; how a simulated person can be erased from one part of the universe and then instantaneously reappear in another, making possible his walking through walls; and even how Jesus could eat or be touched even though he appeared like a ghost.[47] All Tipler does here is say some interesting things about the Easter phenomenon. He sees no proleptic or redemptive power in Jesus' resurrection that has any impact on the rest of us. In sum, for Tipler there is but a loose connection between Jesus' Easter body and our future resurrected forms.

Tipler believes his emulated information processors provide an explanation for what St Paul means by spiritual body.

> Borrowing the terminology of St. Paul, we can call the simulated, improved, and undying body a 'spiritual body', for it will be of the same 'stuff' as the human mind now is: a 'thought inside a mind' ... The spiritual body is thus the present body (with improvements) at a higher level of implementation ... an emulated person would observe herself to be as real, and as having a body as solid, as the body we currently observe ourselves to have. There would be nothing 'ghostly' about the simulated body, and nothing insubstantial about the simulated world in which the simulated body found itself.[48]

Tipler is sensitive to a number of theological concerns here. First, he is sensitive to the need for perfection. Our present state of existence is not sufficient. We do not hunger simply for life beyond death. We hunger for salvation. So, without using the term 'salvation', Tipler announces that the simulated body will transcend the previous model by eliminating bodily defects such as missing limbs, substituting youth for old age; sight for blindness, and so on. Second, continuity of identity will be maintained. Against objections that total death followed by total re-creation denies continuity, Tipler sensitively argues that continuity in conscious self-identity is both necessary and possible. To be resurrected as a replica of one's former self does not deny that it is the same self. The key here is the identity of the information patterns within which we are aware of our experience of the world and ourselves.

> An exact replica of ourselves is being simulated in the computer minds of the far future. This simulation of people who are long dead is 'resurrection' only if we adopt what philosophers call the 'pattern identity theory'; that is, the essence of identity of two entities which exist at different times lies in the (sufficiently close) identity of their patterns. Physical continuity is irrelevant.[49]

This is not simply another soulechtomy in which a non-material soul is extracted permanently from a material base. The simulation so emulates the real that, for all practical purposes, what resurrected souls experience is physically real. Tipler's own version of 'spiritual body' is apt.

> *The simulations which are sufficiently complex to contain observers – thinking, feeling beings – as subsimulations exist physically.* And further, they exist physically by definition; for this is exactly what we mean by existence, namely, that thinking and feeling beings think and feel themselves to exist. Remember, the simulated thinking and feeling of simulated beings are real.[50]

What resurrected souls experience is themselves in their environment, and this environment is experienced as physical. Tipler unabashedly follows Bishop Berkeley on this: to be is to be perceived.[51] If as a computer simulation we perceive physicality, the physicality exists thereby.

Although this replica theory may appear at first to be religiously unsatisfying, it has the advantage of facing squarely the terrifying emphasis of St Paul, namely, we do undergo total death and total recreation. Theologically speaking, neither our physical atoms nor our soul's content perdures beyond death on its own. Despite the apparent coldness of the image of computer processing, Tipler's image has the advantage of correlating squarely with St Paul's image of the seed dying and then sprouting.

The final point I wish to make in this treatment is that neither the resurrection of Jesus nor your nor my individual resurrections stand alone. They play roles in a much larger drama, the consummation of God's redemptive work for the whole of the cosmos. Resurrection and eschatology belong together. Before turning to the tie between the resurrection body and the cosmic scope of the new creation; however, we need to pause to ask about the interim state.

The Interim State

A question which theologians have been compelled to ask in every generation since the close of New Testament times down to the present is this one: what happens to us between the time of our death and the time of Christ's return in triumph? This question is already asked by the Thessalonians. In responding, Paul speaks of the dead as 'asleep', but tells us not to worry. Hope does not die with us. In fact, those who are alive at the advent of the eschaton will not precede those already in their graves. 'The dead in Christ will rise first' (1 Thess. 4:16). But, we might still ask, what happens to the dead prior to that resurrection?

There are different theories. Jerome believes that dead martyrs cannot be kept 'shut up in a coffin', and if the devil and demons can wander the streets, so can the souls of these holy ones.[52] Augustine certainly rejects the idea that the spirits of the dead live on to influence actively the course of normal events.[53] He says that, during the interim between one's individual death and the cosmic consummation, 'the soul dwells in a hidden retreat, where it enjoys rest or suffers affliction in just proportion to the merit it has earned by the life which it led on earth'.[54] Thomas Aquinas goes a bit further, saying that 'as soon as the soul is set free from the body it is either plunged into hell or soars to heaven'.[55] Even though both Augustine and Aquinas insist that resurrection consists in the transformation of our bodies which will occur at the consummate end, they are satisfied that in the meantime our souls are capable of leaving the body and going to a place where they will be occupied with either pain or pleasure.

Calvin objects here. He objects not to the idea of a disembodied soul, which he approves, but to the excessive speculation of these earlier theories. He contends that 'it is neither lawful nor expedient to inquire too curiously concerning the soul's intermediate state'.[56] He fails to follow his own advice, however, and proceeds to argue that, during the interim state, the faithful exist in the presence of Christ while the reprobate suffer the torments they deserve. Calvin differs from Aquinas only in that he does not specifically locate these interim activities in heaven or hell. In our own time, Karl Rahner states unequivocally that the doctrine of the immortality of the soul and the interim state of disembodiment are not mere speculations, but full articles of Catholic faith.[57]

Oscar Cullmann, who has more than a little distaste for the Greek notion of a disembodied soul, will tolerate none of this. He follows Calvin in reiterating the ban against too much speculation regarding the interim state. And like Calvin, he speaks of the faithful as enjoying a 'special nearness to God' even though they are 'still in time' while fast asleep.[58] Such an interim of sleep should not bother us, he argues, because having died in the faith we will continue to exist within the grasp of the Holy Spirit until raised. Though asleep, we are not abandoned. Behind Cullmann is a long tradition of invoking the image of Abraham's bosom in Jesus' parable of Dives and Lazarus, according to which the faithful dead lie restfully in the bosom of Christ until awakened by the trumpet blast on the last day. They will not experience the lapse of time during their nap, and when they awaken on the last day it will seem like just a moment beyond their own death.

The Cullmann position has the virtue of being theologically consistent. Thomas Aquinas' position, in contrast, is less consistent. Aquinas works strenuously to defend the doctrine of the resurrection of the body, and in so doing he appeals to Aristotle's allegedly convincing argument that the soul cannot exist separated from its body.[59] Once he has convinced the reader with Aristotle's help of the impossibility of a disembodied soul, he then proceeds with his own theological surgery to sever the soul from the body at the moment of death and to send it off temporarily to heaven, hell, limbo or purgatory. In short, Aquinas wants both immortality of the soul and resurrection of the dead, and the concept of the interim state permits him to have them in sequence. The only price is inconsistency. Cullmann avoids the inconsistency because he is willing to stick with the implications to be drawn from understanding just how seriously Paul means it when he says that 'what you sow does not come to life unless it dies' (1 Cor. 15:36). What this means for us at this point in time is that the naturalists are right: when you're dead, you're dead!

But what about widespread belief systems that claim existence for disembodied souls of those who are dead? What about those we discussed earlier who claim to have had an out-of-the-body experience? Before proceeding further down the path in which our theological logic would like to direct us, let us pause to observe and assess some of these potential claims to the contrary. It is not necessarily helpful to march lockstep down the road of doctrinal reasoning without looking occasionally from side to side at common human experience. If we do, it will not be long and we will look back and wonder why no one is following us. In the case of what we have been calling the 'interim' and what other people normally think of as the time 'after death', there are some amazing things to consider. Most of the peoples of the world do not accept the scientific naturalist position that when once you are dead you are simply dead.

The particular question we are concerned with right here is this: during the interim state do disembodied spirits exist and do they have social intercourse with those of us who are still alive? We have already noted that the Akamba (and this is true for both Christian and non-Christian Akamba alike) see the Aimu when they appear. They claim that the Aimu appear less often now than they did before Europeans arrived, but the appearances have by no means ceased altogether. We have also discussed OBEs, where people claim to be able to perceive what is going on in the physical world even if they are unable to affect it themselves while in their disembodied state.

Augustine wrestles with this issue while formulating his own position. He tells of the case of a man named Curma in the town of Tullium, who had the equivalent of an OBE while he lay 'all but dead for several days'. While engaged in astral-like travel, he met up with other previously deceased souls as well as living people in geographically removed locations. He also approached the gates of paradise, but there he was told that he should return to his earthly body and become baptized. Augustine is skeptical about Curma's account, but he wishes to examine it with care rather than dismiss it out of hand. He wishes to handle with equal gingerliness the more widespread claims that dead people have at times either in dreams or in other ways appeared to their living descendants and communicated astonishing information. Then he raises the question: is there really social intercourse taking place between disembodied souls and those of us who still live corporeally? Augustine answers negatively. But rather than dismiss these anecdotal reports, he speculates that perhaps these appearances of the dead are due to the work of God-directed angels who wish to communicate with us mortals.[60] Rahner asks the same question and, while affirming that the dead still live and denying that we can communicate with them, says that our posture should be one in which we 'open our hearts to the silent calm of God himself, in which they live'.[61]

The problem which we face is this: our evangelical explication of Paul's discussion of resurrection of the body seems either to ignore or to preclude the possibility of supraphysical personal existence after death, yet there exist many philosophies of soulechtomy, and there are widespread claims that people have experienced communication from just such disembodied beings. Have we come to a point of showdown where the Christian view is either right or wrong? Or is there any hope of merging horizons to form a larger more comprehensive integration of views?

Para-eschatology

In working our way through this problem, two resources can aid us: first, the observation that the Bible in general gives no sign of conflict between belief in disembodied spirits and eschatology; second, John Hick's helpful concept of pareschatology for organizing our thoughts.

Contact with the spirits of the dead through witchcraft is simply assumed to be possible when the frustrated Saul asks the medium at Endor to raise the dead Samuel so he can consult with him (1 Sam. 28), although the Old Testament in general outlaws necromancy and divination (Ex. 22:18; 1 Sam. 15:23, 28:3; Micah 5:12). The New Testament seems to assume the existence of numerous supranatural beings such as cosmic rulers, *archontes* (1 Cor. 2:6,8; Eph. 2:2), powers, *dynameis* (Rom. 8:38; 1 Peter 3:22), authorities, *exousiai* (Eph. 3:10; Col. 1:16; 2:15), elemental spirits, *stoicheia* (Gal. 4:3,9; Col. 2:8,20), along with sundry demons and unclean spirits (Mt. 9:33; Mk. 1:23, 27, 34; 3:11; 1 Cor. 10:20f) and even Satan himself (Mt. 4:1–11; Rom. 16:20; 1 Cor. 5:5). Then, of course, there are the angels, whom we will be like in the resurrection (Mt. 22:30). There may be a difference between some supraphysical beings and the souls of the deceased, however. Demons and unclean spirits, for example, can enter a person and establish possession. In Jesus' parable of Dives and Lazarus, in contrast, it appears that dead people are not permitted to leave their abode to return and influence the course of ordinary events (Luke 16:26). In short, there is no shortage of background presence of supraphysical beings in Scripture. Had there been an intrinsic antipathy between belief in disembodied spirits and the eschatological vision, one would expect that it would have surfaced already within the New Testament. But, such a tension does not seem to exist.

Thus, we might consider the merits of the concept of pareschatology introduced by John Hick. Hick begins by affirming that the Christian doctrine of resurrection refers to the final or ultimate state of human existence. It does not refer to what happens immediately upon death. This opens the door to speculation regarding the interim state. Hick considers the various possibilities we have been discussing here and finds there to be no intrinsic conflict between disembodied existence immediately after death and a final eschatology of the Christian type. Our discussion of what happens in between he dubs 'pareschatology'. The term appears to prefix 'eschatology' with the preposition 'para', meaning 'alongside of'. Whereas eschatology deals with the 'last things', pareschatology permits us to deal with the 'next-to-last things'.[62] As with 'parapsychology' and 'paranormal' we now have a category for dealing with relevant material which hitherto has fallen outside the confines of the discipline.

This category is helpful. The essential commitment of Christian theology is to the explication of the concept of resurrection as it is associated with ultimate destruction and new creation. What the category of pareschatology does is leave open – theologically speaking – considerable room for debate regarding the experience of death and what happens immediately thereafter.

It leaves it open to scientific reflection and discussion, however, not to religious dogma. By this, I mean we should attend honestly and forthrightly – as a scientist would attend to an experiment – to the evidence. This is not the same thing as accepting the beliefs of occultists or Tibetan Buddhists as true on the basis of their traditional authority. Nor is it the same thing as accepting the assertions of modern naturalism, because this '-ism' is really a form of unfounded ideology which is attached to science but not essential to science. If by 'science' we refer to an open-minded appraisal of possible explanations for experience, then this should be our approach in this matter. If the evidence is strong enough to make the naturalist case that when a person dies he or she remains dead, then we will have to accept it. If, on the other hand, reports of life-after-life experiences prove to be unassailable, we will have to assess this theologically. At present, the jury is still out.

In the event that the jury returns with a convincing verdict on behalf of some form of soulechtomy, we need to ask: what could this mean? The preliminary answer I suggest is this: whatever the makeup of this disembodied post-mortem existence, it still belongs to this order of creation. It belongs to the old eon. It is still subject to further destruction and new creation. If death does not occur when the body dies, it still will. Whenever claims are made that the non-physical realm to which the disembodied self goes looks like life on this side – that the living-dead continue their anxieties over the welfare of their descendants, or that in this new realm we find punishments for previous sins and rewards for virtue – we know that things have not changed much. Post-mortem experience is in too much continuity with pre-mortem experience. Death has not yet done its job of annihilating the curse of evil. In other words, should the evidence compel us to affirm the existence of the living-dead now, we must still anticipate that the living-dead, like the rest of us, will be subject to destruction at a later time. The Akamba provide us with an example of how we might conceive of soulechtomy occurring at the point of physical death but annihilation occurring later. Thus the thought is not without some precedent.

One of the difficult tasks conceptually is to coordinate the great divergence of opinions regarding what happens to the self once it is disengaged from the body at death. Does it hang around as a ghost so that we can communicate with it through a medium? Does it proceed gnostic-style up the planes of existence toward some sort of perfection? Does it go immediately to a place of happiness or torment, as Plato or Thomas would suggest? Does it become reincarnated? These are open questions which we will simply leave open at this point. What needs to be affirmed here is that our theological method can and should be open to participating in a discussion of such matters.

The Coming New Creation

Now let us turn to our final point and central thesis: human destiny is inseparable from cosmic destiny. One element in common among the four theories of immortality (or non-immortality in the case of scientific naturalism) as well as interim state speculations is this: they all deal with the question of human destiny in partial isolation from that of cosmic destiny. One's own soul may exercise its philosophical wings and fly to heaven and there enjoy the beatific vision, or through strenuous meditative effort one might attain enlightenment and realize oneness with Brahman, but the affairs of this mundane world will simply go on as a matter of course without these now departed human souls. Not so with the Christian vision. What happens to us depends on what happens to the cosmos. The resurrection to a spiritual body can only occur at the advent of the eschaton. If there is no cosmic transformation, then there is no resurrection, and if there is no resurrection then our faith is in vain and we of all people are most to be pitied (1 Cor. 15:14,19).

Resurrection is indispensably tied to the eschatological parousia – the second coming of Christ. Paul suggests an order to things. First comes Christ, the first fruits (1 Cor. 15:23). This probably refers to Easter. Then, at his coming 'the dead in Christ will rise first, then we who are alive' (1 Thess. 4:16–17). He 'will transform the body of our humiliation that it may be conformed to the body of his glory' (Phil. 3:21; see Rom. 8:29). 'Then comes the end, when he hands over the kingdom to God the Father, after he has destroyed every ruler and every authority and power. ... The last enemy to be destroyed is death' (1 Cor. 15:24,26).

The key to understanding the resurrected body is placing it within the broader horizon of God's promised new creation. As the creation is transformed, so are we. Salvation is creation-wide, our bodies included. This leads Gordon Fee to comment:

The transformed body, therefore, is not composed of 'spirit'; it is a *body* adapted to the eschatological existence that is under the ultimate domination of the Spirit. Thus for Paul, to be truly *pneumatikos* is to bear the likeness of Christ (v.49) in a transformed body, fitted for the new age.[63]

It is a credit to Tipler that he sees the necessary connection between resurrection and new creation. That is the point of his Omega Point. Resurrection is not merely resuscitation to life in the physical universe as we currently know it. Rather, it participates in the arrival of a total cosmic transformation.

Yet, there is something abrasive about Tipler's method that leads to excessive confidence regarding his speculative interpretations. His method is clearly anti-theological. Rather than relying in any way on faith, he restricts himself to reason. 'The Omega Point Theory has the first physical resurrection theory to be fully consistent with the Christian resurrection theory. It is also the first redemption theory justified by reason, not faith.'[64] Tipler wants to engage in 'pure physics. There is nothing supernatural in the theory, and hence there is no appeal anywhere to faith'.[65]

Why this blustering opposition to faith? It is not necessary to eliminate faith completely when employing reason. Non-dogmatic theological method has long consisted of rational speculations rising out of faith commitments. Faith and reason have long been partners. Why does Tipler eschew faith?

Augustine's works provide us with a healthier example of faith seeking understanding through reason. He seeks logical directions for drawing out implications of New Testament commitments. In the final sections of his *City of God*, for example, Augustine asks whether everybody will be raised. Yes, he says; and the resurrection will even include aborted infants. Will we get our own bodies back or will we be issued new ones? He says that the actual physical elements which composed the first body will be retrieved for the new one. What condition will our physical bodies be in? Every blemish and infirmity will be removed. How old will we be? The age at which we die? No. We will be at our healthiest mature age. This Augustine guesses is about 30, about the final age of Jesus.[66] Will some of us be bigger and stronger than others? No, we will all have the same stature. Will there be two sexes in heaven? Yes, but 'we shall enjoy one another's beauty without any lust'.[67] Will we remember our past tragedies and sufferings? Yes, we will remember them intellectually but we will no longer feel the pain.

Augustine does not have apodictic knowledge here. He is not delivering irreversible dogma. Rather, he is speculating. But, then, that is what theologians are supposed to do. On the basis of faith, we as theologians try to construct reasonable answers to questions rising out of the scriptural witness but which need further speculative pondering. What Augustine says is a carefully thought out explication of the New Testament. His thoughts regarding the great transformation have been quite widely accepted in subsequent centuries. But, they are just thoughts, carefully considered, to be sure, but they are his thoughts. This is what we ask of our theologians. But rather than see himself in the great tradition of St Augustine by adding reason to faith, Frank Tipler sees himself as promulgating an onto-theological dogma, a dogma derived from the field of physics. Why claim such apodictic status for one's speculative thoughts? Most theologians are a good deal more timid. Despite the confidence persons of faith put in the promise delivered to us through the Easter resurrection, our understanding of that resurrection is shrouded in so much mystery that even the angels dare not dogmatize too quickly.

Conclusion

Despite the mystery, faithful Christians pray and sing at funerals. Just before entrusting Ethel Mae to the 'never failing love' of God, our congregation prayed:

> Help us, we pray, in the midst of things we cannot understand, to believe and trust in the communion of saints, the forgiveness of sins, and the resurrection to life everlasting.

Now, I just do not know for sure if Ethel Mae will rise at the Omega Point as an eternal information processor. Maybe Frank Tipler will be proved correct. Or maybe not. Maybe it is beyond our precise understanding at the moment. Yet to pursue further understanding is what theologians and physicists – together or separately, with or without faith – ought to do. In the meantime, I take some comfort in knowing that Ethel Mae knew what I know, namely, that 'in the midst of things we cannot understand' we find ourselves with a divine promise that the future new creation will include the resurrection of our bodies, the redemption of our souls and everlasting life in the spirit.

Notes

1 *Lutheran Book of Worship* (Minneapolis: Augsburg Fortress, 1979), 206.
2 Frank J. Tipler, *The Physics of Immortality* (New York: Doubleday, 1994), 220; italics in original.
3 Ibid., ix. 'Science has taken the last independent stronghold of theology. Thus, theological research in the twenty-first century will require a Ph.D. in particle physics' (ibid., 329).
4 Ibid., xiv; see 294.
5 Ibid., 339.
6 Jack London, *John Barlycorn* (New York: Signet, 1990), 218–19.
7 Bertrand Russell, 'A Free Man's Worship', *Mysticism and Logic* (New York: Doubleday, 1957), 44–5.
8 Tipler, *Physics of Immortality*, 310.
9 Plato, *Phaedo*, 66.
10 Plato, *Gorgias*, 523.
11 Plato, *Phaedrus*, 249–50; *Republic*, X, 614–21.

12   Cited by Karl Rahner (ed.), *The Teaching of the Catholic Church as Contained in her Documents* (Staten Island, NY: Alba House, 1966), 124.

13   John P. Newport, *Life's Ultimate Questions* (Waco TX: Word, 1989), 277.

14   Tipler, *Physics of Immortality*, 124. 'The human soul is *nothing but* a program being run on a computer called the brain' (ibid., xi). This is an example of what Arthur Peacocke calls 'nothing buttery' reductionism: *Theology for a Scientific Age* (Minneapolis: Fortress, enlarged edn, 1993), 40.

15   Tipler, *Physics of Immortality*, 127.

16   Ibid., 293.

17   Three broad paths or *margas* make up the complex history of Hinduism: the path of ritual action (*karma marga*), knowledge (*jnana marga*) and devotion (*bhakti marga*). The second, the path of knowledge, most emphasizes the ultimate identity of the self (*atman*) with the All (*Brahman*). See Thomas J. Hopkins, 'Hindu Views of Death and Afterlife', in *Death and Afterlife: Perspectives of World Religions*, Hiroshi Obayashi, volume ed., number 33 of *Contributions to the Study of Religion*, Henry Warner Bowden, series ed. (New York: Greenwood Press, 1992), 143–56.

18   Some non-dualist theists within Hinduism claim to stop short of oblivion. 'Moksha for the nondualist (*advaitin*) does not mean that the self merges into Brahman as a river merges into the sea, but that the self realizes itself as it eternally exists; i.e., in perfect identity with the Absolute. Hence liberation is not a state to be newly attained but is the very nature of the Self become conscious of its identity with the All-One,' Mariasusai Dhavamony, 'Death and Immortality in Hinduism', in *Death and Immortality in the Religions of the World*, ed. by Paul and Linda Badham, (New York: Paragon House, 1987), 106.

19   In another work I attempt to show that the Western interest in reincarnation as we find it in New Age spirituality is due to the conflation of the notion of karma with that of trauma in psychotherapy and its use in so-called reincarnation therapy. See Ted Peters, *The Cosmic Self: A Penetrating Look at Today's New Age Movements* (San Francisco: Harper, 1991), 71–4.

20   Tipler, *Physics of Immortality*, 273–4.

21   Ibid., 274.

22   Ibid., 154.

23   Ibid., 255.

24   John S. Mbiti, *New Testament Eschatology in an African Background* (Oxford: Oxford University Press, 1971), 139.

25   Tipler, *Physics of Immortality*, 280–81.

26   Raymond A. Moody, *Life after Life* (Atlanta: Mockingbird Books, 1975 and New York: Bantam, 1977), 48; see also his *Reflections on Life after Life* (New York: Bantam & Mockingbird, 1977) and Elizabeth Kübler-Ross, *Death, the Final Stage of Growth* (New York: Macmillan 1975). Ordinarily, interpreters of NDEs speak modestly about subjective survival beyond physical death. On a much more grand scale, however, Kenneth Ring connects NDEs with UFO experiences, sees both as initiation rites into a cosmic reality, and then projects a near eschatological vision of a new level of evolutionary development. He says, 'the world of the dead and the world of the living are ones between which there may eventually no longer be a sharp distinction. Veils will be lifted from the face of the nonphysical, and we ourselves will become diaphanous beings, with bodies of light', Kenneth Ring, *The Omega Project: Near-Death Experiences, UFO Encounters, and Mind at Large*, (New York: William Morrow, 1992), 239.

27   John Newport summarizes critical assessments of NDOBE claims such as attempts to explain them physiologically as hallucinations created by the brain owing to the

trauma of approaching death: *Life's Ultimate Questions*, 289. Questions of authenticity lead to controversy. Author Betty Malz published a book, *My Glimpses of Eternity* (Grand Rapids: Zondervan, Chosen Books, 1977), which has sold nearly a million copies, describing her alleged 1959 death of 28 minutes on a hospital operating table, her OBE, plus her trip to heaven and back. The doctors involved – H. Clark Boyd, Henry Bopp and James Bopp – reported to *Christianity Today* investigator Lorna Dueck, however, that Betty Malz nee Upchurch did not die as she claimed. They describe what she writes as 'almost a complete fabrication' and say 'this didn't happen'. Her editor defends her by saying that, whether actually dead or not, Betty Malz has 'a marvelous ministry'. See Ken Sidey, 'Doctors Dispute Best-Selling Author's Back-to-Life Story', *Christianity Today*, 35 (22 July 1991), 40–42.

28 This expands a discussion begun in my book, *GOD – the World's Future: Systematic Theology for a Postmodern Era* (Minneapolis: Fortress, 1992), 310–16.

29 Over against the neo-orthodox theologians for whom death belongs naturally to human finitude, evangelical theologians hold that human death is the result of human sin. John Newport writes, 'humans were created with contingent or conditional immortality. They could have lived forever, but it was not certain that they would. Upon sinning, they lost this status', *Life's Ultimate Questions*, 296.

30 By adding this role of death in the plan of salvation, I move a bit beyond the interpretation of John Newport, who writes, 'we must experience physical death simply because it has become one of the conditions of human existence' (*Life's Ultimate Questions*, 296).

31 Oscar Cullmann, 'Immortality of the Soul or Resurrection of the Dead?', in *Immortality and Resurrection*, ed. by Krister Stendahl (New York: Macmillan, 1965), 14–15.

32 'The post-resurrectional confession is not simply "We have seen Jesus" but "We have seen *the Lord*" (John 20:18, 25; 21:7; Luke 24:34). Since "Lord" is a Christological evaluation of Jesus, the evangelists are telling us that the witnesses enjoyed not only the *sight* of Jesus but also and even primarily *insight*,' Raymond E. Brown, *The Virginal Conception and Bodily Resurrection of Jesus*, (New York: Paulist, 1973), 112, italics in original.

33 I am particularly indebted to Patricia Codron, my research assistant, for her aid in thinking through the issues associated with the spiritual body.

34 Gordon D. Fee, '*The First Epistle to the Corinthians*' in *The New International Commentary on the New Testament*, F.F. Bruce, general ed. (Grand Rapids: Eerdmans, 1987), 785.

35 Roy A. Harrisville, '*I Corinthians*' in *Augsburg Commentary on the New Testament* (Minneapolis: Augsburg, 1987), 276.

36 Roy Harrisville notes that Paul's seed analogy emphasizes the discontinuity between death and resurrection. 'But in neither instance is the move from agronomy to Christian existence, but exactly the reverse. The analogy is warped to what it serves, and here it is made to fit the assertion of discontinuity, the contention that there is no resurrection unless "from the dead". What that warping and twisting of the figure to serve its topic means is that there is, after all, no analogy in nature to the activity of God envisioned here, but only a refraction; no possibility of inferring the "wisdom of God" from what can be observed in the world,' *I Corinthians*, 274–5.

37 My assumption is that the Easter body of Jesus is the prototype of the eschatological bodies of the faithful. John Newport, however, is reluctant to make the equation. He drives a wedge between the body of Jesus immediately after

Easter and Jesus' ascended reality which comes later: 'Our resurrection body will be like Jesus' present body, not necessarily like the body he had between his resurrection and ascension. We will not have those characteristics of Jesus' postresurrection earthly body which appear inconsistent with our resurrection bodies, which the apostle Paul calls "spiritual bodies" (1 Cor. 15:44). The characteristics we will need will not necessarily include physical tangibility and the need to eat,' *Life's Ultimate Questions*, 305–6. I gather this means that in heaven there will be no Big Mac Attacks.

38 'The idea that the soul is naturally immortal, deathless by definition, is at home in much of Greek thought but not in the New Testament.... The New Testament has a unique idea of immortality: The whole person will become immortal by resurrection,' Leander E. Keck, 'Death and Afterlife in the New Testament', in *Death and Afterlife*, 84. This seems to be the consensus. Thomas Deidun sees Paul as refuting a presupposed dualism of spirit and body among the Corinthians and proposing in contrast to see the resurrection and transformation of the body as the completion of God's work of salvation: 'The *soma* is to be eschatologically changed by God's *power*. It will become *soma pneumatikon*. Yet it remains *soma* – the substantial point of *continuity* between now and then.' Deidun proceeds to argue that this affirmation of the body in resurrection has an impact on sexual morality, because 'the mutual love of sexual union is capable of eschatological transformation without losing its deepest significance' ('Beyond Dualisms: Paul on Sex, Sarx, and Soma', *The Way*, 28:3 (July 1988), 203. Brendan Byrne similarly argues that affirmation of bodily resurrection has an impact on morality: 'Paul derives from the heart of the gospel an eschatology of resurrection that endows bodily life with lasting moral value' ('Eschatologies of Resurrection and Destruction: The Ethical Significance of Paul's Dispute with the Corinthians', *The Downside Review*, 104 (October 1986), 295.

39 Cullmann, 'Immortality of the Soul or Resurrection of the Dead?', 25. Walter Wink would tend to agree with Cullmann in dubbing *sarx* a transcendent power. The transcendent power in Wink's case has to do with fallen social–psychological structures, not necessarily a supernatural power: 'Life lived "according to the flesh" (*kata sarka*) denotes the self externalized and subjugated to the opinions of others. It is the self socialized into a world of inauthentic values, values that lead it away from its own centeredness in God.... "Fleshly" or "carnal" refers to a life that has abandoned the transcendent and become fixated on personal satisfactions.... The best paraphrase I can render for *kata sarka* is "dominated existence".' *Engaging the Powers* (Minneapolis: Fortress, 1992), 62–3.

40 Justin, *On the Resurrection*, II and VII in *Anti-Nicene Fathers*, I, 194 and 297.

41 Augustine, *Enchiridion*, Chap.91 in *Nicene and Post-Nicene Fathers*, 1st: III, 266.

42 Hans Conzelmann, *I Corinthians* (Philadelphia: Fortress, 1978), 282.

43 Resurrection will include a dialectic between transformation and continuity. Our personal identity cannot be obliterated completely; otherwise, transformation would consist of simple destruction. Something subjective and identifiable must continue. Newport reminds us that this continuity is a gift of divine grace, however, not a natural propensity: 'Our personal identity is not a predication we can make based on our creaturely nature. Rather, it is predicated upon the initiative of God, who addresses us and upholds us as the persons we are before him and with each other' (*Life's Ultimate Questions*, 303).

44 'A panoramic view of the Pauline writings shows no special apologetic preoccupation in the presentation of the resurrection of Jesus. However, on the relatively few occasions when the question came up, Paul did have to come to grips

with the problem of the risen body and with the law of conformity to Christ in all aspects of his life and destiny,' Giuseppe Ghiberti, 'Contemporary Discussion of the Resurrection of Jesus', in *Problems and Perspectives of Fundamental Theology*, ed. by René Latourelle and Gerald O'Collins, translated by Matthew J. O'Connell (New York: Paulist, 1982), 231.

45 Tipler, *Physics of Immortality*, 305, 309–13.
46 Ibid., 225.
47 Ibid., 244.
48 Ibid., 242.
49 Ibid., 227.
50 Ibid., 210 italics in original.
51 Ibid., 211.
52 Jerome, *Against Vigilantius*, vi.
53 Augustine, *On Care to be had for the Dead*, 12,18.
54 Augustine, *Enchiridion*, 109.
55 Thomas Aquinas, *Summa Theologia*, III, Q,69, A,2.
56 John Calvin, *Institutes of the Christian Religion*, III, 6.
57 Karl Rahner, *On the Theology of Death* (New York: Crossroad, 1973), 16; 'The Life of the Dead', in *Theological Investigations*, 21 volumes (New York: Crossroad, 1961–88), IV, 352.
58 Cullmann, 'Immortality of the Soul or Resurrection of the Dead?', 39. A similar position is taken by Paul Althaus, *Die Letzten Dinge* (Gutersloh: Bertelsmann, 8th edn, 1961), 155–7.
59 Thomas Aquinas, *Summa Theologia*, III, Q,75, A,1; Aristotle, *On the Soul*, II:2 (414a,12).
60 Augustine, *On Care to be had for the Dead*, 12–15.
61 Rahner, 'The Life of the Dead', 353–4.
62 John Hick, *Death and Eternal Life* (New York: Harper, 1976), 22.
63 Fee, *First Epistle to the Corinthians*, 786. Ben F. Meyer asks if corporeal participation in the final salvation is ruled out. Then he answers: 'No; the issue is not "body versus spirit" but "body in the present age" – be it the flesh and blood of the living or the decayed body of the dead – versus body transfigured and immortal in the reign of God.' 'Did Paul's View of the Resurrection of the Dead Undergo Development?', *Theological Studies*, 47:3 (Summer 1986), 381.
64 Tipler, *Physics of Immortality*, 347.
65 Ibid., 16.
66 Augustine, *City of God*, XXII:15.
67 Augustine, *City of God*, XXII:24.

Name Index

Index

1964 Civil Rights Act, Title VII 141

a se 91
abnormal occurrences 264
abortion 143, 183, 195, 201, 204, 206
   controversy (debate) 142, 181, 182,
     197, 198
   elective 185
   selective 191, 192, 195, 196, 197, 198,
     201, 206
   spontaneous (natural) 183, 185
absorption into infinity 297, 300
accident insurance fund 264
acid rain 220
acidification 259
actualization 239
acupuncture 285
Adam 152, 153, 306
Adam and Eve 304
adaptation (adaptability) 231, 232, 233,
   234
Adenosine Deaminase Deficiency 214
adoption 194, 202, 203
adventus 69
adversity 240, 243
advertising 287
advocacy 287
AFR *see* away-from-reactor facilities
   253
afterlife 299, 301, 312
Agathon 257, 258
agriculture 260
AID *see* Artificial Insemination with
   Donor Sperm
AIDS 180, 243, 271
AIH *see* Artificial Insemination by
   Husband
Aimu 300, 301, 312
Akamba people 66, 71, 72, 73, 74, 300,
   301, 312, 315
Alabama-Coushatta 274
Alamoudi, Abdurahman 145
ALARA *see* as low as reasonably
   achievable

alcoholism 206
Algeny 146, 156
alleles 180, 192
alpha particle-emitting nuclides 253
altruism 220
Alzheimer's disease 140, 142, 146, 192,
   215
America 251, 255
American culture 207
American Indians 286
American Medical Association 285
American Scientific Affiliation 44, 45
American Society for Reproductive
   Medicine 170
amniocentesis 196
angels 126, 313, 317
angina 180
Anthropic Principle, the 6, 7, 43
anthropocentric 242
anthropology 11, 27, 32, 79, 155,
   213
   theological 8, 10
antibodies 232
anti-reductionistic 87
anti-semitism 191, 217
anxiety 177, 241, 255, 256, 305
AOs *see* abnormal occurrences
apeiron 106
aperoi kosmoi 122
aplastic anemia 179
apocalyptic 68, 69, 223
apocalyptic fatalism 68
apodictic knowledge 316
Apostles' Creed 308
aqueous solution 253
archetypes, Jungian 303
archonic view 83
archontes 313
arenavirus 231
arms race 54
arterioscleriosis 142
artificial insemination 172, 201, 203,
Artificial Insemination by Husband 202,
   210